Mastering Citrix® XenDesktop®

Design and implement a high performance and efficient virtual desktop infrastructure using Citrix® XenDesktop®

Govardhan Gunnala

Daniele Tosatto

[PACKT] enterprise

professional expertise distilled

PUBLISHING

BIRMINGHAM - MUMBAI

Mastering Citrix® XenDesktop®

First published: June 2015

Production reference: 1270615

Published by Packt Publishing Ltd.
Livery Place
35 Livery Street
Birmingham B3 2PB, UK.

ISBN 978-1-78439-397-7

www.packtpub.com

Credits

Authors
Govardhan Gunnala

Daniele Tosatto

Reviewer
Robert Ljunggren

Commissioning Editor
Julian Ursell

Acquisition Editor
Reshma Raman

Content Development Editor
Ajinkya Paranjape

Technical Editor
Mitali Somaiya

Copy Editors
Janbal Dharmaraj

Vikrant Phadke

Rashmi Sawant

Trishla Singh

Project Coordinator
Harshal Ved

Proofreader
Safis Editing

Indexer
Priya Sane

Graphics
Sheetal Aute

Production Coordinator
Shantanu N. Zagade

Cover Work
Shantanu N. Zagade

About the Author

Govardhan Gunnala is a Technical Architect with knowledge of cross-platform technologies understanding and applying them to complex business requirements. He is a computer science graduate and a Microsoft and Citrix® Certified professional specialized in server, desktop, and application virtualization technologies. He is a skilled IT network security analyst and is highly regarded for sophisticated automation using Perl and PowerShell scripting. He has designed and delivered various cloud software solutions based on web, Citrix®, and VMware technologies. He is also responsible for data center architecture and network security administration. He earlier worked as a senior systems engineer and member of IT systems at a global investment and technology development firm. He is also a technical blogger, corporate and institutional trainer with more than 9 years of experience in the IT software industry.

You can follow his blog at `http://gunnalag.com/`.

I would like to deeply thank each of my family members. My parents, Markandeyulu Gunnala and Durgamma Gunnala, for supporting me to write this book. My beloved wife, Sarika, who has been the motivation for this undertaking, and without her support, I wouldn't have completed this book. All the others who have made my stay comfortable while I was occupied with writing this book.

I would like to thank my mentor and manager, Andy Poulter, who encouraged me to achieve every milestone that I reached while writing this book. I would also like to thank Ravi Koppara for being my personal mentor and motivator.

I would like to express my special thanks to Daniele Tosatto for joining me as a coauthor on this title and to the entire Packt team and technical reviewers for all their diligent work on this book.

Daniele Tosatto is a Windows Infrastructure Architect specialized in Citrix®
and Microsoft technologies with 15 years of experience. He is a Microsoft Certified
Solutions Expert, Microsoft Solutions Associate, and Citrix® Certified Administrator.
He has been working with Microsoft products since 2000 as a systems administrator.
He currently works as a project manager for the Italian Citrix® Platinum Partner in
medium to large Citrix® and virtualization projects.

About the Reviewer

Robert Ljunggren is a system/network administrator, who is in charge of keeping the systems functional and running smoothly. He has over 10 years of experience in the technology field. He brings his knowledge of virtualization and customer support to the table. He was a lead data center technician and technical assistance call center manager. He is certified in Microsoft MCTS, MCITP, and Citrix® CNA. He has produced training materials and instructed end users in a formal setting. He has an extensive background in network performance assessment and strong end user support skills. He also has a wide knowledge of Cisco and SonicWall switches and router configurations.

I would like to thank my wife, Jamie; my son, Connor; and my two daughters, Katrina and Viktoria, for giving me the time to work on the book. I would also like to thank the rest of my family.

www.PacktPub.com

Support files, eBooks, discount offers, and more

For support files and downloads related to your book, please visit www.PacktPub.com.

Did you know that Packt offers eBook versions of every book published, with PDF and ePub files available? You can upgrade to the eBook version at www.PacktPub.com and as a print book customer, you are entitled to a discount on the eBook copy. Get in touch with us at service@packtpub.com for more details.

At www.PacktPub.com, you can also read a collection of free technical articles, sign up for a range of free newsletters and receive exclusive discounts and offers on Packt books and eBooks.

https://www2.packtpub.com/books/subscription/packtlib

Do you need instant solutions to your IT questions? PacktLib is Packt's online digital book library. Here, you can search, access, and read Packt's entire library of books.

Why subscribe?

- Fully searchable across every book published by Packt
- Copy and paste, print, and bookmark content
- On demand and accessible via a web browser

Free access for Packt account holders

If you have an account with Packt at www.PacktPub.com, you can use this to access PacktLib today and view 9 entirely free books. Simply use your login credentials for immediate access.

Instant updates on new Packt books

Get notified! Find out when new books are published by following @PacktEnterprise on Twitter or the *Packt Enterprise* Facebook page.

Disclaimer

Table of Contents

Preface

The adoption of Cloud computing and the maturity of server virtualization have led many enterprises to consider transforming their traditional desktop infrastructures from physical to virtual. Desktop virtualization has become one of the new top priorities for IT. Many organizations are now approaching or evaluating desktop virtualization solutions. Having virtual desktops centrally maintained in your data center using desktop virtualization, your users can gain Cloud computing capabilities, such as freedom to work from anywhere and from any device at any time. This increases user productivity and overall IT operational efficiency, while reducing the total cost of ownership of the desktop infrastructure.

Citrix® XenDesktop® is the industry leader in Virtual Desktop Infrastructure (VDI) solutions to implement a scalable and high-performance virtual desktop environment. Citrix® XenDesktop® delivers end-user experience that rivals traditional physical desktop environments, while supporting most of its features, such as audio/video conferencing, media streaming, and high-end 3D graphics rendering. Whether you are new to desktop virtualization or an IT professional with expertise, as you work through this book, you will quickly learn the technical skills you need to successfully design, set up, and maintain a XenDesktop® environment, meeting the emerging requirements for your organization and your business.

Mastering XenDesktop® gives you a practical approach to achieve the advanced desktop virtualization requirements using XenDesktop®. The detailed use case analysis, step-by-step instructions that are supplemented with screenshots makes it easier to understand and implement the discussed solution in real time. You'll notice that this book also covers the other Citrix® (such as NetScaler) and non-Citrix® technologies (such as Amazon Cloud, NVidia GRID, and so on) to the extent they are relevant to the use case with XenDesktop®. You will be able to master both the basic functions and the advanced features and configurations of XenDesktop®. You will also gain the strong technical skills needed to start-off or resume desktop virtualization projects using XenDesktop® technology. As always, you should validate the advanced configurations discussed in the book in a test lab, since they involve multiple technologies.

What this book covers

Chapter 1, Evolution and Core Strengths of XenDesktop®, walks you through the evolution of XenDesktop® from the start to its current latest version. It also introduces the core strengths and future roadmap of XenDesktop®, which help you understand why you need to choose XenDesktop® for your desktop virtualization.

Chapter 2, Understanding the XenDesktop® Architecture in Detail, introduces the core and additional components of XenDesktop® in detail. It explains the XenDesktop® architecture (FMA) and features in great depth. This basic knowledge gives you a strong foundation to easily understand the advanced configurations discussed in the later chapters.

Chapter 3, Designing XenDesktop® for Complex Environments, describes the process of designing XenDesktop® using a layered approach and Citrix® design tools. It exclusively covers how to design XenDesktop® for highly available and scalable enterprise environments. It also discusses how to design and deploy XenDesktop® for complex environments, including multisite XenDesktop® environments, using application orchestration for multi-forest Active Directory environments, and deploying XenDesktop® in private, public, and AWS hybrid Cloud environments.

Chapter 4, Implementing a XenDesktop® Environment, gives you practical knowledge through a step-by-step presentation of implementing the XenDesktop® environment. You'll learn how to install XenDesktop® core components, configure them, and verify the XenDesktop® site and its setup. This basic knowledge helps you quickly start your XenDesktop® deployments.

Chapter 5, Delivering Virtual Desktops and Optimizing XenDesktop®, provides you with advanced skills on how to configure additional instances of XenDesktop® core components to build highly available environments. It covers how to configure VDA, machine catalogs, and delivery group entities to deliver virtual desktops. It also explains how to optimize XenDesktop® for performance, through Citrix® policies at server side and VDA performance optimizations at client side.

Chapter 6, Configuring XenDesktop® for Advanced Use Cases, exclusively covers how to configure XenDesktop® for a unique compilation of advanced use cases by enterprises and businesses. You'll master how to configure XenDesktop® for these advanced use cases, which include high-end 3D applications, streaming media applications, web filtering, and so on. It also covers advanced fine-tuning and customization of XenDesktop® capabilities, including virtual display, Local App Access integration, and seamless and in-browser session interfaces. This unique content would be highly useful for Desktop-as-a-Service (DaaS) providers.

Chapter 7, Networking for XenDesktop®, describes the various layers of networking required for the successful functioning of your deployment and connectivity of sessions from users in detail. It explains the sequence of steps that occur during a user connection with a virtual desktop from an external access in detail. It makes you aware of all the required networking concepts and their configuration, to the extent that they are relevant to the scope of XenDesktop® networking. This knowledge effectively helps you understand, plan, and implement the networking for your deployment.

Chapter 8, Monitoring and Troubleshooting XenDesktop®, focuses on the usage and features of Citrix®-provided tools for the effective monitoring and troubleshooting of XenDesktop® environments. You'll gain deep understanding of the functionality and usage of Citrix® Director and EdgeSight®, Citrix® Studio, and Citrix® Insight Services using Citrix® Scout to effectively monitor and troubleshoot XenDesktop® environments. It also covers the various advanced Citrix® tools available for troubleshooting to efficiently handle real-time issues.

Chapter 9, XenDesktop® PowerShell SDK for Automation, introduces the PowerShell SDK provided by Citrix® for automating XenDesktop® tasks and operations. It covers the detailed usage and functioning of commonly-used SDK command-lets and how to author your own PowerShell scripts for automation. This knowledge empowers you with the most sought-after skill of automating XenDesktop® tasks using the PowerShell SDK.

Chapter 10, XenDesktop® and App-V Integration, focuses on implementing and integrating Microsoft App-V technology-based application delivery with XenDesktop®. It discusses how you can quickly learn to deliver App-V-based applications with an easy-to-follow practical approach. It also covers all the prerequisite configuration steps needed for you to start off.

Chapter 11, XenDesktop® Licensing, discusses the Citrix® licensing for XenDesktop®, including the license types, and the editions of licenses available for Citrix® XenDesktop®. It provides you with a deep understanding of the process of license discovery and allocation.

What you need for this book

Mastering XenDesktop® covers the ins and outs of achieving various advanced and complex deployment and use cases, apparently involves referring to and using a wide range of other technologies. The following is a quick list of what you need along with the citation of the use case.

The following are the software and hardware requirements for XenDesktop®
deployment:

- Windows 8 desktop operating system
- Citrix® XenDesktop® 7.5 with Platinum Edition License
- Hardware systems compatible with and/or certified for Microsoft
  Windows Server
- Windows Server 2012 operating system with Standard and above License
- Active Directory environment to create users, groups, and computer accounts

The following are the software requirements for XenDesktop® Cloud deployment:

- Amazon Web Services account
- Windows Server 2012 Instances to deploy XenDesktop® environment
- Citrix® XenDesktop® 7.5 with Platinum Edition License
- NetScaler VPX running NetScaler Gateway and CloudBridge
- On-premises Citrix® NetScaler running NetScaler Gateway and CloudBridge

The following are the software and hardware requirements for XenDesktop® 3D
Graphics support:

- Citrix® and NVidia GRID certified server hardware
- NVidia GRID Software for NVidia Virtual GPU Manager
- XenServer 6.2 Service Pack 1 and above, which includes Citrix® 3D
  Graphics Pack

The following are the software and hardware requirements for XenDesktop®
UCS support:

- Microsoft's Lync Server and VDI plug-in
- Citrix® HDX RealTime Optimization Pack for Microsoft Lync
- Citrix® GoToMeeting
- Good quality headset with mic, along with proper drivers

The following is the software requirement for XenDesktop® Streaming
Media support:

- Adobe Flash Player

The following are the software and hardware requirements for XenDesktop®
integration with web filter:

- Any of the popular web filter appliances (list available in *Chapter 6, Configuring XenDesktop® for Advanced Use Cases*)
- Any software-based web filter such as GFI WebMonitor

The following are the software requirements for XenDesktop® External access:

- A publicly accessible domain name, an IP address, and SSL certificate from Internet Service Provider
- An external Name Server based on Linux with DNS role and a zone
- A network firewall with NAT support
- Citrix® NetScaler running GSLB, NetScaler Gateway, and load balancing features

The following are the software requirements for XenDesktop® troubleshooting:

- Citrix® MyAccount
- Internet access to upload files to the CIS website
- Citrix® Scout pre-installed with Citrix® Controller or Studio software
- Citrix® troubleshooting tools (list available in *Chapter 8, Monitoring and Troubleshooting XenDesktop®*)

The following are the software requirements for XenDesktop® PowerShell SDK:

- Windows PowerShell 4.0 pre-exists on the latest Windows systems (Windows 8.1 and Windows Server 2012 R2)
- Dell PowerGUI

The following are the software requirements for XenDesktop® App-V integration:

- Windows Server 2012 for hosting App-V components
- Microsoft Desktop Optimisation Pack (MDOP), which includes App-V
- Microsoft Remote Desktop Server Client Access License

Who this book is for

This book is intended for IT administrators who want to use Citrix® as a desktop virtualization solution or for IT architects who have the desire to learn how to design and implement highly available and scalable XenDesktop® environments. Whether you are new to desktop virtualization or you are a skilled IT professional, you will be able to master both the basic functions and the advanced features of XenDesktop®. It is assumed that you have prerequisite intermediate-level knowledge of virtualization concepts, Windows desktop operating systems, and Windows Server technologies. You will gain the technical skills needed to start off or resume desktop virtualization projects using XenDesktop® technology. If you are a Desktop-as-a-Service provider based on XenDesktop®, this will be a must-have book, which can help you service advanced real-time customer requirements.

Conventions

In this book, you will find a number of text styles that distinguish between different kinds of information. Here are some examples of these styles and an explanation of their meaning.

Code words in text, database table names, folder names, filenames, file extensions, pathnames, dummy URLs, user input, and Twitter handles are shown as follows: "The Controller SID can be obtained by using the XDPing command."

Any command-line input or output is written as follows:

```
XenDesktop®VdaSetup.exe /components VDA /controllers "xd-ctxdc1.contoso.
local xd-ctxdc2.contoso.local" /enable_remote_assistance /enable_hdx_
ports /optimize /enable_real_time_transport
```

New terms and **important words** are shown in bold. Words that you see on the screen, for example, in menus or dialog boxes, appear in the text like this: "Select the URL of the desired Store and then click on **Manage Delivery Controllers**".

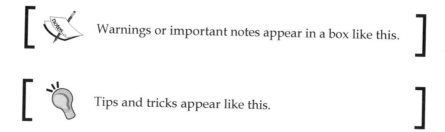

Warnings or important notes appear in a box like this.

Tips and tricks appear like this.

Reader feedback

Feedback from our readers is always welcome. Let us know what you think about this book—what you liked or disliked. Reader feedback is important for us as it helps us develop titles that you will really get the most out of.

To send us general feedback, simply e-mail feedback@packtpub.com, and mention the book's title in the subject of your message.

If there is a topic that you have expertise in and you are interested in either writing or contributing to a book, see our author guide at www.packtpub.com/authors.

Customer support

Now that you are the proud owner of a Packt book, we have a number of things to help you to get the most from your purchase.

Errata

Although we have taken every care to ensure the accuracy of our content, mistakes do happen. If you find a mistake in one of our books—maybe a mistake in the text or the code—we would be grateful if you could report this to us. By doing so, you can save other readers from frustration and help us improve subsequent versions of this book. If you find any errata, please report them by visiting http://www.packtpub.com/submit-errata, selecting your book, clicking on the **Errata Submission Form** link, and entering the details of your errata. Once your errata are verified, your submission will be accepted and the errata will be uploaded to our website or added to any list of existing errata under the Errata section of that title.

To view the previously submitted errata, go to https://www.packtpub.com/books/content/support and enter the name of the book in the search field. The required information will appear under the **Errata** section.

Piracy

Piracy of copyrighted material on the Internet is an ongoing problem across all media. At Packt, we take the protection of our copyright and licenses very seriously. If you come across any illegal copies of our works in any form on the Internet, please provide us with the location address or website name immediately so that we can pursue a remedy.

Please contact us at copyright@packtpub.com with a link to the suspected pirated material.

We appreciate your help in protecting our authors and our ability to bring you valuable content.

Questions

If you have a problem with any aspect of this book, you can contact us at questions@packtpub.com, and we will do our best to address the problem.

Evolution and Core Strengths of XenDesktop®

A product's evolution, its roadmap, and its performance in the respective industry play an important role for businesses while adopting a product for a technology. We will begin by learning the XenDesktop evolution and looking at its core strengths, which will pave the path for the journey of mastering XenDesktop.

The following is an overview of the topics that we'll be learning in this chapter:

- The evolution of XenDesktop
- XenDesktop releases and improvements across
  - All major versions
  - All feature packs
- The core strengths of XenDesktop

As part of its evolution, you'll learn about the company that owns the XenDesktop technology, the company's vision that led to the XenDesktop development, and it's early relationship with Microsoft, where the company worked on Windows technologies. You'll also learn about the roadmap of XenDesktop, which is part of Project Avalon. A great place containing resources and showcasing a consolidated list of the XenDesktop features and capabilities that were uncovered in each release, alongside with a detailed timeline. This will help you find out more about the releases when XenDesktop implemented a new feature or a few new capabilities.

The core strengths will explain the benefits that the business can reap from XenDesktop technology's unique features. It will enable you to build a deeper understanding of all the core strengths of the XenDesktop technology. This will help you to understand the positioning and the roles of certain components discussed in the next chapter, which will cover the detailed architecture of XenDesktop. Readers with this knowledge will be able to easily assess the XenDesktop architecture across different versions of XenDesktop, and possibly, even the future versions.

The evolution of XenDesktop®

Knowing about the evolution of XenDesktop is not only about knowing when XenDesktop started, but about knowing everything that has come together to make this product. I've covered the technologies that have been bought over and built into the XenDesktop product. You'll also come across the feature packs of the XenDesktop versions that have uncovered major capabilities. As you read more, you will come across a summarized table, which shows the healthy and active development of the XenDesktop technology and provides a detailed timeline diagram as an easy reference to XenDesktop releases.

Citrix® and its vision

XenDesktop is a desktop virtualization product from Citrix Systems, and it plays a vital role in its vision. Citrix Systems Inc. is publicly listed as **CTXS** and is an American multinational company founded on April 17, 1989, and it is headquartered in Fort Lauderdale, Florida. It has over 10,000 partners across 100 countries. All of the Global Fortune 100 companies use Citrix solutions.

Citrix's vision is to empower people to work better and live better by making IT simpler and enhancing the productivity of people. In its vision statement, Citrix aims at building mobile workspace solutions that give people new ways of working better, providing secure and seamless access to apps, desktops, files, and services that they need on any device at any time.

Citrix®'s relationship with Microsoft

Citrix developed its first product and brought multi-user access to the IBM OS/2 platform. This product included the OS/2 source code, which was licensed by Microsoft alone, thereby bypassing IBM. However, this product failed to find a market when Microsoft removed their support to OS/2 in 1991.

Later, Citrix worked with Microsoft and obtained the license to Microsoft's Windows NT source code and then released its first product called Citrix Multiuser v 2.0 for the Windows platform in 1993. In 1997, under the Cross-Licensing and Development agreement, Microsoft and Citrix agreed to cooperate in the development of multi-user base capabilities for Windows, where each would develop, and then market, the additional components that would be built upon
these base services.

This early and strong relationship with Microsoft shows a key capability of Citrix's ability to deliver a new class of multi-user and virtualization solutions for Windows technologies.

Citrix® XenDesktop® virtualization solutions

Citrix expanded its application delivery (XenApp) capabilities to include the virtualized Windows desktops, which were delivered securely from the data centre. Citrix started its initial desktop virtualization product called Citrix Desktop Server 1.0. Citrix later entered the data center and desktop virtualization markets with its acquisition of XenSource, a leader in the enterprise-grade virtual infrastructure solutions. Citrix announced the XenDesktop 2.0 for desktop virtualization in October 2007. Since its inception, Citrix has been actively enhancing the XenDesktop product. Citrix has made the XenDesktop solution robust and efficient by adding more capabilities to every major release. On average, a new version of XenDesktop has been released every 6 months. This indicates Citrix's dedication and active priorities, when it comes to developing the product.

The following is Citrix XenDesktop's major, sub-version, and feature packs release track:

Sr. No	Released Version	Release Date (mm-yyyy)	Difference (in Months)
1	Citrix Desktop Server 1.0	04-2007	0
2	XenDesktop 2.0	05-2008	13
3	XenDesktop 2.1	09-2008	4
4	XenDesktop 3.0	02-2009	5
5	XenDesktop 3.0 Feature Pack 1	05-2009	3
6	XenDesktop 4.0	11-2009	6
7	XenDesktop 4.0 Feature Pack 1	03-2010	4

Sr. No	Released Version	Release Date (mm-yyyy)	Difference (in Months)
8	XenDesktop 4.0 Feature Pack 2	09-2010	6
9	XenDesktop 5.0	12-2010	3
10	XenDesktop 5.5	08-2011	8
11	XenDesktop 5.6	03-2012	7
12	XenDesktop 5.6 Feature Pack 1	06-2012	3
13	XenDesktop 7.0 (Excalibur)	06-2013	12
14	XenDesktop 7.1	10-2013	4
15	XenDesktop 7.5	03-2014	5
16	XenDesktop 7.6	09-2014	6
17	XenDesktop 7.6 Feature Pack 1	03-2015	6
	Average (in Months)		6

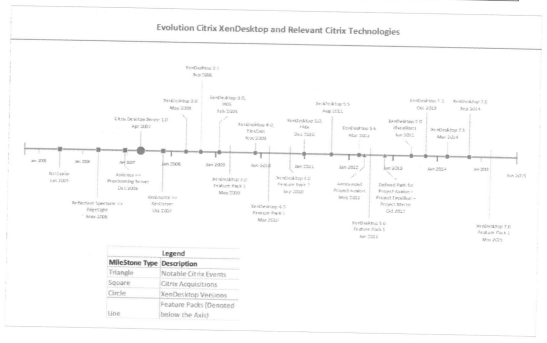

The XenDesktop® and Project Avalon roadmap

In May 2012, Citrix first announced Project Avalon during a Citrix Synergy conference. Project Avalon is a highly optimized and tuned integration of XenDesktop and CloudStack. CloudStack is an open-source Cloud computing software, which is used for implementing and managing the infrastructure of Cloud services. Project Avalon's objective is to empower businesses to rapidly deploy personalized Windows apps and desktops in a private Cloud across single or multiple sites, and to utilize the public Clouds in a "capacity on demand" fashion. It supports business initiatives, such as business continuity, integrating mergers and acquisitions, or offshoring projects.

At the October 2012 Synergy, Citrix laid out the path to the Project Avalon delivery in two major releases:

- The Excalibur release; key features included:
    - A simple and unified service delivery by using FlexCast 2.0, which will integrate XenApp and XenDesktop
    - Reinventing **HDX (High-Definition Experience)** for mobile and video
    - New HDX EdgeSight for real-time analytics and service visibility
    - Support for Windows 8 and Windows server 2012

- The Merlin; key features included:
    - Self-service provisioning, management, and service orchestration
    - An architecture that is open and scalable; it also supports any-site and any-Cloud architecture
    - Uninterrupted and easy service upgrades that support mix-and-match product releases

In June 2013, Citrix released the Project Avalon Excalibur with the XenDesktop 7 release. It was the first release of Project Avalon, and it integrated both XenApp and XenDesktop technologies into a unified **FlexCast Management Architecture (FMA)** for delivering Windows applications and desktops as Cloud services. Project Avalon makes and drives the XenDesktop roadmap along the way. The following screenshot taken from the Citrix website will give you an overview of Project Avalon:

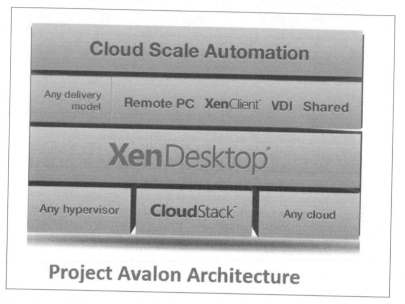

Project Avalon Architecture

XenDesktop® releases and improvements

Knowing the track record of how XenDesktop, its features, and its components have come about will help you to build a deeper understanding of the XenDesktop releases, and the ability to correlate them with the ultimate XenDesktop Project Avalon roadmap. You'll also be able to assess when a specific XenDesktop feature was released. However, this chapter doesn't include the details of the mentioned features or components.

Citrix® Desktop Server 1.0

Released in April 2007, **Citrix Desktop Server** 1.0 **(CDS)** was previously code-named Project Trinity. Citrix Desktop Server was the first purpose-built solution with the *DynamicDelivery* technology, which automatically selected the right type of virtual desktop, and thus enabling IT administrators to deliver the best desktop for each user according to their needs. It supported all three of the most popular ways of installing a desktop operating environment in a data centre. It included **Windows Terminal Server (TS)**, the server-hosted **virtual desktop infrastructure (VDI)**, and blade PCs-based assigned workstation desktops (blades). It featured two desktop delivery models:

- The server desktops, which were based on the Terminal Server
- The workstation desktops, which ran on VMware, Microsoft virtual server, the physical blade servers in a data centre, or any other end user PC

Workstation desktops can be *pooled* or *assigned*. The 32-bit Windows XP OS was supported for desktops. The product was priced starting at $75 per named user.

XenDesktop® 2.0

Released in May 2008, after the acquisition of Ardence and XenSource, Citrix announced the release of XenDesktop 2.0. Citrix combined the desktop virtualization capabilities of XenEnterprise v4 with its Citrix Desktop Server product line, thereby forming a new product called XenDesktop. XenDesktop 2.0 used to be shipped in five editions.

- Express
- Standard
- Advanced
- Enterprise
- Platinum

It featured the Active Directory authentication, Desktop Delivery Controller, XenApp for Virtual Desktops, Provisioning Server, Desktop Receiver for Windows XP, and Windows Vista. It also supported the 32-bit Windows XP SP2 and the Windows Vista desktop operating systems. It supported hypervisor versions, such as Citrix XenServer 4.1, SCVMM 1.0, and VMware Infrastructure 3 (VMware ESX). The pricing model has been changed to concurrent user's mode, which begins at $75 per concurrent user.

XenDesktop® 2.1

Released in September 2008, XenDesktop 2.1, in addition to enhanced components, it featured a **Software Development Kit** (**SDK**) and a way of creating disabled desktop groups. It supported the 64-bit version of Windows XP SP2 and the Windows Vista desktop operating systems. The hypervisor support was extended to the Windows Server 2008 Hyper-V and the respective SCVMM version.

XenDesktop® 3.0

Released in February 2009, XenDesktop 3.0 introduced the HDX technologies, including HDX MediaStream, HDX Plug-and-Play, and HDX Broadcast. At that time, the other new features were smart card support, profile management, local peripheral support, and user-driven desktop restart. It supported Windows XP SP3 and the Windows Vista 32-bit desktop operating systems. The hypervisor support remained the same. The pricing began at $75 per concurrent user.

XenDesktop® 3.0 Feature Pack 1

Released in May 2009, in this feature pack, Citrix enhanced XenDesktop 3.0 smart card support, display performance with CGP, and audio functionalities. It introduced HDX RealTime, which delivers voice-over-IP to the on-premises users and HDX MediaStream for Flash, which is a trial version released for evaluation and not for production use.

XenDesktop® 4.0

Released in November 2009, XenDesktop 4.0 introduced the FlexCast technology for improving scalability across multiple virtual desktop delivery models and for enabling enterprises to deliver virtual desktops to more users at a far lower cost. XenDesktop 4 includes all the functionalities of XenApp as an integrated feature, and it makes delivering on-demand applications a seamless part of the overall desktop management strategy.

The new features, such as active directory multi-forest support, site roaming and site failover for disaster recovery, IPv6 support, password manager, branch repeater integration, and alternate protocols /RDP integration have been included in this version. Enhancements have also been made to EdgeSight and profile management components. The HDX enhancements, such as plug-n-play USB Support, plug-n-play multi-monitor support, IntelliCache, and HDX 3D Pro graphics have been included in this version. The desktop support is extended to operating systems, such as Windows 7 (non-Aero) 32-bit or 64-bit, and 64-bit Windows XP and Windows Vista. The hypervisors support included Citrix XenServer 5.5, VMware Infrastructure 3, and VMware vSphere 4/4.1, and SCVMM 2008 & SCVMM 2008 R2.

Citrix changed the licensing to the named user pricing model. The XenDesktop 4 pricing began at $75 per named user for the standard edition. The VDI edition was priced at $95 per named user or $195 per concurrent user. The enterprise and the platinum editions were tagged at $225 and $350 per named user respectively. Citrix also started trade-up to XenDesktop 4 program, through which XenApp customers can trade their existing XenApp concurrent user licenses for a better version of XenDesktop. For one XenApp license, the customers would receive two XenDesktop 4 user licenses. Moreover, the trade-up starts at $45 per user.

XenDesktop® 4.0 Feature Pack 1

Released in March 2010, the Feature Pack 1 offered significant improvements to the Windows 7 image quality, the HDX plug and play audio for VoIP, and profile management. It has been built on the XenDesktop scalability enhancements, which allow the users to access the virtual desktop five times faster. It incorporated all the XenApp 6 features, including integration with Microsoft App-V and support for the Windows Server 2008 R2 for delivery controller.

XenDesktop® 4.0 Feature Pack 2

Released in September 2010, it featured the addition of two new technologies: Citrix XenClient and Citrix XenVault. The new XenClient technology was a groundbreaking client-side hypervisor developed in close collaboration with Intel, and it was optimized for the Intel Core vPro technology. It supports Citrix XenClient 1.0 for the XenDesktop 4 Enterprise and Platinum versions. The new XenVault technology automatically and transparently saves any user data created by corporate apps into an encrypted folder. This is ideal for contractors and businesses based on the **BYOC (Bring Your Own Computer)** model. XenVault automatically encrypts the data created by any corporate app that is delivered by Citrix XenApp or Microsoft App-V.

XenDesktop® 5.0

Released in December 2010, XenDesktop has been re-written and re-architected, bringing unprecedented levels of simplicity for both the users and IT professionals and developers. XenDesktop moved away from **Independent Management Architecture (IMA)** to a new architecture called FMA, which has been written almost completely in .NET. A remote desktop service (formally Terminal Services) is no longer required on **Desktop Delivery Controllers (DDC)** and it doesn't use the IMA data store.

For end users, an entirely redesigned virtual desktop viewer makes the workspace feel familiar and inviting. The powerful new HDX enhancements include the support for 32-bit color, dynamic color compression, HDX RealTime video conferencing, and large-file printing optimizations. These would dramatically improve the performance of the system even over low bandwidth connections. It has improved the smart card single sign-on from the non-domain-joined user devices. It also supports an entirely new generation of web and **software-as-a-service (SaaS)** apps. Citrix unveiled an extensive new initiative to help customers move from the *wow* of desktop virtualization to the *how* of successful implementation.

For IT, its role-based features have greatly simplified the management tasks and reduced the total number of management consoles. The new Desktop Studio console has been designed for administrators, and the new Desktop Director console has been designed for Helpdesk users. The new installer makes it faster and more powerful, so much so that you can complete a new installation in 10 minutes. It introduced a new technology for easily creating virtual desktops, called **Machine Creation Services (MCS)**, and single image desktop management. Microsoft remote assistance is now used for shadowing user desktop sessions. It has simplified policy administration by integrating Active Directory group policies. It has extended the FlexCast technology for supporting the new XenClient hypervisor and it has also extended the hypervisor support to XenServer 6, VMware vSphere 5.0, and SCVMM & Hyper-V for Windows Server 8 and SCVMM 2012. In addition, it introduced a comprehensive new SDK, which enables customers and partners to integrate and automate solutions with third-party systems management tools. The virtual desktop supported 64-bit Windows XP, Vista SP2, and Windows 7 (non-Aero).

The pricing for the VDI-only edition starts at $95 per user or device. The whole desktop and application virtualization in Enterprise and Platinum editions cost $225 and $350 respectively.

XenDesktop® 5.5

Released in August 2011, it introduced the Personal vDisk technology, acquired from RingCube, which made the virtual desktops personal. XenDesktop 5.5 witnessed 150 new features, and these are the most significant enhancements ever to have been made to HDX technology, resulting in three times faster (HDX Broadcast) delivery of virtual desktops over the WAN to mobile and branch office workers. Printing and scanning became six times faster, and app launching became two times faster. There have been new **Quality of Service (QoS)** controls for ensuring superior user experience across any network conditions. It included significant multimedia, voice and video enhancements. It also comes with a new flash redirection technology, which delivers stunning video and audio experience even over WAN.

The HDX components included the following:

- HDX MediaStream - Second generation flash redirection, server-rendered video, Windows media redirection, multi-stream ICA - including UDP for audio
- HDX RichGraphics - Microsoft RemoteFX Support, Windows 7 Aero Redirection, and 3D Pro Enhancements
- HDX Plug-n-Play Enhancements
- HDX Monitor to monitor and analyze HDX performance

It supports faster application delivery with the inclusion of the new Citrix XenApp 6.5 as an integrated feature. The new instant app access feature reduced the application launch times by almost 50 percent. It unveiled unparalleled native user experience on smart phones and tablets. It has enhanced the support for Microsoft technologies, including Microsoft RemoteFX, which provides Aero-based Windows 7 desktops, and App-V management tools integration. Hypervisor support has remained almost the same. The virtual desktop support was extended to Windows 7 Aero 32-bit or 64-bit.

XenDesktop® 5.6

Released in March 2012, this new version has fully integrated personalization technology with the addition of two new types of catalogues. The new catalogue are "pooled with the help of personal vDisk" (for pooled-static virtual desktops), which you can manage with the help of Desktop Studio, and "streamed with personal vDisk", which you can manage with the help of provisioning services. It has fully integrated the support for Microsoft System Center 2012 Configuration Manager (SCCM 2012) and for Microsoft System Center 2012 Virtual Machine Manager (SCVMM 2012). Citrix also announced the release of Citrix AppDNA 6 software, which enables the rapid assessment and migration of applications.

The virtual machines with personal vDisks are supported by Windows XP 32-bit with SP3 and Windows 7 (non-Aero). The supported virtual machines without personal vDisks include Windows XP, Windows Vista (non-Aero) with SP2, and Windows 7 (non-Aero).

XenDesktop® 5.6 Feature Pack 1

Released in June 2012, this is installed only as an upgrade to a XenDesktop 5.5 or a XenDesktop 5.6 deployment. This release unveils new features, such as remote PC access, a universal print server, the Citrix mobility pack, and the XenDesktop Collector support tool. It introduces enhancements for HDX 3D Pro and leverages the GPU hardware acceleration for the 3D applications based on OpenGL and DirectX. It enables replacing complex and expensive workstations with much simpler user devices, moving graphics processing into the data centre for centralized management. The other HDX enhancements include the HDX RealTime optimization pack for Microsoft Lync and HDX RealTime webcam video compression support for Cisco WebEx.

XenDesktop® 7.0

Released in June 2013, XenDesktop 7 is the first product release of the Project Avalon. It is called the Excalibur release. Project Avalon is a multi-phased initiative by Citrix for delivering Windows apps and desktops as Cloud services. XenDesktop 7 integrates both XenApp and XenDesktop technologies into a new unified and Cloud-style FMA. It has enabled scalable, simple, efficient, and manageable solutions for delivering Windows applications and desktops.

Citrix released new and redesigned management and delivery components, which provide administrators with a unified management experience. It has made XenDesktop 7 available in app edition. It has devised a new, streamlined installer, which will guide you through the installation of all of core components, such as delivery controller, StoreFront, license server, studio, director, and **Virtual Delivery Agents (VDAs)**.With EdgeSight integration, the web-based director user interface has been redesigned. StoreFront replaced the Web Interface component and featured enhancements including desktop appliance sites. MCS supported the creation of desktops and server OS VMs. For XenApp administrators, the entire XenDesktop FMA architecture brings a lot of new concepts, features, component mappings, and learnings.

XenDesktop 7 featured new HDX mobile technologies, which deliver an intuitive and mobile-friendly experience. The fully incorporated H.264 compression raised the WAN bandwidth efficiency, added innovative touch screen capabilities, and provided support for translating multi-touch gestures and finger swipes into smooth navigation and scrolling commands. New compression capabilities for supporting the dynamic optimization of the full HD video (webcam) bit rate has made HD videos viewable on 3G mobile networks. It included Windows Server 2012 and Windows 8 support, desktop composition redirection, Windows media client-side content fetching, multicast support, real-time multimedia transcoding, **User Datagram Protocol (UDP)** audio for server OS machines, HDX 3D Pro, rich graphics and video rendering from the server side, and improved flash redirection.

XenDesktop 7 is built as an open platform, and it supports deployment on any hypervisor or Cloud management solution, including the Citrix Cloud platform (which is powered either by Apache CloudStack) or **Amazon Web Services (AWS)**. It introduced the addition of new capabilities, such as the following:

- Universal print server functionality included within the delivery controller
- New machine catalog options, applications, and desktops
- Local App Access
- Microsoft app-V integration
- IPv6 support
- AppDNA
- Improved profile management
- Configuration logging
- Delegated administration
- VDAs auto-update delivery controller details
- Client folder redirection
- Improved VDA management settings
- Enhanced and integrated error reporting
- Support for group policies configured in the Citrix mobility pack
- Personal vDisk enhancements
- Support for Microsoft **Key Management Services (KMS)** activation with **Machine Creation Services (MCS)**
- Support for fast user switching by using RDP connections
- Remote PC access support for Windows 8

The Citrix Ready partners deliver XenDesktop 7 optimized solutions, such as:

- CA technologies to support the new infrastructure management capabilities
- Dell introduced DVS-Enterprise Integrated Storage
- The NVidia Grid vGPU technology enabled enhancements, which made a new Citrix HDX 3D technology that supports an unmatched direct GPU access

The Host hypervisor support included:

- XenServer 6.2
- VMware vSphere 5.1 Update 1
- SCVMM 2012 and 2012 SP1

The virtual desktops support the following:

- Windows Desktop OS
    - Windows 7 SP1
    - Windows 8

- Windows Server OS
    - Windows Server 2012
    - Windows Server 2008 R2 SP1

The minimum supported provisioning services version is 7.0, and the License Server is v11.11.

Citrix has discontinued most of the legacy features in this release, including:

- Legacy printing
- Direct SSL connections
- Secure ICA encryption below 128-bit
- Secure Gateway
- Web interface
- Shadowing users-to-users and supporting Microsoft remote assistance
- Anonymous users
- Session pre-launch
- Power and capacity management
- The initial Flash v1 redirection

- Local text echo
- Loopback support for virtual IP
- Smart auditor
- **Single sign-on (SSO)**
- Oracle database support
- **Health monitoring and recovery (HMR)**
- Custom ICA files
- The management pack for **System Center Operations Manager (SCOM)** 2007
- CNAME function
- The quick deploy wizard
- Native device drivers on delivery controllers
- Remote PC service configuration files and PowerShell script for automatic administration and Workflow Studio

The XenDesktop 7 editions were available in licensing modes, such as per-user, per-device, or on a concurrent basis. The new XenDesktop app edition was made available only for XenApp customers who were using the entire hosted-shared (RDS) app and published desktop workloads. The upgrade to the XenDesktop app edition was offered without any additional charge for XenApp Enterprise and Platinum customers with an active subscription.

XenDesktop® 7.1

Released in October 2013, Citrix termed XenDesktop 7.1 as a platform. The XenDesktop platform is based on the new architecture Simplified FlexCast Management, which is compatible with the latest Microsoft technologies. The new features include the **Virtual Graphical Processing Unit (vGPU)**, which allows multiple VMs to access a single physical GPU, and provides full support to 3D graphics. The **Graphical Processing Unit (GPU)** capabilities redirect flash- graphics for OS, such as Windows 8.1, Windows 8, Windows Server 2012, and 2012 R2. It supports virtual desktops and applications for the operating system Windows 8.1 and Windows Server 2012 R2.

It supports the following hypervisor solutions:

- XenServer 6.2
- VMware vSphere 5.1 Update 1
- SCVMM 2012, 2012 R2 and 2012 SP1

XenDesktop® 7.5

In March 2014, along with XenDesktop 7.5, Citrix released XenApp 7.5 as a separate product, which shared the unified FMA architecture and management. XenDesktop takes the enterprise desktop virtualization deployments to hybrid provisioning by allowing businesses to use public Clouds, such as AWS or any Citrix Cloud Platform that is powered by the Apache CloudStack Cloud. This improves their flexibility and leads to the growth or transformation of their virtual desktop infrastructure. While the hypervisor's support is extended to VMware vSphere 5.5, neither VMware vSphere 5.5 nor Hyper-V hypervisors are supported by the Citrix CloudPlatform. The Citrix CloudPlatform only supports XenServer 6.2. On the other hand, AWS doesn't offer the desktop operating system instances. So, you can provision the applications and desktops only on supported Windows server operating systems.

The remote PC access is enhanced such that it supports the Wake on the LAN for PCs that support Intel **Active Management Technology (AMT)**, or PCs with the Wake on the LAN option enabled in the BIOS. Also included full AppDNA support for the automated analysis of Windows application suitability for application virtualization through XenApp, App-V, or XenDesktop. It also features StoreFront 2.5 and supports Web Interface 5.4 without providing support for any additional operating systems or enhancements. The virtual desktops operating system support remains the same.

Citrix announced two new Citrix Ready programs for driving the hybrid Cloud and low-cost initiatives. The new Citrix Ready **Infrastructure-as-a-Service (IaaS)** Cloud for XenDesktop supports businesses by helping them find a Cloud operator whose infrastructure supports XenDesktop. Citrix Ready low-cost converged infrastructure verified solutions are tested for their scalability deployments, which range from a few hundred to a few thousand desktops. These provide performance and maintain a high availability of resources. Citrix also introduced a limited time XenMobile promotion, which included a free XenMobile MDM or 20 percent off the XenMobile enterprise for XenApp and XenDesktop platinum edition customers, which was valid until September 30, 2014.

XenDesktop® 7.6

Released in September 2014, XenDesktop is built on third-generation FMA, and it is designed to be deployed in the Cloud and in hybrid environments. It features instant access to virtual apps by retaining the application pre-launch, session linger, and anonymous logon features that were made popular by the earlier versions of XenApp. The new connection leasing feature enables high availability and provides resilience in withstanding the temporary loss of database. It delivers an unmatched user experience through improved graphics performance, which includes improved image sharpening, visually enhancing the lossless compression, and extending the DirectX/2D rendering capabilities. It is also USB 3.0 ready, and it provides the generic redirection of the latest USB 3.0 peripherals, such as webcams, headsets, and Lync phones. To enhance the user experience of Windows apps on the mobile devices, Citrix released a new update for the HDX Mobile SDK. The new enhancements in provisioning services employ commodity servers and the RAM so that the IOPS load on storage is dropped by 99 percent, which obliterates the cost barriers for delivering high-performance storage.

It's the only unified platform which is **Federal Information Processing Standards (FIPS)** compliant under the **Common Criteria (CC)** evaluation. It features the security enhancements that enable the granular policies over clipboard content filtering and directional control, so that potentially malicious data, perhaps embedded in the Rich Text Format, cannot be pasted to the secured environment. It supports the secure connections between users and VDAs. The Platinum edition includes the full power of the Citrix AppDNA application migration technology, which simplifies app migrations to the latest versions of Windows. In close partnership with Microsoft, Citrix developed the Citrix Connector 7.5 for **System Center Configuration Manager (SCCM)**, and it has released a new reference architecture for deploying XenApp and XenDesktop on Microsoft Azure, which materializes the Citrix Workspace Services vision on Azure. It integrates and enhances the existing XenApp 6.5 deployments, and it also streamlines the Cloud deployments with the verified IaaS providers.

Enhancements have been made to Citrix Studio and Citrix Director. The new features in Studio include enhanced reporting and application folders. The new features in Director include licensing alerts, the view hosted applications usage, monitoring hotfixes, an expanded filtering feature, and the Director has also been made compatible to XenApp 6.5. The enhanced connection throttling settings provide control and they improve host performance.

They support both the virtual IP and the virtual loopback for the applications published on machines running Windows Server 2008 R2 and Windows Server 2012 R2. The Remote PC access enhancement limits a local user from disconnecting a remote session without the permission of a remote session user. It provides support for the HDX Real-Time Optimization Pack 1.5 for Microsoft Lync. It also provides support to the receiver for Chrome 1.4 and the Receiver for HTML5 1.4. These receivers include the ability to convert document files into PDF files from hosted applications or applications running on the virtual desktops, so that users can view and print them from their local device.

The new Citrix StoreFront 2.6 has the following features:

- Simplified store configuration in the administration console
- A receiver for the Web My Apps Folder View
- Support for the pass-through authentication by XenApp 6.5 through the Kerberos constrained delegation
- Support for smart card authentication by XenApp Services
- Single **Fully Qualified Domain Name (FQDN)** access
- Receivers for mobile platforms, such as iOS and Android

The virtualization resource support has been extended to XenServer 6.2 SP1 with hotfixes. The virtual desktops operating system support remains the same. The Citrix CloudPlatform supports XenServer 6.2 SP1 with hotfixes, VMware vSphere 5.5, and it does not support the Hyper-V hypervisors.

XenDesktop® 7.6 Feature Pack 1

The XenDesktop 7.6 feature pack 1 was released in March 2015, and it features the Session Recording capability, which lets admin users record the on-screen activity of any user's session. It is accompanied by a new Citrix Director, version 7.6.200, through which the session recording can be enabled or disabled. The Session Recording is based on Citrix's popular SmartAuditor technology. Using Session Recording, one can instantly record difficult to reproduce errors and provide faster resolutions for the users' issues. The feature pack includes the latest HDX Real-Time Optimization Pack 1.7, which has further enhanced the performance of Microsoft Lync in XenDesktop environment for the users of Linux and Windows devices. It also has a new version of Citrix Licensing 11.12.1, which is equipped with the Citrix Licensing **Customer Experience Improvement Program (CEIP)**, and the Call Home capability.

Core strengths of XenDesktop®

A technology product's core strengths/capabilities make it stand out in the competitive industry market. XenDesktop comes with a set of core strengths that make it a preferred choice across various business verticals. The following are the core strengths of XenDesktop technology:

- Any device, anytime, anywhere
- HDX user experience technology
- FlexCast delivery technology
- Open architecture - Cloud-ready FMA
- On-demand applications by XenApp
- Automated Application Migration with AppDNA
- High security and compliance standards

The following figure is a diagrammatic representation of the XenDesktop core strengths:

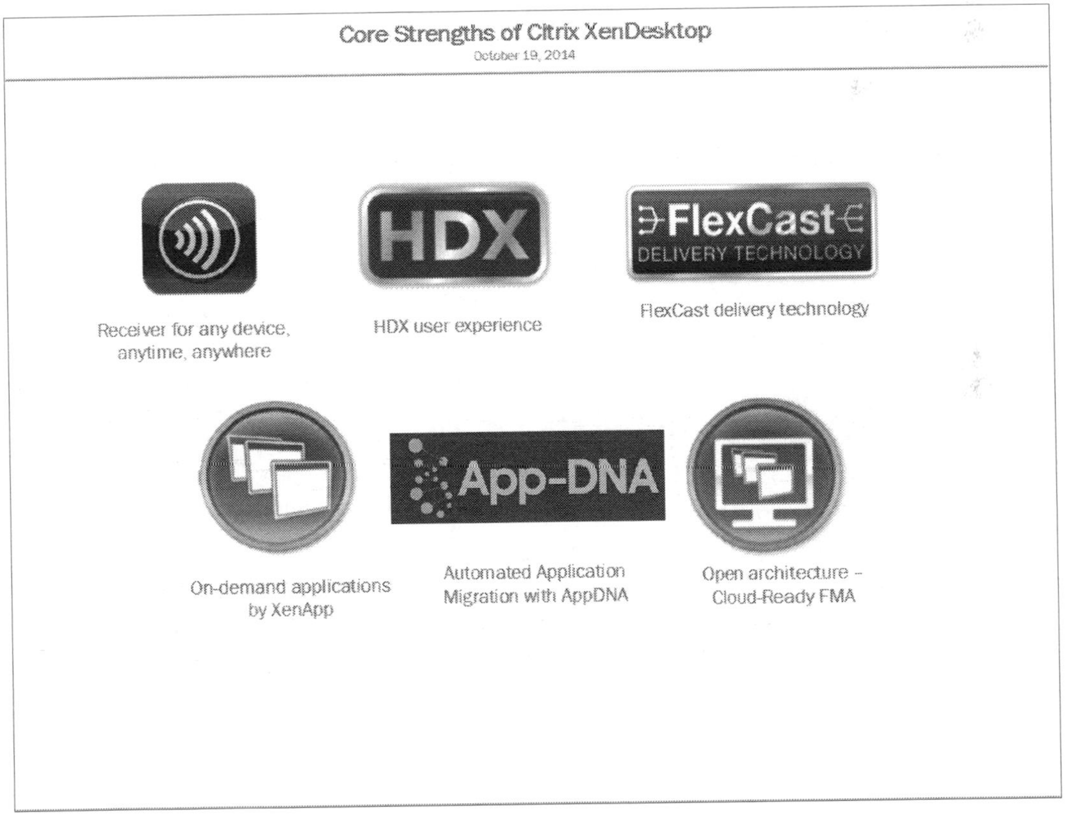

XenDesktop administrators, technologists, and architects know all of these very well. For mastering XenDesktop, it is important to understand how these core strengths matter for businesses. We'll discuss these core strengths in detail, and also get to know the other key strengths of XenDesktop that have significant business value.

Citrix® Receiver for any device, anytime, anywhere

Citrix XenDesktop uses the Citrix Receiver, which is a universal client built with a vision of supporting any device and any platform. It currently supports all mobile and desktop device platforms, including Windows, Mac, Linux, iOS, Android, ChromeOS, and Blackberry. It also supports Thin Client environments, which require a zero-install option and a clientless HTML5 Receiver, which is available for web-based access. It works natively on a broad range of physical devices, including desktops, laptops, tablets, and smart phones. Citrix Receiver has been made available on many popular online application stores, which has made it simpler to install and use on BYOD or corporate devices. It has been designed to easily adopt the features of the native device, including scrolling the native menus, multi-touch, and pop-up controls, GPS, and cameras, specifically on touch based mobile devices.

XenDesktop users can access their desktops, corporate applications, web, SaaS, and their secure ShareFile integrated user data on any device, at anytime and from anywhere. This enables complete workplace flexibility, business continuity, and user mobility.

HDX user experience technology

Citrix High Definition (**HDX**) user experience technologies have been built on top of the Citrix ICA protocol, which is renowned for the best-of-breed networking. It represents 25 years of innovation and excellence. The ICA protocol in itself is based on the basic TCP/IP and RTP/UDP protocols, and it has been uniquely designed for traversing the difficult network topologies that range from variable mobile networks to high latency low-bandwidth WANs. HDX is a unique strength of XenDesktop, and it makes the virtual desktop delivery experience extremely responsive and fast.

The Citrix ICA protocol was primarily used for streaming application and terminal session screen updates by XenApp. Citrix ported this ICA protocol for delivering a Windows desktop operating system, and they had initially named it PortICA. The underlying architecture of PortICA remained the same. It uses the virtual channels. PortICA was turned into the HDX technology in the later releases. HDX has been a part of Project Avalon Excalibur, and it has been enhanced by enormous capabilities.

The Citrix HDX technologies are the foundation of the Citrix application (XenApp) and desktop delivery (XenDesktop) platforms. They provide superior high-definition user experience on any device, over any network. It delivers an unparalleled experience, even while using real time audio and video collaboration, rich multimedia, the latest USB peripherals and 3D graphics. As Windows apps became optimized for mobile devices, they improved their support for touch gestures and other native device features. The integrated WAN optimization capabilities of HDX deliver a satisfying user experience, even over challenging low-bandwidth and high-latency networks. When using XenDesktop and the HDX technologies, IT departments can successfully extend the delivery of the virtual desktops beyond the corporate headquarter offices to remote, mobile, and branch office users.

Knowing the HDX internals involves understanding the three technical principles that it is made of. These are:

- Intelligent redirection
- Adaptive compression
- Data de-duplication

At run time, these work towards delivering an optimized user experience, reduced bandwidth consumption, and improved scalability of the rendering server.

Intelligent redirection

This involves examining user screen activity, application commands, and the user endpoint device, which connects the network and hosting server capabilities, so that they can dynamically determine how and where to render an application or a desktop activity. The redirection operation can occur on either the local client or the central VDA. Redirection at the client offloads all the processing from the server and places it on the client's device. The device and the peripheral redirection lets the peripherals, such as webcams, printers and scanners, to be terminated locally, so that users can interact with these devices at native USB speeds.

The following figure is a diagrammatic illustration of the steps that were used in the intelligent redirection process. It also indicates the various virtual channels, the network layers, and the protocols that were involved in the HDX technology.

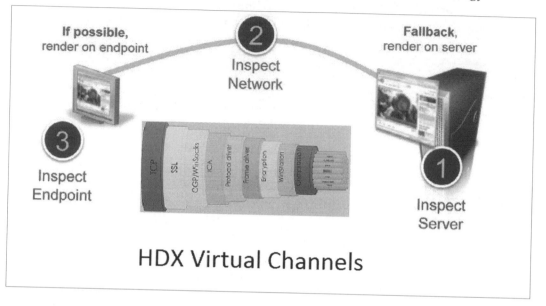

Adaptive compression

Adaptive compression is a core intellectual property of the ICA protocol. It determines the intelligent usage of system resources, including CPUs and/or GPUs. It also configures the appropriate codecs that can be used, based on different network conditions.

De-duplication of network traffic

This is implemented through multicasting and caching techniques. The HDX caching de-duplicates frequently accessed data, including files, bitmap graphics, print jobs, and streamed media. HDX supports the multicasting of multimedia streams, where the delivery of a single transmission from the source to many users creates one-to-many communications.

The Citrix HDX technology ensures the following:

1. The delivery of smooth audio, video, and multimedia performance.
2. HDX 3D Pro optimizes 2D and 3D professional graphics.
3. HDX mobile provides a native look and feel to the Windows applications on the mobile.

4. The HDX SoC embedded technology enhances the thin clients support.

5. Accelerated printing and scanning.

6. Support for a broad variety of USB devices.

7. Highest quality of service and reliability.

FlexCast® delivery technology

As in the case of traditional physical desktops, it is not possible to meet every user's requirements with a single desktop type because different types of business users need different types of desktop setups. This has been the greatest limitation for businesses when it comes to adopting desktop virtualization technologies. In a business organization, some users will require simplicity and standardization, while other users will require a highly personalized and more performance equipped system. If a single desktop virtualization model is implemented across an entire organization, it will inevitably lead to reduced user productivity.

FlexCast is a delivery technology which enables IT to deliver every type of virtual desktop, such as hosted, local, physical, or virtual- each specifically tailored to meet the performance, security, personalization, mobility and flexibility requirements of each user. This approach is unique and it is dramatically different from the way in which most other vendors look at desktop virtualization. Six FlexCast models are available, and each one provides different capabilities,
based on the unique user group requirements.

- Hosted shared
- Hosted VDI
    - Random/Non-persistent
    - Static/Non-persistent
    - Static persistent

- Remote PC
- Streamed VHD
- Local VM
- On-demand apps

It is very important to assess the business user requirements, and then choose the right FlexCast model for using resources efficiently and for providing the best end user experience.

Hosted shared

A single server based operating system equipped with high end resources is provisioned by using machine creation services, or by provisioning services provided by XenDesktop. Multiple user desktops are delivered by a single server, which uses Microsoft **Remote Desktop Services (RDS)**. This is similar to the Published Server Desktop in XenApp environments. This model provides a low-cost, high-density solution. However, it can only support the applications that are compatible with a multi-user server operating system.

Hosted VDI

In this model, each user is provided with a true desktop operating system. This removes the limitation of the applications that requires them to be multi-user aware and binds them to support the server operating systems. Since the complete desktop instance is rendered, it is easier for administrators to define a granular level of control over desktop resources, including a number of virtual processors and memory assignments.

It offers the following sub categories. In all of the sub categories, the desktops are based on a single master image and they are provisioned by using machine creation services or provisioning services.

Random/Non-persistent

In this model, the user changes made to the desktop will be lost when it is rebooted. There will be a pool of desktop instances and users will be dynamically connected to one of them when they log on.

Static/Non-persistent

In this model, the user changes made to the desktop will be lost when it is rebooted. However, the users will always be connected to the virtual desktop instance that was allocated to them at the time of their first access.

Static persistent

In this model, the user changes made to the desktop will be stored in a personal vDisk and it will be retained in-between reboots. Also, the users will always be connected to the virtual desktop instance that was allocated to them at the time of their first access. However, the desktops with a personal vDisk cannot be shared among multiple users and each user will require their own desktop. It is recommended to host a personal vDisk on a shared storage for high availability requirements.

Remote PC

This model lets users connect to their already existing physical desktop, which is on the corporate network, is a recent addition to FlexCast. It has been done to facilitate a secured and a controlled access to corporate systems by users from remote locations. It assumes that the physical desktop management should be taken care of, either manually or by using third party tools.

Streamed VHD

This is a primary model, which employs the provisioning services for delivering desktops. In this model, virtual desktops are provisioned for being run locally on the user's desktop computer hardware. This is a great solution for businesses, and using this will let them leverage their investments on desktop systems with high resources. This solution requires a LAN connection to be in place between the desktop and Provisioning Servers. In this, changes made to the desktops will be lost upon rebooting.

Local VM

The centrally managed virtual desktops image is delivered to VMs running locally within a hypervisor on the client computer, and this enables offline connectivity. This model uses Citrix XenClient for providing the Local VMs.

On-demand apps

The on-demand apps FlexCast model centralizes the Windows applications in the data centre, and enables instant accessing through high-speed protocol (requires connection), or it can also be streamed (offline support) through Microsoft App-V. It does not provide users with virtual desktops, but provides them with Windows applications.

The following figure is a very informative comparison table, which covers the various FlexCast model supports that have been provided by XenDesktop version 7.x. Using this table, you can easily opt for a FlexCast model for a given user case requirement.

FlexCast Model Comparison

FlexCast Model		User Installed Apps	Image Delivery Technology	Virtual / Physical	Access	Desktop to User Ratio
Hosted shared: Non-Persistent		No	MCS / PVS	Physical / Virtual	HDX	1:Many
Hosted VDI:	Random / Non-Persistent	No	MCS / PVS	Virtual	HDX	1:Many
	Static / Non-Persistent	No	MCS / PVS	Virtual	HDX	1:1
	Static / Persistent	Yes	MCS / PVS	Virtual	HDX	1:1
Remote PC		Yes	Installed	Physical	HDX	1:1
Streamed VHD		No	PVS	Physical	Local	1:1
Local VM		Yes	XC	Virtual (XenClient)	Local	1:1
On demand apps		No	MCS / PVS	Physical / Virtual	HDX	1:Many

Open architecture - Cloud-ready FMA

In today's businesses, IT prioritizes the centralization and simplification of desktop infrastructure for reducing the total cost of ownership. This leads to the move of desktop infrastructure to a Cloud that enables maximum benefits and capabilities for businesses. However, at present, businesses have made huge investments in various hypervisors, storage, and Microsoft infrastructures. Most of the businesses need a hybrid solution, which would leverage the existing infrastructure, as well as pave the path for migrating to Cloud solutions.

The XenDesktop architecture, FMA, adds the hybrid Cloud provisioning capability, which lets the customers use Cloud services, as well as the traditional virtual infrastructural deployments. The XenDesktop supports Cloud services with the help of a public AWS or Citrix CloudPlatform powered by Apache CloudStack Cloud for flexing, growing, or transforming virtual desktop infrastructures.

It also supports the existing hypervisors, storage, and Microsoft infrastructures, and this enables businesses to leverage their current investments, while providing the flexibility for adding or changing alternatives. Support includes all the major hypervisors, such as Citrix XenServer, Microsoft Hyper-V, and VMware ESX. It simplifies the management of networked storage by using Citrix StorageLink technology, which was leveraged and supported by XenServer. XenDesktop also closely integrates with Microsoft App-V and System Center for application management.

Citrix FMA is the XenDesktop architecture that plays a key role in Project Avalon Excalibur by converging XenApp with the XenDesktop solutions. Citrix, with XenDesktop 7.0, has converged the XenApp with XenDesktop. Now, both solutions share a common FMA architecture.

The other key benefits of the FMA architecture include:

- It simplifies the installation and administration by having only two components, delivery controllers, and agents. The agents are the installed worker servers, while the controllers manage users, resources, configurations, and they store these in a central SQL server database.
- Agents on the worker servers communicate with delivery controllers and they do not require a direct access to either the site's database or the license servers.
- FMA is now the common underlying architecture for both XenApp and XenDesktop products. This makes it easier for XenApp customers to migrate to XenDesktop.
- Management consoles have been consolidated and reduced to only two programs: the Studio and the Director. The Studio is for IT administrators so that they can administer and manage the XenDesktop infrastructures. The next generation Director is for Cloud-enabled management and operations of the Helpdesk support teams.

The following figure is a diagrammatic representation of the XenDesktop FMA architecture:

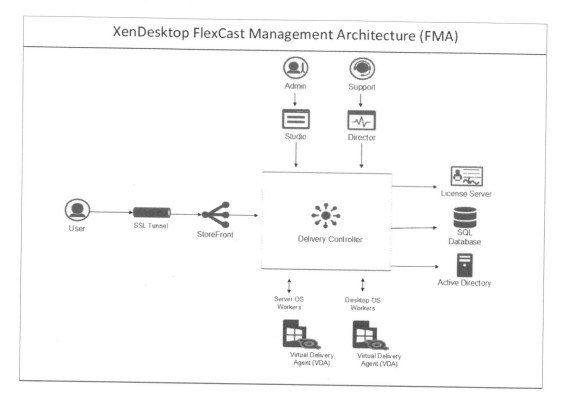

On-demand applications by XenApp®

To reduce the desktop management cost and complexity, XenDesktop includes the integration of a range of Citrix application virtualization technologies with on-demand applications by Citrix XenApp. With application virtualization, IT can control data access, manage fewer desktop images, eliminate any system conflicts, and reduce the application regression testing, by making it a requirement for successful desktop virtualization. Adding, updating, and removing applications has now become simple as XenDesktop now includes a self-service app store, which has been made available through the storefront, and lets users access applications instantly from any location.

Automated application migration with AppDNA®

The XenDesktop Platinum edition includes the Citrix AppDNA application migration technology, which simplifies app migrations to the latest versions of Windows. The Citrix AppDNA application management software combines insight about the application portfolios with an accurate application testing, compatibility, and remediation. It lets enterprises discover, automate, model, and manage the applications for migrations. It also deploys new virtualization technology and daily application management. Automating the application migration process saves enterprises time, labor, and cost, while reducing risk. It greatly helps the desktop transformations to be completed on time, within budget, and with lesser end user disruption. The AppDNA software also provides the knowledge that guides business decisions about application compatibility, migration, management, and building a long-term application portfolio evolution.

The Citrix AppDNA software simplifies the following key areas of application management:

- Discovering application issues with the help of sophisticated testing methods
- Application portfolio modeling for determining the best plan of action
- Automating both the application remediation and the packaging processes
- Eases the management of ongoing application evolution after the launch of the migration or the virtualization project

High security and compliance standards

When deploying Citrix XenDesktop within large organizations and government environments, security standards are an important consideration. Citrix is committed to making sure that the technology is fully secure and adheres to government standards for encryption and accessibility.

For businesses, XenDesktop currently offers the following security and compliance capabilities:

- A centrally secured desktop in the data centre that can be delivered to any device.
- Centrally secured apps in the data that centre can be delivered to any device.
- It provides high security with multi-factor authentication, the latest FIPS Compliance, the Common Criteria Evaluation certifications, and activity logging for compliance support.

- It provides SmartAccess fine grained context based policy controls for scenario based access restrictions.

- The Session Recording capability provides enhanced security through logging and monitoring. It allows organizations to record on-screen user activity for applications that deal with sensitive information, which is critical in regulated industries, such as health care and finance.

- The **Mobile Device Management** (**MDM**) suite for configuring and securing the enterprise user mobile devices ensures the authenticity and safety of users who access the XenDesktop sessions from their mobile devices.

- The Citrix ShareFile product integration provides optimized and on-demand on-premises or off-premises data sync and sharing.

Summary

We saw a detailed XenDesktop evolution timeline from its initial version to its latest version and its roadmap, which is part of Project Avalon. From the roadmap, we learned the key objectives of Project Excalibur and Project Merlin, which make up Project Avalon. This understanding will help you in knowing what to expect in the future releases of the XenDesktop. We also learned the core strengths that have expanded the XenDesktop usability and dependability by businesses. This chapter will help the businesses to easily and clearly understand the reliable data points and technical strengths in choosing XenDesktop. From reading this chapter, you'll be able to assess whether or not you should consider XenDesktop for your desktop virtualization projects.

In the following chapter, we'll go through the detailed architecture that includes the core and additional components of the XenDesktop. We'll learn the role of each component and its orchestration in serving the users of the XenDesktop sessions.

2
Understanding the XenDesktop® Architecture in Detail

In the previous chapter, we saw the evolution of XenDesktop from its early days to its latest versions. We discussed the various capabilities and features of XenDesktop across the different versions. We learned their core strengths and their technological details. In this chapter, we'll learn the key benefits of the XenDesktop architecture for enterprise businesses. We will also discuss its evolution, its components, and the XenDesktop architecture's workflow.

The architecture covers layers such as:

- Site database
- The client side receiver
- Delivery controllers
- NetScaler for networking
- StoreFront for web services
- Active Directory for authentication
- XenDesktop editions for licensing
- Hypervisors supporting the backend **Virtual Machine (VM)** instances

We'll discuss the XenDesktop internals in detail. In this chapter, the following topics will be covered:

- Site
- Store
- Delivery groups
- Machine catalogs
- Machine creation services
- Master images and their management
- Virtual desktop agents
- Working with the Director and the Studio consoles for managing the XenDesktop infrastructure

We'll also cover additional components such as:

- EdgeSight
- Branch repeaters
- NetScaler
- Provisioning services

 The XenDesktop architecture is now shared by the XenApp product as well. However, the scope of this chapter is limited to the details of XenDesktop.

Key features of the XenDesktop® architecture for businesses

Before we explore the XenDesktop architecture in detail, let's discover the key features of the XenDesktop architecture that benefit enterprises and businesses. The following is a quick list of the features of the XenDesktop architecture that benefit enterprises and businesses:

Here are the business driven enterprise capabilities of the XenDesktop architecture:

- FMA is developed from scratch for XenDesktop
- No dependency on the Microsoft Terminal Services
- Supports scalability and extensibility of the overall solution
- Shared architecture for XenApp and XenDesktop

- Simplified installer with guided quick deploy
- Reduced management consoles
- Configuration logging for change management
- Delegated administration
- Integration with Active Directory for MCS and AD Group Policies for managing XenDesktop policies
- Real-time monitoring and reports generation
- SDK for custom automations

The evolution of XenDesktop® architecture

XenDesktop has gone through a long journey, and it has passed through major architectural changes. Citrix introduced a new intuitive way for businesses to manage enterprise Windows applications through a centralized application delivery technology (the XenApp). Later, it was expanded to cover virtual desktops as well (the XenDesktop). Lately, Citrix has unified both of these technologies for delivering mobile users a complete workspace with support for Cloud infrastructures under Project Avalon. This sequence of high-level integrations has led to the dissection and convergence of both the XenApp and XenDesktop architectures.

What this means for businesses its going to be a faster step to adopt one of these technologies if they already own one. Say, if a company already has the XenApp technology in place, then it's a familiar step to adopt the XenDesktop technology, since both of the products use the same HDX protocols and other networking components, such as StoreFront, NetScaler, and so on.

As mentioned in *Chapter 1, Evolution and Core Strengths of XenDesktop®*, Citrix launched its very first virtual desktop delivery technology called Citrix Desktop Server 1.0 in 2007, and its later versions came to be known as XenDesktop.

XenDesktop® 2.0 and Independent Management Architecture (IMA)

It's very important for the XenDesktop masters to know how XenDesktop worked in its previous versions and the pros and cons that led to the changes in its architectural design. We'll go through an overview of the IMA and discuss the data points on how it was before IMA, since it's closely related to XenApp.

In 2008, the initial version of XenDesktop 2.0 was built on Citrix's pre-existing flagship technologies, including the networking protocol and architecture. It featured the following:

- The PortICA (now HDX) extended the ICA protocol for client to server communication. The ICA protocol for Windows was introduced in 1990. The PortICA allows only a single ICA session at a time whereas ICA protocol supports multiple concurrent ICA sessions to RDSH in XenApp.
- The IMA was introduced with Citrix MetaFrame XP (now called XenApp) for internal server management in 2001.

Prior to IMA, in the versions before MetaFrame XP, the server configuration settings were saved in the registry. They have been replicated across the MetaFrame servers by the ICA Browser Service (installed on each server locally) through the UDP broadcasts and remote calls. The MetaFrame XP was launched with IMA in which IMA replaced the ICA browser service. It had features such as:

- Data store: An ODBC compliant database, which contained the configuration settings of all the MetaFrame servers, including licenses, zone configurations, printers and drivers, published apps, load evaluators, trust relationships, and so on. These are accessible to all MetaFrame servers.
- A protocol: It is a TCP-based event-driven messaging bus, and it is used for transferring the ever-changing background information among the MetaFrame servers, and these include the server load, the current users and connections, and the licenses that are in use. It uses port 2512 for server to server communication and port 2513 for management console communication with the data store.

The IMA for XenDesktop had the following scalability limitations:

- Single Farm Master: the IMA constitutes a master desktop delivery controller for the zone, and it is referred to as the Farm Master. It has specific duties that only it can perform. The duties include handling all the connection requests from the users, performing desktop resolution operations during desktop startup, managing the backend hosting infrastructure, and so on. This has caused Farm Master to become a bottleneck in large enterprise deployments, as the desktop groups grow. Furthermore, a Farm Master can't be scaled out by adding more servers. It can only be scaled up by upgrading to a system with higher processing power.

- Proprietary database: the IMA data store was built on the proprietary database structure, that is, it has evolved from its legacy, the MetaFrame technology, which was based on encrypted LDAP. It was not built on the SQL features or capabilities though it supports the SQL database as a container. The IMA data store has not been designed for scaling thousands of desktops and for holding a huge configuration data. IMA caches the data store locally on every XenDesktop server as **Local Host Cache (LHC)**. As the desktop count grows, the data that has to be replicated for each member controller server LHC increases, thus affecting performance and scalability.

The following figure is an architectural diagram of XenDesktop with IMA:

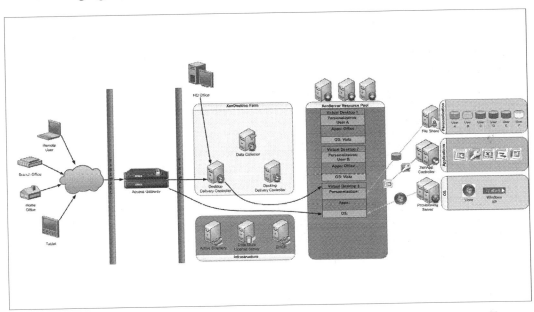

XenDesktop® 5.0 and FlexCast® Management Architecture

In 2010, Citrix released XenDesktop 5.0 designed with a completely revamped new framework architecture called **FMA (FlexCast Management Architecture)**. FMA is primarily comprised of the delivery controller, the server side component, the virtual desktop agent, the client side component. This greatly simplified and the XenDesktop setup compared to the previous version of XenDesktop, which was based on IMA. We'll discuss the FMA components, including the delivery controller and the virtual desktop agent in the next section.

Here is how FMA addressed the scalability limitations with the previous IMA:

- To overcome the IMA data store database scalability limitations, FMA has been designed and developed on the standard relational database featuring the Microsoft SQL. This has let the XenDesktop administrators leverage the enterprise capabilities of the SQL server, such as redundancy, backup, high availability, and scalability.

- In FMA, the entire configuration and dynamic data were saved in the central SQL database and there was no LHC that had to be maintained on the member server. With this, the controllers were made truly stateless and there was no need for the master controllers. Thus, in FMA, all the controllers are equal and you can scale XenDesktop to any of the larger deployments.

XenDesktop® 7.0 with FMA - the unified architecture for XenDesktop® 7 and XenApp®

In 2013, Citrix released a new major version XenDesktop 7 as Project Excalibur featuring convergence of the XenApp product. Later in 2014, Citrix released XenApp again as a separate product based on FMA. This has lead to the sharing of the same FMA architecture by the XenDesktop and XenApp products. FMA is now going to be the future of both the product lines. This means that mastering FMA will get you to master the worlds of XenDesktop and the XenApp. However, in this context, we'll only see the comparisons and the benefits of FMA within the XenDesktop versions.

The basics of FMA - the XenDesktop® architecture

FMA is the first architecture from Citrix that has been designed for XenDesktop. Citrix has chosen to develop the new FMA version on the **Microsoft .Net** framework. Also, Citrix played an important role in choosing the relational database for storing the static configuration and the dynamic management information. Citrix FMA is fully based on the Microsoft SQL relational database and its built-in enterprise capabilities. This choice of Microsoft's native application development technologies has become the greatest strength for implementing a flexible and robust FMA. It has also made it easier to automate and integrate them through scripting for tasks, such as automation and reporting.

FMA also supports interoperability and modular management across the various Citrix technologies. FMA is a key player in the Project Avalon roadmap for supporting FlexCast, delivering models with open architecture, and supporting the Cloud infrastructures.

Here, we'll learn about the key features of FMA and discuss all of its components and their inter-workings in detail. We will also define the new concepts and terminologies of FMA.

Concepts and terminologies

The following are the different concepts and terminologies that are used in FMA:

- A delivery site: A delivery site is a top level entity that includes all the components of a XenDesktop deployment in a single geographical location. It serves as an administrative boundary for the XenDesktop deployment. These sites offer applications and desktops to groups of users. In FMA, a domain environment is a prerequisite for deploying a site.

- Host: A host is a server class hardware computer dedicated entirely to running the hypervisor for hosting the virtual machines. These virtual machines are used for hosting applications and desktops in XenDesktop. XenDesktop includes the XenServer hypervisor, and it also supports the other hypervisors, such as Microsoft Hyper-V with SCVMM or VMware vSphere. A host is neither required for providing Remote PC access nor for using PVS instead of MCS.

- A master image: It is a virtual hard disk that is pre-installed and configured with the Windows operating system, applications, the virtual delivery agent, and the other customizations. It is used by the provisioning methods for creating virtual desktops or the applications that need to be delivered to the users. The master image is created and stored on a hypervisor. It is usually joined to the domain and set to use DHCP. A master image can host either the Windows desktop OS or the Server OS with the appropriate VDA software. Depending on the FlexCast model, the user changes (users' environment settings/configuration) made to the desktops are either saved or discarded when the user logs off. It simplifies deploying changes to the desktops or the applications for all the user groups by updating the master image.

- The provisioning method: The provisioning method is a mechanism which automatically creates a specified number of virtual machines on the configured host system's resources from a pre-defined master image. Currently, there are two technologies by Citrix that perform VM provisioning. They are **Machine Creation Services** (**MCS**) and **Provisioning Services** (**PVS**). PVS is available as a separate technology, while MCS is integrated into FMA. FMA also supports delivering the VMs that are provisioned by alternate means or that are created manually.

- Machine type: It is a specification that brings the flexibility of choosing the different types of machines, which can be delivered to end users. Currently, FMA supports three types of machines, which include the Windows Desktop OS, the Windows Server OS, and the Remote PC Access. This specification represents the FlexCast Technology, which indicates delivering the different types of resources through FMA.

- Machine catalog: The machine catalog is a single manageable entity, which specifies a collection of *similar* physical or virtual machines. The machines in a catalog have common specifications, including the operating system and the applications along with the VDA installed on them, the naming convention for respective AD computer accounts, the master image, the type of the machine and the provisioning method. Thus, all the machines in a catalog will be identical and they will deliver the same applications or the virtual desktop to the users.

- Delivery group: The delivery group is the entity through which a collection of users, with similar requirements, are given access to a common group of resources through machine catalogs. The delivery group links a collection of AD users to the machines from machine catalogs. A delivery group can deliver the users' applications, desktops, or both.

- Delivery type: The delivery type is a specification of the delivery group. It is similar to what the machine type is for the machine catalog. It specifies the type of resource that is to be delivered to the users. A delivered resource can be one of desktops only, applications only, or desktops & applications.

- Delivering applications: XenDesktop ships the XenApp as one of its core strengths for delivering applications to virtual desktops. Applications that are available on the master image and the applications that are virtualized by using App-V can be delivered to the users. XenDesktop lets you install the desktop applications on the desktop OS and then deliver them. You can also deliver the applications that are installed on a server OS similar to the hosted shared desktop model. This extends the scope of FlexCast to delivering the applications as well.

- Delegated administrators: The FMA features a very fine grained control in designing the administrative access needed for the various roles across enterprise IT departments. It comes with a set of pre-defined roles, which can be used for providing respective access. Using the custom role, you can define what permissions that role should hold on certain objects by specifying a scope.

- Policies: Policies let you centrally and automatically manage the settings and the configurations of the XenDesktop resources. They form a large part of the operational management of the XenDesktop environments as the settings and configurations need to be updated. Citrix has integrated its policies with the Windows group policies technology. You can manage XenDesktop policies from both XenDesktop as well as Windows group policies.

- Configuration logging: This is yet another enterprise feature that lets the administrators track the changes made to the XenDesktop configuration. By default, its data is logged into the site database and it can be configured such that it uses a separate database at any time.

The components of FMA

FMA includes various technologies that have been developed as well as acquired or merged by Citrix. The technologies involved in accomplishing its respective tasks are combined together to form a component in FMA. The FMA components are conveniently classified into two modes:

- Based on essence: They are classified into the core and the additional components. In this section, we will see all the components that fall in this classification.

- Based on the administration scope: They are classified into the server side components and the client side components. In this classification, all the components except the receiver fall under the server side components.

Core components

The following is a quick description of the FMA core components:

- Delivery controller: It is the server that centrally manages the XenDesktop site. The delivery controller communicates with the database and runs several services that manage the hypervisor resources, the user authentication and access, the broker between the user requests and their virtual desktops and applications, monitoring, and the shutting down of virtual desktops when needed, and so on. At least one delivery controller is installed on a site.

- Database: It is a Microsoft SQL server that stores the static configuration and the ever -changing data of the site components status. This database can be accessed by the controller and all the services that make up the controller. There needs to be at least one database in a site that is accessible by the controller.

- Studio: It is the management console that is made available for the XenDesktop administrators for configuring and managing the sites. It's a consolidated console that provides the features required for the administration of the desktops and the application deliveries. The Studio is typically installed on the delivery controller servers. Using Studio, you can manage your hosts, track your licenses, create and assign the resources to the user's groups, configure the policies, manage the user's sessions, and so on.

- License server: It stores the licenses of all of the Citrix products and allocates the licenses to each user's session requests from the controller. At least, one license server is needed for storing and managing the licenses. It consumes relatively less computing resources.

- Hypervisor: It has been defined in the previous section. It is referred to as the host.

- Machine Creation Services: It is one of the VM provisioning technologies. MCS includes a collection of services which automatically creates virtual machines (either servers or desktops) from a master image on demand. MCS uses the snapshot copying for creating new VMs as clones. MCS is a newly built technology by Citrix. It was introduced along with FMA and it is fully integrated and administered through Studio.

- Virtual Delivery Agent: The VDA is installed on each physical or virtual machine on the site that you want to make available to the users. VDAs are available for the Windows desktop OS and the Windows server OS. The VDA for the Server OS is designed from scratch for dynamic provisioning with MCS and PVS. It has a smaller footprint as it consists of the components that are needed for delivering the hosting sessions. It has been made such that it is multi-user aware, unlike the desktop OS systems that are single-user aware. It communicates only with the delivery controllers, and it does not need to access the site's database or the license server directly. It enables the machine to register with the controller, which in turn, allows the machine and the resources it is hosting to be made available to the users. The VDAs establish and manage the connection between the machine and the user's device, verify the license file with the controller, and apply whatever policies have been configured to the session. The VDA communicates the session information to the broker service in the controller through the broker agent included in the VDA. XenApp and XenDesktop include VDAs for the Windows server and the desktop OS. VDAs for the Windows server operating systems let multiple users connect to the server simultaneously. VDAs for the Windows desktops let only one user connect to the desktop at a time.

- StoreFront: It is an IIS web application that lets you create stores of desktops and applications that the users can access over the web. It handles user authentication to the delivery site hosting the resources and communicates with delivery controller to route the user requests. The users can access their applications, desktops, or any other allocated resources at the Site. It provides the self-service access to the users for all the resources that are made available by the administrator for them.

- Director and EdgeSight: Director is a web-based portal that lets the support/helpdesk teams access the real-time status update information from the delivery agents, which helps in troubleshooting the issues proactively. Director includes the Citrix monitoring software called EdgeSight, which forms an integral component. The integrated EdgeSight features include performance management for health and capacity assurance, and historical trending and network analysis. The EdgeSight features in Director are currently limited to the Platinum license of XenDesktop. Director brings up-to-date real time data from the agents and historical data from the site's database. It features more detailed network level debugging information from the HDX insight from NetScaler. The NetScaler HDX insight feature is available only to the Enterprise or Platinum license users of NetScaler 10.1 and above. By default, Director is installed as a web site on the delivery controller. Helpdesk and support teams can access the Director website by using the supported browsers on their desktop systems. It can connect to and monitor multiple XenDesktop sites. It lets you view and interact with the user sessions for providing remote support.

- Receiver: It is the only client side component of FMA and is installed on user devices. The usable features of a receiver depends on the OS the receiver is installed on. Using a receiver on supported Windows desktop systems, users can access the complete features of the XenDesktop resources and their integration with the client device. Users can access their assigned applications, desktops, Remote PCs, web sites, and any other resources. Receiver software is a universal client built for virtually any device including desktops, smart phones, tablets and so on. For devices that can't install a receiver, a new receiver for HTML5 provides connection through HTML5-compatible web browsers.

Additional components

The following is a quick description of the FMA additional components:

- Citrix AppDNA: It is an optional component, which can be integrated with XenDesktop for automated application migration. AppDNA analyzes the application portfolio in terms of criteria, such as the determination of conflicts, compatibility, and then it provides remediation steps. AppDNA analyzes the application portfolio for the accurate determination of conflicts, compatibility, and remediation steps. It's currently only available for the XenDesktop Platinum edition users.

- Provisioning Services: PVS is an independent solution acquired by Citrix. Before FMA, PVS was used for provisioning the VMs on-demand and it is still supported by FMA. It can be integrated with both the XenApp and the XenDesktop technologies. Provisioning services employs streaming of the master image to the user device and it can be run on hard disk-less devices as well. In addition to provisioning the VMs on the hypervisors, it can also be used for streaming OS to the physical machines. When PVS is used as a provisioning method, the delivery controller communicates with PVS for the VM provisioning.

- NetScaler Gateway: It is a networking device to let the users access the resources from the external world, which is outside of your corporate intranet firewall. NetScaler can help in securing the external connections through SSL. It's available as a physical appliance and as a **virtual appliance** (**VPX**). It's usually deployed in DMZ to provide a secure access through the firewall. It requires a separate license from Citrix.

- Citrix CloudBridge: It is an acceleration solution used for delivering optimized virtual desktop performance to the users in remote/branch offices over WAN, so that they experience LAN-like performance. It was formerly called Citrix Branch Repeater or WANScaler. CloudBridge intelligently prioritizes the virtual channels of the different parts of the user experience. It's available as a physical appliance as well as a virtual appliance. The XenDesktop Platinum license includes the VPX version of CloudBridge.

A pictorial representation of the XenDesktop FMA components is shown here:

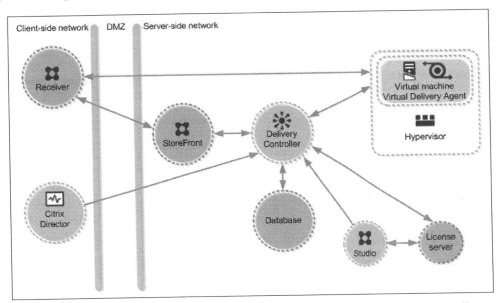

The features of FMA

The following is a detailed explanation of the features of FMA:

- Business driven enterprise capabilities: We have already covered these at the beginning of this chapter, under the *Key Features of XenDesktop architecture for businesses* section.

- Intuitive user experience: It instantly delivers fresh desktops to the users with their personal settings and applications on any device. The integrated application delivery ensures the availability of the business and the productivity applications to the users at anytime. A user profile layer ensures retaining the user preferences and applies them to virtual desktops and to the applications every time. This makes the experience consistent and seamless for the users across any device.

- The HDX performance and the multimedia support: The Citrix HDX technology intelligently calculates and optimizes the virtual channels according to the network changes at runtime. This best optimizes the display and boosts the performance of the overall sessions delivered to the users over any network, including the low-bandwidth and the high-latency WAN connections. The HDX leverages the server-side compute resources and thus, delivers a high multimedia performance to end users, regardless of the capabilities of their device. The HDX bundles many technologies that deliver a high definition experience and the local peripheral support over the high latency and the low bandwidth networks. It includes technologies such as the HDX MediaStream, the HDX Flash Redirection, the HDX Plug-n-Play Multi-Monitor, the HDX Plug-n-Play USB Support, and so on. It enhances the multimedia experience, which is richer than that of the local device performance. Users can reconnect to their disconnected virtual desktops and resume working across the devices.

- The integrated on-demand applications by XenApp: With the unified architecture, XenDesktop now, by default, supports the publishing of the applications that are available on the master image. Furthermore, the built-in integration of the XenApp capabilities for delivering the virtual applications on-demand makes it possible to separate the applications from the virtual desktop layer. This separation of the applications from the virtual desktop increases the virtual desktop's density and provides it with greater flexibility in the deployment and management of applications to the virtual desktops.

- The FlexCast delivery options: With FMA, it not only supports the virtual desktop delivery, but it also supports delivering the other resources access, such as the virtual applications, and the Remote PC access. It has been designed for supporting the flexibility of managing the desktops, the applications, the user profiles, the user data, and so on.

- Open architecture: The FMA supports integration with the various on-premise hypervisor hosts as well as with the Cloud computer resources. It is not restricted to specific hypervisor software, but rather it supports all the leading hypervisors, including Citrix XenServer, the Windows Server 2008 Hyper-V with SCVMM, and the VMware vSphere. This lets businesses to either leverage their existing investments on on-premise hypervisors or cloudify their deployment by using the public Cloud providers. It also supports building on the hybrid resources that include both on-premise as well as Cloud resources. This lets your deployment easily scale out or scale in by just adding more host resources to support the additional user load.

- The simplified desktop image management: Use of the master desktop image in the data center makes it possible to instantly deliver up-to-date fully configured desktops to the users. The application deployments, patch management, and maintenance efforts are drastically reduced as it involves making changes only to the master image, and then updating the virtual desktops to pick up on those changes. This drastically reduces the desktop support and storage costs, by almost 90 percent.

- Integrated provisioning: The FMA includes MCS as the integrated provisioning method, which simplifies and makes XenDesktop implementation drastically faster. This lets enterprises not to worry about setting up and integrating PVS if they don't already have it. MCS in FMA is available out-of-the-box without needing any additional setup. Using MCS also reduces troubleshooting and support issues.

- Controlled and secured data access: FMA lets you configure the centralized control policies and it tightly integrates with Active Directory for user authentication. By default, the FMA network protocol, ICA, securely delivers the virtual desktop through only screen updates, mouse clicks, and key strokes over the network to the authorized users. The high performance standard encryption is used for delivering the desktops by using the SSL integration, for the users using the internal and external networks. Multi-factor authentication is also supported through the smart card integrations.

- Simplified upgrade and maintenance of the controller servers: FMA with its worker and agent model, supports the co-existence of the different versions of the XenApp and the XenDesktop controller servers within the same site. This has been a great benefit for the enterprises in working with their Windows server platforms and the XenDesktop product updates. This has been made possible with the delivery agent developed consisting of only the broker agent components.

- SDK for easy integration: As FMA is developed completely in .Net, it exposes the interfaces (API) for automation and the extension of the overall solution. This reduces the development efforts of building the products around the FMA XenDesktop and the XenApp technologies. Along with .Net interaction, Citrix has made a PowerShell SDK for the IT administrative tasks automation. This helps in improving the monitoring and the automation of the manual tasks.

- Lower total cost of the ownership: FMA with FlexCast delivery and support for MCS and PVS provisioning technologies drastically reduces the overall cost of the entire desktop lifecycle management. It lowers the device/hardware maintenance, power/energy consumption, cooling requirements, software maintenance, storage requirements, migrations to newer operating systems, and so on. It also reduces the overall IT staff and it ensures high availability of the business applications for greater productivity.

Terminology change from the IMA to the latest FMA

Here is a quick mapping of the terminology change from the IMA to the latest FMA. This mapping would come in handy for the administrators of the previous versions of XenDesktop, which are based on the IMA. It also enables the IMA-based XenApp administrators in getting familiar with the equivalent terms of the XenDesktop environment:

Parameter	XenDesktop with IMA (up to XenDesktop v4)	XenDesktop with FMA (XenDesktop v5 and above)
Architecture	IMA	FMA
Database	IMA DataStore - Encrypted LDAP-based; Supports SQL, Oracle and the Access database	Only SQL DataBase – the Microsoft SQL Server
Administrative Boundary	Farm	Site
Data collector role	Zone data collector	Merged into delivery controller; Does not use Terminal Services
Desktop Delivery Controller (DDC) role	Zone Master/Member desktop delivery controller	Delivery controller
Worker software	Worker	**Delivery Agent (DA)** for both the server OS machines and the desktop OS machines
Worker grouping	Worker groups	Machine catalogs and delivery groups
Desktop Assignments to users	Desktop groups	Delivery groups
VM pool management	Idle pool management	Power management
Admin consoles	Delivery services console	Citrix Studio new director for helpdesk support
Load management	Load evaluator	Load management policies

Parameter	XenDesktop with IMA (up to XenDesktop v4)	XenDesktop with FMA (XenDesktop v5 and above)
User roles	Pre-defined administrator roles only	Delegated and custom administrators based on roles and scopes
Application management	Publishing applications	Delivering applications
Web access for session launch	Web interface	StoreFront
Remote support	Session shadowing - ICA	Microsoft remote assistance
Connectivity during DB offline	**Local Host Cache (LHC)**	Connection Leasing (XML files)
Dependencies	Built on top of the Microsoft Terminal services	Built from scratch. Doesn't depend on the Terminal Services on the controller servers.

Advanced FMA - the XenDesktop® architecture in detail

So far, we have learned about the FMA components, concepts, and features. We'll now dive into FMA, representing the positioning and functioning of its components and their communications, which deliver the virtual desktops to the end users.

FMA exhibits elasticity and expandability by design. It supports the components across the varying infrastructures. These features reflect in its layered/modular architecture by grouping the common components to ease the understanding of the overall communication flow. The modular architecture consists of the five layers that cover all the key design decisions. This makes it easier for the architects to focus on the technologies involved in each layer of the overall architecture, it also helps in streamlining their assessment and design decisions. In the image shown later, you can see a high level description of FMA, its five layers, and their importance.

The five layers of FMA

We'll start with the conceptual diagram of FMA representing all the five layers along with the respective components, as shown in the following figure. This will help you in understanding the positioning of the FMA components within the scope of the FMA layers that we will be discussing in this section:

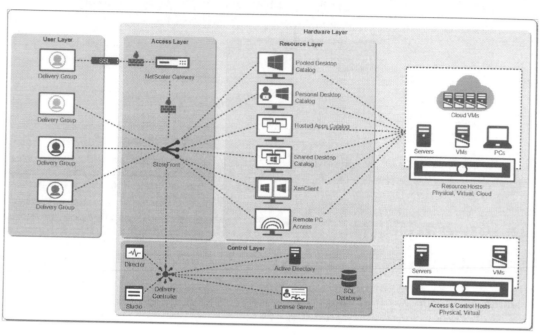

The following image shows the logical representation of the five layers of FMA at a high level:

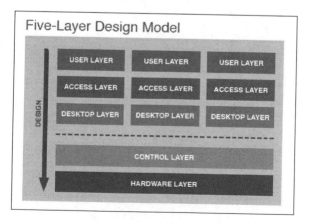

The following is a quick description of each layer of FMA:

- User layer: It is the top layer that defines the recommended strategies for the end-point devices and the Citrix receiver for them. The assessment criteria used in this layer primarily assesses the business priorities and the user group requirements. The decisions made in this layer impact the flexibility and functionality of each user group.

- Access layer: Defines user's access to the virtual desktops. It handles the user validation, and orchestrates access across all the components involved in establishing a secure virtual desktop session. Decisions in this layer are based on the mobility requirements and the end-points used across the user groups. Decisions include choosing between options, such as local versus remote access, the firewall and the SSL secured access.

- Desktop/resource layer: Defines the user's virtual desktop. This layer is divided into three sections, and these are personalization, application, and the overall desktop image. These include the FlexCast model, the application requirements, the user policy, and the profile requirements. These decisions play a key role in the user acceptance of the chosen virtual desktop.

- Control layer: In this layer, all the decisions related to the management and the maintenance of the overall solution are defined. The control layer components include the access controllers, the desktop controllers, and the infrastructural controllers. The access controllers support the access layer, the desktop controllers support the desktop layer, and the infrastructural controllers provide the underlying support for each component within the architecture. Determining the capacity, the configuration, the topology, and the redundancy for the respective components creates a control environment capable of supporting user requirements.

- Hardware layer: This is the last layer and it comprises of the physical devices required for supporting the overall solution, including the servers, the processors, the memory, and the storage devices. The devices are grouped and they are classified into three groups for allocating the resources to specific parts of the entire solution, such as the first group of servers for XenApp and its components, the second group for the XenDesktop components, and the third group for supporting the underlying infrastructure of the control layer components.

The first three layers are defined for each user group. They specify the user's virtual desktop characteristics, and how they access them. This is derived by assessing the business user group's requirements. The architects should thoroughly understand the various factors of the user requirements, including the type of applications, their compatibility, the criticality of the data, nature of employment, access locations, performance requirements, and so on. Then, decide the respective type of desktop that would be appropriate for them.

Based upon the decisions made in the first three layers, the back end foundational layers are designed for the entire solution. The aforementioned defined layered process streamlines the design thinking such that the decisions made in the first three higher level layers impact the design decision made in the two lower level layers.

Working of FMA components to deliver virtual desktops

The following is a sequence of steps that takes place at the high level for delivering a virtual desktop session to the end user, in single site XenDesktop deployment. For starting a XenDesktop session, a two phase process takes place in the background.

Phase 1 - User authentication and resources enumeration

The sequence of actions shown here take place during phase 1:

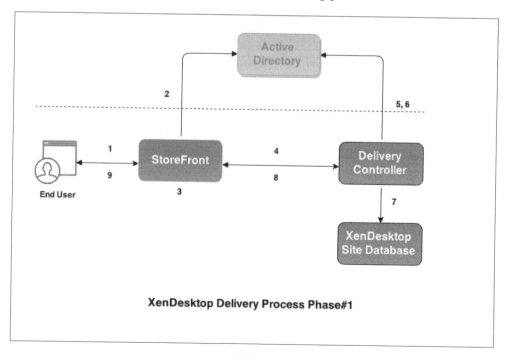

XenDesktop Delivery Process Phase#1

1. The user logs into the StoreFront web store URL.

2. StoreFront validates the user credentials with the help of the Active Directory domain controller.

 This is a new step in this process and it was introduced in StoreFront. This step was not performed in the web interface.

3. Upon successful authentication, StoreFront will check the application subscription data store for the existing user subscriptions and then store those in the memory.

4. StoreFront will forward the user credentials, as a part of the XML query, to the controller.

 To secure this sensitive information over the network, it's recommended that you configure the StoreFront site to use the secure SSL connections so that the user credentials are encrypted, while they reach StoreFront from their device.

5. The controller will query Microsoft Active Directory with the end user's credentials to verify the user authorization. That is, the controller will fetch the user security group memberships to find the resources that the user had access to.

 Active Directory validates the credentials and issues a Kerberos authentication token for the user. This token will be valid for a defined period of time and it can be re-used across any of the Active Directory domain resources for authenticating the user against. For further reading on the Kerberos authentication in Windows, please refer to the topic, **How the Kerberos Version 5 Authentication Protocol Works**, which can be found at `https://technet.microsoft.com/en-us/library/cc772815(v=ws.10).aspx`.

6. Upon successful validation, the controller will query the user security group memberships.

7. The controller will then query the site database and then determine which applications and desktops the user will be allowed to access.

8. The controller sends an XML response to the StoreFront site, which contains the enumerated list of all the resources (desktops or apps) that are available for the user within that XenDesktop site.

9. The StoreFront web store pages display the desktops and the applications, which the user can access.

Phase 2 - Virtual Desktop allocation and connection establishment

The following image displays the sequence of actions that takes place during phase 2:

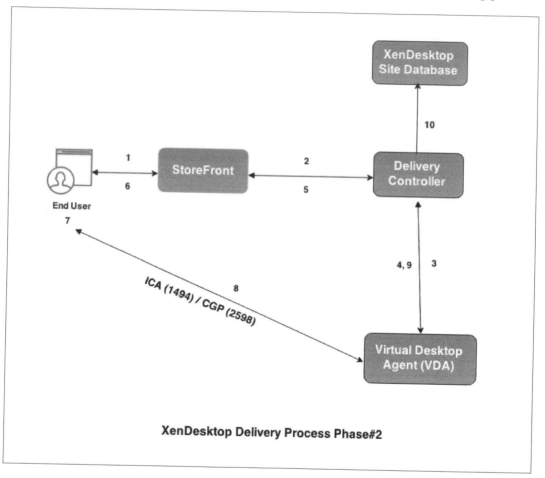

XenDesktop Delivery Process Phase#2

1. The user selects an application or a desktop from the list.
2. StoreFront passes the user resource selection to the controller.
3. The controller queries the status of the desktops within that group. It determines the proper VDA for hosting a specific application or a specific desktop. Then, it communicates the user credentials and all the data about the user and the connection to the VDA.

4. The VDA of the selected desktop accepts the connection and then sends all the information that is needed for establishing the session back to the controller.

5. The controller forwards this connection information to the StoreFront site.

6. StoreFront delivers this information to the receiver.

7. The receiver combines all the connection information generated in the session request and saves it in the **Independent Computing Architecture** (.ICA) file on the user's device. If the receiver is not available on the client's device, then the receiver for the web will handle this activity.

8. Using the saved connection settings in the .ICA file, the receiver establishes a direct connection between the user's device and the ICA stack which runs on the VDA. This connection bypasses the entire management infrastructure, including StoreFront and the controller. This connection takes place over the ICA port 1494 on the virtual desktop. It will take place over the **Citrix Gateway Protocol (CGP)** port 2598, if the session reliability is enabled.

9. Once the user connects to the VDA, the VDA will notify the controller about the logged in user.

10. The controller will write this connection information into the site's database and then it will start logging the data into the monitoring database.

Designing FMA for your XenDesktop® deployment

While we know the FMA that makes up your XenDesktop technology in detail, it critical for you to know how to design the FMA for your XenDesktop deployment. FMA for a XenDesktop version remains the same globally, yet each enterprise according to its business requirements will have its own design for FMA. To make this designing simpler, faster, and more effective, Citrix has devised an automated system called Project Accelerator. Project Accelerator extensively covers all the possible specifications that are required for a XenDesktop deployment for the chosen requirements. Working with Project Acceleration for designing your FMA deployment should be your first step toward building your deployment plan.

Project Accelerator

Project Accelerator is a web solution that is available for all Citrix customers. It lets you specify all the high level steps, and the real time values for completing your XenDesktop deployment. It's an easy to use web based tool with limited documentation, which is available online. In this section, we'll cover the vast set of options and parameters that come with the latest version of the tool (that is 0.7). This understanding will help you in becoming familiar with the tool, and it will help you in using it in your XenDesktop deployment planning.

The Project Accelerator is divided into three phases as follows:

- Assess
- Design
- Result

The assess phase

The assess phase lets you provide the custom business requirements for desktop virtualization. It involves specifying the various types of information in five sections as follows:

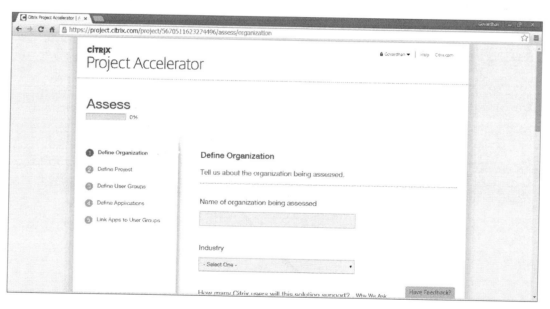

It resembles the steps that you would follow in reality for resource creation and allocation to user groups in XenDesktop deployment.

1. **Define Organization**: It specifies the business priorities when deploying the XenDesktop solution.

2. **Define Project**: It specifies the XD version, the licensing, and the scope of support/consultation.

3. **Define User Groups**: It specifies the user group along with the number of users, personalization, security, mobility, the workload of the applications used by the users, and the desktop loss criticality.

4. **Define Applications**: It specifies the list of the applications along with their high level resource requirements, the application setup complexity, and the usage of the application by other companies.

5. **Link Apps to User Groups**: This final step specifies all the user's groups that would be using the defined business applications.

At the end of the assessment phase, you'll be automatically presented with **Sizing & Deployment Plan** and a **Recommended Architecture** based on the basic details. To make your design more realistic, you can choose the option of stepping into the design phase.

The design phase

The design phase consists of three steps. This phase gathers the information to profile the user's environments so that your design becomes more accurate and closer to real time. As in real time, the parameters in the later steps are dependent on the previous steps, and if you change the decision values in step 1, then you will need to re-define the relevant data points in the later steps.

Following is the screenshot of design phase options to be defined:

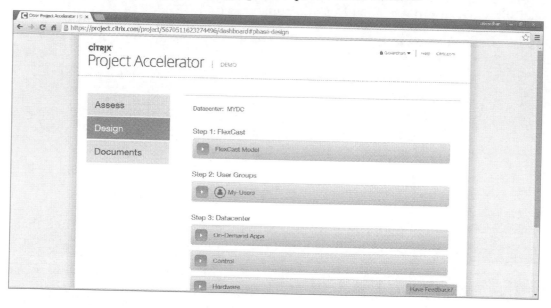

We'll learn the design phase steps along with the possible values here:

1. **FlexCast**: This will lead you to the decision on FlexCast model for users. You can choose among the FlexCast models from the following. For the sake of this content, I am choosing the Pooled VDI mode, which will affect the options in the later steps.

    ○ **Assigned VDI**

    ○ **Hosted Shared**

    ○ **Local VM**

    ○ **On-Demand Apps**

    ○ **Pooled VDI**

    ○ **Remote PC**

2. **User Groups**: This defines the user's device/end point capabilities (a decision based on Primary End Point) and their business application delivery modes (decision based on application deployment method). Depending on the FlexCast model, chosen in step 1, you'll see various options, which you will need to specify here. Relatively, the On-Demand Apps mode has the least user level parameters. Most of the parameters that are available for the other FlexCast models are as follows:

- ◦ The user's **Primary End Point** can be one of these: **Corporate Desktops**, **Corporate Laptops**, **Personal Devices**, **Shared PCs** or **Thin Clients**.
- ◦ **vCPU per Desktop**: Select from a range of 1 to 8 cores.
- ◦ **RAM per Desktop**: Select from a range of 1 to 8 GB.
- ◦ **Steady State IOPS per User**: A value of IOPS.
- ◦ **User Profile Type**: Citrix user profiles, roaming, and others.
- ◦ **User Security and Safety Policy**: You will specify the XenDesktop Baseline, the policy to be used for the WAN users of XenDesktop, and also specify XenDesktop's Low Security & High Security Policies.
- ◦ **Applications**: Installed on the base image, On-Demand App (Dedicated Server), On-Demand App (Shared Server), and Deliver with the Microsoft App-V.
- ◦ **Desktop Image Selection**: New.
- ◦ **Desktop Operating Systems**: Windows XP, Windows 7, Windows 8, and Windows 8.1.
- ◦ **Desktop Image Size**: Specify the value in GBs (in other words, it is the size of the base disk).
- ◦ **Desktop Cache Size**: Specify the value in GBs (forms the differential disk). Usually, this will be in the 2-25 GB range.
- ◦ **Computer Policy**: You will specify the XenDesktop Baseline for the WAN user, the XenDesktop LAN or XenDesktop WAN, and the XenDesktop Low Security & XenDesktop High Security Policies.

3. **DataCenter**: This step involves defining your data center resources, which would be available for use on your virtual desktops and on the XenDesktop controller. It includes the hardware resources of the hosts, the storage, and the operating system requirements for the controller, applications and their sizes.

The following is a quick list of the decisions involved which should be considered when choosing the possible options:

- ◦ **On-Demand Apps**:
  - ◦ **On-Demand Apps Operating System**: Choose one of the supported server operating systems listed as follows:
    - ◦ **Windows Server 2008 R2**
    - ◦ **Windows Server 2012**
    - ◦ **Windows Server 2012 R2**

- **On-Demand Apps Profile Type**: This refers to the type of user profiles to retain the user-specific application settings. Supported profile types include the following:
  - **Local**
  - **Mandatory**
  - **Roaming**
  - **Citrix User Profile**
  - **Other**

- **On-Demand Apps Image Size**: It's the size of image that includes the operating system and the applications that are to be installed. Usually specified in GBs, Citrix recommendation is 60 GB for Windows Server 2012.

- **On-Demand Apps Cache Size**: Any changes made to On-Demand Apps server during normal operations are stored within the cache and cleared during a reboot. Cache size must be large enough to contain the changes, should be specified in GBs and have a default value of 40 GB .

- **Control**:
  - **Image Controllers**:
    - **Preferred Imaging Solution**: PVS, MCS and Manual.
    - For MCS, you can specify its **Storage Type** among **Shared CIFS**, **Shared NFS**, **Shared iSCSI** or **Share FC**.
  - For PVS, you can specify its PVS server network capacity (1 or 10 Gbps) and the **Storage Type** for its image, and these can be **Local PVS Server Disk**, **CIFS**, **NFS**, **iSCSI per PVS**, **FC per PVS**, **Shared iSCSI** or **Shared FC**.

- **Hardware**:
  - **VDI Pool Hardware Design**:
    - **VDI Pool Hypervisor**: XenServer, Hyper-V, and vSphere
    - **VDI Cores per Server**: A range of 8-24 Cores
    - **VDI RAM per Server**: A range of 32-256 GBs

- ○ **VDI Resource Pool Storage Location**: Shared
- ○ **VDI Resource Pool Storage Type**: NFS and iSCSI/FC

- ○ **Shared Pool Hardware Design**:
  - ○ **Shared Pool Hypervisor**: XenServer, Hyper-V, vSphere
  - ○ **Hosted Shared Pool Cores per Server**: A range of 8-24 Cores
  - ○ **Hosted Shared Pool RAM**: A range of 32-256 GBs
  - ○ **Hosted Shared Resource Pool Image Size**: A value in GBs
  - ○ **Hosted Shared Resource Pool Storage Location**: Shared
  - ○ **Hosted Shared Resource Pool Storage Type**: NFS and iSCSI/FC

- ○ **Control Pool Hardware Design**:
  - ○ **Control Pool Hypervisor** (Control servers): XenServer, Hyper-V, vSphere
  - ○ **Control Cores per Server**: A range of 8-48 Cores
  - ○ **Control Hardware (RAM)**: A range of 32-320 GBs
  - ○ **Control Resource Pool Storage Location**: Shared
  - ○ **Control Resource Pool Storage Type**: NFS and iSCSI/FC

Results along with an example

For example, I choose to deliver the Microsoft Office application suite to a group of 10 users through a pool of 10 virtual Windows 7 Desktops. I would deliver these desktops to the users from remote locations as well.

The results will give you two pages: **Sizing & Deployment Plan** and **Recommended Architecture**. One can further customize these two pages and make any changes that are needed and then export them in order to share them with the business heads and management officials so that they can work on an implementation proposal.

Here is how the resulting **Sizing & Deployment Plan** page looks:

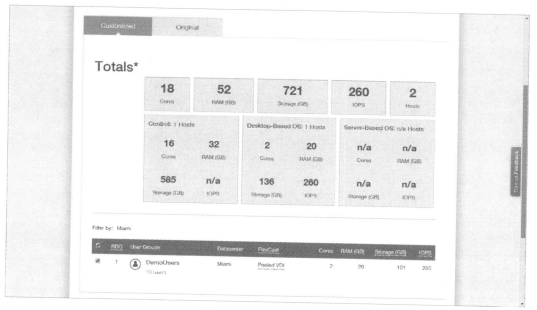

Sizing and deployment plan

The following image displays the resulting **Recommended Architecture** page:

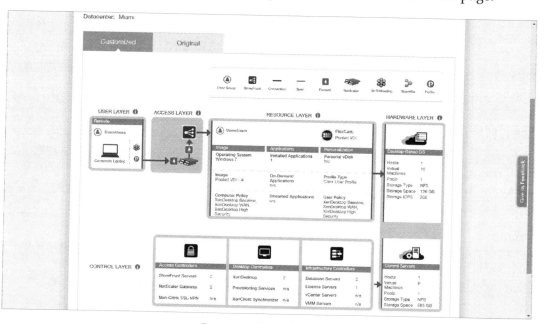

Recommended architecture

Summary

We saw how XenDesktop architecture has evolved. We began with the limitations of IMA and how those were addressed in FMA. We learned the basics of FMA, including the concepts, the terminology, all the components, its classification, and the FMA features. Then, we discussed the advanced FMA and explained the working of FMA as a whole. We also looked at the detailed architecture of all the important components. Finally, we moved onto the Project Accelerator for designing an FMA for your business custom requirements and capabilities. We learned that only knowing the architecture in detail won't help you in building an efficient deployment plan. You will need the knowledge of designing it, which involves the other key technologies.

In the next chapter, you'll learn how to design XenDesktop for the deployments in a layered approach. You'll also discover the design considerations for complex business requirements, such as high availability, scalability, App Orchestration for multi forest AD environment and deploying XenDesktop in Cloud infrastructures.

3
Designing XenDesktop® for Complex Environments

In the earlier chapters, we saw the evolution and core strengths of XenDesktop. We also discussed the history and FMA (the architecture) of XenDesktop. These foundational chapters have helped you in building a deep understanding of the working of the XenDesktop and its design. In this chapter, we'll learn the application of that knowledge to designing XenDesktop deployment as per your business requirements. Designing a XenDesktop deployment involves establishing the critical path and making decisions at each stage of it. The deeper your understanding of the business requirements and the XenDesktop technology is, the better your XenDesktop design would be.

We'll start off by discussing the role of the desktop environments in various businesses. We will look at the enterprise features that businesses will ascertain in choosing a technology for transforming those desktop environments. We'll also learn how XenDesktop can be a better fit for businesses with specific requirements across the various verticals. Then, we'll learn about the XenDesktop features that will enable businesses to take their desktop environments to the Cloud. The following is a list of the topics that we'll cover in this chapter:

- The desktop environments
- How the XenDesktop transforms the desktop environments
- Process of designing the XenDesktop deployments

- Designing XenDesktop for complex environments, including:
    - XenDesktop architecture designed for high availability
    - Design considerations for a scalable deployment
    - App Orchestration – the multi forest Active Directory environment
    - The XenDesktop deployment in public and hybrid Cloud by using AWS

We are going to cover the complex environments involving advanced configurations, so we are assuming that you have an intermediate and above level of understanding of technologies, including Active Directory, DNS, NetScaler, failover clusters, and AWS Cloud.

Desktop environments

We have assumed that you are aware of the traditional desktop environments and their limitations, and that you have kept up with the ever-changing computing industry and business requirements. We'll cover the technological aspects of a desktop environment, which will be transformed or replaced by a desktop virtualization technology.

The essential elements of a desktop environment

Irrespective of the traditional physical or modern virtual infrastructure used for the desktops, a Windows desktop intended for business users is expected to support these basic features:

- Windows Operating system
- The Windows applications (typically business and productivity)
- The user profile and preferences
- The user data files
- Access to the peripheral devices

Business expectations of a desktop environment

Every business organization expects that its desktop environments will always be available for its users for continuing the business. Considering this, businesses expect the desktop environments to feature the following:

- **High availability (HA)**
- Scalability
- **Disaster recovery (DR)**
- Security and compliance
- Ease of administration
- Operations automation
- Support for the Cloud capabilities
- Support for the increasing mobile work styles
- Reduced **TCO (Total Cost of Ownership)**

For businesses, the desktop environment is not just a technology, it's a strategy to serve the current business requirements and to take the business to the future.

XenDesktop® – Transforming desktop environments

XenDesktop with the FlexCast architecture brings most of the required methods of delivering the desktops to various user groups across a business. It separates and enables you to manage the essential elements of the desktop environments, including the OS layer, application layer, user layer, and data layer. It features the separate components and integrates with the other technologies for managing each layer of the desktop elements effectively.

XenDesktop®

As a leading desktop virtualization solution, XenDesktop offers a great and a unique flexibility in transforming the traditional desktop environments into virtualized data center environments. Its core strengths are—anydevice-anytime-anywhere, FlexCast delivery technology, Open architecture – Cloud Ready FlexCast Management Architecture (FMA), on-demand applications by XenApp, automated application migration with AppDNA, high security and compliance standards, and a broader scope of its adoption in Project Avalon by Citrix. All this helps XenDesktop in providing businesses with all the enterprise features that are needed for the future Cloud era.

Essentially, you can incorporate the enterprise features, such as HA, scalability, DR, and so on, in the individual components of FMA at each of its layers.

Additional technologies

Knowing the XenDesktop architecture and how it works alone won't help you in building an efficient XenDesktop deployment for your business requirements. For developing an enterprise-capable XenDesktop deployment, it involves the use of other technologies across various layers of the FMA to achieve the required enterprise features. These primarily include storage, intranet and Internet networking, hypervisors, Windows servers, and Active Directory, and so on. The more hands on experience you have with these technologies, the faster and more effective your XenDesktop implementation would be. Usually in large enterprises, the XenDesktop designing and implementation spreads across various technical teams.

Process of designing XenDesktop® deployments

The uniqueness of the XenDesktop architecture is its modular five layer model. It covers all the key decisions in designing the XenDesktop deployment (as we saw in the previous chapter).

- User layer: Defines the users and their requirements
- Access layer: Defines how the users will access the resources
- Desktop/resource layer: Defines what resources will be delivered
- Control layer: Defines managing and maintaining the solution
- Hardware layer: Defines what resources it needs for implementing the chosen solution

While FMA is simple at a high level, its implementation can become complex depending on the technologies/options that are chosen for each component across the layers of FMA. Along with great flexibility, comes the responsibility of diligently choosing the technologies/options for fulfilling your business requirements.

Importantly, the decisions made in the first three layers impact the last two layers of the deployment. It means that fixing a wrong decision anywhere in the first three layers during/after implementation stage would have less or no scope, and may even lead to implement the solution from the scratch again. Your design decisions speak for your solution's effectiveness in helping with the given business requirements.

The layered architecture of the XenDesktop FMA, featuring the components at each layer is given in the following diagram. Each component of XenDesktop will fall under one of the layers shown in the succeeding diagram. We'll see what decisions are to be made for each of these components at each layer in the next sub section.

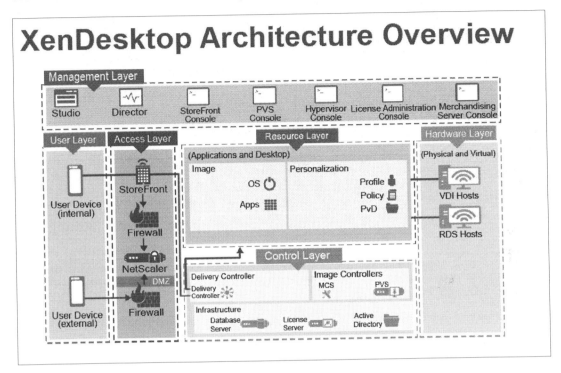

Decisions to be made at each layer

I will have to write a separate book for discussing all the possible technologies/options that are available at each layer. Following is a highly summarized list of the decisions to be made at each layer. This will help you in realizing the breadth of designing XenDesktop. This high level coverage of the various options will help you in locating and considering all the possible options that are available for making the right decisions and avoiding any slippages and missing any considerations.

User layer

The user layer refers to the specification of the users who will utilize the XenDesktop deployment. A business requirement statement may mention that the service users can either be the internal business users or the external customers accessing the service from Internet. Furthermore, both of these users may also need mobile access to the XenDesktop services.

The Citrix receiver is the only component that belongs to the user layer, and XenDesktop is dependent on it for successfully delivering a XenDesktop session. By correlating this technical aspect with the preceding business requirement statement, one needs to consider all the possible aspects of receiver software on the client devices.

This involves making the following decisions:

- Endpoint/user devices related: What are the devices that the users are supposed to access the services from? Who owns and administrates those devices throughout their lifecycle?

    ○ Endpoints supported: Corporate computers, laptops, or mobiles running on Windows or thin clients. User smart devices, such as Android tablets, Apple iPads, and so on. In case of service providers, the endpoints can usually be any device and they need to be supported.

    ○ Endpoint ownership: Device management includes security, availability, and compliance. Maintaining the responsibility of the devices on network.

    ○ Endpoint lifecycle: Devices become either outdated or limited very quickly. Define minimum device hardware requirements to run your business workloads.

    ○ Endpoint form factor: Choose the devices that may either be fully featured or have limited thin clients, or be a mix of both to support features, such as HDX graphics, multi-monitors, and so on.

    ○ Thin client selection: Choose if the thin clients, such as Dell Wyse Zero clients, running on the limited functionality operating systems would suffice your user requirements. Understand its licensing cost.

- Receiver selection: Once you determine your endpoint device and its capabilities, you need to decide on the receiver selection that can be run on the devices. The greatest thing is that receiver is available for almost any device.

    ○ Receiver type: Choose the receiver that is required for your device. Since the Receiver software for each platform (OS) differs, it is important to use the appropriate Receiver software for your devices while considering the platform that it runs on. You can download the appropriate Receiver software for your device from `http://www.Citrix.com/go/receiver.html` page.

- Initial deployment: Receiver is like any other software that will fit into your overall application portfolio. Determine how you would deploy this application on your devices. For corporate desktops and mobiles, you may use the enterprise application deployment and the mobile device management software. Otherwise, the users will be prompted to install it when they access the StoreFront URL, or they can even download it from Citrix for facilitating the installation process. For user-managed mobile devices, you can get it from the respective Windows or Google Apple stores/marketplaces.

   - Initial configuration: Similar to other applications, Receiver requires certain initial configuration. It can be configured either manually or by using a provisioning file, group policy, and e-mail based discovery.

- Keeping the Receiver software up-to-date: Once you have installed Receiver on user devices, you will also require a mechanism for deploying the updates to Receiver. This can also be the way of initial deployments.

Access layer

An access layer refers to the specification of how the users gain access to the resources. A business requirement statement may usually state that the users should be validated for gaining access, and the access should be secured when the user is connected over the Internet.

The technical components that fall under this layer include firewall(s), NetScaler, and StoreFront. These components play a broader role in the overall networking infrastructure of the company, which also includes the XenDesktop, as well as complete Citrix solutions in the environment. Their key activities include firewalling, external to internal IP address NATing, NetScaler Gateway to secure the connection between the virtual desktop and the user device, global load balancing, user validation/authentication, and GUI presentation of the enumerated resources to the end users.

It involves making the following decisions:

- Authentication:
   - Authentication point: A user can be authenticated at the NetScaler Gateway or StoreFront.

- Authentication policy: Various business use cases and compliance makes certain modes of authentication mandatory. You can choose from the different authentication methods supported at:

    - StoreFront: Basic authentication by using a username and a password; Domain Pass-through, the NS Gateway pass-through, smart card, and even unauthenticated access.

    - NetScaler Gateway: LDAP, RADIUS (token), client certificates.

- StoreFront: The decisions that are to be made around the scope of StoreFront are as follows:

    - Unauthenticated access: Provides access to the users who don't require a username and a password, but they are still able to access the administrator allowed resources. Usually, this fits well with public or Kiosk systems.

    - High availability: Making the StoreFront servers available at all times. Hardware load balancing, DNS Round Robin, Windows network load balancing, and so on.

    - Delivery controller high availability and StoreFront: Building high availability for the delivery controller is recommended since they are needed for forming successful connections. Defining more than one delivery controller for the stores makes StoreFront auto failover to the next server in the list.

    - Security - Inbound traffic: Consider securing the user connection to virtual desktops from the internal StoreFront and the external NetScaler Gateway.

    - Security – Backend traffic: Consider securing the communication between the StoreFront and the XML services running on the controller servers. As these will be within the internal network, they can be secured by using the internal private certificate.

    - Routing Receiver with Beacons: Receiver supports websites called Beacons to identify whether the user connection is internal or external. StoreFront provides Receiver with the http(s) addresses of the Beacon points during the initial connection.

    - Resource Presentation: StoreFront presents a webpage, which provides self-service of the resources by the user.

    - Scalability: The StoreFront server load and capacity for the user workload.

    - Multi-site App synchronization: StoreFront can connect to the controllers at multiple site deployments. StoreFront can replicate the user subscribed applications across the servers.

- NetScaler Gateway: In the NetScaler Gateway, the decision regarding the secured external user access from public Internet involves the following:

  ○ Topology: NetScaler supports two topologies: 1-Arm (normal security) and 2-Arm (high security).

  ○ High availability: The NetScaler Gateways can be configured in pairs to provide high availability.

  ○ Platform: NetScaler is available in different platforms, such as VPX, MDX, and SDX. They have different SSL throughput and SSL **Transaction Per Second (TPS)** metrics.

  ○ Pre-authentication policy: Specifies about the **Endpoint Analysis (EPA)** scans for evaluating whether the endpoints meet the pre-set security criteria. This is available when NetScaler is chosen as the authentication point.

  ○ Session management: The session policies define the overall user experience by classifying the endpoints into mobile and non-mobile devices. Session profile defines the details needed for gaining access to the environment. These are in two forms: SSLVPN and HDX proxy.

  ○ Preferred data center: In multi-active data center deployments, StoreFront can determine the user resources primary data center and NetScaler can direct the user connections to that. Static and dynamic methods are used for specifying the preferred data center.

Desktop/resource layer

The desktop or resource layer refers to the specification of which resources (applications and desktops) users will receive. This layer comes with various options, which are tailored for business user roles and their requirements. This layer makes XenDesktop a better fit for achieving the varying user needs across each of their departments. It includes specification of the FlexCast model (type of desktop), user personalization, and delivering the application to the users in the desktop session.

An example business requirement statement may specify that all the permanent employees would require a desktop with all the basic applications pre-installed based on their team and role, with their user settings and data to be retained. For all the contract employees, provide a basic desktop with controlled access to the applications on-demand and do not retain their user data.

It includes various components, such as profile management solutions (including Windows profiles, the Citrix profile management, AppSense), Citrix print server, Windows operating systems, application delivery, and so on.

It involves making decisions, such as:

- Images: It involves choosing the FlexCast model that is tailored to the user requirements, thereby delivering the expected desktop behavior to the end users, as follows:

    ○ Operating system related: It requires choosing the desktop or the server operating systems for your master image, which depends on the FlexCast model that you are choosing from.

        ○ Hosted Shared

        ○ Hosted VDI: Pooled-static, pooled-random, pooled with PvD, dedicated, existing, physical/remote PC, streamed and streamed with PvD

        ○ Streamed VHD

        ○ Local VM

        ○ On-demand apps

        ○ Local apps

    In case of the desktop OS, it's also important to choose the right OS architecture according to the 32-bit or 64-bit processor architecture of the desktop.

    ○ Computer policies: Define the controls over the user connection, security and bandwidth settings, devices or connection types, and so on. Specify all the policy features similar to that of the user policies.

    ○ Machine catalogs: Define your catalog settings, including the FlexCast model, AD computer accounts, provisioning method, OS of the base image, and so on.

    ○ Delivery groups: Assign desktops or applications to the user groups.

    ○ Application folders: This is a tidy interface feature in Studio for organizing the applications into folders for easy management.

    ○ StoreFront integration: This is an option for specifying the StoreFront URL for the Receiver in the master image so that the users will be auto connected to the storefront in the session.

- Resource allocation: This defines the hardware resources for the desktop VMs. It primarily involves hosts and storage. Depending on your estimated workloads, you can define the resources, such as number of virtual processors (vCPU), amount of virtual memory (vRAM), storage requirements for the needed disk space, and also the following resources

    - Graphics (GPU): For the advanced use cases, you may choose to allocate the pass-through GPU, hardware vGPU, or the software vGPUs.

    - IOPS: Depending on the operating system, the FlexCast model, and estimated workloads, you can analyze the overall IOPS load from the system and plan the corresponding hardware to support that load.

    - Optimizations: Depending on the operating system, you can apply various optimizations to Windows that run on the master image. This greatly reduces the overall load later.

- Bandwidth requirements: Bandwidth can be a limiting factor in case of WAN and remote user connections of slow networks. Bandwidth consumption and user experience depend on various factors, such as the operating system being used, the application design, and screen resolution. To retain high user experience, it's important to consider the bandwidth requirements and optimization technologies, as follows:

    - Bandwidth minimizing technologies: These include Quality of Service (QoS), HDX RealTime, and WAN Optimization, with Citrix's own CloudBridge solution.

    - HDX Encoding Method: HDX encoding method also affects the bandwidth usage. For XenDesktop 7.x, there are three encoding methods that are available. These will appropriately be employed by the HDX protocol. These are Desktop Composition Redirection, H.264 Enhanced SuperCodec, and Legacy Mode (XenDesktop 5.X Adaptive Display).

    - Session Bandwidth: Bandwidth needed in a session depends on the user interaction with desktop and applications.

    - Latency: HDX can typically perform well up to 300 ms latency and the experience begins to degrade as latency increases.

- Personalization: This is an essential element of the desktop environment. It involves the decisions that are critical for the end user experience/acceptance and for the overall success of the solution during implementation. Following are the decisions that are involved in personalization.

  - User profiles: This involves the decisions that are related to the user login, roaming of their settings, and seamless profile experience across overall Windows network:

    - Profile type: Choose which profile type works for your user requirements. Possible options include local, roaming, mandatory, and hybrid profile with Citrix Profile Management. Citrix Profile Management provides various additional features, such as profile streaming, active write back, and configuring profiles using an .ini file, and so on.

    - Folder redirection: This option saves the user's application settings in the profile. Represents special folders, such as AppData, Desktop, and so on.

    - Folder exclusion: This option is for setting the exclusion of folders that are to be saved in the user profile. Usually, it refers to the local and IE Temp folders of a user profile.

    - Profile caching: Caching profiles on a local system improves the user login experience and it occurs by default. You need to consider this depending on the type of virtual desktop FlexCast mode.

    - Profile permissions: Specify whether the administrator needs access to the user profiles based on information sensitivity.

    - Profile path: The decision to place the user profiles on a network location for high availability. It affects the logon performance depending on how close the profile is to the virtual desktop from which the user is logging on. It can be managed either from Active Directory or through Citrix Profile Management.

    - User profile replication between data centers: This involves making the user profiles highly available and supporting the profile roaming among multiple data centers.

  - User policies: Involves the decision regarding deploying the user settings and controlling those using management policies providing consistent settings for users, such as:

- Preferred policy engine: This requires choosing the policy processing for the Windows systems. The Citrix policies can be defined and managed from either Citrix Studio or the Active Directory group policy.

- Policy filtering: The Citrix policies can be applied to the users and their desktop with the various filter options that are available in the Citrix policy engine. If the group policies have been used, then you'll use the group policy filtering options.

- Policy precedence: The Citrix policies are processed in the order of LCSDOU (Local, Citrix, Site, Domain, OU policies).

- Baseline policy: This defines the policy with default and common settings for all the desktop images. Citrix provides the policy templates that suit specific business use cases. A baseline should cover security requirements, common network conditions, and managing the user device or the user profile requirements. Such a baseline can be configured using the security policies, connection-based policies, device-based policies, and profile-based policies.

- Printing: This is one of the most common desktop user requirements. XenDesktop supports printing, which can work for various scenarios. The printing technology involves deploying and using appropriate drivers.

  - Provisioning printers: These can either be a static or dynamic set of printers. The options for dynamic printers do and do not auto-create all the client printers and auto-create the non-network client printers only. You can also set the options for session printers through the Citrix policy, which can include either static or dynamic printers. Furthermore, you can also set proximity printers.

  - Managing print drivers: This option can be configured so that printer drivers are auto-installed during the session creation. It can be installed by using either the generic Citrix universal printer driver, or the manual option. You can also have all the known drivers preinstalled on the master image. Citrix even provides the Citrix universal print server, which extends XenDesktop universal printing support to network printing.

  - Print job routing: It can be routed among client device or through the network server. The ICA protocol is used for compressing and sending data.

    ° Personal vDisk: Desktops with personal vDisks retain the user changes. Choosing the personal vDisk depends on the user requirements and the FlexCast Model that was opted for. Personal vDisk can be set to thin provisioned for estimated growth, but it can't be shrunk later.

- Applications: The application separation into another layer improves the scalability of the overall desktop solution. Applications are critical elements, which the users require from a desktop environment:

    ° Application delivery method: Applications can be installed on the base image, on the Personal vDisks, streamed into the session, or through the on-demand XenApp hosted mode. It also depends on application compatibility, and it requires technical expertise and tools, such as AppDNA, for effectively resolving them.

    ° Application streaming: XenDesktop supports App-V to build isolated application packages, which can be streamed to desktops.

    ° 16-bit legacy application delivery: If there are any legacy 16-bit applications to be supported, then you can choose from the 32 bit OS, VM hosted App, or a parallel XenApp5 deployment.

Control layer

Control layer speaks about all the backend systems that are required for managing and maintaining the overall solution through its life cycle. The control layer includes most of the XenDesktop components that are further classified into categories, such as resource/access controllers, image/desktop controllers, and infrastructure controllers. These respectively correspond to the first three layers of FMA, as shown here:

- Resource/access controllers: Supports the access layer
- Image/desktop controllers: Supports the desktop/resource layer
- Infrastructure controllers: Provides the underlying hardware for the overall FMA components/environment

This layer involves the specification of capacity, configuration, and the topology of the environment. Building required/planned redundancy for each of these components enables achieving the enterprise business capabilities, such as HA, scalability, disaster recovery, load balancing, and so on.

Components and technologies that operate under this layer include Active Directory, group policies, site database, Citrix licensing, XenDesktop delivery controllers, XenClient hypervisor, the Windows server and the Desktop operating systems, provisioning services, which can be either MCS or PVS and their controllers, and so on.

An example business requirement statement may be as follows:

Build a highly available desktop environment for a fast growing business users group. We currently have a head count of 30 users, which is expected to double in a year.

It involves making the following decisions:

- Infrastructure controllers: It includes common infrastructure, which is required for XenDesktop to function in the Windows domain network.
  - Active Directory: This is used for the authentication and authorization of users in a Citrix environment. It's also responsible for providing and synchronizing time on the systems, which is critical for Kerberos. For the most part, your AD structure will be in-place, and it may require certain changes for accommodating your XenDesktop requirements, such as:
    - Forest design: It involves choosing the AD forest and domain decisions, such as multi-domain, multi-forest, domain and forest trusts, and so on, which will define the users of the XenDesktop resources.
    - Site design: It involves choosing the number of sites that represent your geographical locations, the number of domain controllers, the subnets that accommodate the IP addresses, site links for replication, and so on.
    - Organizational unit structure: Planning the OU structure for easier management of XenDesktop Workers and VDAs. In the case of multi-forest deployment scenarios (as supported in App Orchestration), having the same OU structure is critical.
    - Naming standards: Planning proper conventions for XenDesktop AD objects, which includes users, security groups, XenDesktop servers, OUs, and so on.
    - User groups: This helps in choosing the individual user names or groups. The user security groups are recommended as they reduce validation to just one object despite the number of users in it.

- ° Policy control: This helps in planning GPOs ordering and sizing, inheritance, filtering, enforcement, blocking, and loopback processing for reducing the overall processing time on the VDAs and servers.

- ° Database: Citrix uses the Microsoft SQL server database for most of its products, as follows:

  - ° Edition: Microsoft ships the SQL server database in different editions, which provide varying features and capabilities. Using the standard edition for typical XenDesktop production deployments is recommended. For larger/ enterprise deployments, depending on the requirement, a higher edition may be required.

  - ° Database and Transaction Log Sizing: This involves estimating the storage requirements for the Site Configuration database, Monitoring database, and configuration logging databases.

  - ° Database Location: By default, the Configuration Logging and the Monitoring databases are located within the Site Configuration database. Separating these into separate databases and relocating the Monitoring database to a different SQL server is recommended.

  - ° High availability: Choose from VM-level HA, Mirroring, AlwaysOn Failover Cluster, and AlwaysOn Availability Groups.

  - ° Database Creation: Usually, the database is automatically recreated during the XenDesktop installation. Alternatively, they can be created by using the scripts.

- ° Citrix licensing: Citrix licensing for XenDesktop requires the existence of a Citrix license server on the network. You can install and manage the multiple Citrix licenses.

  - ° License type: Choose from user, device, and concurrent licenses.

  - ° Version: Citrix's new license servers are backward compatible.

  - ° Sizing: A license server can be scaled out to support a higher number of license requests per second.

- High availability: License server comes with a 30 day grace period to usually help in recovering from failures. High Availability for license server can be implemented through Window clustering technology or duplication of the virtual server.

- Optimization: Optimize the number of the receiving and processing threads depending on your hardware. This is generally required in large and heavily-loaded enterprise environments.

- Resource controllers: The resource controllers include the XenDesktop, the XenApp controllers, and the XenClient synchronizer, as shown here:

  - XenDesktop and XenApp delivery controller.

    - Number of sites: It is considered to have been based on network, risk tolerance, security requirements.

    - Delivery controller sizing: Delivery controller scalability is based on CPU utilization. The more processor cores are available, the more virtual desktops a controller can support.

    - High availability: Always plan for the N+1 deployment of the controllers for achieving the HA. Then, update the controllers' details on VDA through policy.

    - Host connection configuration: Host connections define the hosts, storage repositories, and guest network to be used by the virtual machines on hypervisors.

    - XML service encryption: The XML service protocol running on delivery controllers uses clear text for exchanging all data except passwords. Consider using an SSL encryption for sending the StoreFront data over a secure HTTP connection.

    - Server OS load management: The default maximum number of sessions per server has been set to 250. Using real time usage monitoring and loading analysis, you can define appropriate load management policies.

    - Session PreLaunch and Session Linger: Designed for helping the users in quickly accessing the applications by starting the sessions before they are requested (session prelaunch) and by keeping the user sessions active after a user closes all the applications in a session (session linger).

- ° XenClient synchronizer: It includes considerations for its architecture, processor specification, memory specification, network specification, high availability, the SQL database, remote synchronizer servers, storage repository size and location, and external access, and Active Directory integration.

- Image controllers: This includes all the image provisioning controllers. MCS is built-into the delivery controller. We'll have PVS considerations, such as the following:

  - ° Farms: A farm represents the top level of the PVS infrastructure. Depending on your networking and administration boundaries, you can define the number of farms to be deployed in your environment.

  - ° Sites: Each Farm consists of one or more sites, which contain all the PVS objects. While multiple sites share the same database, the target devices can only failover to the other Provisioning Servers that are within the same site. Your networking and organization structure determines the number of sites in your deployment.

  - ° High availability: If implemented, PVS will be a critical component of the virtual desktop infrastructure. HA should be considered for its database, PVS servers, vDisks and storage, networking and TFTP, and so on.

  - ° Bootstrap delivery: There are three methods in which the target device can receive the bootstrap program. This can be done by using the DHCP options, the PXE broadcasts, and the boot device manager.

  - ° Write cache placement: Write cache uniquely identifies the target device by including the target device's MAC address and disk identifier. Write cache can be placed on the following: Cache on the Device Hard Drive, Cache on the Device Hard Drive Persisted, Cache in the Device RAM, Cache in the Device RAM with overflow on the hard disk, and Cache on the Provisioning Server Disk, and Cache on the Provisioning Server Disk Persisted.

  - ° vDisk format and replication: PVS supports the use of fixed-size or dynamic vDisks. vDisks hosted on a SAN, local, or Direct Attached Storage must be replicated between the vDisk stores whenever a vDisk is created or changed. It can be replicated either manually or automatically.

  - ° Virtual or physical servers, processor and memory: The virtual Provisioning Servers are preferred when sufficient processor, memory, disk and networking resources are guaranteed.

- ◦ Scale up or scale out: Determining whether to scale up or scale out the servers requires considering factors like redundancy, failover times, datacenter capacity, hardware costs, hosting costs, and so on.

- ◦ Bandwidth requirements and network configuration: PVS can boot 500 devices simultaneously. A 10Gbps network is recommended for provisioning services. Network configuration should consider the PVS Uplink, the Hypervisor Uplink, and the VM Uplink. Recommended switch settings include either Disable Spanning Tree or Enable Portfast, Storm Control, and Broadcast Helper.

- ◦ Network interfaces: Teaming the multiple network interfaces with link aggregation can provide a greater throughput. Consider the NIC features TCP Offloading and **Receive Side Scaling (RSS)** while selecting NICs.

- ◦ Subnet affinity: It is a load balancing algorithm, which helps in ensuring that the target devices are connected to the most appropriate Provisioning Server. It can be configured to Best Effort and Fixed.

- ◦ Auditing: By default, the auditing feature is disabled. When enabled, the audit trail information is written in the provisioning services database along with the general configuration data.

- ◦ Antivirus: The antivirus software can cause file-locking issues on the PVS server by contending with the files being accessed by PVS Services. The vDisk store and the write cache should be excluded from any antivirus scans in order to prevent file contention issues.

Hardware layer

The hardware layer involves choosing the right capacity, make, and hardware features of the backend systems that are required for the overall solution as defined in the control layer. In-line with the control layer, the hardware layer decisions will change if any of the first three layer decisions are changed.

Components and technologies that operate under this layer include server hardware, storage technologies, hard disks and the RAID configurations, hypervisors and their management software, backup solutions, monitoring, network devices and connectivity, and so on.

It involves making the decisions shown here:

- Hardware Sizing: The hardware sizing is usually done in two ways. The first, and the preferred, way is to plan ahead and purchase the hardware based on the workload requirements. The second way to size the hosts to use the existing hardware in the best configuration to support the different workload requirements, as follows:

  - Workload separation: Workloads can either be separated into dedicated resource clusters or be mixed in the same physical hosts.

  - Control host sizing: The VM resource allocation for each control component should be determined in the control layer and it should be allocated accordingly.

- Desktop host sizing: This involves choosing the physical resources required for the virtual desktops as well as the hosted server deployments. It includes estimating the pCPU, pRAM, GPU, and the number of hosts.

- Hypervisors: This involves choosing from the supported hypervisors that include major players, such as Hyper-V, XenServer, and ESX. Choosing from these requires considering a vast range of parameters, such as host hardware - processor and memory, storage requirements, network requirements, scale up/out, and host scalability. Further considerations to be made also include the following:

  - Networking: Networks, physical NIC, NIC teaming, virtual NICs—hosts, virtual NICs—guests, and IP addressing

  - VM provisioning: Templates

  - High availability:

    - Microsoft Hyper-V: Failover clustering, cluster shared volumes, CSV cache

    - VMware ESXi: VMware vSphere high availability cluster

    - Citrix XenServer: XenServer high availability by using the server pool

  - Monitoring: Use the hypervisor specific vendor provided management and monitoring tools for hypervisor monitoring; use hardware specific vendor provided monitoring tools for hardware level monitoring.

  - Backup and recovery: Backup method and components to be backed up.

  - Storage: Storage architecture, RAID level, numbers of disks, disk type, storage bandwidth, tiered storage, thin provisioning, and data de-duplication

- Disaster recovery

    ○ Data center utilization: The XenDesktop deployments can leverage multiple data centers for improving the user performance and the availability of resources. Multiple data centers can be deployed in an active/active or an active/passive configuration. An active/active configuration allows for both data centers to be utilized, although the individual users are tied to a specific location.

    ○ Data center connectivity: An active/active data center configuration utilizing GSLB (Global Server Load Balancing) ensures that the users will be able to establish a connection even if one datacenter is unavailable. In the active/active configuration, the considerations that should be made are as follows: data center failover time, application servers, and StoreFront optimal routing.

    ○ Capacity in the secondary data center: Planning of the secondary data center capacity is determined by the cost and by the management to support full capacity in each data center. A percent of the overall users, or a percent of the users per application, may be considered for the secondary data center facility. Then, it also needs the consideration of the type and amount of resources that will be made available in a failover scenario.

Tools for designing XenDesktop®

In the previous section, we saw a broad list of components, technologies, and configuration options, and so on, which we learned are involved in the process of designing the XenDesktop deployment. Obviously, designing the XenDesktop deployment for large, advanced, and complex business scenarios is a mammoth task, which requires operational knowledge of a broad range of technologies. Understanding the maze of this complexity, Citrix constantly helps the customers with great learning resources through handbooks, reviewer guides, blueprints, online eDocs, and training sessions. To ease the life of technical architects and XenDesktop designing and deployment consultants, Citrix has developed an online designing portal called Project Accelerator, which automates, streamlines, and covers all the broad aspects that are involved in the XenDesktop deployment.

Project Accelerator

Citrix designed the Project Accelerator web based designing tool, and it is available to the customers after they login. Its design is based on the Citrix consulting best practices for the XenDesktop deployment and implementation. It follows the layered FMA and allows you to create a close to deployment architecture. It covers all the key decisions and facilitates modifying them and evaluating their impact on the overall architecture. Upon completion of the design, it generates an architectural diagram and a deployment sizing plan, as discussed in the previous chapter. One can define more than one project and customize them in parallel to achieve multiple deployment plans. I highly recommended starting your Production XenDesktop deployment with the Project Accelerator architecture and the sizing design.

Virtual Desktop Handbook

Citrix provides the handbook along with new XenDesktop releases. The handbook covers the latest features of that XenDesktop version and provides detailed information on the design decisions. It provides all the possible options for each of the decisions involved, and these options are evaluated and validated in an in-depth manner by the Citrix Solutions lab. They include the Citrix Consulting leading best practices as well. This helps architects and engineers to consider the recommended technologies, and then evaluate them further for fulfilling the business requirements.

The Virtual Desktop Handbook for latest the version of XenDesktop, that is, 7.x, can be found at: `http://support.Citrix.com/article/CTX139331`.

XenDesktop® Reviewer's Guide

The Reviewer's Guide is also released along with the new versions of XenDesktop. They are designed for helping businesses in quickly installing and configuring the XenDesktop for evaluation. They provide a step-by-step screencast of the installation and configuration wizards of XenDesktop. This provides practical guidance to the IT administrators for successfully installing and delivering the XenDesktop sessions.

The XenDesktop Reviewers Guide for the latest version of XenDesktop, that is, 7.6, can be found at `https://www.citrix.com/content/dam/citrix/en_us/documents/products-solutions/xendesktop-reviewers-guide.pdf`.

XenDesktop® deployment architectures for complex environments

In the previous section, we saw how broad the scope of designing the overall XenDesktop environment for implementation is. We'll now see the XenDesktop architectures that are designed for certain complex and advanced business use cases. These architectures, at their core, consist of all the factors that were discussed earlier. Additionally, they involve advanced configurations and components.

XenDesktop® architecture designed for high availability

High availability is also referred to as HA, and it is a key enterprise feature, which is expected for business continuity. HA is a strategy for businesses to consider/ expect failures in a system and build an alternate auto failover at all the possible failure points. An HA design should eliminate all the points of failures and increase the reliability of each layer of FMA, and consequently, increasing the reliability of the overall system. HA for XenDesktop refers to building redundancy for all the components that are involved in serving a successful session to the end user and the configuration framework that lets failover and failback automatically.

Overview

XenDesktop is built around the fault tolerant components that can be enhanced by Citrix NetScaler for providing disaster recovery and a high availability for business continuity. The high level overview of the XenDesktop architecture design for HA includes the following:

- Deploying at least two NetScaler appliances configured as a HA pair to provide external user access
- Deploying at least two StoreFront servers configured in the load balanced mode by using NetScaler
- Deploying at least two controller servers per site and configuring them for the stores in StoreFront
- Implementing the NetScaler load balancing for the controller servers to achieve the active/active load balancing mode

- Deploying the site SQL databases in the failover clustering mode either in the AlwaysOn Availability Groups or in the AlwaysOn Failover Cluster instances; SQL mirroring is also recommended—mirroring was announced to be discontinued in future releases

- Implementing the backup and restore strategy for the license server if it runs in a virtual environment

- Utilizing the hypervisor clustering and the HA features for making the virtual infrastructure HA for XenDesktop

- Ensuring redundancy at the physical layer that provides the computer network and storage systems to the overall XenDesktop infrastructure.

The following is a high level conceptual architectural diagram representing the HA capability at the level of each component of FMA:

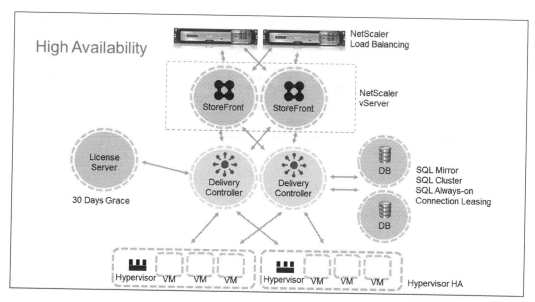

In-depth analysis of the HA architecture at each layer of FMA

We will analyze each of these components according to their respective layers in detail.

User layer

The user layer involves the business users with their respective endpoints running the Receiver software.

- The business user's technical knowledge: The users of business organizations have varying technical expertise when it comes to operating virtual desktops and addressing any of the endpoint environment issues. It is important to build a trained support staff that can assist, guide, and resolve issues for the end user environments.

- Endpoints and bandwidth: They are managed either by the IT staff, or the users themselves, with the help of respective hardware vendor warranty support. In case of the business endpoints, you may plan for a pool of spare devices to support the users. The user experience for an endpoint also depends on the bandwidth that is available for the user while connecting to the virtual desktop. The bandwidth requirements vary across applications.

- Receiver software: Receiver software needs to be properly installed and configured on endpoints. You can install a full version of receiver on corporate fully-featured endpoints. In case of external access and service provider based scenarios, you can either use the reduced plugin version of Receiver or the HTML5 browser Receiver. Whenever users access the StoreFront URL, and if the Receiver software is still unavailable on endpoints, they are directed to download and install this software from the StoreFront or the Citrix downloads page (`http://www.citrix.com/downloads/citrix-receiver.html`).

Access layer

The access layer involves the networking components for external access. Alongside the XenDesktop components, HA also requires the existing corporate network systems as well be configured for HA.

Existing network configuration: HA needs to be supported and configured in several of the existing network components that may fall in the path of connecting to your NetScaler/StoreFront servers. These usually include the following:

- Multiple Name Servers (NS) need to be configured for your external domain name resolution

- The corporate firewalls are the entry points that facilitate communication with your internal systems; firewalls using NAT feature resolves your external domain names to your internal systems

- If a load balancer exists, it also needs to be configured for HA

- The external **Domain Name Servers (DNS)** which resolves your external host names

- Internal Windows DNS as well are required for natively locating and resolving the Windows Active Directory services

- Active Directory services are needed for the user validation requests that come from the NetScaler and StoreFront services

NetScaler Gateway HA pair: Citrix NetScaler offers extensive networking features and controls over the Citrix ICA/HDX connections. NetScalers completely isolate your internal system locations by building a virtual IP for all the external requests and intelligently resolves them as per the internal resources. This plays a key role for all the secured external access to the Citrix resources.

NetScalers are network appliances and they can be configured to run as a pair representing the HA pair. In an HA pair, the appliances operate in the active/passive mode. The NetScalers are configured as two nodes; each of them will have a remote node pointing to the NetScaler IP (NSIP) address of other node. The HA pair synchronizes the configuration from the primary to the secondary appliance. The secondary NetScaler monitors the first NetScaler by sending a periodic heartbeat message, which performs health checks that determine whether the first NetScaler is accepting connections. If this health check fails for a period beyond the configured dead interval, then the secondary NetScaler takes over the primary node and that primary node becomes secondary after the failover. In the event of both nodes failing the health checks, if configured on individual nodes, then the fail-safe mode will ensure that the configured node will always act as the primary node.

The NetScalers HA pair specifications are as follows:

- Both the appliances must be of the same model (that is, configuring a 10010 model along with a 7000 model as an HA pair is not supported)
- All the paired NetScaler appliances must have the same license
- All the paired NetScaler appliances must run on the same version of the NetScaler Gateway software
- All `ns.conf` must match both the appliances except for their NSIPs and HA pair associate IPs

StoreFront HA: User connection requests land on StoreFront web site, upon crossing over NetScaler in case of external user access. StoreFront is critical for the users to logon, and thus, the StoreFront web service and system hosting is expected to be highly available for the users to connect to. There should always be an extra StoreFront server, which has been configured in redundancy.

To configure the StoreFront services for HA, you can choose any one of the following options:

- The NetScaler StoreFront aware intelligent load balancing: An intelligence network appliance, such as NetScaler, has a built-in capability of verifying the availability of the StoreFront service, and it can also actively load balance the user requests. The NetScaler intelligent load balancing automatically removes the failed services and includes them when the service turns functional. The NetScaler pre-configured StoreFront health checks dramatically simplify configuring the load balance checks. All the participating HA StoreFront servers need to be the members of the same StoreFront Server group.

- Windows Network Load Balancer (NLB): This is a less sophisticated mechanism in which a Windows Service checks and verifies whether the listed server is available (Up/Down), but it doesn't verify the status of the individual services. The drawback of this is that the users can be forwarded to a StoreFront server, where the store service is not processing the requests.

- The Traditional DNS round robin: This is a traditional DNS configuration option. It provides rudimentary load balancing across multiple servers, which are configured for a single DNS host record entry. It doesn't perform any checks concerning the availability of the server or the required services.

StoreFront Database HA: The StoreFront servers have a database component, that is, application subscription database. It stores users' personalized application subscription data. This information is automatically either synchronized or replicated to the other StoreFront servers in the group. This ensures that the users have a consistent experience when they connect to the multiple StoreFront servers within an environment. You need to plan for having an appropriate disk space for this database on each of the StoreFront servers for accommodating your users. It typically requires 3 KB to store per user per app details. The size required for this proportionally increases with the increase in both the number of applications used by the user and the number of users.

Desktop/resource layer

The desktop/resource layer includes the resources that can be delivered for user access. It usually includes choosing the desktop and application delivery models and managing the user profiles. The components in this layer don't affect the entire deployment, rather they specifically affect their respective user groups, desktops, or applications delivery. This layer doesn't include any Citrix specific HA configuration doesn't need to be maintained for the components in the layers. However, here are certain recommendations for ensuring that this layer is configured to be more reliable:

- The desktop images: Ensure that your master image is saved to the network storage instead of the host's local disks, so as to overcome host disk failures. Use appropriate naming for each snapshot of your master image.

- Applications delivery: To ensure faster provisioning and high availability of applications, all the common applications may be installed on the master image. You may use XenApp for delivering applications common to large groups. Also utilize the App-V for streaming the isolated applications. Both the XenApp and the App-V applications have to be maintained for HA.

- User profiles: Save the user profiles on the network location that is located on the protected storage with the RAID configuration to overcome disk failures. You may use Windows DFS for the distributed environments that can also overcome the hardware failures on one site.

Control layer

The control layer is the foundation layer containing most of the critical components that are needed for the delivery of the XenDesktop solution. Each component in this layer should be highly available, as they impact the overall deployment. We'll learn how to configure HA for the control layer components, as follows:

Existing network configuration: The control layer involves the use of the existing Windows network components, which need to be configured for HA, as briefed here:

- The Active Directory Services: The AD services are needed for the delivery controller servers for enumerating the user properties and the security group memberships. The AD services also provide time for virtual desktops. There should be primary and secondary AD servers in the network.

- The Active Directory DNS: The DNS service is required for resolving service requests. There should be at least two DNS servers in the site.

- DHCP: DHCP should be configured with the HA features, such as a split scope or a clustered DHCP implementation.

Delivery controllers HA: The delivery controllers are required for both the StoreFront services as well as the VDA on the virtual desktops. It is critical to maintain both the StoreFront and the VDA configurations, which point to a working delivery controller. Based on the user load, there should be at least two delivery controller servers (with N+1redundancy) deployed on the different physical servers to ensure that it withstands the host's physical failures as well as the single controller server's failures.

Configuring the Delivery Controllers for HA at StoreFront: Multiple controllers (at least two) can be configured for each store in StoreFront. StoreFront will automatically failover to the second server in the list if the first server is unavailable (active/passive). For large infrastructures or environments that have a high logon load, an active distribution of the user load (active/active) is required. An active/ active load balancing for controllers (in specific XML service) can be configured by using NetScaler. NetScaler comes with a built-in XML monitoring and session persistency for intelligently load balancing the user requests across the available controllers.

Configuring the Delivery Controllers for HA at VDA: VDAs are configured with the list of all the controllers in the site, during the installation or through the policy setting. VDA automatically fails over if communication with a delivery controller is unavailable. VDA stops at the first place where it finds that an active controller is available. The active controller list for VDA can be configured by using the options shown here:

- A persistent storage location maintained for the VDA auto-update feature — this location is updated with the controller information when an auto-update is enabled and VDA successfully registers for the first time upon installation
- Policy settings (Delivery Controllers, Delivery Controller SIDs)
- The ListofDDCs registry key values are populated by the VDA installer, based on the information specified while installing VDA
- Using `Personality.ini` file created by **Machine Creation Services (MCS)**
- The Active Directory OU-based discovery is a legacy method maintained for providing backward support
- Do not use external load balancing for the Controller address for VDA

Site database HA: The site database is a key repository, which by default holds all the databases, including site configuration, configuration logging, and monitoring. For the production and enterprise deployments configuration, logging and monitoring databases needs to be separated from the site configuration database. While all three databases can be hosted on either the same or different SQL servers, relocating the monitoring database to a different server is recommended as it generates a high load and it is not as important as the other databases.

HA for the site SQL Database can be configured by using SQL server high availability solutions detailed below. In case of the SQL server running on a virtual machine, HA can also be configured at hypervisor level.

- The VM Level HA: This is applicable only to the virtual SQL servers and it can be enabled at the hypervisor level. In case of either an unexpected VM shutdown or underlying host failures, the hypervisor will restart the VM on a different host. This will protect the SQL servers from power outages and host failures, but it cannot protect them from operating system corruption.

- Mirroring: The SQL mirroring creates a standby/mirror database for their respective production database. Mirroring can be a synchronous (provides high safety) or an asynchronous (provides high-performance) operation. For automatic failover, a third server called the Witness server is required. This will let the mirror server act as a hot standby. In case the primary database fails, the failover to the mirror database will happen automatically and it will usually be completed in a few seconds.

- AlwaysOn Failover Clustering: The failover cluster provides an HA for the entire SQL instance of the SQL server. The SQL server 2012 features the AlwaysOn Failover Cluster instance, which appears as a single computer on the network but has the functionality that provides automatic failover from one node to another if the current node becomes unavailable. This failover transition will be seamless to the clients connected to the cluster. A failover cluster consists of two or more nodes, which use a shared storage.

- AlwaysOn Availability Groups: This is a new enterprise level high availability and disaster recovery feature of the SQL server 2012. It maximizes the availability of one or more user databases. It exposes a single virtual IP/network name to the database users. All of the SQL instances should reside on the **Windows Server Failover Clustering (WSFC)** nodes. It doesn't involve using a shared storage, but it involves using the replicas copied locally to each node. Both synchronous and asynchronous replication to one or more secondary servers is supported. Unlike in mirroring or clustering, the secondary servers can be actively used for processing the incoming read-only requests along with the other checks. The data on the active secondary server will lag behind the primary server by multiple seconds.

The XenDesktop comes with a built-in capability called **Connection Leasing**, which lets users connect or reconnect to their most recently used applications and desktops, even when the site database is unavailable. However, this doesn't help new or first time user scenarios.

Licensing server HA: The licensing server provides licensing for all of the Citrix products in an environment. The Citrix licenses are hostname dependent. To make your license files work on multiple systems, a CNAME record in DNS can be used for referencing the license server. CNAMEs allow the license server's name to be changed without updating the Citrix products.

- Built-in grace period: In case of the license server unavailability, the dependent Citrix products enter a 30-day grace period during which the XenDesktop components function normally. The Citrix products enter a grace period if they are unable to communicate with the license server within 2 heartbeats. Once communication with the license server is re-established, the license server will reconcile the temporary licenses with the actual licenses.

- Windows clustering: The cluster servers are groups of computers that work together in order to increase availability. Clustering allows the license server role to automatically failover in the event of a failure.

- Duplication of the license server: This is applicable only if the license server is running on a VM. This creates a backup of the VM and stores it on an HA storage. A failed license server can easily be rebuilt and restored from the backup without impacting the operations of the XenDesktop infrastructure.

Provisioning Services (PVS) HA (Optional Component): If implemented, then the PVS technology has its own components and it requires HA for all the components that are needed for provisioning the desktops. Following is a quick and high level list of the required PVS components for HA:

- Provisioning Server HA: Deploy at least two Provisioning Servers per site. Up to four PVS servers can be configured in the boot file and the boot file should be configured for HA. These servers can be configured for load balancing.

- The database HA: You may choose either offline database or database mirroring.

- vDisks and storage: For the vDisk stores that are hosted on DAS, use replication for synchronizing the vDisks, and in the case of the NAS host, use the vDisks on the HA network share.

- The networking HA: You may use NIC teaming.

- The TFTP service HA: The options to implement HA for TFTP service includes DNS round robin, hardware load balancer, and in case of non-Microsoft DHCP environments you can configure multiple entries for the DHCP option 66.

- Alternates to TFTP: These includes the proxy DHCP or the boot device manager.

Hardware layer

The hardware layer includes all the physical compute, network, and storage systems. The virtualized infrastructure environments includes the Hypervisor and the virtual resources for the compute, network, and storage systems. Building an HA involves building a redundancy at the physical hardware and enabling the respective hypervisor HA features.

Existing infrastructure expertise can be utilized for choosing the appropriate physical components and ascertaining their availability. Following are the common considerations for the hardware HA:

*   The redundant server chassis
*   The redundant power supplies and fans
*   **Uninterruptible power supplies** (UPS)
*   The multiple fiber connects/HBAs
*   The hardware RAID levels for the disk subsystems
*   The multiple diversely routed network interfaces and switches, and NIC teaming with link aggregation for greater throughput

All the major hypervisors (Hyper-V, XenServer & ESX) support the HA features, which should be configured for all the virtualized components of XenDesktop. They employ heartbeats for detecting the VM status and fails over in case of host failures.

Best practices of HA

The best practices for the HA XenDesktop deployments are as follows:

*   Consider HA for every XenDesktop component at each layer
*   Deploy at least two NetScaler appliances for achieving the HA pair
*   Deploy at least two StoreFront servers in a load balance mode
*   If NetScaler exists in the environment, then always prefer it when configuring the StoreFront services for HA
*   Avoid the use of the DNS round robin for configuring the HA of any of the XenDesktop components, such as StoreFront
*   Deploy at least two delivery controller servers (N+1 redundancy) per site on the different physical servers
*   Multiple controllers (at least two) should be configured for each store in StoreFront

- Do not use the external load balancing for the controller addresses with VDA

- Separate the secondary configuration logging and monitoring databases from the primary site configuration databases

- Relocate the monitoring database to a separate SQL server — the monitoring database doesn't fall in the critical path of serving the session to users, and thus, it is not critical for HA

- For the site database HA, the SQL Mirroring is recommended — however, Microsoft is planning to discontinue mirroring in the future versions of the SQL server

- Connection leasing should not be considered as an HA, as it only allows the active users to access their recently accessed resources

Design considerations for a scalable deployment

For any business, the growth of a desktop infrastructure is inevitable and it is critical for running successful businesses. Thus, businesses expect the desktop virtualization solutions to quickly and predictably scale with their business growth. The solution should also be cost effective by minimizing the datacenter hardware requirements, including server hardware, rack space, power supply, and cooling facilities.

A scalable design involves the IT departments, which determine the number of users, the desktop load based on the user requirements, purchase hardware, and integrate and maintain the overall infrastructure for supporting the desktops for the users. The consideration of the peak loads (storms of operations such as logon, reboot, and so on), how many users concurrently request for desktops, and how fast the desktops start, play a significant role in the overall scalability of the solution. It caters to the diligent job of choosing the right backend hardware and highly optimizing XenDesktop and Windows software components for achieving the expected scalability. We'll cover the major XenDesktop scalability features and hardware considerations for large deployments.

XenDesktop® scalability

Scalability is built into a five layer modular architecture of the XenDesktop that makes it adoptable to any size of deployments. The XenDesktop environments can scale to a large number of virtual desktops, and there isn't a limiting size on the XenDesktop site growth. The recent developments supporting the Cloud infrastructures have taken the overall XenDesktop solution to new heights of Scalability. To gain high performance, more user density, and more scalability, updating your XenDesktop software to the latest version is recommended. We will discuss the key concepts that are required for designing a scalable environment around the business requirements.

StoreFront

The number of the concurrent Receiver users supported by StoreFront depends on the StoreFront resources. While StoreFront supports multiple controllers being aggregated into a single store, it's not recommended to have more than ten controllers configured. The additional StoreFront servers can be setup in a load balanced mode for scaling up the overall StoreFront services. Furthermore, the StoreFront servers synchronize the users' personalized application subscription details so that the users have the same seamless experience, despite the StoreFront server that they logon to.

Delivery controllers

The delivery controllers are CPU intensive, as most of the critical services run on them. In FMA, all the controller servers are stateless and equal in their role. Thus, in the virtualized environments, you can easily scale up the controllers either by adding the additional CPU resources or by building the additional controller servers itself. In case of the additional virtual controllers, ensure that they are placed on different physical hosts so that they gain higher performance levels and become highly available. For the non-virtual environments, more controller servers can be added to the site as needed.

Database

The site database supports all the SQL server scalability features. The SQL databases run both CPU and memory intensive loads. The virtualized SQL servers make it easier to scale up or scale out the compute resources. The transaction log files can become large and then they may need to be placed on a separate network storage drive with adequate IOPS capacity. A simple SQL mirror configuration (high resourced principal & mirror servers and low resources witness servers) can sufficiently scale up the medium and large scale deployments.

For the large enterprise environments, scalability can be addressed by placing the database on an SQL failover cluster or an SQL server AlwaysOn availability group. As you grow, you can add more nodes (SQL servers) to the SQL server AlwaysOn availability groups.

Provisioning technologies—MCS and PVS

A common concern among the XenDesktop administrators is to decide on a provisioning method when designing XenDesktop for the large scale deployments. While both MCS and PVS can scale up to large deployments, each of them has their own advantages. Choosing from these options depends on the business use case requirements.

MCS is built-in, simple, and primarily designed for a faster deployment of XenDesktop for small scale deployment, without needing any additional infrastructural setup. MCS possess various limitations that affect the scalability.

- MCS mandates the Master image to be made available on the storage repository that hosts the provisioned virtual machines. This leads to additional manual/automated efforts in copying the master image to each of the host storage repositories.

- MCS results in the need for extra storage and the IOPS load on the storage subsystems, since both the master disk and the difference disk exist on the same storage and are accessed constantly. In this case, MCS generates 1.2x extra IOPS compared to that of PVS.

- In MCS, the hypervisors are also loaded with all the VM copying activities, and this results in a bottleneck when a large number of desktops are provisioned concurrently.

However, most of the preceding limitations can be overcome by employing the appropriate technologies and advanced automation, except that it can't provision the physical systems in achieving large scale deployments.

PVS, on the other hand, is primarily designed for streaming the operating systems to the endpoint devices. It supports both the virtual and the physical systems. Although, it involves additional hardware and advanced infrastructural setup, it seamlessly scales to any size (up to many thousands of desktops) once it is properly deployed. Being a streaming technology, it offloads the processing load to the endpoint devices and increases the desktop density per PVS server. PVS supports deploying the multiple Provisioning Servers to scale for the large scale deployment.

The common bottlenecks in the PVS deployments are the network IO of the Provisioning Server, and the disk IO of the vDisk and the WriteCache file. To scale PVS for the larger deployments, the PVS server network IO can be improved by adding more NICs to it and by teaming them up. Write Cache when configured as typically to **Cache on device hard drive** will cause high IO in virtual environments. It is recommended that the PVS provisioned virtual machines be configured with the storage pools that are designated with the RAID 10 configuration.

Open architecture and Cloud support

In *Chapter 1*, *Evolution and Core Strengths of XenDesktop®*, we learned that the open architecture Cloud ready FMA is one of the core strengths of XenDesktop. XenDesktop is supported on all the popular hypervisors. This is a key feature, and it benefits the businesses that invested in the existing hypervisors' infrastructures. Its support for integration with Cloud the infrastructure providers, such as Amazon EC2, and Citrix CloudPlatform, makes the architecture broader. With the cloud infrastructure integration, the XenDesktop deployments can be classified into private, hybrid, or public Cloud deployments. Similar hypervisor hosts can be grouped into clusters and resource pools to form a modular system that can be easily scaled by adding more hypervisors to the cluster/resource pool. The Cloud integration architectures provide scalability, as well as sustainable solutions in case of disaster recovery.

Windows operating system and applications optimization

A virtual desktop scalability at run time depends on the load generated within a desktop, which contributes to the overall desktop load. It's recommended that we follow the respective Windows operating system optimization guidelines for the virtual environment. The operating system security and monitoring software, such as antivirus, can affect the desktop performance. Keeping the security and the monitoring software CPU usage to just what is absolutely required will make your solution not only scalable, but it will also provide faster response times. Furthermore, the application types and their resource access also need to be considered since the CPU, memory, or IOPS intensive applications can also limit the desktop's scalability. The application deployment when done through Streaming can increase the IOPS. The application delivery method should be diligently chosen for reducing the run time load. It's preferred to install all the common applications on the master/gold image itself, which avoids the application deployment load.

Site capacity and multi-site deployments

A XenDesktop site scales up as the controllers and the database processing capacity grows in the environment. However, the risk of a site failure impacting a significant portion of the user population increases as the size of an individual desktop site increases. The XenDesktop layered modular architecture lets businesses scale out by deploying the multi-site configurations (deploying a second site alongside the initial site within the same geographical location). In the multi-site deployments, the components are shared and combined together through the access and control layers. This results in an environment that can serve the needs of both the large and the small scale deployments, providing resiliency and high availability in case a single site structure fails.

Following is the XenDesktop multi-site architecture diagram showing the control layer components connecting to the multiple XenDesktop sites:

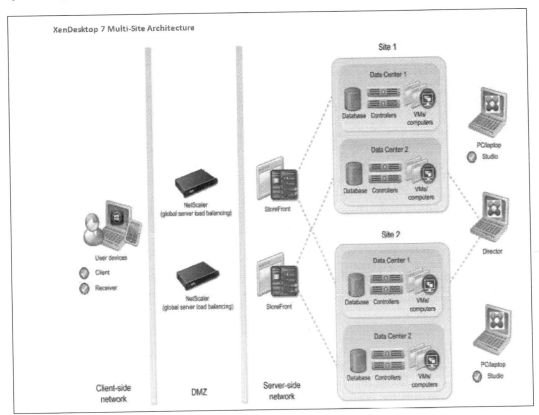

Hardware scalability

Scaling up the virtual desktop environments from a single server to a modular block/cluster of the resources requires a deep understanding of the hardware and the knowledge of its capacity, performance capabilities, and limitations.

Single server scalability

Single server scalability refers to determining the number of the desktops that a single hypervisor host server can load. This forms the basis for determining the scalability of a hypervisor resource pool and the overall scalability of a single pod. Once the single server scalability is determined, it becomes easier to scale your deployment for meeting the estimated user growth with the addition of the proportional host/servers to the infrastructure. It is recommended to adhere to the scalability best practices that are given by the chosen hypervisor vendor.

Scalability with hardware assisted server technologies

The server hardware technologies are constantly evolving in such a way that they are able to achieve low cost and high scalability. Currently, there are three emerging technologies which can change the future of the desktop virtualization and the data center consolidations. They are hardware-assisted system virtualization, hardware-assisted system security, and hardware servers physicalization.

Today's server consolidation through virtualization effectively reduces network, memory, and the IO bandwidth, which makes the large IO problem worse. The server physicalization is a new approach in many of the small one-socket servers that are built into a single Microserver, which shares the chassis, fans, the power supplies and a common interconnect for achieving improved flexibility, higher efficiency, and density. Up to four Intel Atom SoC nodes can be added to a Server System Infrastructure (SSI) module. A single microserver chassis supports the addition of the multiple SSI modules for expanding the number of nodes. This optimizes and increases the rack density compared to the other single unit servers. Citrix actively works with the hardware vendors for bringing these new advantages early to XenDesktop. The HP Moonshot hyperscale microservers are built under strong collaboration with Citrix and AMD.

Storage considerations

Similar to the server hardware, the storage architecture plays a key role in the performance that affects the end user experience, thereby affecting the overall solution. The storage technologies are advancing and need to be considered in accordance with the vendor recommendations. The major storage architectures include local storage, **Network-attached storage (NAS)**, **Direct-attached Storage (DAS)**, **Storage-attached Network (SAN)**, and hybrid. It's recommended that a storage system should be chosen according to the FlexCast deployment type used in your environment. From the available storage architectures, SANs are highly scalable and they provide no noticeable changes in performance when more storage is added or more devices are connected.

App Orchestration – multi forest Active Directory Environment

App Orchestration (AO) has been designed for **Citrix Service Providers (CSPs)** for orchestrating and automating the delivery of applications and desktops in multi-tenant environments and across multiple locations, sites, Active Directory domains, and datacenters. AO supports delivering the shared and the isolated hosted applications and desktops for the tenant users. AO is a part of the **CloudPortal Services Manager (CPSM)**. Using AO with the CPSM hosted service providers can support the multi-tenant self-service of the app and desktop offerings and empower the tenants and resellers by giving them the ability of supporting themselves and delegating control to the tenant or the reseller administrator for managing their user subscription offerings. AO has been built around a desired state configuration paradigm that involves define, design, deliver stages, and these enable the repeatable processes and the self-service administration of the desktop and app services.

We'll see the deployment considerations of AO in a complex multi forest Active Directory environment. It is assumed that you possess the knowledge of how AO works and what its role in the cloudscale **Desktop-as-a-Service (DaaS)** model is. Deploying AO in these environments involves doing the additional configurations manually. Many of these configurations are based on the XenDesktop multi-forest active directory deployments. The primary requirement of the multi-forest XenDesktop deployments is to enable the communication and access to the desktop resources (VDAs) in the cross forests and domains for the users. These, at a high level, include configuration setting up at Active Directory, DNS, and VDAs.

Active Directory requirements

The following Active Directory requirements are to be in-place or configured for achieving the cross multi-forest Windows domain resources communication:

- Configure either a two-way transitive or an external transitive trust between the primary and the secondary forests

- Create an organizational unit (OU) in the secondary forest, which is identical in structure to the one in the primary forest

- Delegate security in the secondary forest so that the AO administrator account can create the machine accounts in that forest

- Add the orchestration service account or group (domainname\AOAdmins) to the local administrators group on the local VDA machine, which will be added to the machine catalog

DNS requirements

In the Windows environment, DNS is closely integrated with Active Directory, and it is critical for establishing proper communication between the systems. You need to ensure that the following DNS configuration exists for supporting the multi-forest systems communications:

- Configure the DNS resolution between the primary and the secondary forests

- DNS forwarders can be configured for the name lookup and the DNS registrations between the forests, if there exists either one-way or two-way trusts between the forests

- Reverse DNS zones are not required if the appropriate DNS forwarders are in place between the forests — a reverse DNS configuration may be required if the DNS namespace is different from that of Active Directory

VDA requirements

The VDA that is running on the virtual desktop needs to be configured so that it can communicate with delivery controllers of the different forests, as follows:

- If the VDA and the delivery controllers are in separate forests, then regardless of any differences between the Active Directory and the NetBIOS names, the following registry key on the VDA will need to be created and the value will need to be set to 1. You will have to restart the Citrix desktop service to apply the change.

  ```
  HKEY_LOCAL_MACHINE\SOFTWARE\Citrix\VirtualDesktopAgent\
  SupportMultipleForest
  ```

- In case the external trusts are in place, create the following registry key on the VDA and set the value to the security identifier (SID) of the Delivery Controllers. The Controller SID can be obtained by using the `XDPing` command.

`HKEY_LOCAL_MACHINE\SOFTWARE\Citrix\VirtualDesktopAgent\ListOfSIDs`

Additionally, modify the `brokeragentconfig.exe.config` file (it is usually located at `C:\Program Files\Citrix\Virtual Desktop Agent\` directory) on the VDA so that it allows the Microsoft **NT LAN Manager (NTLM)** authentication. Restart the Citrix Desktop Service to apply both the changes.

SSL requirements

AO configuration server communicates with the other servers in the deployment, and the SSL protocol can be used to secure this traffic. In multi-domain environments, an SSL certificate from a trusted domain must be present in the trusting domain to enable the AO configuration across domains. This would be easier in the case of the single-domain environments, where you can use the server certificate that is signed by the certificate authority of that domain. The certificate can be installed on the AO configuration server for enabling the communication with the agents on various machines in an AO deployment.

Following is a conceptual diagram representing the AO that is in the common Global Shared domain, the Active Directory users, and the XenDesktop resources that are in their own Active Directory forests with the appropriate Active Directory trusts.

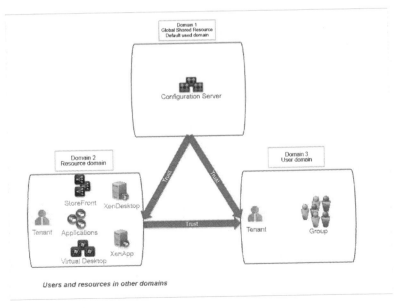

XenDesktop® and Cloud computing integration

There are many interpretations and much buzz about the Cloud and the Cloudifying technologies in the IT industry. It is important to understand what the Cloud is, and how it benefits businesses in the desktop virtualization. Learn the features of XenDesktop that help in Cloudifying the desktop virtualization. We'll cover the advance deployment of XenDesktop in Private Cloud by using CloudPlatform and in Public Cloud by using AWS EC2. Amazon EC2 has set the standards for the Public Cloud services and it's assumed that the readers are aware of the Cloud domain terminology, including regions, availability zones, Pod, VPC, multi-tenancy, and so on.

Cloud computing for desktop virtualization

Cloud computing is a collection of a large (boundless) group of remote servers networked to provide a centralized data storage and online access to the compute resources and services. Cloud computing services possess key characteristics, such as agility, high availability, multi-tenancy, performance, reliability, scalability, and API. It also increases user productivity by making the service device independent and accessible from anywhere. Cloud computing relies on resource sharing and supports the pay-as-you-go billing model. These key benefits of Cloud computing address major and common concerns for businesses and it helps in reducing the capital investment for businesses. There are three primary Cloud service models that offer different services along with the entire Cloud computing characteristic. They are **Infrastructure as a service (IaaS)**, **Platform as a service (PaaS)**, and SaaS. Based on the deployment mode, Cloud Computing is classified into Private Cloud, Public Cloud, and Hybrid Clouds.

Transforming the desktop virtualization into the Cloud service enables all the Cloud capabilities to the desktop virtualization solution. The true cloud service of the virtualized desktop solution forms the **Desktop-as-a-Service (DaaS)** model.

XenDesktop® Cloud support

As we saw in XenDesktop and the Project Avalon roadmap discussed in *Chapter 1, Evolution and Core Strengths of XenDesktop®*, Citrix is constantly enhancing, redesigning XenDesktop, and building more technologies that make the XenDesktop deployments integrate with any of the cloud infrastructures. XenDesktop has been redesigned with the built-in support for the industry leading Citrix CloudPlatform, as well as the public cloud services from the **Amazon Web Services (AWS)** EC2. Citrix is also working with Microsoft for integration of their cloud infrastructures services Windows Azure. This capability will significantly turn the XenDesktop deployments into private, public, or hybrid Clouds. Also, Citrix started a new certification program called the Citrix Ready IaaS Cloud for XenDesktop, which gives businesses the confidence that XenDesktop will run on a particular Cloud operator's infrastructure. This lets businesses quickly adopt the public or the hybrid cloud deployments for their XenDesktop environment.

Following is a pictorial representation of XenDesktop showing support for integrating with the traditional hypervisors, CloudPlatform for Private cloud, and Amazon AWS for the public cloud deployments:

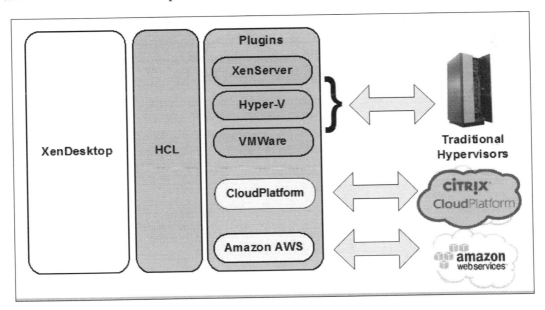

CloudPlatform

Citrix CloudPlatform is a key solution from Citrix for building and managing the public, private and hybrid IaaS cloud environments. CloudPlatform has specifically been architected for supporting the enterprise cloud success capabilities, such as compatibility, scalability, and flexibility. The architecture is inherently redundant, without any single points of failure, making the product ready for hosting business critical workloads. While the architecture provides sustainability over a single point of failures, there may be a possible service interruption if a simultaneous failure occurs over multiple points, as seen with the public Cloud service providers in the recent past. CloudPlatform is powered by Apache CloudStack, which is a community-led open source cloud orchestration project. The industry standard APIs that are compatible with Apache CloudStack, as well as with the Amazon Web Service's APIs, enable the CloudPlatform powered Clouds to interface with the third parties for value added solutions, such as PaaS, monitoring, capacity management, and hybrid Clouds.

CloudPlatform facilitates easy scaling of the infrastructure by providing the modular desktop Cloud architecture. It allows the infrastructure to be modularly structured as hosts, clusters, pods, zones, and regions. This approach enables administrators to develop design and deploy them based on the current needs. It also helps them in adding infrastructure, such as new hosts, clusters, and zones on demand, based on the requirements. This ensures that the environment is neither under-provisioned, which can impact the performance, nor over-provisioned.

The key benefits of CloudPlatform for businesses is adoption to an industry standard based on the open source platform, which enables a variety of choices in the hypervisor, storage, and network technologies, and it offers the Amazon AWS compatibility. It provides businesses with the flexibility of supporting either the traditional workloads or the Cloud era workloads, however it can't support both of these at the same time. CloudPlatform is massively scalable. It can orchestrate the provisioning of thousands of physical or virtual servers in multiple geographically distributed data centers, which allows the resultant Cloud(s) to be easily managed through a user-friendly single-pane-of-glass interface delivered by a single management server. No individual component is a single point of failure, and the periodic maintenance of the management server can be performed without affecting the VMs that run in the Cloud.

A high level Cloud deployment conceptual diagram representing CloudPlatform, which is supporting the orchestration of the resources from the various infrastructure providers, has been shown here:

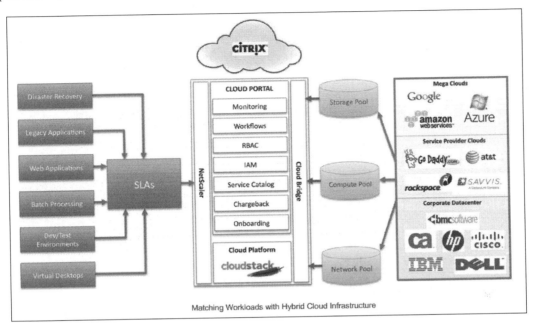

Matching Workloads with Hybrid Cloud Infrastructure

Using CloudPlatform, businesses can turn their enterprise infrastructure into their own private Cloud, which can be used by XenDesktop. CloudPlatform is used by the service providers for building the large scale Cloud service infrastructures. We'll learn how to build the private cloud deployment by using CloudPlatform.

Amazon Web Services (AWS) Elastic Computing (EC2)

AWS emerged as the industry's leading public Cloud platform and defined the various standards of a public Cloud, which businesses and technologies require for faster integration and migrations. Following is the high level architecture and terminology of Amazon Web Services (AWS) Elastic Computing (EC2):

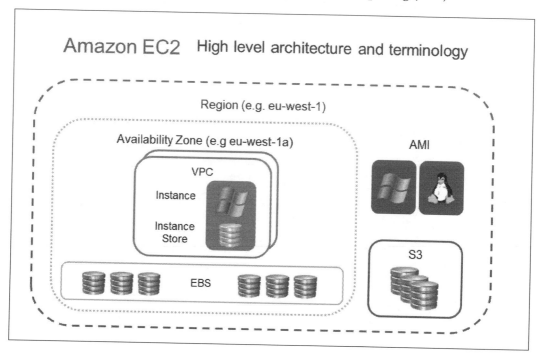

The XenDesktop parallel site deployment in AWS involves a sequence of defined steps for creating and configuring multiple instances along with their roles. AWS has the provision for automating the defined steps for quickly provisioning a stack of instances and then configuring them. It's called CloudFormation. It is a JSON scripted way of deploying the servers and configuring them in AWS. Citrix provides its own CloudFormation template on AWS for quickly provisioning the XenDesktop deployment in AWS. The latest Citrix CloudFormation template has been enhanced with a support for multi-region availability and a simplified installation. You can create your own template script to customize the deployment.

Creation of the XenDesktop stack by using the CloudFormation template creates a complete VPC, which includes the following:

- The availability zone
- The public (DMZ) and private (internal) subnets
- The DMZ network:
    - A NAT instance
    - A NetScaler VPX and its associate IPs, include two public IPs (SNIP and VIP) and two private IPs (NSIP & SNIP)
    - The Bastion server in the DMZ network, which allows the external administration
- The private network:
    - An Active Directory instance
    - The VDAs master image instance
    - XenDesktop Delivery Controller
    - The Hosted Desktop services server
- NetScaler features, including NetScaler Gateway and CloudBridge Connector, for the Site-to-Site VPN access

AWS limitations for XenDesktop® deployment

The XenDesktop deployment on AWS is limited only to the server-based desktop and the application delivery, since AWS doesn't support the Windows Desktop operating system instances. AWS currently only supports the machine provisioning through MCS and not through PVS.

As many businesses consider deploying XenDesktop with AWS, we have covered the XenDesktop deployment with AWS in both the modes that form the public and hybrid Cloud deployment scenarios. This shall help businesses in adopting, as well as migrating to the AWS Cloud deployments for XenDesktop.

Private Cloud

The private Cloud is the collection of an on-premise infrastructure, desktops, applications and the data delivered on demand by the enterprise IT. The private Clouds can also be hosted off-premise. In this case, a service provider offers a portion of its public infrastructure for the exclusive use by a single customer, also known as a tenant. Private Clouds are commonly used when direct control on the services provided and on the backend infrastructure is needed. The CloudPlatform deployment works better for the large enterprises or the Service Providers organizations that span across the multiple datacenters with the advanced infrastructure hosting the hardware servers, Storage, and Network resources. The XenDesktop deployment with the CloudPlatform forming a private Cloud can be configured in various modes. Here, we'll see a XenDesktop deployment architecture that is used in the Hybrid deployments when configured with the AWS public Cloud.

The deployment architecture

The XenDesktop deployment extended with CloudPlatform enables businesses to build an agile private cloud, which can provide the cloud infrastructure for each data center. With the CloudPlatform private cloud, the datacenter infrastructure is consolidated, and they can just run the Active Directory that hosts the users. Within CloudPlatform, the multiple XenDesktop deployment sites are deployed for each data center respectively for building better management. The Citrix licensing can be consolidated into a system, which supports licensing for all of the XenDesktop sites.

Following is an architectural diagram representing the consolidated XenDesktop deployment in the CloudPlatform private Cloud:

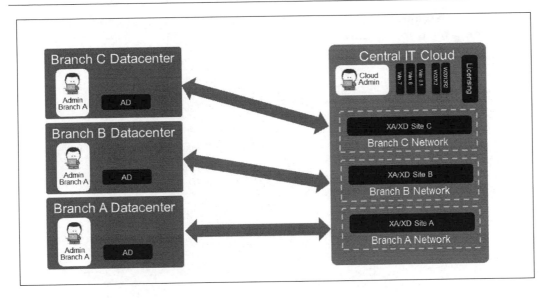

Public Cloud (using Amazon AWS)

The public Cloud is a collection of the off-premise multi-tenant infrastructure, storage, and computing resources, and the SaaS applications and data, which are delivered on demand by the external Cloud service providers. Public Clouds allow multiple customers, or tenants, to share the underlying resources with each paying only for the resources that it consumes. However, the public Cloud deployments don't provide a direct physical access to the systems or the devices that are involved in building the infrastructure. We'll discuss how to deploy the complete XenDesktop infrastructure on the AWS infrastructure, which forms the public Cloud.

The deployment architecture

The XenDesktop deployment on the AWS public cloud involves the complete XenDesktop site deployment in a **virtual private cloud** (VPC) in AWS. In the public Cloud deployment, all XenDesktop components and common Windows infrastructure services, such as Active Directory, DNS, DHCP, and so on, run on the AWS Cloud. This site functions completely independent of your on-premise Citrix and Windows infrastructure and the users can directly access the desktop sessions in AWS. The business users can access XenDesktop from anywhere, including their corporate office or home networks.

An architectural diagram representing a typical full XenDesktop deployment on AWS forming the public Cloud is as follows:

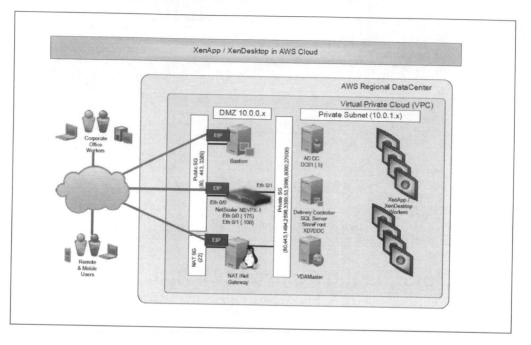

Deployment functional overview

The XenDesktop deployment in the AWS public cloud provides a seamless provision of the AWS server-based desktops to the end users. The NetScaler VPX running on the NetScaler Gateway provides the external access over the AWS EIP that is highly available. All the XenDesktop servers are made the members of the Active Directory, which enables Windows level access and communication between the systems. The NetScaler Gateway hosted in DMZ is configured with the internal StoreFront store URL and the Active Directory for the LDAP authentication with a public certificate that secures the connections to the desktop sessions. Use of the public trust certificate SSL connection ensures a secure connection from anywhere. The master VDA AMI with all the applications installed, domain membership, dynamic IP address assignment, and so on, is used for the VM provisioning by MCS. This complete infrastructure can either be scaled up or be scaled out in accordance with the business needs.

Detailed deployment procedure

Following is a detailed procedure explaining the XenDesktop deployment in the AWS public Cloud by using the preceding detailed architecture:

- Create the XenDesktop stack on AWS by using the CloudFormation template.
  - Review and note the public and the private IP ranges. The NetScaler public and private IPs are used in the later steps of configuring the XenDesktop deployment in AWS.

- Build and configure Windows Active Directory domain controller server on AWS infrastructure for user authentication:
  - Install the Active Directory services roles along with DNS and DHCP roles required for Windows infrastructure
  - Join all the Windows servers to the new Active Directory domain with respective DNS entries

- Build and configure the XenDesktop site on the AWS infrastructure, as shown here:
  - Install the XenDesktop delivery controller with the local database and all the core components
  - Setup the licensing from the Studio
  - Setup the hosting connection to the AWS Cloud by using the access credentials for provisioning the instances on AWS
  - Choose the AWS region, availability zone, private subnet for hosting your instances
  - Complete the XenDesktop site

- Configure the master image by configuring the master VDA machine, as follows:
  - This involves installing the VDA for the Windows server on the system
  - Configuring it as the master image with the delivery controller, which is installed in AWS
  - After installing VDA, install any application that can be delivered to the users
  - Then, shut down the instance
  - Create an AMI from the master VDA, which can be used for the machine creations

- Provision the machines in AWS by using the master VDA AMI with MCS and assign the users, as shown here:
    - Create a machine catalog with the following options:
        - **Operating system** as the **server OS**
        - **Machine management** to use **Citrix Machine Creation Services (MCS)** provisioning
        - Select the master VDA AMI
        - Select the required Domain and Private security groups that contain your users and select **use hardware that is dedicated for my account**
        - Specify the number of machines to be provisioned and their AWS instance type
        - Choose the network settings that indicate your private network range
        - Specify the **account naming scheme** for the AD computer accounts and the OU path
    - Create the delivery group and assign the users the applications or desktops, as it is usually done in a regular XenDesktop deployment
- Set up the NetScaler Gateway remote access, as follows:
    - Add the NetScaler Gateway to the StoreFront remote access by doing the following:
        - On the Delivery Controller, launch the StoreFront console and select **Enable Remote Access** for the default created store
        - Use **No VPN Tunnel** option, and then add the NetScaler Gateway parameters, such as the **NetScaler Gateway URL**, Private SNIP, and so on, as requested by the **Add NetScaler Gateway Appliance** wizard
        - In the **Secure Ticket Authority URLs**, add the AWS Delivery Controller URL
    - Configure the NetScaler Gateway settings in NetScaler.
        - Log on to the AWS NetScaler VPX web console (over Private NSIP) from the machine on your AWS private network.

- Create the Network connections under **Network**, the **IPs** section.

  - Create a VIP pointing to IP within the public range. It will be used for configuring the NetScaler Gateway in the steps discussed here. Create an SNIP pointing to the IP within the private range. This IP address is used while configuring the NetScaler Gateway in the StoreFront Remote Access wizard.

- Enable the **NetScaler Gateway** option by navigating to **System | Settings | Configure Basic Settings**.

- Setup a new NetScaler Gateway by going to the **NetScaler Gateway, Configure NetScaler Gateway for enterprise store** with parameters, such as **Name**, **IP-Address**, and **Port**

- Ensure that the VIP that has been used is of the type AWS Elastic IP. If not, then use an AWS elastic IP, which points to VIP.

- At DNS, create an entry for your NetScaler Gateway FQDN, and ensure that it resolves to VIP of NetScaler from your StoreFront and in the private network.

- Under the **Certificate** section, use a publicly trusted certificate, which matches the FQDN DNS name used while specifying the NetScaler Gateway details in StoreFront.

- Authentication method as the **LDAP** Policy pointing to the AD service in AWS.

- In the **Enterprise Store settings**, select **StoreFront** as the **deployment type**, then specify the StoreFront FQDN, and select the HTTPS, and then add the **STA URL** (that is your delivery controller).

- Now, verify by logging on to your NetScaler Gateway URL, which validates the user credential against the Active Directory server in AWS.

Hybrid Cloud (using Amazon AWS)

The hybrid Cloud deployment features orchestration of both on-premise (private) and off-premise (public) infrastructure resources. This gives business the benefits of both the worlds of the Cloud deployments and builds an agile, highly available, and scalable (up/down) solution for meeting the ever-changing user demands. This lets the businesses with flexibility to support the best fit cloud deployments for the usage scenarios that may either need a public or a private cloud. We'll see a high level architecture detailing of what it involves in achieving the XenDesktop hybrid Cloud deployment by using AWS.

The deployment architecture

Extending the XenDesktop deployment to the Cloud involves the deployment and integration of a parallel XenDesktop site, which is positioned inside a VPC in AWS. In a hybrid deployment, the Citrix StoreFront access, domain authentication, and licensing components will run on the existing on-premise corporate site, and it will be shared by the parallel site in the AWS cloud. To establish a secure connectivity between the on-premise site and the AWS site, deploying the NetScaler VPX's and the Citrix CloudBridge components in both the sites is required. Then, configuring the Citrix CloudBridge connection over the NetScaler VPX's enables a secure connectivity between the sites.

The architectural diagram of the XenDesktop hybrid Cloud deployment representing the on-premise private Cloud components and the off-premise public AWS resources is as follows:

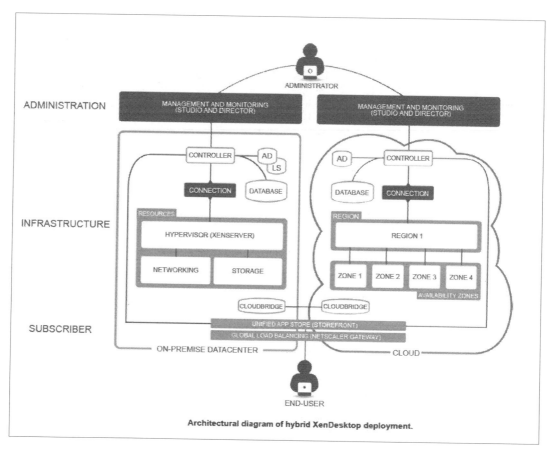

Architectural diagram of hybrid XenDesktop deployment.

Deployment functional overview

XenDesktop extended AWS hybrid cloud deployment provides a seamless provision of the AWS VMs to the end users. This is achieved by retaining the end user accessible StoreFront store URL unchanged and extending it by the addition of the delivery controller setup in the AWS. The network level bi-directional secure connectivity between the on-premise XenDesktop components and the AWS XenDesktop site is achieved by deploying the NetScaler VPX in both the networks and then configuring the NetScaler's CloudBridge connection feature. The Windows domain level access and communication is established by making the delivery controller and Master VDA systems to be the members of the existing on-premise Active directory domain and DNS. Then, the AWS XenDesktop site can be configured to use the existing on-premise Citrix license server.

The AWS delivery controller configured with the hosting connection to the customer AWS infrastructure and the VDA master image AMI lets the delivery controller provision the virtual machines in AWS and it lets enumeration of the users and the security groups from the on-premise Active Directory. By ensuring that the master image, with consistent updates in the on-premise and AWS, will enable the users to have a seamless experience across the VMs delivered either from the AWS Cloud or by the On-premise infrastructure.

Detailed deployment procedure

Following is a detailed procedure explaining the XenDesktop deployment in the hybrid AWS Cloud by using the preceding architecture:

- It's assumed that the on-premise Citrix component NetScaler and shared components, including StoreFront, Active Directory, and licensing are existing in-place.
- Create the XenDesktop Stack on AWS by using the CloudFormation template, as shown here:
  - Review and note the public and the private IP ranges, the NetScaler public & private IPs used in the later configuration of the setup
- Configure the AWS NetScaler VPX with the required network connections, as follows:
  - Connect to the AWS NetScaler VPX by connecting from any machine in the AWS private network.

- ° Create the three SNIP Network connections that correlate and connect to the private, Public, and CloudBridge networks. Enable the management across all of the three SNIPs. Once the configuration is complete, the management access is required only on the public SNIP for the management access from the on-premise environment.
- ° Bind an EIP (Elastic IP) to the public SNIP of the NetScaler from the AWS console.
- ° Verify that the default route on the AWS NetScaler points to the public Gateway.

- Configure the access connection rules required for CloudBridge connector in Amazon AWS, as shown here:
  - ° Verify and configure the inbound & the outbound TCP and UDP rules for all the AWS security groups which contain **NATSecurityGroup**, **PublicSecurityGroup**, & **PrivateSecurityGroup** in their names. The ports and the protocols majorly include the Active Directory LDAP, DHCP, and so on.
  - ° In the AWS **Route Tables**, for the private subnet add a new private route that directs the traffic destined for the private on-premise subnet to the private **Elastic Network Interface (ENI)** of the AWS NetScaler.

- Configure the On-premise Internet router with the following rules, which are required for the CloudBridge connector.
  - ° The inbound UDP traffic on the 500 & 4500 ports to the private SNIP of the on-premise NetScaler
  - ° The outbound traffic destined for all the three cloud bridge networks, the AWS public subnet, and the AWS private subnet, should be routed to the private SNIP on the on-premise NetScaler

- Install and configure the CloudBridge connector between the on-premise and the AWS NetScalers SNIPs. At the On-premise NetScaler VPX, create the CloudBridge connector with the following parameters:
  - ° Select the **Amazon Web Services**
  - ° Connect by using the AWS access and the secret key IDs
  - ° Specify the AWS NetScaler EIP address and the AWS NetScaler credentials
  - ° Configure the connection strings, including:
    - ° The public and private SNIPs of the on-premise NetScaler

- EIP (which is bound to the public SNIP) and the private SNIPs of the AWS NetScaler
- Specify the security settings for the encryption and the hash algorithms
- Choose to auto-create keys
- Review the connection settings, including name, local and remote IP settings

- Configure the AWS delivery controller and the VDA master instances to communicate with the on-premise Windows Active Directory infrastructure, as shown here:
    - Configure the delivery controller with a static IP address, which is within the private AWS subnet range.
    - Configure the DNS resolution between the delivery controller and your corporate DNS infrastructure. Set up the secondary DNS server to the on-premise DNS server.
    - Rename the delivery controller server as per your naming convention requirements.
    - Join the delivery controller with the Active Directory domain.
    - Run all the preceding steps for the VDA master instance.

- Create the desktop server base image by doing the following:
    - Create an AWS image from the VDA master instance
    - The newly created base image will appear on the AMI list

- Create the XenDesktop site on a delivery controller in AWS, as follows:
    - Install the XenDesktop delivery controller with the local database. The shared components, such as Citrix license server and StoreFront are not required.
    - Configure the licensing to use the existing on-premise license server, as follows:
        - Specify the on-premise licensing server's name
        - If prompted, then select **Connect Me** to trust the license server certificate
        - Select **Use an Existing License** and then choose an appropriate license for the XenDesktop site

- Configure the hosting connection to the AWS Cloud by using the access credentials for provisioning the instances on AWS by using MCS
- Select the appropriate AWS region, VPC, availability zone, and the AWS private subnet for hosting your instances
- Select **No** to **App-V publishing**
- Complete the XenDesktop site

- Provision the machines in AWS by using the Master VDA AMI with MCS and assign the users, as shown here:
  - Create a machine catalog with the following options:
    - **Operating system** as the **Windows Server OS**.
    - **Machine management** to use **Citrix Machine Creation Services** (**MCS**) provisioning.
    - On **Machine Template** screen select your Master VDA AMI.
    - Select the appropriate AWS Private Security group that facilitates the respective access rules. The **use shared hardware** is the default option, which can be changed if required.
    - Specify the number of the virtual machines to be provisioned and their AWS instance type.
    - Select the network and the network interface associated with the AWS private subnet.
    - Specify the **account naming scheme** for the AD computer accounts and the OU path.
  - Configure the delivery group:
    - Click on **Create delivery group**.
    - Select the previously created machine catalog.
    - Specify the number of VMs that are to be allocated to these delivery group users.
    - Select the **delivery type** to be **Desktops**.
    - Specify the AD domain users or the user group under the **Users** section.

- ° Configure the StoreFront list for Receiver by selecting the automatically configure Receiver with a list of the StoreFront servers. This is for the Receiver that runs on the VDAs.
  - ° Provide a friendly name and description for finishing the delivery group creation.

- Configure the on-premise StoreFront server with the AWS delivery controller for providing the AWS desktops, as follows:
  - ° Select the URL of the desired Store and then click on **Manage Delivery Controllers**
  - ° Click on **Add** and then enter the private IP address of the AWS delivery controller with the default http port 80

Summary

We learnt the decision making that is involved in designing the XenDesktop in general, and we also saw the deployment designs of the complex environments involving the cloud capabilities. This understanding will help you in appreciating the existing XenDesktop deployments. It will also enable you to easily identify the short falls of a given XenDesktop environment. You shall be able to build the XenDesktop deployments in the Cloud infrastructures based on the Citrix CloudPlatform as well as the industry leading Amazon Web Services EC2 infrastructures.

In the next chapter, we'll learn how to deploy XenDesktop, including both the core and the additional components, followed by its configuration. We will also discuss the verification process of the deployment.

Implementing a XenDesktop® Environment

4

In the last chapter, we discussed the XenDesktop design and the XenDesktop infrastructure components.

Now it is time to start the setup of our first XenDesktop environment. At the end of this chapter, you will be able to install and configure a basic infrastructure, and this will give you the ability to deliver applications and desktops to your users.

In this chapter, we will cover the following topics:

- Installing of the main components of XenDesktop
- Configuring and verifying the XenDesktop setup
- XenDesktop site database concepts and configuration

Installing of XenDesktop®'s main components

As we saw in the previous chapter, a XenDesktop infrastructure includes many components, and some of them are essential for successfully installing XenDesktop.

In this chapter, we will install and configure the essential elements of XenDesktop, such as:

- Citrix Licensing
- Citrix Delivery Controller
- Citrix Studio

- Citrix Director
- Citrix Storefront

At the end of the installation process, you will be able to install a XenDesktop deployment, as shown here:

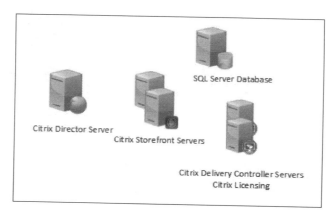

When installing the components, you will have to satisfy some of the system requirements. You can find these on the Citrix web page, which can be found at `http://support.citrix.com/proddocs/topic/xenapp-xendesktop-75/cds-system-requirements-75.html`.

Here you can find a table listing the main requirements and operating systems support:

XenDesktop component	Supported operating systems	Disk space	Features
Delivery Controller	Windows 2012 R2	100 MB	Microsoft .NET 3.5 SP1 (only for Windows 2008 R2)
	Windows 2012		Microsoft .NET 4.5 (only for Windows 2012 and 2012 R2)
	Windows 2008 R2 SP1		Windows Powershell 2.0 (Windows 2008 R2) or Windows Powershell 3.0 (Windows 2012 and 2012 R2)
			Visual C++ 2005, 2008 SP1 and the 2010 Redistributable packages

XenDesktop component	Supported operating systems	Disk space	Features
Studio	Windows 2012 R2	75 MB	Microsoft .NET 3.5 SP1 (only for Windows 2008 R2 and Windows 7)
	Windows 2012		Microsoft .NET 4.5 (only for Windows 2012, 2012 R2 and Windows 8.x)
	Windows 2008 R2 SP1		Windows Powershell 2.0 (Windows 2008 R2) or Windows Powershell 3.0 (Windows 2012 and 2012 R2)
	Windows 8.x		
	Windows 7		
Director	Windows 2012 R2	50 MB	Microsoft .NET 4.5
	Windows 2012		Microsoft IIS 7.0 and ASP.NET 2.0
	Windows 2008 R2 SP1		
StoreFront	Windows 2012 R2		Microsoft .NET 3.5 SP1 (only for Windows 2008 R2)
	Windows 2012		Microsoft .NET 4.5 (only for Windows 2012, 2012 R2)
	Windows 2008 R2 SP1		Microsoft IIS 7.0 and ASP.NET 2.0
Database	SQL Server 2012 SP1, Express, Standard and Enterprise Editions		
	SQL Server 2008 R2 SP2, Express, Standard, Enterprise and Datacenter Editions		

As you can see, the table doesn't list any information about processor and memory requirements. Citrix doesn't provide any guidelines about this, but it does recommend a minimum allocation of 3 GB of memory if all the components are to be installed on a single server.

Based on my working experience and the XenDesktop implementations, allocating two processors and 4 GB of memory for each system hosting infrastructure component is sufficient for obtaining a good performance.

In any case, sufficient resources should be assigned to the infrastructure's server in order to avoid bottlenecks.

The database server sizing is quite different. We will discuss it later.

When you install the XenDesktop components, make sure to also consider the infrastructure that you have to implement and the business requirements you have to satisfy.

For example, if you plan to serve very few users, or a laboratory for testing, you can choose to install all the components on a single server.

On the contrary, if you have to provide access to virtual desktops or applications to many users, you should consider splitting the components across different systems.

Now we can begin the installation of each component.

Installing Citrix® Licensing

The Citrix Licensing component is used for managing the Citrix licenses. This component is required for many Citrix products.

Citrix Licensing is available as a Windows installer and a virtual appliance (format .xva), and you can import these into a Citrix XenServer host.

> If you decide to use the virtual appliance, note that XenServer 6.1 and 6.2 are the only supported platforms.

The installer is available on the XenDesktop ISO, or on the Citrix website at http://www.citrix.com/downloads/licensing.html.

> You need a MyCitrix account for downloading either the installer or the appliance. You can create an account for free.

At the time of writing this chapter, the release 11.12.1 was available for downloading from the Citrix website.

For the successful installation of Citrix Licensing on a Windows server, you need to satisfy the following requirements:

Supported operating systems	Disk space	Features
Windows 2012 R2	55 MB	Microsoft .NET 3.5 SP1 or later
Windows 2012		
Windows 2008 R2		
Windows 2008		

Updated information about the system requirements are available at
`http://docs.citrix.com/en-us/licensing/11-12-1/lic-`
`licensing-prerequisites.html`.

Citrix Licensing is a light workload, so you don't need to install or configure a dedicated server for a medium sized environment. You can also manage the different Citrix products (for example, Citrix XenDesktop, XenApp, provisioning services, and so on) with the same unique license server.

 If you plan to manage many Citrix XenDesktop environments alongside thousands of users/licenses, you should install a dedicated machine with one processor and 2 GB memory.

You could be thinking that installing a single license server could be a single point of failure, but you should remember that if the license server is unavailable, then Citrix XenDesktop (and other products) will continue to work for 30 days (grace period). So, it is not vital to provide high availability for this component.

If you have to provide high availability for the Citrix Licensing component, note that the Citrix license server installation is also supported by a cluster environment.

You can find more information regarding this at `http://support.citrix.com/` `proddocs/topic/licensing-11121/lic-cl-citrix-environment-c.html`.

We can now approach the Citrix Licensing installation.

We will install the latest version of the component on the server named `XD-CtxDC`, which is based on Windows 2012 R2. It will also act as a delivery controller for the XenDesktop environment.

 Citrix recommends using the latest version of Citrix Licensing, especially if you are upgrading or installing new versions of the products.

The installation process will execute the CTX_Licensing installer, as shown here:

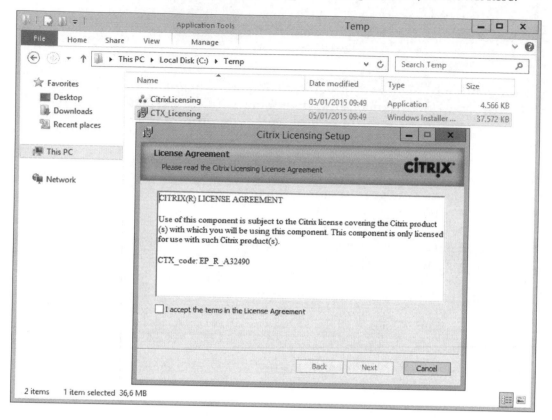

The process is very easy. Begin by accepting the license agreement and then select the installation folder. When you are ready, click on the **Install** button.

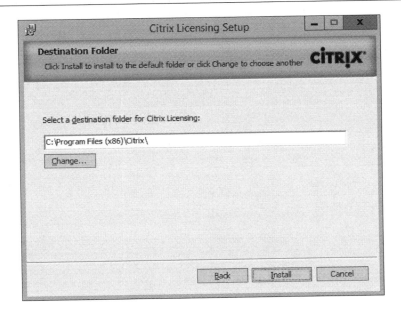

The setup will complete the installation of Citrix Licensing. To exit the installation wizard, click on the **Finish** button.

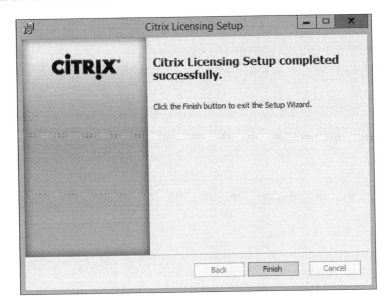

At the end of the installation process, the configuration page will be displayed.

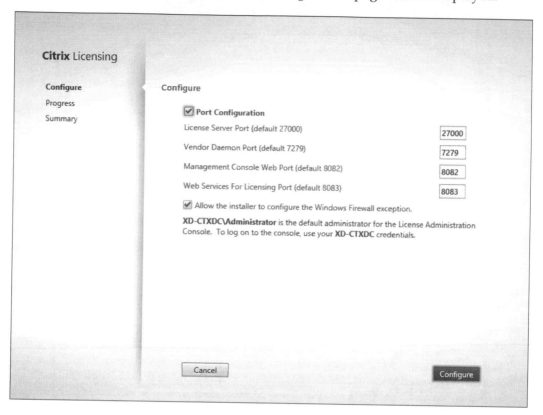

By default, Citrix Licensing uses the TCP port numbers **27000**, **7279**, **8082**, and **8083** for communicating with other Citrix products.

The configuration wizard will require you to confirm or change the aforementioned TCP ports.

If the Windows firewall has been enabled on the machine, where you are installing Citrix Licensing, the installer will create the necessary firewall exceptions.

If you plan to install Citrix Licensing and the other XenDesktop components on different networks and a firewall appliance has been configured, create the rules for the Citrix Licensing communication.

It is recommended to only change the default ports if necessary.

Furthermore, the user performing the installation will be configured as the default administrator. In this example, it is **XD-CTXDC\Administrator**.

You will be able to add more administrators by using the License Administration Console.

When you are satisfied with the configuration, click on the **Configure** button.

The wizard will apply your desired configuration, and it will also give you an option between License Administration Console and the Simple License Service, as shown in the following screenshot:

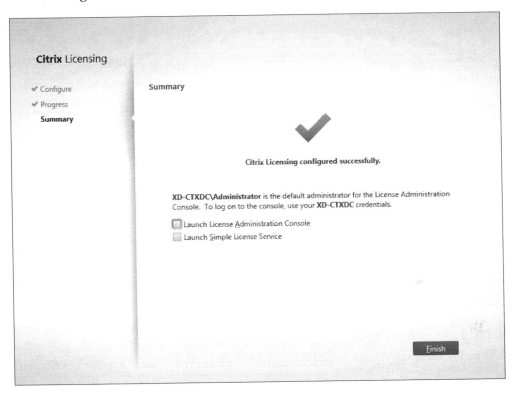

 Simple License Service is a tool which enables the installation of license files on a license server with the help of a web browser.

We have installed the first component of the XenDesktop infrastructure.

Remember that you need to install the Citrix license files for XenDesktop to work. We will discover how to install them in *Chapter 11, XenDesktop® Licensing*.

Understanding the site database

In the previous section, we discussed the Citrix Licensing installation.

Before we go any further, it is important to have a look at the site database. This plays a key role in a XenDesktop environment.

Earlier in this chapter, we discovered that XenDesktop supports different editions of the Microsoft SQL Server.

The installer for the SQL Server 2012 Express edition has been included in the ISO image of XenDesktop, and if you don't have database server in your company, you can install it on the same machine while the first delivery controller is created.

Installing SQL Express is a good choice for installing a testing environment and for providing virtual desktops to a few non-critical users.

For medium and large deployments, it is better to install the site database on a dedicated database server.

A database server with two processors and 4 GB memory will support an environment of up to 5000 users.

 When deciding the size of your database server for the XenDesktop environment, also consider the future growth of the deployment. It is better to allocate more hardware resources so as to ensure the expected performance and stability.

Because the database contains all the data of the XenDesktop deployment, the database server could be a single point of failure.

If the site database fails, or if it is not available, then you cannot manage your XenDesktop environment, the users will not be able to start new ICA sessions, and existing connections to the virtual desktops will continue to function until a user either logs off or disconnects.

If you need to provide high availability for your environment, then you should configure your site database with the help of any one of the following SQL Server features:

- SQL clustering
- SQL mirroring
- AlwaysOn Availability groups

> Standard Edition is recommended for hosting a site database that is in the production environment. You can either create a 2-nodes SQL cluster or use the SQL Mirroring/AlwaysOn Availability group for protecting the Citrix database.
>
> SQL Express doesn't support any of the high availability features.
>
> You can find more about the SQL high-availability solutions at `https://msdn.microsoft.com/en-us/library/ms190202(v=sql.110).aspx`.

Typically, the size of the site database is small and it is based on a number of virtual desktop agents and active sessions in the environment. The size can reach up to 400 MB in very large deployments, which have thousands of users.

The following two databases are used by XenDesktop and are created during the setup.

- The monitoring database: This contains all the monitoring information about the deployment
- The configuration logging database: This records all the administrative changes that are performed on the XenDesktop site

> For more information about database sizing, refer to the *XenDesktop 7.x Database Sizing* document, which can be found at `http://support.citrix.com/article/CTX139508`.

Typically, the site database is created during XenDesktop site creation. You need the *dbcreator* and the *securityadmin* server rights in order to complete this task.

If your account does not have the required SQL server permissions for creating the site database, you can generate some scripts for the manual database creation and ask your database administrator to use them when creating the needed databases for the XenDesktop environment.

We will learn how to use these scripts later in this chapter.

You need the `Latin1_General_100_CI_AS_KS` collation when creating the database.

Installing the Delivery Controller

After we have installed the Citrix Licensing, we can start the installation of the first server acting as the delivery controller of the XenDesktop site.

In this example, we will configure XenDesktop as a typical environment for a medium sized enterprise. Here, each component will be distributed across the different servers.

We will start the installation process by using the ISO image of XenDesktop on the server named `XD-CtxDC`. This server is based on Windows 2012 R2.

 You can download the XenDesktop ISO image from `http://www.citrix.com/downloads/xendesktop/product-software.html`.

1. Click on the **Delivery Controller** area for starting the installation wizard, as shown here:

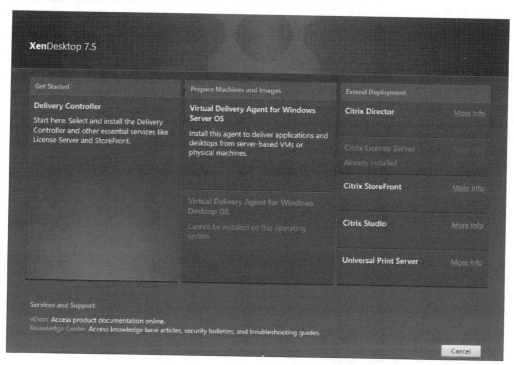

2. Accept the license agreement, and then click on the **Next** button to continue, as shown in the following figure:

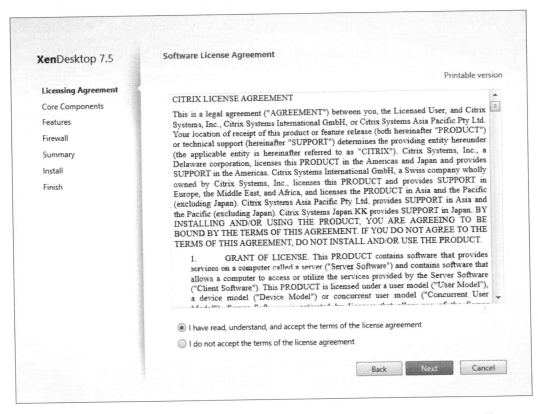

3. We will install the **Delivery Controller** and **Studio** components. **Director** and **Storefront** will be installed on different machines.

> You can also install Citrix Studio on your Windows client machine.
>
> It is the best practice, especially for large deployments that have more Citrix administrators, to configure one or more XenDesktop management machines to avoid performance impact on the servers that act as Delivery Controllers.

By default, `C:\Program Files\Citrix` folder would have been used as the location. If you want, you can change the installation directory.

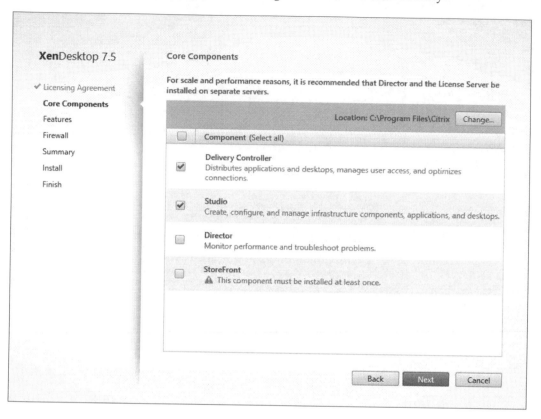

4. Click on the **Next** button to continue. The wizard tells you to install the Microsoft SQL Server Express on the server. We will deselect the checkbox because we want to use a different machine as the database server.

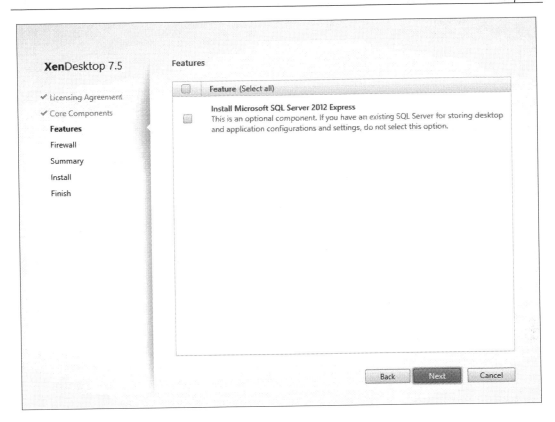

5. Click on the **Next** button to continue.

6. The wizard will ask you how to configure the Windows firewall. You can either leave the default selection, which will be **Automatically,** or select the other option, which will be **Manually**.

If you have a firewall appliance on your network, remember to check that the TCP ports 80 and 443 have been opened.

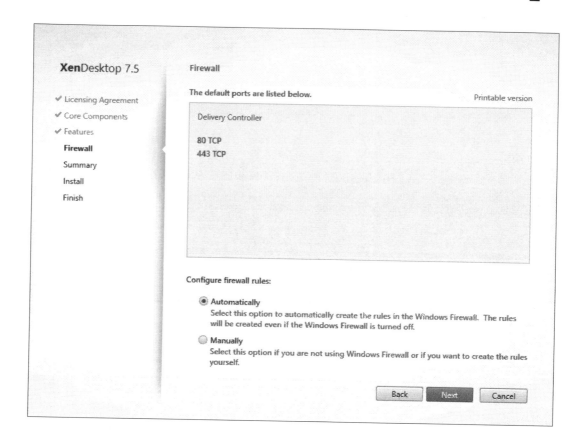

7. Click on the **Next** button to continue.

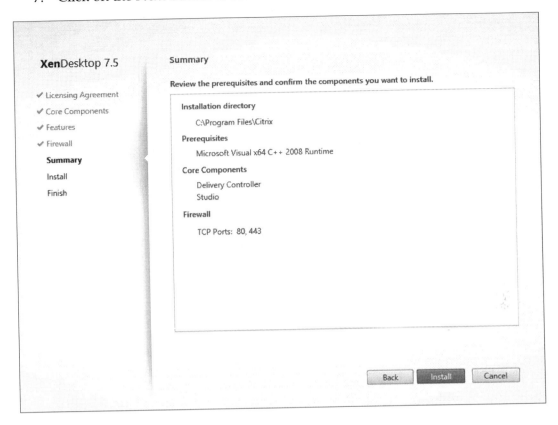

The wizard will show you a summary of the configuration that you have selected for reviewing. When you are satisfied with the selections, you can click on the **Install** button to start the installation process.

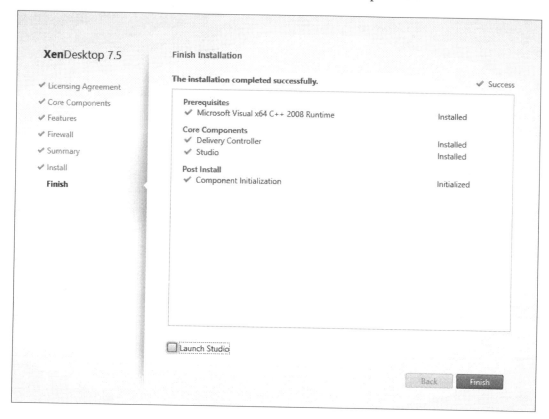

At the end, you will receive a summary reporting that the installation has finished successfully. This summary will also report any errors or give warnings regarding any errors that might have occurred during the setup.

By default, the **Launch Studio** checkbox would have been selected. In this example, it has been deselected.

8. To close the wizard, click on the **Finish** button.

Later in this chapter, we will discover how to install a second Delivery Controller for providing high availability.

Creating the XenDesktop® site

After the installation of the Delivery Controller and Citrix Studio, we will be ready for creating the XenDesktop site that will be providing virtual desktops and applications to users.

We will start the creation process by launching **Citrix Studio**, which is on the **Start** menu, on the XD-CtxDC server:

1. To create the site, click on the **Deliver applications and desktops to your users** option on the Studio console.

Now, the wizard will start and it will ask you whether you want to create **A fully configured, production-ready Site (recommended for new users)** or if you want to create **An empty, unconfigured Site**.

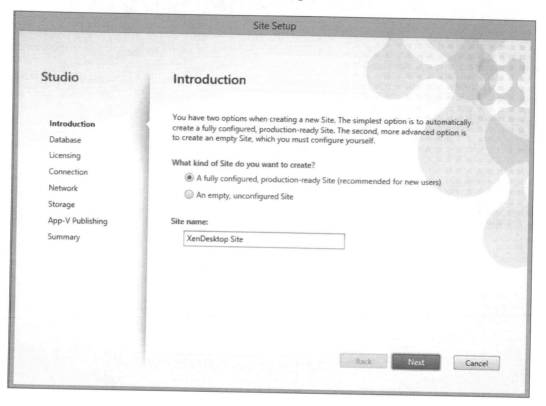

2. In this example, we will create **A fully configured, production-ready Site (recommended for new users)** to explore all the options that you can select during the wizard.

 If you choose to create an empty site, the wizard will require you to insert the information about the database and the licensing.

3. On this page, the wizard will ask you to type the site's name. In the example, we have typed **XenDesktop Site** as the site's name. The site's name will identify your XenDesktop deployment and it will be shown in the Citrix Studio console. When you work with different deployments, because you have data centers located in different regions or countries, it is the best practice to use a friendly name.

When you are ready, click on the **Next** button to continue.

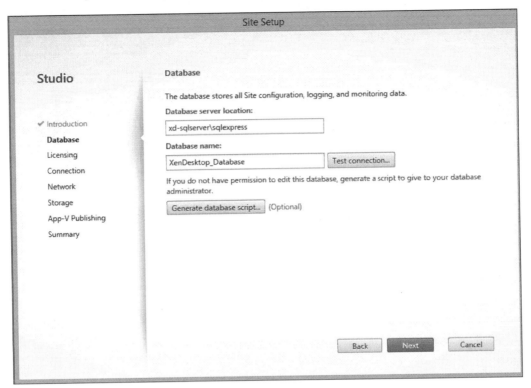

4. Now, you will be required to insert the database connection information. In the **database server location** field, type the name of the database server and the SQL Server instance name. In this example, the XenDesktop database will be created on the SQL Server instance named sqlexpress, which is hosted on the server name xd-sqlserver.

5. The wizard will also ask you to type a name for the site's database. In the example, we will create a database named XenDesktop_Database.

6. You can click on the **Test connection...** button to test the database server connection.

7. If the database that you have specified is not accessible, you will receive the following information:

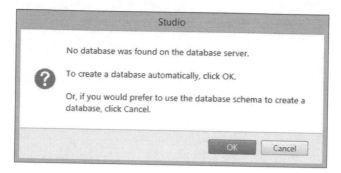

8. If your user does not have sufficient privileges for accessing the database's server, or for creating the database, you will have to ask a database administrator to perform the task, as shown here:

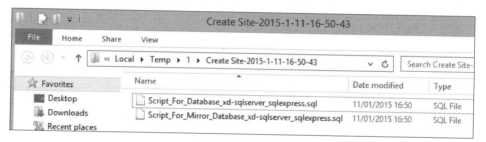

You can click on the **Generate database script** button for creating the two SQL files named `Script_For_Database_SQL-Server_Database-Name` and `Script_For_Mirror_Database_SQL-Server_Database-Name`, where `SQL-Server` is the name of the database server and `Database-Name` is the name of the database that you have to create. Note that the second script will only be used if you have to create a mirrored database.

You can find more information about the SQL roles and permissions that are required for creating a site on the addresses `http://support.citrix.com/article/CTX132269` and `http://support.citrix.com/article/CTX127998`.

You can also find more about how to create a mirrored database on the web address `http://support.citrix.com/proddocs/topic/xenapp-xendesktop-75/cds-plan-high-avail-rho.html`.

9. When you are ready, click on the **Next** button to continue.

10. Later, the wizard will require you to configure the **Licensing**, as shown in the following screenshot:

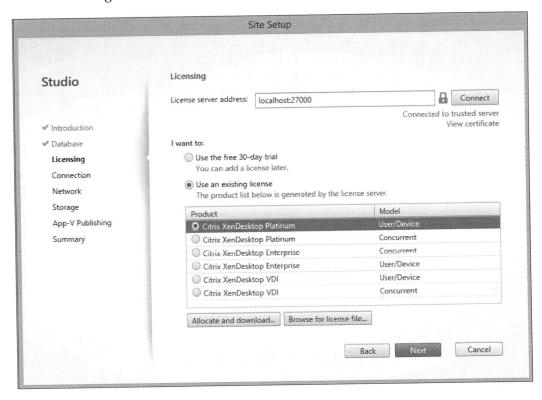

11. You will have to provide the name of the license server and then select the existing license you want to use.

    ○ If the Citrix licensing has been installed on the same server, it is automatically discovered, and `localhost` will be inserted in the field **License server address**

    ○ If no licenses are discovered, you can continue configuring the XenDesktop site and use the free 30-day trial

12. Click on the **Next** button to continue.

13. Now, the wizard will require you to create a connection to a Cloud environment or a virtualization environment, such as **Citrix XenServer**, **VMware Vsphere**, or **Amazon EC2 cloud**.

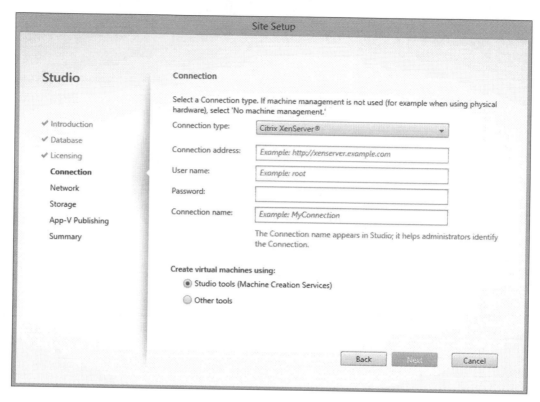

XenDesktop 7.5 supports the following virtual hypervisor and Cloud environments:

- Citrix XenServer 6.02, 6.1 or 6.2
- Vmware Vsphere 5.0 Update 2, 5.5 Update 2 or 5.5
- Microsoft System Center Virtual Machine Manager 2012, 2012 SP1 or 2012 R2
- Amazon Web Services
- Citrix CloudPlatform 4.2.1 with hotfixes 4.2.1-4

According to your selection, you have to provide some information for creating the connection.

For example, if you select Citrix XenServer, VMware vSphere or Microsoft Virtual Machine Manager, you will have to type the following:

- **Connection address**: This is the address that XenDesktop will use to connect to your virtual infrastructure. For XenServer and VMware, you will have to use HTTP (or HTTPS for secure communications).

- **Username**: This is the name of the user that you will use for connecting to the virtual infrastructure.

- **Connection name**: This is the name that you want to use for identifying the connection in Citrix Studio.

> Use a friendly name for naming the connection. This will help you to identify them quickly.

If you select the Cloud environment option on the **Connection Type**, you will have to provide the API and secret key to complete the connection wizard successfully.

> Visit the following web addresses to learn more about the requirements for creating connections to virtual environments:
>
> Citrix Xenserver: `http://support.citrix.com/proddocs/topic/xenapp-xendesktop-75/cds-install-create-site.html`
>
> VMware vSphere: `http://support.citrix.com/proddocs/topic/xenapp-xendesktop-76/xad-install-prep-host-vmware.html`
>
> Microsoft System Center Virtual Machine Manager: `http://support.citrix.com/proddocs/topic/xenapp-xendesktop-76/xad-install-prep-host-msscvmm.html`

Furthermore, you are required to select if you want to use **Machine Creation Services** or any other tools for creating machines in the virtualization environment.

Machine Creation Services are based on a master image, which is present within your environment. This option will offer the possibility of delivering virtual machines (desktop or server), managing and updating the target devices through a master image.

In the example shown here, we will create a connection with a Citrix XenServer host.

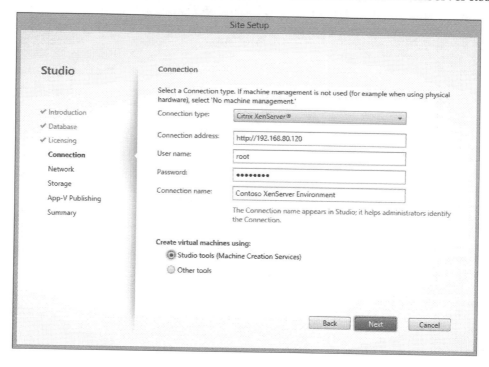

1. Click on the **Next** button to continue.

If you are creating a connection with Microsoft System Center Virtual Machine Manager, then install the Virtual Machine Manager console on the Delivery Controller.

Citrix Studio could generate a fatal error when creating a connection to Virtual Machine Manager.

If you experience the error shown here, check the registry value. `HKLM\Software\Microsoft\Microsoft System Center Virtual Machine Manager Administrator Console\ Settings\IndigoTcpPort`

The value has to be `REG_DWORD` with 1FA4 (which is the hexadecimal of 8100).

Export the registry key before changing it for backup.

2. Now, the wizard will ask you to type a name for identifying the resources and for selecting a virtual network for virtual machines. These network resources have been discovered by the wizard by using the connection we have already created.

   Now, click on the **Next** button to continue.

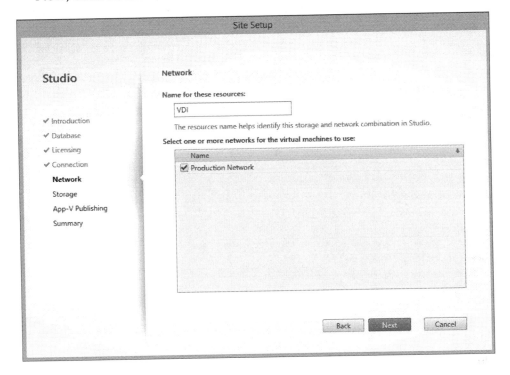

3. Now, configure the storage for the XenDesktop environment. The wizard displayed here will show the storage that is available on the virtual environment.

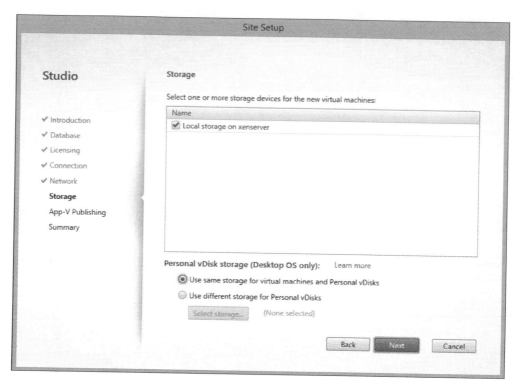

In this example, we have used **Local storage on xenserver**. If it is available here, you will also find the shared storage repository that is configured on the NAS or SAN systems.

 The shared storage repository is not available for the environment that we have used in this book. This is not a limitation of the wizard.

You have to decide if you want to use different storage devices for Personal vDisk storage.

The Personal vDisk feature was introduced by Citrix in XenDesktop version 5.6. The administrators can manage the base virtual machines, while providing the users with a customized and personalized desktop experience. The users do not lose their customizations and personal applications when the Citrix administrators change or update the base image.

In the example shown here, we will not change the default selection, which is **Use same storage for virtual machines and Personal vDisks**.

If you select a different storage, you will be required to select it. To do this, click on the **Select storage** button and then choose an available storage. When you are ready, click on the **OK** button to close the box, as shown in the following screenshot:

4. Now, click on the **Next** button to continue.

5. The wizard will prompt you to select if you want to add an **App-V publishing server**.

App-V is an application virtualization and streaming solution provided by Microsoft. You will learn more about App-V in *Chapter 10, XenDesktop® and App-V Integration*.

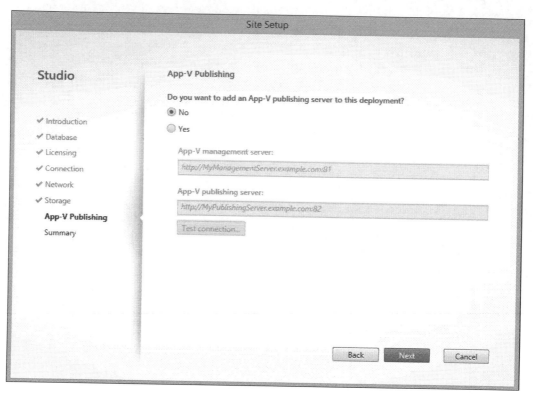

In this example, we have decided not to add an App-V publishing server.

6. Next, click on the **Next** button to continue. The wizard will display the summary page. Here, you can review the decisions that were made regarding the environment.

7. Now, click on the **Finish** button to start the XenDesktop site creation process.

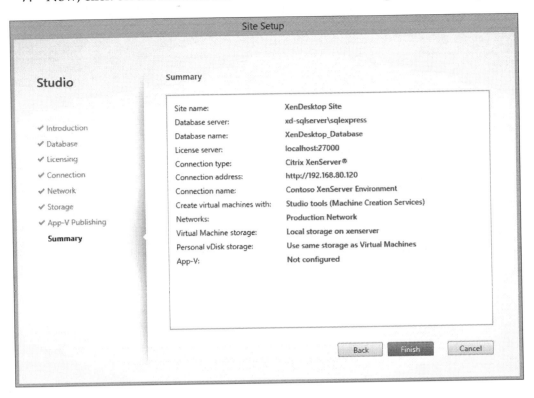

8. During the setup, the wizard will create the database, and configure the services and resources. At the end of the process, the main page of Citrix Studio will be displayed.

9. You can test your configuration by clicking on the **Test site configuration** button.

10. Next, Citrix Studio will perform some tests on the environment and generate a status report, which will display the results of the performed tests.

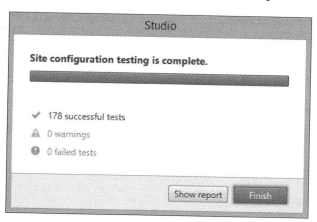

Installing Citrix® Director

In the previous sections, we installed Citrix Licensing, Citrix Delivery Controller, and Citrix Studio. We also configured a basic XenDesktop site. In this section, we will discover another component of a XenDesktop environment, Citrix Director.

Director is a web management portal, that provides an overview of the virtual desktops, applications, and users' sessions.

You will also use it for performing maintenance tasks, such as remotely assisting a user, disconnecting a user, killing processes, monitoring deployment, and troubleshooting any system issues.

The following Internet browsers are supported for viewing the Citrix Director:

- Internet Explorer 9, 10, or 11
- Firefox ESR
- Chrome

At the beginning of the chapter, we identified the system requirements for installing the Citrix Director.

In a production environment, you should install this component on a dedicated machine because Director is a processor and memory intensive application, especially when you have many administrators working on it at the same time.

The server hosting Director should be configured with four processors and a minimum of 4 GB memory.

 In my deployments, I always configure the Director machine with 8 GB memory.

Citrix Director requires Microsoft Internet Information Services. This role gets automatically installed during the setup.

When installing Citrix Director, you must visit `http://support.citrix.com/article/CTX139382` in order to understand the best practice.

Now, we will install Director on the server named XD-CtxDir, which is based on Windows 2012 R2 by using the installer included in the XenDesktop ISO image.

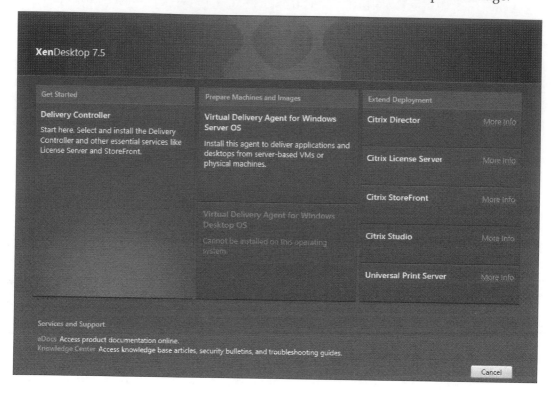

1. You can begin the installation process by clicking on **Citrix Director** in the **Extend Deployment** section.

2. Accept the license agreement, and then click on the **Next** button to continue.

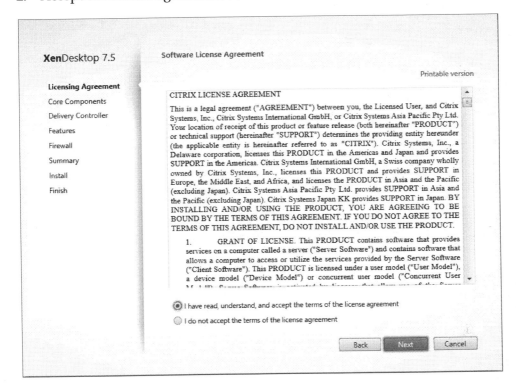

3. The wizard will display the component that is going to be installed and will then provide the option of changing the installation directory. By default, the C:\Program Files\Citrix folder will be used as the location by the wizard.

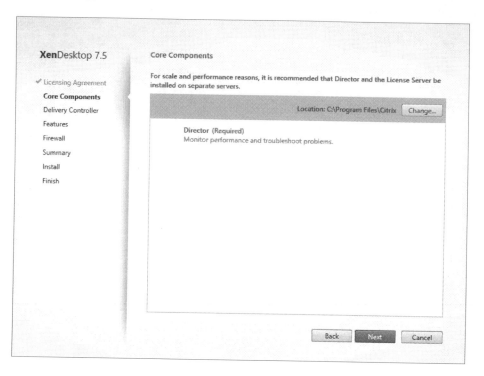

4. Now, click on the **Next** button to continue.
5. The wizard will ask you to enter the address (by using Fully Qualified Domain Name) of an existing Delivery Controller.

   Here, we will insert the name of the first Delivery Controller that we created, which would be XD-CTXDC.contoso.local.

If you want to provide high availability, add two or more Delivery Controllers. If you have configured two or more Citrix Delivery Controllers in your deployment, you should know that they auto balance themselves.

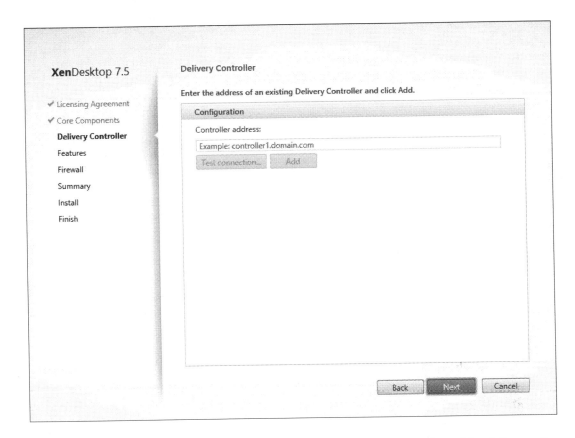

6. After you enter the name, click on the **Add** button to confirm. The Microsoft Active Directory domain hosting the XenDesktop environment is named Contoso.local.

You can also click on the **Test Connection** button to verify that the Delivery Controller which you have added is reachable.

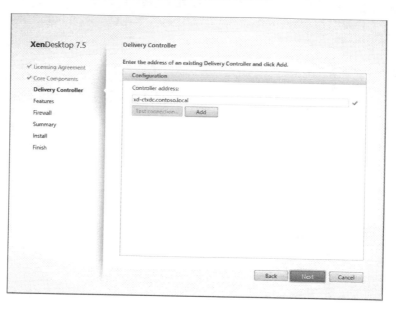

7. Now, you can click on the **Next** button to continue.

8. In the **Features** screen, the wizard will require you to choose to either enable or disable Windows Remote Assistance. This option is enabled by default.

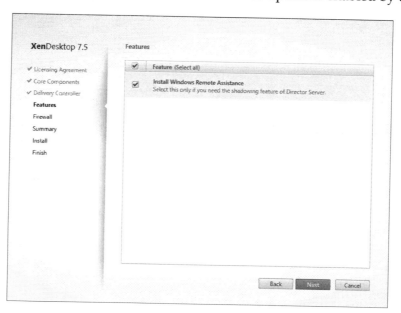

The help-desk staff uses Windows Remote Assistance for shadowing and helping connected users.

9. Now, click on the **Next** button to continue.

10. The wizard will ask how you want to configure the Windows firewall. You can either leave the default selection as it is (**Automatically**) or change it to **Manually**.

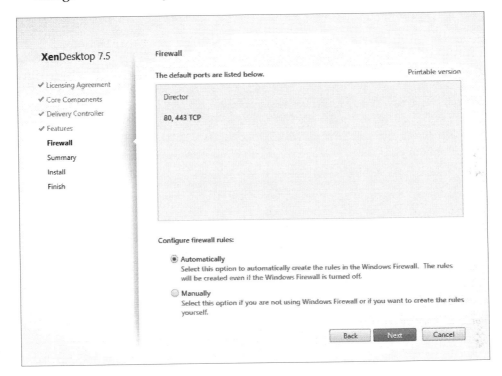

 If you have a firewall appliance on your network, remember to check that TCP ports 80 and 443 have been opened.

11. Click on the **Next** button to continue.

12. The wizard will display the **Summary** page. Review it, and then click on the **Install** button to start the installation process.

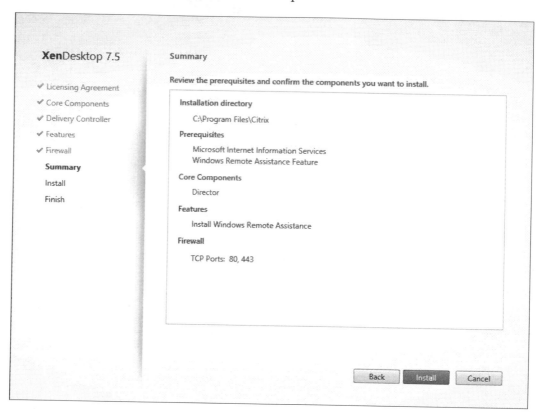

13. At the end of the installation process, you will receive a status report. After receiving it, you can launch the Citrix Director.

You can open Director either from the Start menu or from the web address `http://server_name/Director,` where the `server_name` is the name of your Director's server.

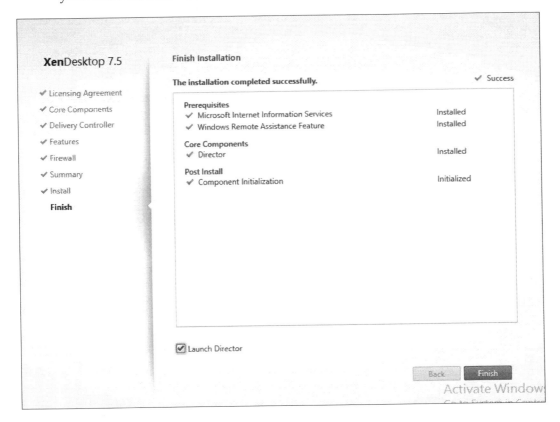

In the screenshot shown here, you can see the main page of Citrix Director:

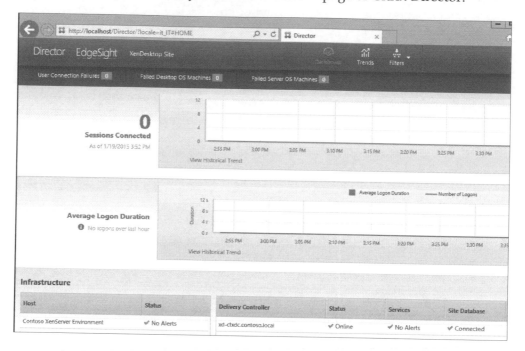

When you try to login to Citrix Director, you might experience the following error:

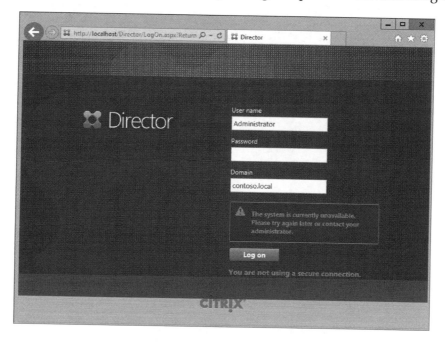

Furthermore, you can find the Event ID 7 recorded on the Application log of the
Director server, as shown in the following example:

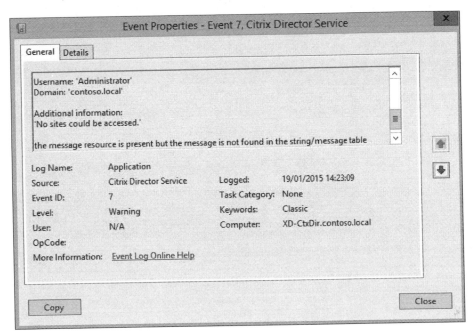

To solve this issue, you can perform the following steps:

1. Open **Internet Information Services (IIS) Manager** on the Director server.

2. On the IIS manager console, navigate to the **Director** application (by default,
   it will be located in **Default Web Site**), and click on it.

3. Open the **Application Settings** feature.

4. Double click on `Service.AutoDiscoveryAddresses`, and then type the hostname of the Delivery Controller in the **value** field.

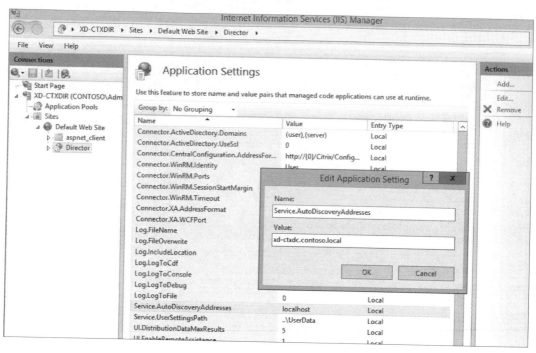

5. Click on the **OK** button, and then open a command prompt (which has admin rights).

6. Run the `iisreset` command.

Installing Citrix® StoreFront

One of the last steps for configuring your XenDesktop environment is installing Citrix StoreFront.

Citrix StoreFront is a web application which gives users access to the virtual desktops and applications that are delivered by XenDesktop, with the help of Citrix Receiver.

> Citrix StoreFront also aggregates resources that are provided by other Citrix products, such as XenApp, XenMobile App Controller, and VDI-in-a-Box.

StoreFront is built on Microsoft Internet Information Services and the Microsoft .NET framework. These roles and features get installed during the setup.

You can learn more about the system requirements by reading the introduction to this chapter and by navigating to `http://support.citrix.com/proddocs/topic/dws-storefront-25/dws-system-requirements.html`.

 Reserve at least 2 GB RAM for the StoreFront services. A server with 4 GB RAM can serve up to 10,000 user connections per hour.

The users can access their desktops and applications through different ways by using StoreFront, such as Citrix Receiver or an HTML5-compatible web browser.

A list of compatible devices and browsers is available at `http://support.citrix.com/proddocs/topic/dws-storefront-25/dws-system-requirements-client.html`.

In this section, you will learn how to install and perform a basic setup of Storefront. In the next chapter, you will discover how to configure it in detail.

In a production environment, it is the best practice to install more than one Citrix StoreFront server in order to provide load balancing and high availability. If you install only one server and the server is not available, users will not able to access your XenDesktop environment.

Installing StoreFront in a multiple server deployment creates a server group, wherein the servers belonging to the same group share the same configuration.

If a server becomes unavailable, for example, because of network or hardware issues, the configuration data on the failed server will automatically get updated when it is reconnected to the server group.

 The StoreFront servers belonging to the same group must have the same operating system and locale. They must also be joined to the same Active Directory domain.

In the following procedure, we will discover how to install this component on a server named XD-CtxSF1, which is based on Windows Server 2012 R2:

1. You will start the installation process by using the XenDesktop ISO image, and then you will click on **Citrix StoreFront**, which is in the **Extend Deployment** section.

2. Accept the license agreement, and then click on the **Next** button to continue, as shown here:

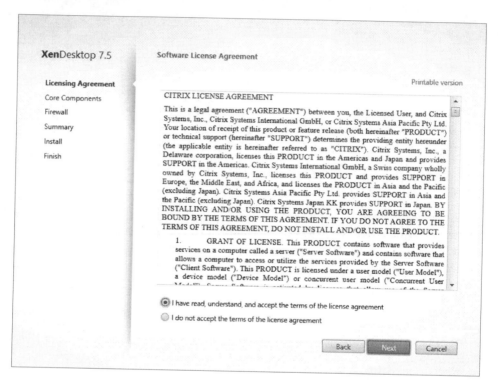

The wizard will display the component that is going to be installed. Here, it will give you the option of changing the installation directory's location, which, by default, would have been the `C:\Program Files\Citrix` folder.

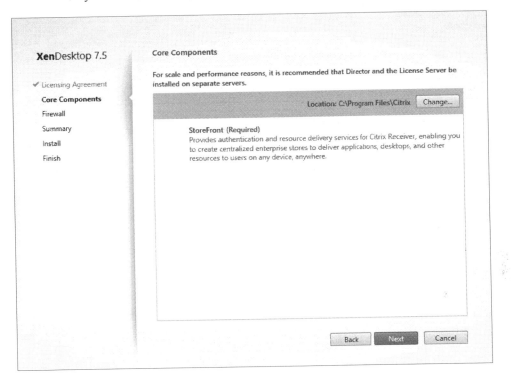

3. Now, click on the **Next** button to continue.

4. The wizard will give you the option of configuring the Windows firewall. Here, you can leave the default selection (**Automatically**).

In a production environment, Citrix recommends using HTTPS for securing the communications between StoreFront and users' devices. If you want to access your StoreFront from the Internet, you will have to deploy Citrix Netscaler Gateway.

Furthermore, the TCP port 808 is used for communications among StoreFront servers. The TCP port 8008 is used when users connect to StoreFront through an HTML5-compatible web browser.

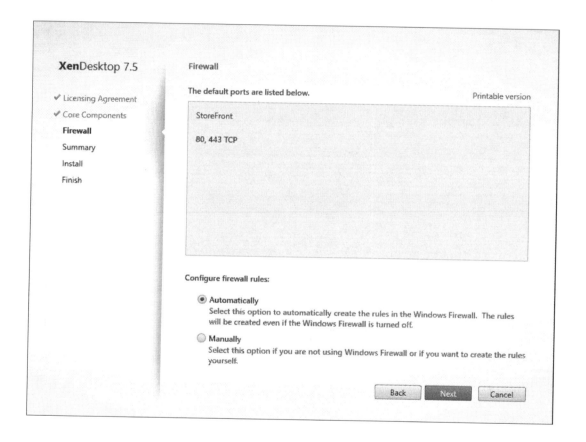

5. Make your selection, and then click on the **Next** button to continue.

6. The wizard will display the **Summary** page. Review it, and then click on the **Install** button to start the installation process.

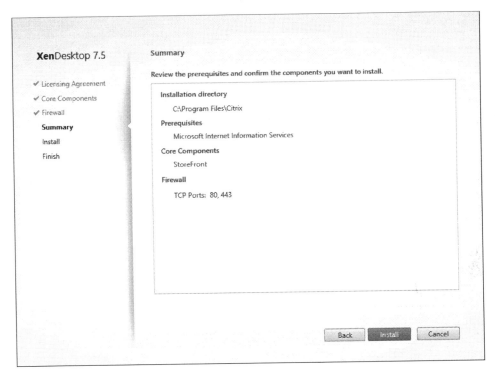

7. At the end of the installation process, you will receive a status report. Then, you will be able to open the Citrix StoreFront management console for setting up the initial configuration.

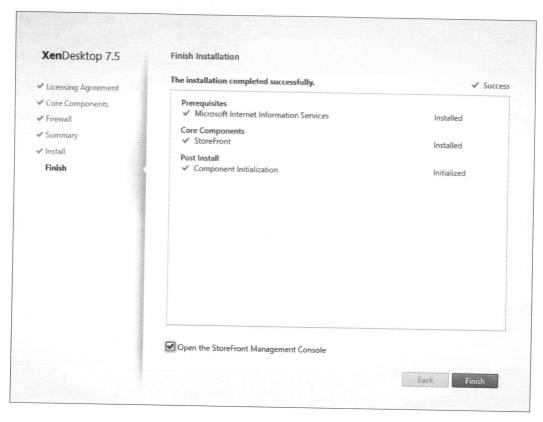

Creating a Citrix® StoreFront store

In this section, you will learn how to perform the initial configuration of Citrix StoreFront.

In this scenario, we will create a new deployment and then connect it to the XenDesktop site, which we configured earlier in the chapter.

1. To start the configuration, click on the **Create a new deployment** section in the StoreFront console.

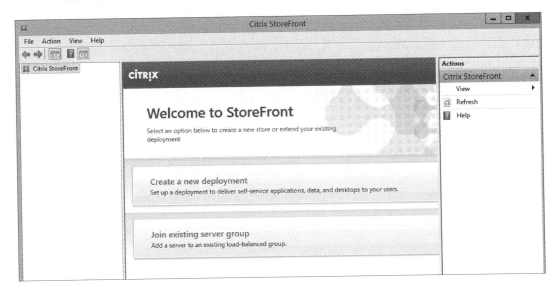

2. In the **Base URL** field, confirm the web address for the deployment. If need be, you can change this value in the future.

    In the example shown here, we will use `http://xd-ctxsf1.contoso.local`.

Type the FQDN of the server, or specify the load-balanced URL if you are using a balancer such as Citrix Netscaler.

You can also use Alias (CNAME record) for the Citrix Storefront URL. After this if, you change your Storefront server, you won't have to reconfigure the new address for Citrix Receiver clients.

Note that the Citrix Receiver uses HTTPS by default. The wizard will advise you to configure StoreFront by using the HTTP protocol. If you want to use HTTPS here, then SSL should be configured before starting the wizard.

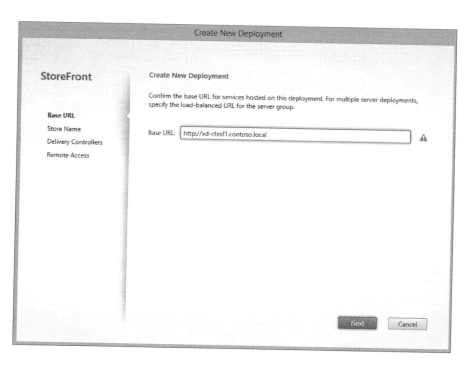

3. Click on the **Next** button to continue.

4. Now, the wizard will prompt you to type a name for the store. A store is used for aggregating desktops and applications; it also makes them available to users.

   In our example, we will use the name **CitrixStore**. You can use the name that you prefer, but keep it simple and friendly.

   The name of the store will be displayed on Citrix Receiver.

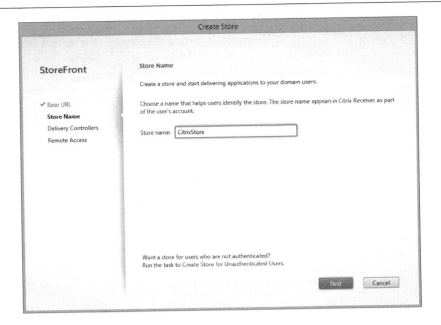

5. Now, click on the **Next** button to continue.

6. Next, set the Delivery Controller that StoreFront has to connect to by clicking on the **Add** button:

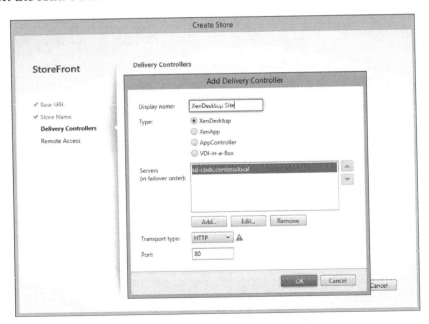

In the **Add Delivery Controller** box, enter a **Display Name**. For this, use a friendly name that will help you to identify the XenDesktop environment. In this example, we have used `XenDesktop Site`. In the **Servers** area, click on the **Add** button, and then insert either the DNS name or the IP address of one or more Delivery Controllers.

If you want to provide fault tolerance, add at least two Delivery Controllers. StoreFront will automatically contact the second server given in the list in case the first server is not reachable. In this example, we will add the Delivery Controller that was created earlier in the chapter, `xd-ctxdc.contoso.local`. By default, HTTPS was used as the transport type. In this example, we have selected **HTTP**.

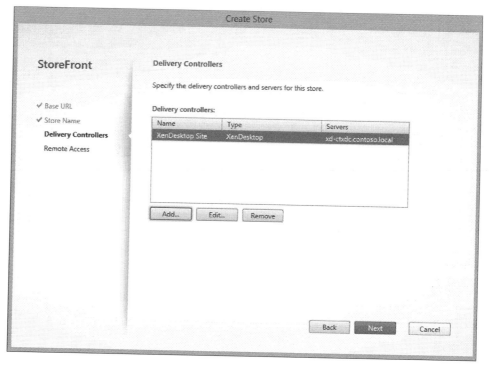

7. After you have finished configuring the Delivery Controllers, click on the **Next** button to continue.

8. Now, you can set how the users should connect to StoreFront from the Internet by using the Citrix Netscaler Gateway appliance. For the moment, Netscaler Gateway is out of scope, so we will not change the default setting, which is **None**.

When configuring the external access, you can select either **No VPN Tunnel** or **Full VPN Tunnel**. The first option is used when you only desire to provide users access to applications and desktops, whereas, if you want to provide users access to the applications and resources that are on your private network, **Full VPN Tunnel** is used.

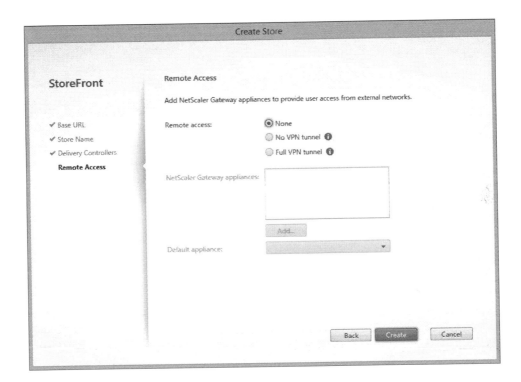

9. When you click on the **Create** button, the wizard will create the store for you.

At the end of the process, a screen similar to the following will be displayed:

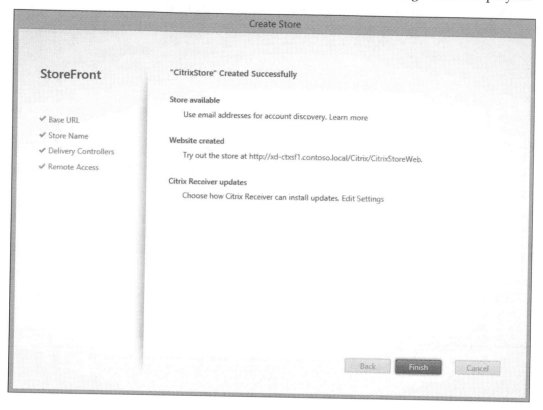

Note the web address. You can use it to connect to the store. In our example, `http://xd-ctxsf1.contoso.local/Citrix/CitrixStoreWeb` has been used as the web address.

Summary

In this chapter, we learnt how to install the core components of Citrix XenDesktop. We also discovered some useful information and tips about the system sizing and initial configuration.

In the next chapter, we will learn how to create machine catalogs and delivery groups. We will also understand how to optimize Citrix XenDesktop. We will discuss some of the customizations that are used for providing the best experience to the users.

5
Delivering Virtual Desktops and Optimizing XenDesktop®

In the last chapter, we discovered how to install a XenDesktop deployment and we learnt the basics of sizing and configuration.

Now, it is time to understand how we can deliver virtual desktops and applications to users using delivery groups.

At the end of this chapter, you will be able to configure and optimize XenDesktop environments.

In this chapter, we will cover the following topics:

- Configuring the XenDesktop components for high availability
- Installing the Virtual Desktop Agent
- Configuring machine catalogs and delivery groups
- Configuring Citrix Policies

We will also introduce some concepts about performance and best practices.

Configuring XenDesktop® components for high availability

In the previous chapter, we learnt how to install a Citrix Delivery Controller and StoreFront in a XenDesktop environment.

In this section, we will discover how to install a second Delivery Controller in order to provide high availability and load balancing.

Installing an additional Delivery Controller

We discussed the importance of Citrix Delivery Controller in earlier chapters. If a server acting as Delivery Controller is unavailable, users will not be able to access either their virtual desktops or the published applications.

For this reason, it is the best practice to configure at least two Delivery Controllers on the different physical servers in order to prevent this component from becoming a single point of failure.

Also, adding more Citrix Delivery Controllers to a XenDesktop environment is very important because, by doing this, you can increase scalability and performance.

Note that the user connections, virtual desktops startup and launch are processor-intensive tasks.

In this example, we will configure a second Citrix Delivery Controller named XD-CtxDC2 in our XenDesktop environment. To do this, consider the following procedure:

Refer to *Chapter 4, Implementing a XenDesktop® Environment* for the installation procedure.

1. Open Citrix Studio on the Delivery Controller.
2. Double click on **Connect this Delivery Controller to an existing Site**, which will be available in the **Scale your deployment** section of Citrix Studio, as shown in the following screenshot:

3. Type the name of an existing Delivery Controller in the site that you want to join. In this example, we will specify the `xd-ctxdc.contoso.loocal` Delivery Controller of the XenDesktop Site. Now, we will click on the **OK** button.

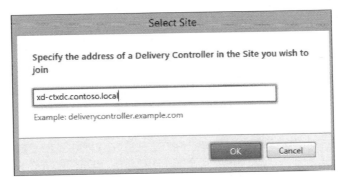

4. The wizard will ask you to update the database automatically. Click on the **Yes** button to continue.

5. Wait while the wizard adds the new Delivery Controller. At the end, the Citrix Studio console will be displayed.

6. Click on **Configuration | Controllers** in the **Citrix Studio** console. Here, you will find your Delivery Controllers.

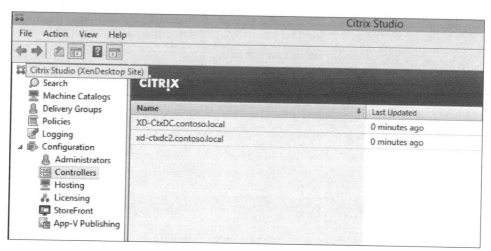

Installing an additional Citrix® StoreFront

After learning how to install an additional Delivery Controller, we will learn how to install an additional Citrix StoreFront server in the XenDesktop environment.

In this example, we will configure a second Citrix StoreFront named XD-CtxSF2 in our XenDesktop environment, as shown here:

[Refer to *Chapter 4, Implementing a XenDesktop® Environment* for the installation procedure.]

7. Open the Citrix StoreFront management console on the Citrix StoreFront server.

8. Click on **Join existing server group,** as shown in the following screenshot:

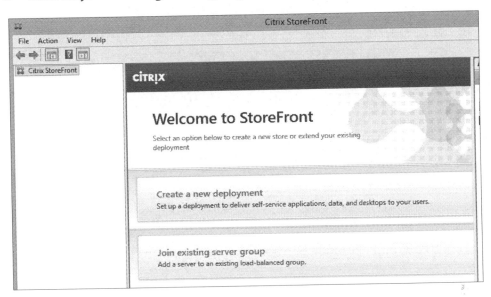

9. Now, the wizard will ask you to insert the name of an **Authorizing server** and an **Authorization code**.

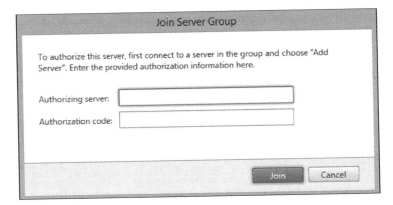

10. To complete this task, you will need to open the StoreFront console on an existing StoreFront server, and then click on the **Add Server** by navigating to the **Actions** panel of the **Server Group** section.

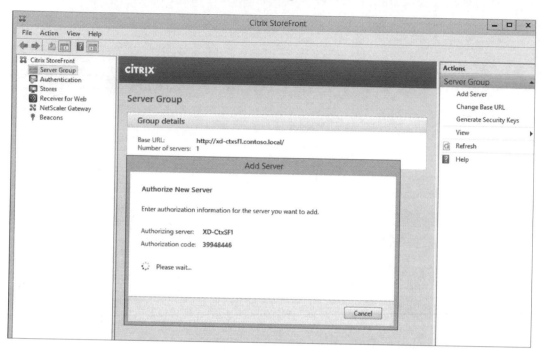

11. When you get the requested information, insert it in the **Join Server Group** box, and then click on the **Join** button, as shown here:

12. Now the server will join the server group.

13. Next, click on the **OK** button to finish.

14. Now, on the StoreFront console of the XD-CtxSF2 server, you will get a message informing you that the server has been added successfully, as shown here:

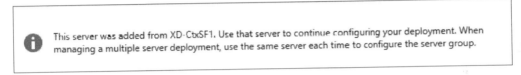

Note that you will be requested to use the same server each time you make any configuration changes to StoreFront.

 Ensure that the Citrix StoreFront management console is not running on any of the other StoreFront servers.

On the XD-CtxSF1 server, a message informing you that a new server has been added, and that the configuration has been synchronized, will appear as follows:

Making configuration changes in StoreFront

In the previous sections, we configured a new Delivery Controller and a new StoreFront server.

Now, we will discover how to make the configuration changes that will reflect this new environment.

The first change that we will make is to add the additional Delivery Controller to StoreFront.

To do this, follow this procedure:

1. Open the Citrix StoreFront management console.

2. Click on **Stores** and then select a store. In this example, we only have the store named CitrixStore, which we had created in the previous chapter.

3. Click on the **Manage Delivery Controllers** link by navigating to **CitrixStore**, which is on the right-hand side of the screen.

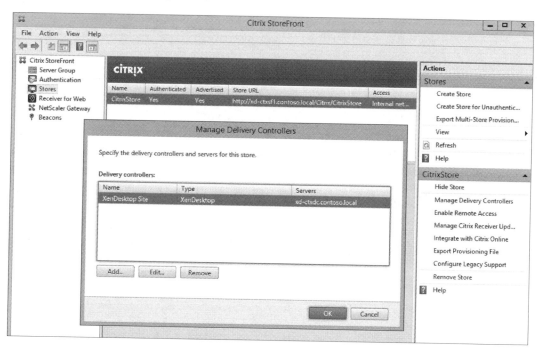

4. Select the deployment that you want to configure, and then click on the **Edit...** button. In this example, we will make changes to the XenDesktop Site deployment.

5. On the **Edit Delivery Controller** screen, click on the **Add...** button for adding the additional Delivery Controller to the environment.

6. On the **Add Delivery Controller** screen, type the **Fully Qualified Domain Name (FQDN)** of the additional Delivery Controller. In this example, we will use `xd-ctxdc2.contoso.local`.

7. Click on the **OK** button, as shown here:

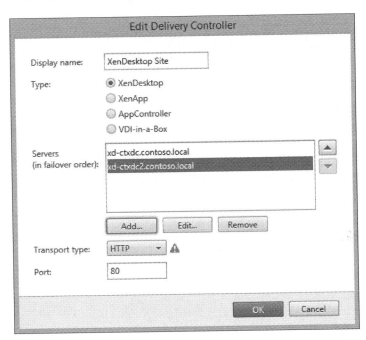

8. Click on the **OK** button twice to confirm the changes that were made, and then return to the main page of the StoreFront console.

The task of adding an additional controller gives me the opportunity to talk to you about replication in StoreFront.

In StoreFront, there is a built-in replication engine, which synchronizes the configuration among the multiple StoreFront servers of the same server group.

For this reason, it is essential to propagate the changes that have been made to the other Citrix StoreFront servers when the configuration is updated.

In order to propagate the changes, follow this procedure:

1. Navigate to the StoreFront management console, and then click on **Server Group**.

2. Now, click on **Propagate Changes**, which will be in the **Actions** menu on the right hand side of the screen, as shown here:

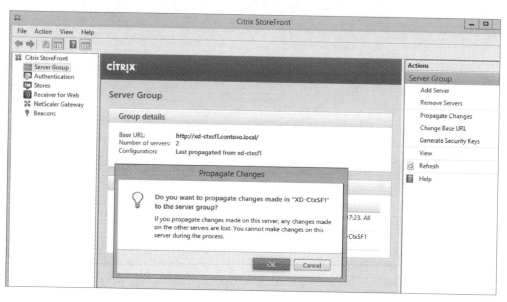

3. Click on the **OK** button to confirm the operation.

4. Configuration will be synchronized between the two storefront servers. The wizard will report you the final result of the synchronization.

 Always propagate a change when you make it. If you update the configuration of a server without propagating the changes that have been made to the other servers in the group, you might lose your updates.

Installing Virtual Desktop Agent

In this section, we will discover how to install Virtual Desktop Agent on the machines that we want to make available to users in a XenDesktop environment.

Virtual Desktop Agent (VDA) is the software that enables a machine to connect to a XenDesktop. VDA can be installed on a desktop or a server operating system.

When you install VDA on a server machine, you can deliver not only a shared hosted desktop, but also applications.

You can deploy VDA through the following ways:

- The graphical user interface
- The command line
- Software management systems
- Active Directory scripts

We will install VDA by using the graphical user interface in a Windows 8 virtual machine called XD-Win8.

Later, we will also learn how to use command line for installing VDA.

For completing this task, follow this procedure:

1. Either insert or mount the XenDesktop ISO image.

2. Double-click on the **Virtual Delivery Agent for Windows Desktop OS** link, which will be in the **Prepare Machines and Images** section. If you are installing it on a server machine, then click on **Virtual Delivery Agent for Windows Server OS**:

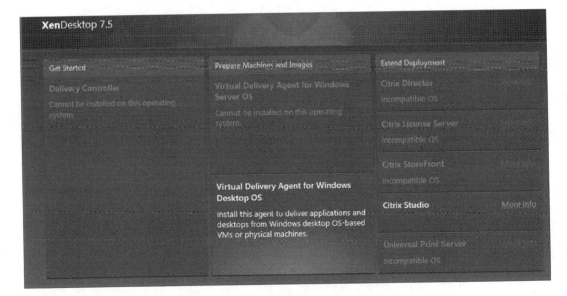

3. The wizard will ask you to select the environment that is related to VDA. The **Create a Master Image** option is the default selection. Use this option for installing the agent on a master image managed either by MCS or by PVS.

Use Remote PC Access when you install the agent on a physical or a virtual machine.

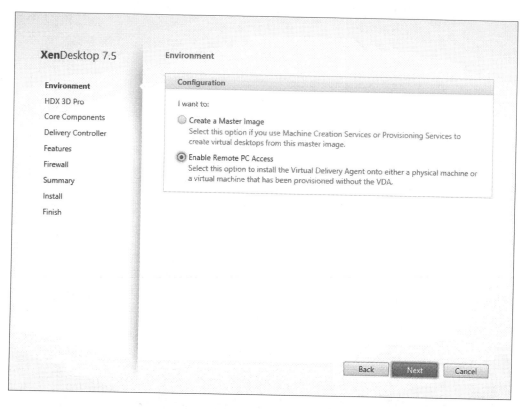

In this example, we will select **Enable Remote PC Access**. We will discover how to use a master image in this chapter.

 Citrix Provisioning Services is based on the software-streaming technology developed by Ardence. It was acquired by Citrix in 2006. This technology allows computers to be provisioned by a single shared-disk image. Administrators can completely eliminate the need for managing and patching individual systems because image management is done on a single master image.

You will find more information about Citrix Provsioning Services at `http://support.citrix.com/proddocs/topic/technologies/pvs-provisioning.html`.

4. Click on the **Next** button to continue.

5. The wizard will then ask you if you want to install the standard VDA (**No, install the standard VGA**) or the VDA for HDX 3D Pro (**Yes, install the VDA for HDX 3D Pro**):

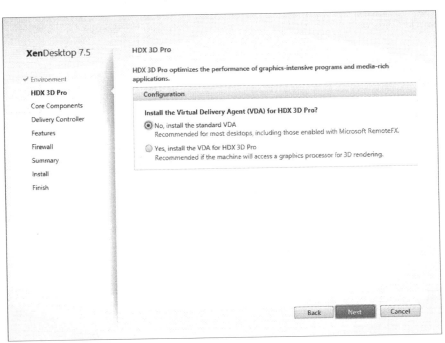

By default, the standard VDA will get installed. In this example, we have used the default selection.

HDX 3D Pro has been developed by Citrix for supporting the higher end application needs that utilize OpenGL, OpenCL, WebGL, and the newer versions of DirectX 11. HDX 3D Pro enables the delivery of the 3D professional applications, such as the CAD\CAM applications by using hardware graphic acceleration, which is available with GPU display cards such as NVidia GRID.

You can find a list of tested hardware for HDX 3D Pro at http://support.citrix.com/article/CTX131385.

You can find more information regarding hardware acceleration with the NVIDIA GRID display cards at https://www.citrix.com/go/private/vgpu.html and http://www.nvidia.com/object/virtual-gpus.html.

In the next chapter, you will learn more about HDX 3D Pro.

For using HDX, review the system requirements, which can be found at `http://support.citrix.com/proddocs/topic/xenapp-xendesktop-75/hdx-sys-reqs.html#hdx-sys-reqs`. You have to satisfy these in order to provide the best user experience:

Now, to continue the process, follow these steps:

1. Click on the **Next** button to continue.
2. The wizard will show you the component that is about to be installed and it will offer you the possibility of changing the installation directory. By default, the **C:\Program Files\Citrix** folder will be used as the location.

   By default, **Citrix Receiver** will be installed. You can leave this selection if your users would need to connect to any other Citrix Farms, such as a XenApp farm.

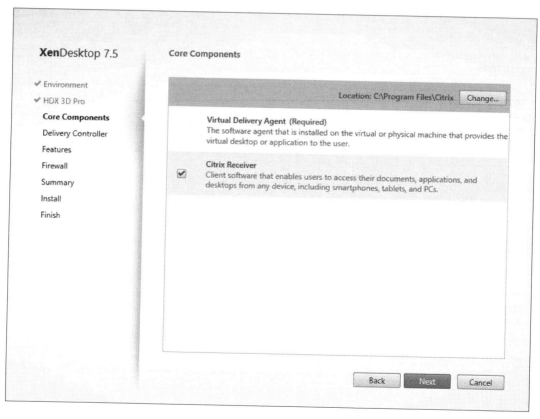

3. Click on the **Next** button to continue.

4. Now, you will need to specify the Delivery Controller locations that were used by VDA for connecting to the XenDesktop environment.

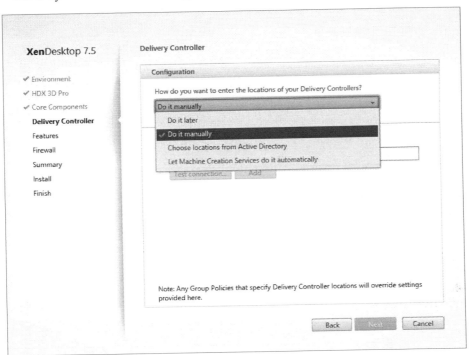

You can select a path from the following options:

- **Do it later**: You can set the Delivery Controller locations by using a Citrix policy.

- **Do it manually**: This is the default selection and it will require you to enter the FQDN of one or more Delivery Controllers. You can use the **Test Connection...** button for checking if the controllers are reachable. If you choose this option, note that the references made to the entered Delivery Controllers would have been hard-coded in the Windows registry.

You can find more about the windows registry values that are used by VDA at http://support.citrix.com/article/ctx118976.

- **Choosing locations from Active Directory**: Using this option, a Virtual Desktop Agent can discover a Delivery Controller's location by searching in an Active Directory domain.

Note that this option is used for backward compatibility. You can find more information at `http://support.citrix.com/proddocs/topic/xenapp-xendesktop-75/cds-mng-cntrlr-intro.html`.

- **Letting Machine Creation Services do it automatically**: Select this option if you plan to provision the virtual desktops by using a single image. Machine Creation Services will configure the Delivery Controller locations when you create the machines.

In this example, we will select the **Do it later** option. We will set the Delivery Controller locations by using a Citrix policy. Let's do this by following these steps:

1. Click on the **Next** button to continue.

2. From the **Features** screen, the wizard will require you to select the features that you want for configuring VDA. You should know that **Optimize performance**, **Use Windows Remote Assistance.** and **Use Real-Time Audio Transport for audio** are the default options.

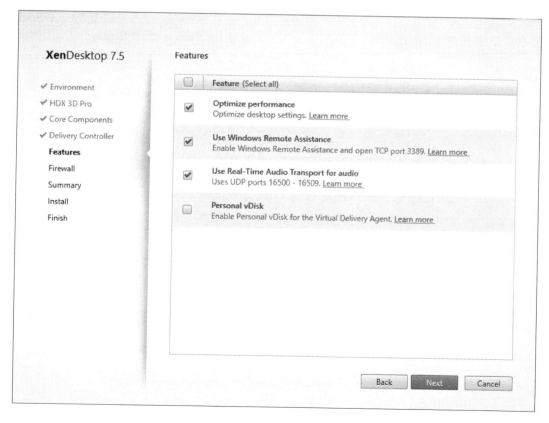

If you plan to use Personal vDisk, you can either select it now or select it later.

Personal vDisks provide the users the opportunity to install applications and change their desktop settings while saving them on a separate disk attached to the virtual machine.

 Go to `http://support.citrix.com/proddocs/topic/ xenapp-xendesktop-75/cds-pvd-intro.html` for learning more about Personal vDisks.

3. Click on the **Next** button to continue.
4. The wizard will ask how you want to configure the Windows firewall. You can either use the default selection, which will be **Automatically** or you can select **Manually**.

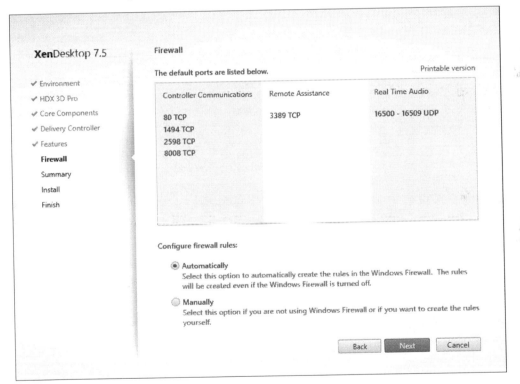

 Remember to check all the required TCP and UDP ports, and ensure that they have been opened on the firewall, especially if you have a segmented network.

5. Click on the **Next** button to continue.

6. The wizard will display the summary page, where you can review your decisions. Click on the **Install** button for starting the installation process.

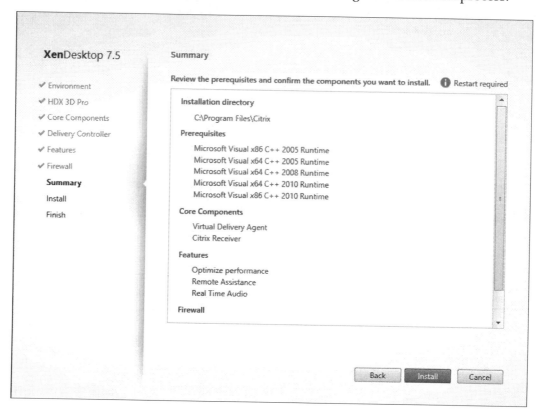

7. When the VDA installation finishes, the desktop machine will restart.

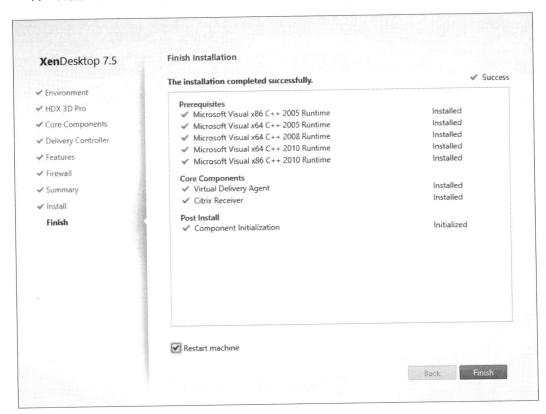

We can install Virtual Desktop Agent by using the command line as well.

For example, if you want to install VDA without Citrix Receiver, you can connect it to specific Delivery Controllers and then select the same features that we selected by using the graphical user interface. For this, you will use the following command line:

```
XenDesktopVdaSetup.exe /components VDA /controllers "xd-ctxdc1.contoso.
local xd-ctxdc2.contoso.local" /enable_remote_assistance /enable_hdx_
ports /optimize /enable_real_time_transport
```

Here, we have the following parameters:

- /components: This parameter is used for specifying the components that are to be installed. You can use the VDA value for installing Virtual Desktop Agent and the PLUGINS value for installing Citrix Receiver for Windows. Separate them by a comma. If you want to install both of them, you will need to omit this parameter.

- /controllers: This parameter is used for specifying the FQDNs of the Delivery Controllers with which VDA communicates. Separate them by using a space and enclose them by using quotation marks.

- /enable_remote_assistance: This parameter enables Windows Remote Assistance.

- /enable_hdx_ports: This parameter configures the Windows firewall by opening the required ports by using features that you have specified.

- /optimize: This parameter enables the optimization of VDA running on a virtual machine.

- /enable_real_time_transport: This parameter enables Real-Time Audio Transport for audio.

The XenDesktopVdaSetup.exe file is available in the \x64\XenDesktop Setup folder, which is present on the XenDesktop ISO image.

> You can find more information about the command line parameters at http://support.citrix.com/proddocs/topic/xenapp-xendesktop-75/cds-install-prepare.html.

You can also install Virtual Desktop Agent by using Active Directory or software distribution systems, such as Microsoft System Center Configuration Manager. In the \Support\AdDeploy folder, which would be available on the XenDesktop ISO image, you can find simple scripts for either installing or uninstalling VDA.

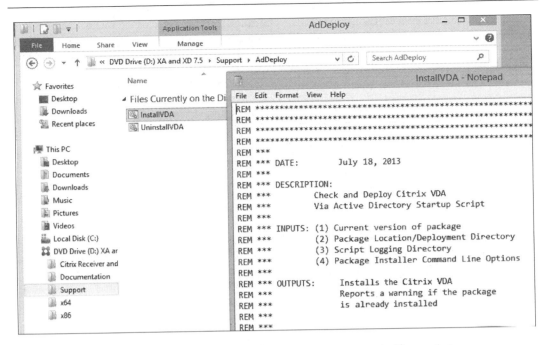

If you use them, remember to set the following parameters in the script:

- `SET DESIREDVERSION`: Set the version of the VDA that you want to install. For XenDesktop 7.5, use version 7.5.0.4523

- `SET DEPLOYSHARE`: Set a network shared folder from where the installer will be executed

- `SET LOGSHARE`: Set the network share location where the installation logs will be saved

Creating and configuring machine catalogs and delivery groups

In the previous section, we learned how to install Virtual Desktop Agent in a Windows Desktop machine.

Now, let's discover how to create machine catalogs and delivery groups in order to provide virtual desktops to the users.

A machine catalog is a collection of identical machines. They can be either virtual or physical. They can host either a supported desktop or server operating system.

You create delivery groups to provide desktops and applications to the users; in a delivery group, you can mix machines from different machine catalogs.

 Visit `http://support.citrix.com/proddocs/topic/xenapp-xendesktop-75/cds-manage-delivery-groups-wrapper.html` for obtaining more details.

Machine catalogs and delivery groups are created by using Citrix Studio.

Before discovering how to create the machine catalog, we need to learn how to create a master image for Machine Creation Services.

The creation process is very simple; to create the master image, follow this procedure:

1. On your Hypervisor, create a new virtual machine, and then install an operating system, desktop, or server.

 While doing this, take the hard disk size into consideration. Select the size of the hard disk carefully because you cannot change it after you have created the master image.

2. On the new virtual machine, install the hypervisor tools (VMware Tools, Hyper-V Integration Services, or XenServer Tools).
3. Install the Virtual Desktop Agent. Remember to select the **Optimize Performance** feature for achieving the best experience of the virtual desktop.
4. Install the third-party tools and applications, such as anti-virus, e-mail client, utilities, and so on, according to the user's need.
5. If you plan to use Microsoft App-V, install the App-V client.
6. Install any language pack or locale if necessary.
7. Join the machine to your Active Directory domain.

8. Create a snapshot of the master image. Use a friendly name so that you can identify it easily.

 The snapshot creation is recommended for Machine Creation Services. If you do not create it, Citrix Studio will create it during the machine catalog creation process.

You can find more details about the master image at `http://support.citrix.com/proddocs/topic/xenapp-xendesktop-75/cds-prep-master-vm-rho.html`.

In the next example, we will create a machine catalog, which will be based on Machine Creation Services. Here, we will introduce this feature, and then we will learn how it works.

To do this, follow these steps:

1. Connect to a Delivery Controller and then start Citrix Studio.

2. On Citrix Studio, select **Machine Catalogs**.

3. Click on **Create Machine Catalog** by navigating to the **Actions** panel, as shown here:

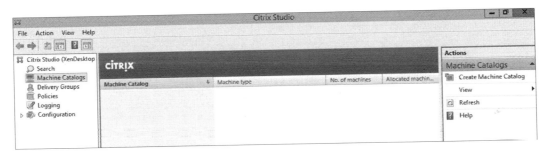

4. Now, the **Machine Catalog Setup** wizard will show you the **Introduction** page. Review it, and then click on the **Next** button.

5. First, the wizard will ask you to select the operating system to be used for the machine catalog. The **Windows Server OS** option would be the default selection. In this example, we will create a catalog based on Windows 8, so we will select **Windows Desktop OS**.

Select **Remote PC Access** when you want to create a machine catalog based on physical machines, and then connect to them by using a secure connection.

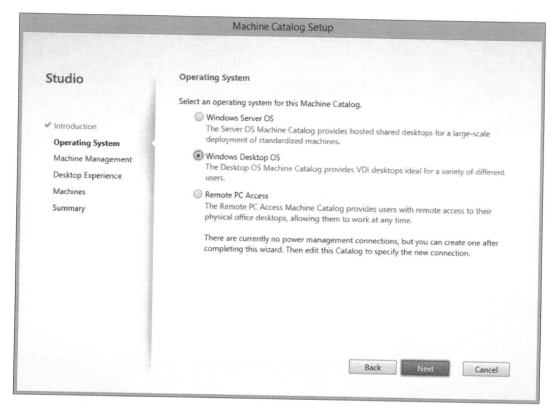

6. Click on the **Next** button to continue.

7. The wizard will now require you to decide how to manage the machines.

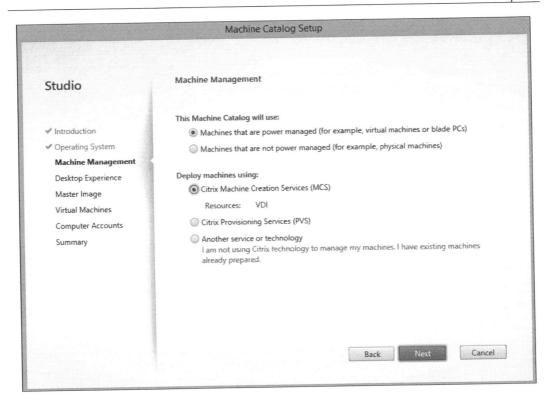

First, you have to select whether the machine catalog will use the machines that are power managed or not.

Note that Citrix Machine Creation Services is available only when you select the use power-managed machines option. Secondly, you have to select the deployment method that you want to use for deploying the machines.

Here, you will have three different options:

- **Citrix Machine Creation Services (MCS)**: By using a master virtual machine within your environment, you can manage the virtual machines.

- **Citrix Provisioning Services (PVS)**: You can manage the target devices as a collection. Machines will be deployed by using a vDisk, a virtual hard drive streamed to virtual machines and imaged from a master image.

- **Another service or technology**: Select this option if you want to use the non-Citrix services for deploying the machines.

In this example, we have used the machines that are power managed and use Citrix Machine Creation Services.

8. Click on the **Next** button to continue.

9. The wizard will display the **Desktop Experience** page.

Here, you can configure how the users connect each time they log onto the XenDesktop environment.

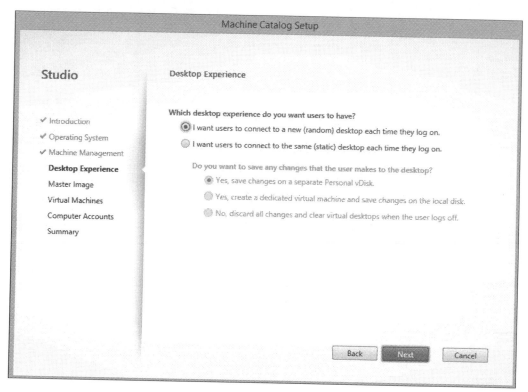

You can choose between these two options:

- ° **I want users to connect to a new (random) desktop each time they log on.**: If you select this option, all changes applied to the desktop by the user will be discarded when the user logs off.

- ° **I want users to connect to the same (static) desktop each time they log on.**: Select this option if you want to save the changes that were made to the desktop by a user.

For selecting a static desktop, the wizard will require you to choose the option for saving the performed changes to the desktop. You can save them by using either Personal vDisks, or a dedicated virtual machine, and then you can save the changes to a local disk.

In this example, we have selected **I want users to connect to a new (random) desktop each time they log on.**.

10. Click on the **Next** button to continue.

11. The wizard will now ask you to select a master image, which will be used as a template for creating the machines.

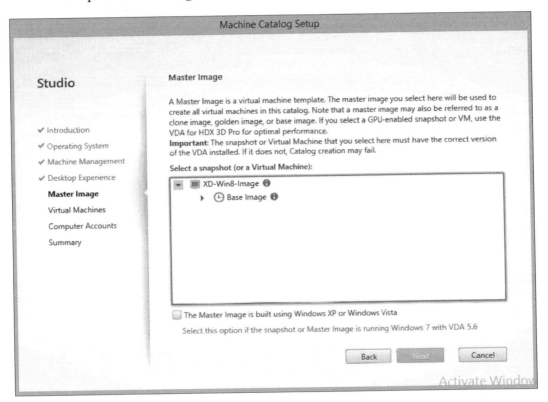

12. Select the snapshot that you want to use. Refer to the master image creation process that we introduced at the beginning of this section.

In this example, we have selected the **Base Image** snapshot. It is related to the **XD-Win8-Image** virtual machine, which is hosted on a XenServer host.

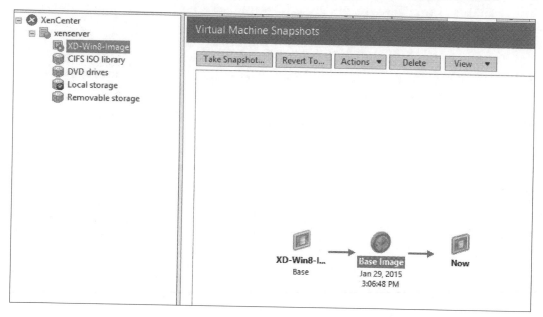

13. If you are using a master image that is based either on Windows XP or on the Windows Vista operating system, select the **The Master Image is built using Windows XP or Windows Vista** option.

14. Click on the **Next** button to continue.

15. The wizard will prompt you to select the number of virtual machines that you want to create. You have the option of changing the number of virtual CPUs. You can also change the memory configuration. However, you cannot change the hard disk size.

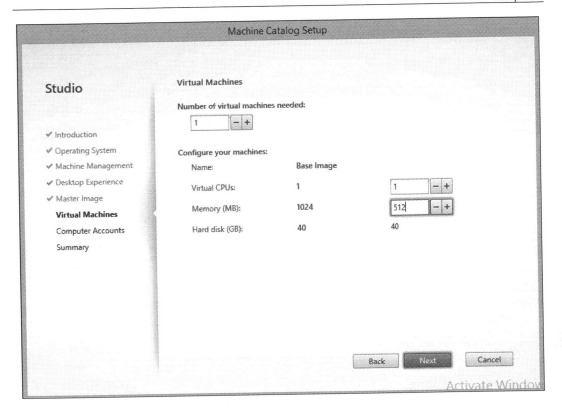

In this example, we have created a single virtual machine with a virtual CPU and a memory of 512 MB.

16. Click on the **Next** button to continue.

17. Now, you will be prompted to select the Active Directory organizational unit, where the wizard will create the virtual machines using the naming convention to name them.

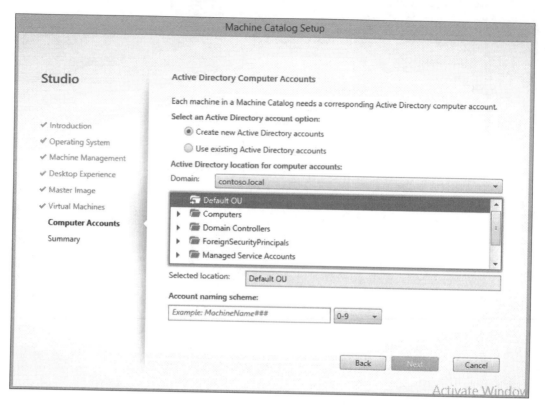

If you do not have the permissions for creating computer accounts in Active Directory, you can instruct your Active Directory administrator to create them for you. After this, select the **Use existing Active Directory accounts** option.

In the **Domain** menu, you can select the Active Directory domain option, where the virtual machines will be created. You can click on the drop-down menu and then select a different domain if needed.

A bi-directional trust must exist between the domain containing the Controller computer accounts and the domain containing the virtual desktop computer accounts.

More information about the supported Active Directory environment is available at `http://support.citrix.com/proddocs/topic/xenapp-xendesktop-75/cds-plan-active-directory-rho.html`.

18. Select the Organizational Unit where you want to create the virtual desktop computer accounts. In this example, we have selected `OU=Virtual Desktop,` `OU=XenDesktop,DC=Contoso,DC=Local`.

19. Set a naming scheme for the computer account according to the `MachineName###` convention, where ### equals either numbers or letters.

    In this example, we will use the "`XD-Win8-PC##`" naming scheme by using the numbers in the range **0-9**.

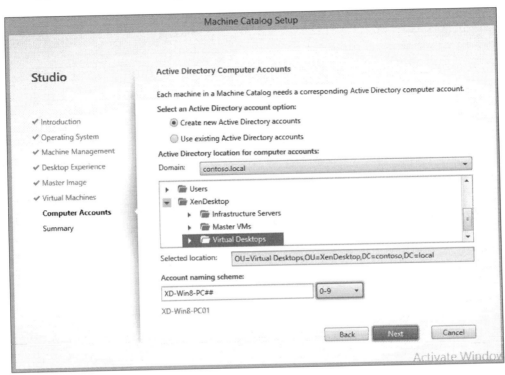

20. Click on the **Next** button to continue.

21. The wizard will display a summary according to your selections, and then it will ask you to type a name and a description for the machine catalog.

In this example, we will name the catalog **Windows 8 Virtual Desktops**, and then insert **Windows 8 Virtual Desktops – Random Assignment** in the **Description** field.

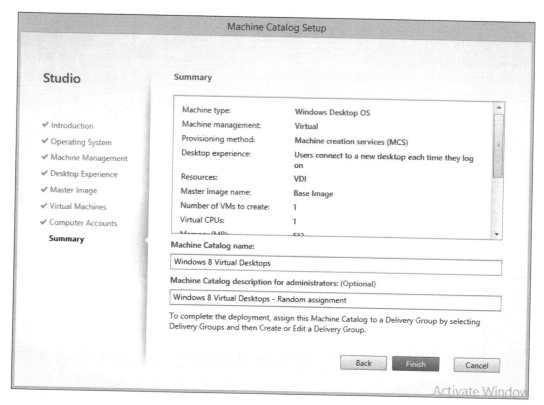

22. Click on the **Finish** button for creating the machine catalog. The wizard will create the virtual machines on your virtual infrastructure and system accounts on Active Directory.

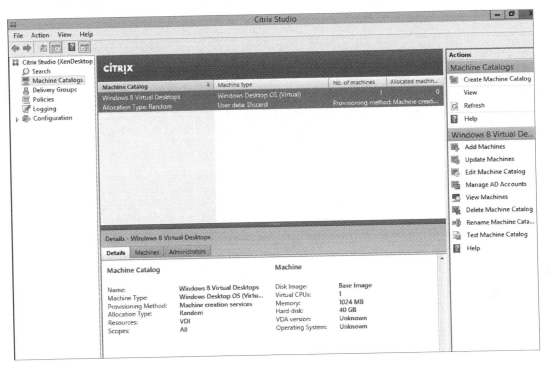

In the previous task, we created a machine catalog. Now, we will create a delivery group. This will be used for delivering applications and desktops.

You can create different types of delivery groups, as follows:

- Desktop Only
- Applications Only
- Desktop and Applications

While creating a delivery group, keep the following in mind:

- You can use a machine in only one delivery group.
- You can only create delivery groups from multiple machine catalogs that have the same characteristics. For example, you cannot mix the machines from static and random catalogs.
- A machine catalog can be associated with one or more delivery groups.
- Multiple catalogs can reference the same delivery group.
- In Remote PC Access delivery groups, any machine that is added to a Remote PC Access machine catalog automatically gets associated with a delivery group.

Delivery groups are created by using Citrix Studio. In the next example, we will create a group for delivering the desktops to users, as shown here:

1. Open Citrix Studio, and then click on the **Delivery Groups** node.
2. Click on the **Create Delivery Group** link, which is available on the **Actions** panel. The wizard will start, and then it will display the introduction page, as follows:

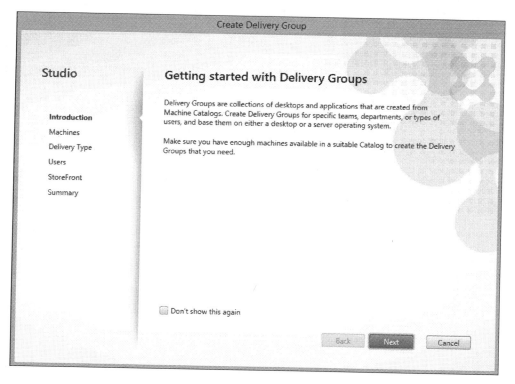

3. Click on the **Next** button to continue.

4. Select the machine catalog that you want to use for this delivery group, and then enter the number of machines that the delivery group will consume from the machine catalog. In this example, we'll choose the machine catalog that we have already created, and then select one machine from it.

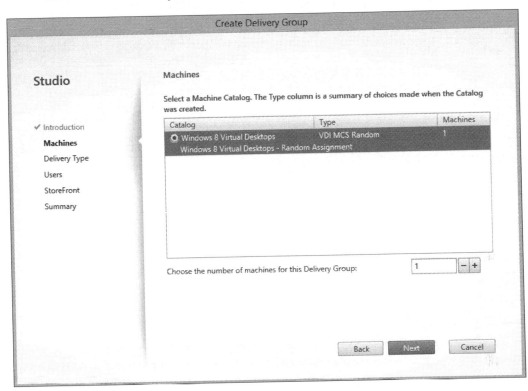

5. Click on the **Next** button to continue.

6. Select the delivery group type that you want to use.

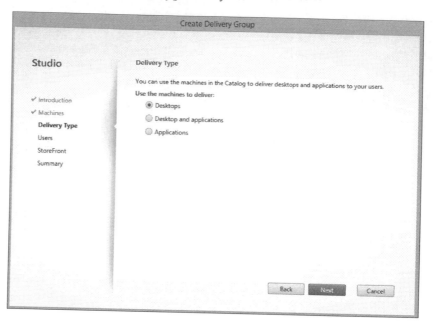

7. Click on the **Next** button to continue.
8. The wizard will ask you to add the users who will be granted permissions to connect to this delivery group. To do this, click on the **Add Users** button.

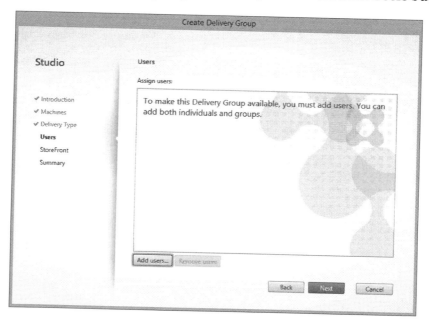

9. You can search the Active Directory domain for users and/or groups. Select the user or group that you want to enable. In this example, we will use the **Random Win8 Users** group, which belongs to the `contoso.local` domain.

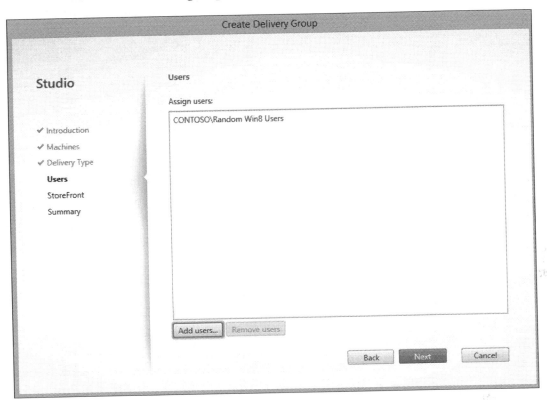

It is a best practice to always select an Active Directory group when adding the users to the delivery groups.

10. Click on the **Next** button to continue.

11. The wizard will now request you to configure the Citrix Receiver installed on the Virtual Desktop Agent.

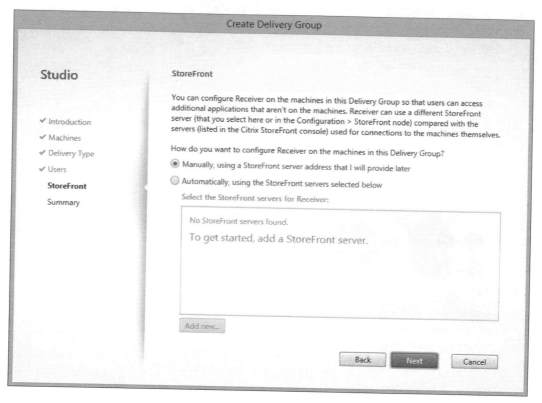

You can configure the Citrix Receiver either manually (**Manually, using a StoreFront server address that I will provide later**) or automatically (**Automatically, using the StoreFront servers selected below**). If you want to choose the automatic option, you will have to add a StoreFront server to the Citrix Studio console.

In this example, we will not change the default selection, which is manual.

12. Click on the **Next** button to continue.

    The wizard will display a summary according to your selections, and then it will ask you to type a delivery group name, a display name, and an optional description. The **Delivery Group name** is to be used only by administrators. Users will see the **Display name**.

    In this example, we will type Win8 Desktop in the **Delivery Group name** field, and then insert Windows 8 Desktop in the **Display name** field.

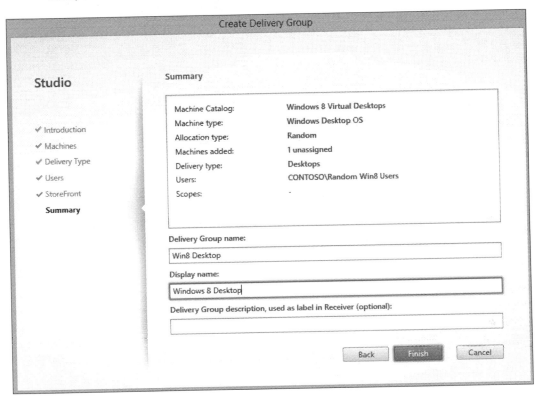

13. Click on the **Finish** button to complete the wizard.

14. On the Citrix Studio console, the new delivery group will be displayed:

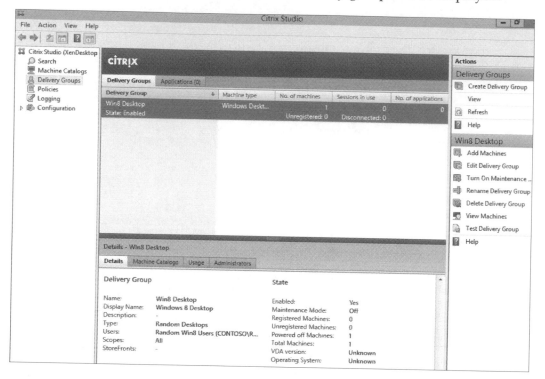

Optimizing XenDesktop® Virtual Desktop Agent for performance

Previously, we learned how to install the Virtual Desktop Agent and how to create machine catalogs and delivery groups.

In the previous chapter, we introduced some tips about sizing the XenDesktop environment.

In this section, we will discover how to optimize VDA so that it provides the best experience to users, delivering them as an optimized and functional environment.

Optimizing VDAs is very important because it increases performance and scalability. Furthermore, applying optimization offers the possibility of lowering the usage of virtual resources, such as virtual CPU, memory, and disks.

Some of these optimizations are based on Windows Registry changes that you can apply manually using Group Policy Preferences; others are automatically applied when you install VDA on a machine.

You can find more details regarding the optimization of the XenDesktop VDA by visiting `http://support.citrix.com/article/ctx125874`.

It is a best practice to apply optimizations based on the editing of the Windows registry by using Windows Group Policy Preferences.

Also, remember to test any changes before applying them in a production environment.

The following optimizations will help you in improving the performances:

- Disable the default system screensaver setting, `HKEY_USERS\.DEFAULT\ Control Panel\Desktop\"ScreenSaveActive"=dword: 00000000`

- Disable the bootlog and the boot animation for speeding up the boot process by running the commands `bcdedit /set {default} bootlog no` and `bcdedit /set {default} quietboot yes`

- Enable the **High Performance** scheme of Windows Power Plans, which is available on the control panel

- Set the initial size of the paging file so that it is equal to the maximum size

- Disable the unnecessary desktop notification icons by using the Group Policy as follows: `Administrative Templates > Start Menu and Taskbar > Hide the notification area`

- Disable the UAC Secure Desktop Prompt setting as follows: `HKEY_LOCAL_ MACHINE\Software\Microsoft\Windows\CurrentVersion\Policies\Syst em\"PromptOnSecureDesktop"=dword: 00000000`

- Increase the Service Startup Timeout setting as follows: `HKEY_LOCAL_ MACHINE\SYSTEM\CurrentControlSet\Control\"ServicesPipeTimeout"= dword:0002bf20`

- Hide the Hard Error Messages setting as follows: `HKEY_LOCAL_MACHINE\ System\CurrentControlSet\Control\Windows\"ErrorMode"=dwo rd:00000002`

- Increase the Disk I/O Timeout to 200 seconds setting as follows: `HKEY_ LOCAL_MACHINE\SYSTEM\CurrentControlSet\Services\Disk\"TimeOutVa lue"=dword:000000C8`

- Disable the Windows Defender Service if you have installed a different anti-virus by using the Group Policy: `Computer Configuration > Administrative Templates > Windows Components > Windows Defender "Turn off Windows Defender`

 Visit `http://support.Citrix.com/article/CTX127030` for browsing the Citrix guidelines regarding the anti-virus configuration. Note that you should backup the registry before making the changes.

If you plan to use a master image with MCS or Citrix PVS, the following should be done to the master image before it is moved to production:

- Update all the virus definitions and perform a full scan on all local hard disks for removing any viruses
- Install the Windows updates and the service packs
- Defragment the hard disk
- Remove unnecessary Windows features

Furthermore, it is a best practice to disable any unnecessary Windows services in order to improve the performances.

For example, you can disable the following services:

- Application Experience
- Application Layer Gateway Service
- Background Intelligent Transfer Service
- BitLocker Drive Encryption Service
- Block Level Backup Engine Service
- Bluetooth Support Service
- BranchCache Service
- Device Association Service
- Device Setup Manager Service
- IP Helper
- Shell Hardware Detection Service
- Volume Shadow Copy Service
- Windows Error Reporting Service
- WLAN Service
- WWAN Service

Optimizations are also necessary for the **Server Message Block (SMB)** protocol, which is used for Microsoft File Sharing.

When a drive is mapped to a shared folder on a Windows machine and Windows Explorer is open in the network drive, the virtual desktop will act as an SMB client.

Depending on what Windows version is being run as the SMB client and the SMB server, you can have different versions that are in use, as shown here:

- SMB 1.0: Operating systems older than Windows Vista/Windows 2008
- SMB 2.x: Windows Vista, Windows 7, Windows Server 2008, 2008 R2
- SMB 3.x: Windows 8.x, Windows Server 2012, and 2012 R2

When you have a mixed environment, you should apply the following optimizations to the SMB 1.0 Client optimization:

- `HKEY_LOCAL_MACHINE\SYSTEM\CurrentControlSet\Services\Lanmanworkstation\Parameters`

  MaxCmds=dword:00002048 (dec)

- `HKEY_LOCAL_MACHINE\SYSTEM\CurrentControlSet\Services\MRxSmb\Parameters`

  MultiUserEnabled=dword:00000001

- `HKEY_LOCAL_MACHINE\SOFTWARE\Microsoft\Windows\CurrentVersion\Policies\Explorer`

  NoRemoteRecursiveEvents=dword:00000001

- `HKEY_LOCAL_MACHINE\SYSTEM\CurrentControlSet\Services\Lanmanserver\Parameters`

  MaxWorkItems=dword:00008192 (dec)

  MaxMpxCt=dword:00002048 (dec)

  MaxRawWorkItems=dword:00000512 (dec)

  MaxFreeConnections=dword:00000100 (dec)

  MinFreeConnections=dword:00000032 (dec)

For SMB 2.x Client Optimization, you can apply the changes shown here:

- `HKEY_LOCAL_MACHINE\System\CurrentControlSet\Services\LanmanWorkstation\Parameters`

  "DisableBandwidthThrottling"=dword:00000001

  "DisableLargeMtu"=dword:00000000

- HKEY_LOCAL_MACHINE\SOFTWARE\Microsoft\Windows\ CurrentVersion\ Policies\Explorer

NoRemoteRecursiveEvents=dword:00000001

> For obtaining more information about the recommended optimizations, read the *Windows 8 and 8.1 Virtual Desktop Optimization Guide*, which is available at http://support.citrix.com/article/CTX140375.

Managing Citrix® policies

The Citrix policies are used for controlling and customizing user access or sessions of the Citrix XenDesktop environment. The Citrix policies are the most efficient methods of controlling connection, user experience, and bandwidth settings.

You can apply the policies by using Citrix Studio or Microsoft **Group Policy Management Console (GPMC)**. Use Citrix Studio when you do not have the permissions for managing the group policies of Active Directory, otherwise the best practice recommends using GPMC.

> Policies created by using Citrix Studio are saved in the site database.
> If you prefer GPMC, then install it on the Citrix Delivery Controller by using Server Manager/Add – Remove Features.

Furthermore, templates are available in the XenDesktop policy. They consist of the pre-configured settings that optimize the performance for specific environments or network conditions, for example, when there is a low bandwidth, or when users require a high quality user experience.

For this, four templates are available, as shown here:

- **High Definition User Experience**: Use this template to deliver a high quality user experience for graphics, audio, and video.

- **High Server Scalability**: Use this template when you want to increase the number of users that are hosted on a single server while offering a good experience.

- **Optimized for WAN**: Use this template when you want to optimize network bandwidth for the remote users; this template can also be used when you have to manage low bandwidth and/or high latency connections.

- **Security and Control**: This template is used for disabling the use of client-side peripheral devices, such as drives mapping, client-side rendering of the media content, and so on

Similar to the Microsoft Group Policy, Citrix policies can be applied either to computers or to users. The computer settings define the behavior of the desktop or server, and they are applied when the machine starts, even when there are no active user sessions.

The user settings define the user experience when connecting to a virtual desktop or to a published application by using the ICA protocol.

You can configure the Citrix policies, or work with templates by clicking on the **Policies** node of **Citrix Studio** console:

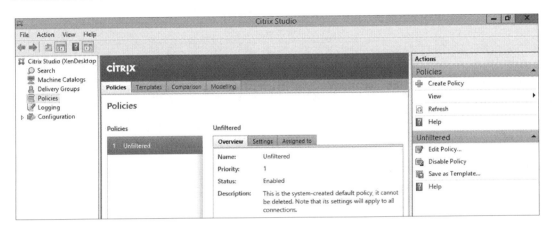

The policies are processed in the following order:

1. Local GPO
2. XenDesktop site GPO (stored in the site database and created by using Citrix Studio)
3. Site-level GPOs
4. Domain-level GPOs
5. Organizational Units

The policies applied last can overwrite those processed earlier.

For example, a Citrix administrator will create a policy (named policy A), and then apply it to an Organizational Unit; this will disable the client printers mapping. The same administrator will later configure a XenDesktop site GPO (named policy B), and this will enable the client printers mapping.

In this scenario, the Policy A will take precedence because it was applied last.

Policies with conflicting settings can be prioritized.

You can prioritize the policies by giving them different priority numbers ranging from 1 to 5, where 1 is the highest priority and 5 is the lowest priority. When you create a new policy, it will be configured with the lowest priority.

A policy with a higher priority overrides a policy with the settings configured in a lower priority.

Sometimes, when multiple policies are in place, it is not easy to understand what the final applied setting is or what the winning policy is. In this case, you can determine how the final policy settings will be merged for a connection by calculating the Resultant Set of Policy.

The resultant Set of Policy can be calculated by using the following:

- The Citrix Group Policy Modeling Wizard will simulate a connection, and it will identify how the Citrix policies can be applied
- Group Policy Results will produce a report describing the Citrix policies that were applied to a user or a machine

The Citrix Group Policy Modeling Wizard is available in Citrix Studio and in the Group Policy Management Console.

 Always start Citrix Group Policy Modeling Wizard in Citrix Studio. Doing so will include the XenDesktop site policy, which was created by using Citrix Studio, in the report.

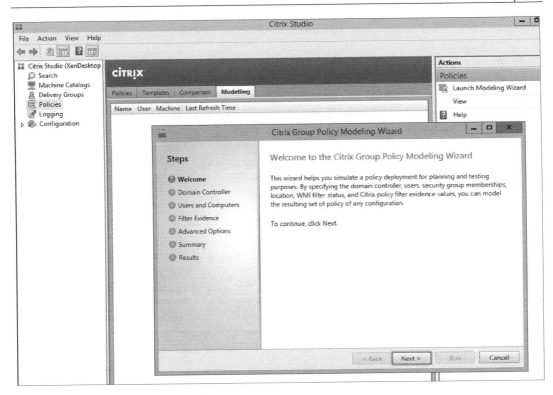

In the following example, we will create a Citrix policy for configuring Delivery Controllers for the virtual desktop agent. We will also introduce more details about policy configurations.

You have to use Group Policy Management Console for configuring the Delivery Controller location by policy.

To create a policy, follow this procedure:

1. Open the Group Policy Management Console (or Citrix Studio) on a Citrix Delivery Controller.

2. Open the Group Policy Objects node, and then create a new policy.

3. Type a name for the new policy. In this example, we will insert the `Citrix XenDesktop Machine Policy` name, as shown here:

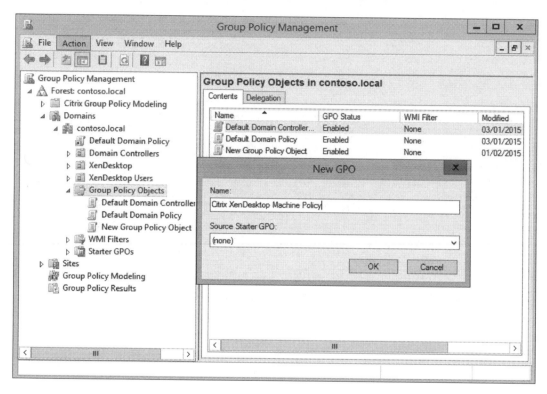

4. Edit the new created policy. Expand the **Computer Configuration** node and click on the **Policies** node.

5. Click on the **Citrix Policies** node. The **Citrix Computer Policies** screen will be displayed, as follows:

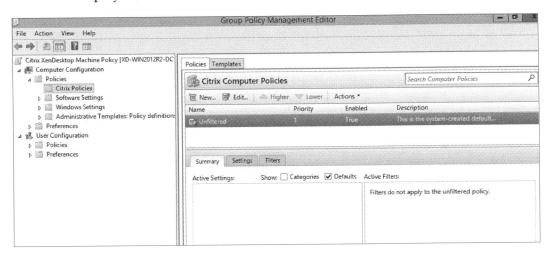

6. As you can see, a policy named **Unfiltered** is already present on the console. This policy was created by default during the setup. The settings added to this policy will apply to all connections.

   You can either modify or disable this policy. You can also create a new one. Normally, it is disabled. For disabling the unfiltered policy, right click on it. and then select **Disable**.

7. Click on the **New...** button for creating a new Citrix policy.

8. Type a friendly name and add a description. This is useful for identifying what the policy does, especially when you are working with many policies. In this example, we will type `Citrix Default Machine Policy`, as shown here:

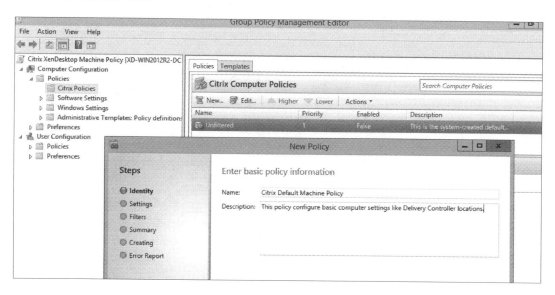

9. Click on the **Next** button to continue.

10. By default, the new policy will include the same settings as the original template.

   You can filter the settings by navigating to **All Products / Versions** and **Categories**. Also, you can run a search for a specific setting by using the **Search** box. In this example, we will filter the settings by using the **Virtual Delivery Agent Settings** category.

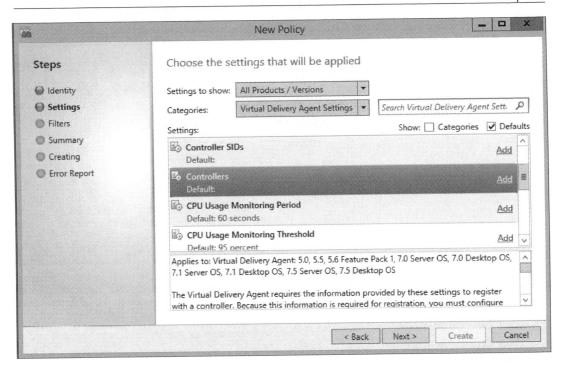

11. The policy settings are not configured by default, but note that some settings can have a default value, while others can only be applied to specific Citrix products or versions. For example, the **CPU Usage Monitoring Period** setting has a default value of 60 seconds and it can only be applied to the Delivery Agent version 5.0 or 5.5.

12. To set the controller location, click on the **Controllers** setting, and then click on the **Add** link.

13. Insert the name of your Delivery Controllers by separating them with a space, as shown here:

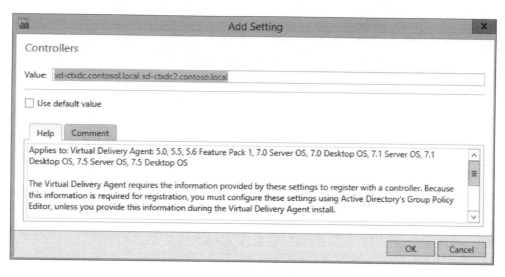

14. Click on the **OK** button to confirm the new setting.

15. If you want to configure any other settings, then you can do this at present, or you can click on **Next** to continue.

16. The filters page will be displayed. Here, you can set the specific criteria in order to filter the policy application, as follows:

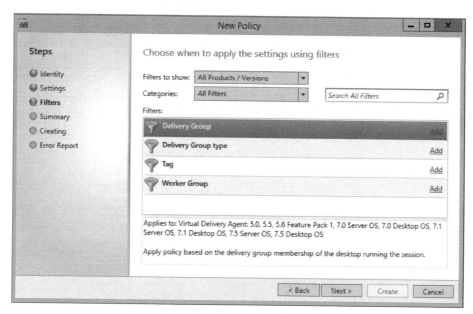

17. If you do not set any filter, the policy will be applied to all the connections. You can apply multiple filters to the same policy. For a given filter, you can set two different modes. If the mode is set to **Allow** (the default), then the policy will only be applied to the connections that match the assignment criteria. When the mode is set to **Deny**, the policy will only be applied if the connection does not match the assignment criteria.

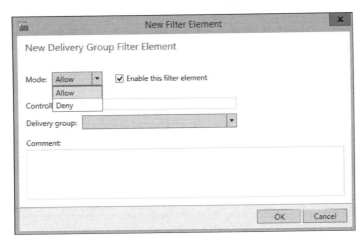

When you set multiple filters on the same policy, keep the following in mind:

- If you set two filters of the same type, the deny mode will take precedence over the allow mode

- If you set two or more filters of different types, the connection must satisfy at least one criteria of each type in order for the policy to be applied

In this example, we will not set any filters because we want to apply the setting to all connections.

18. Now, click on the **Next** button to continue.

19. The **Summary** page will be displayed. Next, click on the **Create** button to complete the policy creation. Note that the policy will automatically be enabled.

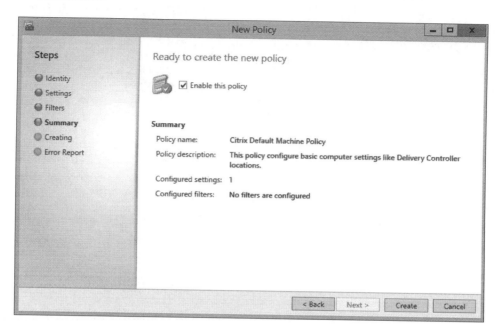

 For more information about the Citrix policies, visit http://support.citrix.com/proddocs/topic/xenapp-xendesktop-75/cds-policies-applying-rho.html.

When you create or apply policies, you can use the following practices:

- Assign the policies to groups rather than to individual users. This will reduce the administrative effort when managing policies.

- Do not enable conflicting or overlapping settings.

- Disable the unused policies.

Summary

In this chapter, we learned how to install the core components of Citrix XenDesktop for providing high availability. We also discovered how to install Virtual Desktop Agent by using graphical interface and command line. In the last sections, we discussed the optimization of the virtual desktop agent for improving performance and managing the Citrix policies.

In the next chapter, we will learn how Citrix XenDesktop can be used for addressing advanced and high end business requirements, such as media streaming, audio and video conferencing, 3D graphics and low bandwidth, remote and mobile user access.

6
Configuring XenDesktop® for Advanced Use Cases

In this chapter, we will learn how to devise the XenDesktop environments for the advanced use cases that are required for businesses. This will include configuring and fine-tuning the policies and settings of both the Windows server and the desktop operating systems from both the Windows and the XenDesktop perspective. The advanced use case scenarios covered in this chapter discuss the common requirements for the advanced high-tech enterprises, as well as the service providers delivering **Desktop-as-a-Service (DaaS)**. There are many more scenarios where XenDesktop can be elegantly configured for fulfilling the use case. Following is a list of major topics, which we'll learn in this chapter:

- Configuring XenDesktop for the advanced business use cases
- The advanced fine-tuning of XenDesktop

It is assumed that you have an intermediate to advanced level of understanding of the HDX technologies and the ICA protocol.

Advanced use cases of XenDesktop®

It is the IT administrators who design, deploy, and deliver the usual virtual desktop service to the users of an enterprise. However, for specific advanced users and use cases, the XenDesktop virtual desktop solution needs to be customized, fine-tuned, and configured as per the user's requirements. These include the use case scenarios, such as configuring the various audio and video based conferencing applications that are used by the management and the engineering staff, the professional high end 3D graphic application for the graphic designers and the creativity department staff, and so on. These require your environment to be equipped with advanced hardware, software updates, and configurations for delivering the solution.

Certain advanced configurations need to be set up for all the users of the virtual desktops. These may include scenarios, such as instantly making the desktop sessions available, delivering the seamless UI, and so on. These usually involve fine-tuning the XenDesktop, as well as the Windows infrastructure, for achieving the required behavior.

Implementing advanced business use cases with XenDesktop®

We'll discuss how to configure XenDesktop for the following advanced use cases:

- The high end 3D business applications that use the GPU technology
- **Unified Communications Solutions** (UCS) – the audio and video conferencing applications
- Streaming Media applications through the HDX technology
- Secure Internet access through web filtering
- Secure virtual desktops through policy restrictions
- Access to the virtual desktops through the low bandwidth remote and mobile user connections
- **High Performance Computing** (HPC) and Citrix XenDesktop

Fine-tuning and customizing XenDesktop® for advanced use cases

We'll cover the fine-tuning of XenDesktop for the advanced use cases listed here:

- The virtual display
- Integrating the local applications
- Controlling the seamless and in-browser access
- Provisioning the instant virtual desktop sessions

Configuring XenDesktop® for advanced business use cases

The focus of this section is on learning the scope of configuring XenDesktop as per specific advanced business use cases. It is possible that more than one of these requirements exist in a single XenDesktop deployment. However, for scenarios such as the DaaS service providers, these requirements may be of specific business cases for fulfilling the customer needs. Understanding these as independent use cases will help you to build specialized knowledge of implementing the XenDesktop based solutions for your business requirements.

High-end 3D business applications using GPU technology

In a business desktop environment, supporting the high end 3D and graphics intensive applications has always been a challenge. We'll see how this has been set up in a traditional desktop environment, and then see its equivalent solution with XenDesktop capabilities and its rich features and benefits for businesses.

Traditional setup for high-end 3D business applications using physical desktops

Delivering the graphics intensive, specifically 3D business applications is usually accomplished by deploying appropriate add-on graphic card (GPU) on the physical systems. Depending on the application requirements, a specified graphic card is installed on the desktops. Furthermore, the physical graphic card installation requires a physical desktop motherboard to support the expansion slot for the selected graphic card model. Supporting the graphic card usually also requires fast and high CPU/RAM equipped systems. In some cases, it turns out that one has to purchase a complete new desktop with the required graphic cards and then install the graphic card drivers, as well as the application integration on top the system.

This additionally incurs business loss if any hardware failures arise. This also causes prolonged periods for the additional deployments and it can't be scaled down once it has been setup.

XenDesktop® provisioning GPU enabled virtual desktops

Citrix introduced a game-changing technology over the past half-decade. Since 2009, Citrix and NVidia have been working together, and they have made exclusive support for the NVidia GRID virtual GPU's in the Citrix XenServer. This has helped businesses in realizing the benefits of moving graphics processing from under the desk to a central data center, both by large and medium enterprises.

 Recently (2014), VMware and NVidia announced the vGPU technology support for VMware Horizon and vSphere.

NVidia GRID – graphics accelerated virtualization

NVidia built the GRID solution after giving it over 20 years of their software and hardware innovations specialized in the accelerated graphics field. Citrix has included the NVidia's low latency remote display technology (called GRID Accelerated Remoting) in the Citrix HDX 3D Pro protocol. All the Kepler GPUs are built with the H.264 encoding high performance engine that can encode the simultaneous streams with superior quality. This has greatly improved the Cloud server efficiency by offloading the CPU from the encoding functions and by allowing the encode function to scale with the number of GPUs in a server. NVidia designed its Kepler based GRID K1 and K2 boards specifically for enabling rich graphics in the virtualized environment. The GRID technology enables businesses to achieve maximum user density, power efficiency, and high reliability. The GRID boards are designed with support for the optimized multi-GPU that comes with them.

The GRID *vGPU* technology made it possible to provision the hardware virtualized GPUs for the first time. It allowed the sharing of a single GPU across multiple users, which further improved the user density. The GRID technologies involve the use of the NVidia GRID vGPU manager, which runs on the hypervisor (say XenServer) and the respective NVidia drivers which are installed on the virtual machines. The vGPU manager assigns the required GPU resources to the virtual machines in a balanced way. The NVidia drivers on the virtual machines directly communicate all the graphic commands to the physical GPU.

Following is the architecture diagram of the NVidia GRID vGPU technology, which supports Citrix XenServer:

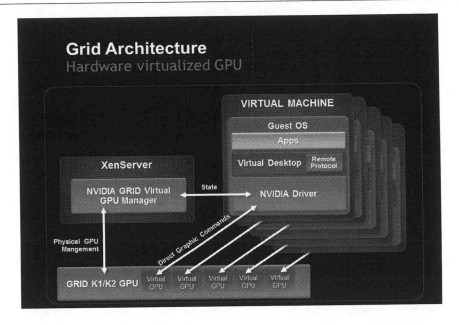

XenDesktop® 3D solution architectures using NVidia GRID technology

The XenDesktop solutions based on the NVidia GRID can be configured either by using the vGPU technology or by using the pass through mode. The NVidia GRID for delivering the server hosted applications and desktops (supported in XenApp, as well as in its previous IMA based versions) provides greater user density per GPU. These various configurations allow IT to design the GPU based virtual desktop and application solutions for meeting the varying GPU processing capacities across the business user groups. In general, the GPU users can be broadly classified into the following categories:

- Knowledge and task workers: They require a limited use of the 3D graphics, such as the Windows 8 style apps, the PowerPoint transitions, and the low end 2D or 3D work.

- Operators and contractors (Power users): They require viewing or editing of the graphics intensive 3D files, or accessing the complex graphics workflows onsite, such as the factory floor or a construction site. The hardware GPU acceleration is recommended.

- Designers and engineers: They require the high end 3D graphic performance for creating and updating the large and complex 3D models. Their use cases may require a dedicated GPU for the graphics acceleration. In some cases, the engineer's requirements may be met by using a high-end vGPU, such as K260Q.

Let's discuss how the XenDesktop solution architectures meet these user group requirements and benefit the business.

- **The GPU pass-through**: It is also called the Dedicated GPU that provisions each physical GPU to single desktop (single user) or server (multi user) virtual machine. The NVidia GPU pass-through technology supports directly connecting a dedicated GPU to a virtual machine through a hypervisor. By using this, the full GPU and the graphics memory capabilities can be allocated to a single virtual machine without any resource compromise. Citrix has built this capability into the XenServer hypervisor, and thus, it can be used for the VMs that run on the XenServer hosts. In case of the graphic cards that have multiple GPUs, the XenServer GPU pass-through will allow a 1:1 physical GPU assignment to the virtual machines. This lets the users connect to the same hypervisor host, and be able to receive a dedicated GPU. This model best suits the professional designing and engineering users who require the ultra-high end 3D graphics capabilities.

- **Virtual GPU (vGPU)**: NVidia GRID vGPU is the advanced technology that enables sharing the true GPU hardware acceleration between multiple virtual desktops without compromising the graphics experience. The physical GPU resources are managed by the NVidia GRID GPU Manager on the hypervisor. In the vGPU technology, the graphics commands of each virtual machine are sent directly to the GPU without involving translation by the hypervisor software. The underlying GPU hardware is time-sliced to deliver the ultimate performance for the shared virtualized graphics requirements. The GRID vGPU supports up to eight users (virtual machines) for sharing each physical GPU in a balanced approach. Thus, an NVidia GRID card having four physical GPUs can support 32 users (virtual machines). This technology provides exceptional graphics performance specifically for the virtual desktops that are equivalent to the local PCs, while sharing a GPU among multiple users. It is recommended for the mid-range to the high-end graphic users, such as operators and contractors (power users).

Following is a pictorial representation of the XenDesktop solution architectures depicting the major user groups and the recommended NVidia GPU models:

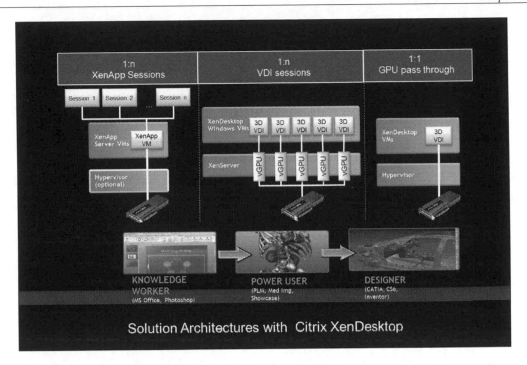

Solution Architectures with Citrix XenDesktop

Implementing XenDesktop® 3D solutions using NVidia GRID technology

Implementing the XenDesktop GPU solution involves various steps, such as choosing the right hardware, configuring the Citrix delivery protocol technology HDX 3D Pro. This also follows the five layer modular architecture designing.

Following are the overall high level steps that are required for achieving a successful implementation of the XenDesktop GPU solution:

1. Choose the Citrix and NVidia GRID certified server hardware.

2. Install or Upgrade your hypervisor to the recommended and the latest version.

3. Install and configure the NVidia GRID manager and the vGPU pack on the hypervisor through **Command Line (CLI)**.

4. Provision a base image (VDA) with the vGPU type by choosing an appropriate vGPU user profile.

5. Install the NVidia GPU guest OS drivers on the base image system (VDA).

6. Install the Hypervisor Tools (that is, the XenServer Tools) on the base image system (VDA).

7. Install the Citrix HDX 3D Pro VDA software on the base image system (VDA).

8. Provision and publish the desktops by using the new base image system (VDA).

9. Verify the GPU sharing by multiple desktops by using the various monitoring tools that are available.

Steps to implement the GPU sharing environment using Citrix® XenDesktop®, XenServer®, and NVidia GRID

Following are the steps for implementing the GPU sharing environment by using the Citrix XenDesktop, XenServer, and NVidia GRID:

1. Choose the Citrix XenServer and NVidia GRID certified server hardware, as follows:

   ○ Refer to the Citrix XenServer hardware compatibility list, as shown here:

     ○ GPU Pass-through Devices: `http://hcl.vmd.citrix.com/GPUPass-throughDeviceList.aspx`

     ○ Virtual GPU Devices: `http://hcl.vmd.Citrix.com/vGPUDeviceList.aspx`

   ○ Refer to the NVidia GRID certified server hardware list by visiting `http://www.nvidia.com/object/enterprise-virtualization-where-to-buy.html`.

   ○ Refer to Citrix Tested Hardware for the HDX 3D Pro Feature in XenDesktop, which can be found at `http://support.Citrix.com/article/CTX131385`.

   ○ Refer to the chosen vendor hardware model documentation to see the GPU options that are available. For example, you can find the various GPU options for Dell PowerEdge R730 by visiting `http://configure.us.dell.com/dellstore/config.aspx?oc=pe_r730_1356&model_id=poweredge-r730&c=us&l=en&s=bsd&cs=04`.

     ○ GPU options will be shown up upon selecting "Upgrade to Two Intel Xeon E5-2603 v3 1.6GHz,15M Cache,6.40GT/s QPI,No Turbo,No HT,6C/6T (85W) [Included in Price]" option in "Additional Processor' section.

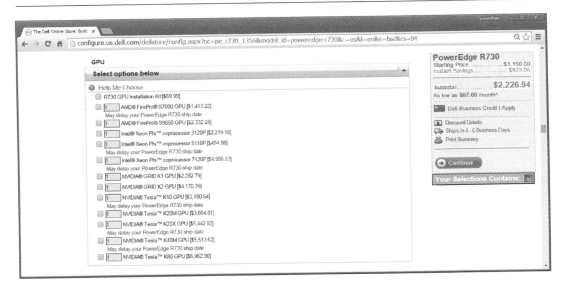

2. Download the Citrix XenServer and NVidia GRID software, as shown here:

   ○ Download the appropriate GRID Drivers from `www.nvidia.com/drivers`. It includes the NVidia Virtual GPU Manager as a `.RPM` drivers installation file (that is Red Hat Package Manager) for XenServer, and the NVidia drivers for Windows 7 32-bit/64-bit.

   ○ Alternatively, you can download the NVidia drivers for Windows 7 32-bit/64-bit from either `http://www.nvidia.in/Download/index.aspx` or `http://www.nvidia.in/Download/Scan.aspx`.

   ○ Download the Citrix 3D Graphics Pack, which is included in the XenServer 6.2.0 Service Pack 1, and it can be found either at `http://support.Citrix.com/article/CTX139788?_ga=1.55055913.3 83094160.1419336296` or you can refer to `https://www.Citrix.com/go/private/vgpu.html`. The latter will give you the up-to-date software versions.

3. Install the Citrix 3D Graphics Pack on the Citrix XenServer, as follows:

   ○ Ensure that you are running the latest/recommended version of BIOS for your server hardware as recommended in the Citrix XenServer Hardware Compatibility list.

- ° Start with a fresh XenServer (minimum version 6.2) or upgrade to version 6.2 if you are running a lower version of XenServer.
- ° Copy and install the Service Pack 1 on the XenServer 6.2, which includes the Citrix 3D Graphics Pack. Following are the XenServer CLI commands for doing so:

```
xe patch-upload -s <XenServer IP> -u root -pw
<rootuserpassword> file-name=XS62ESP1.xsupdate
```

The preceding command will return an UUID of the uploaded update file.

```
xe -s <XenServer IP> -u root -pw <rootuserpassword> patch-
pool-apply uuid=<UUID returned by the above command>
```

4. Install the NVidia Virtual GPU Manager on Citrix XenServer, as follows:
   - ° Login to the XenServer Console (Domain0) through SSH as a root user
   - ° Copy the downloaded GRID Drivers .rpm file (which includes the NVidia Virtual GPU Manager) to the XenServer
   - ° Set the XenServer in the maintenance mode and then reboot
   - ° Install the NVidia Virtual GPU Manager by using the following command, and then reboot.

     ```
     rpm -ivh <filename.rpm>
     ```

   - ° Verify that the GRID package has installed and loaded correctly by using the following command:

     ```
     lsmod | grep nvidia
     ```

   - ° Verify the vGPU types that will be displayed after the driver installation has been completed, as shown here:

     ```
     xe vgpu-type-list
     ```

   - ° Exit XenServer from the maintenance mode

5. In case of the clustered GPU hosts, specify the GPU placement policy that is to be used and the GPU types that are to be made available for the VMs under the XenServer Host GPU section, as follows:
   - ° GPU Placement Policy
   - ° Allow the GPU types that you want to assign to your VMs

Following is a screenshot of the XenServer Host GPU section showing the preceding settings:

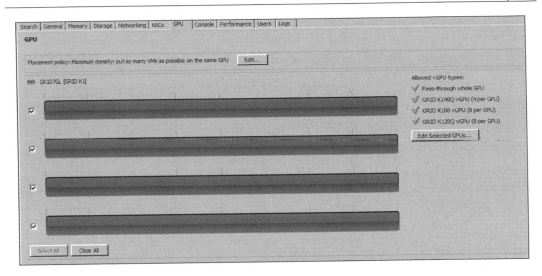

6. Create the Master Image VM with vGPU, as shown here:

   ○ Create a new VM and assign vGPU by selecting the options shown here from the drop down box:

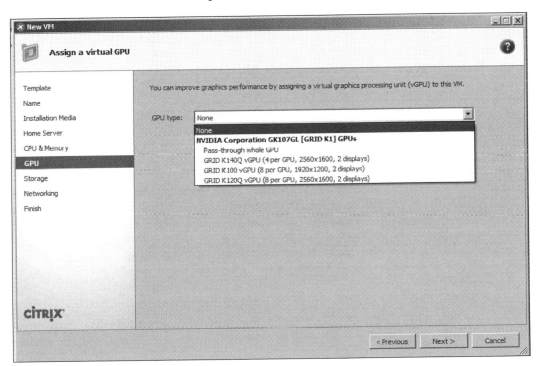

    ◦   Install the Windows OS and NVidia GPU guest OS driver (this is available in the NVidia GRID vGPU Pack, which you have already downloaded for the XenServer installation)

    ◦   Verify the NVidia drivers installation by accessing the NVidia Control Panel and nView Desktop Manager Wizard

7. Install the XenServer Tools.

8. Install the Citrix HDX 3D Pro VDA, as follows:

    ◦   From the XenDesktop source, install Virtual Delivery Agent for the Windows Desktop OS

    ◦   On the HDX 3D Pro screen, click on Yes, then install the VDA for HDX 3D Pro, and then complete the installation

9. Now, publish and verify the new Desktop by using the new GPU based Master Image.

We'll learn how to configure the XenDesktop Graphics and the HDX 3D Pro VDA Policy settings under the *Virtual display* sub-section of *Advanced fine-tuning of XenDesktop* section in this chapter.

Consider the following points carefully while implementing GPU environment:

- Mixing the heterogeneous graphic cards on the server is not recommended.
- The NVidia Display settings will not be available when using Remote Desktop Connection for connecting to the VMs.
- The Citrix HDX 3D Pro doesn't support full screen applications, though there is an experimental support for it, which can be enabled by using registry tweaks.
- Ensure that your business applications are certified or supported with the versions of OpenGL, OpenCL, Microsoft DirectX, CUDA and the other capabilities of your NVidia GPU card.
- The latest version of the NVidia GRID vGPU drivers officially supports OpenGL 4.4 and DirectX 11.
- Refer to the NVidia tested and supported ISV applications. A list of these can be found at `http://www.nvidia.com/object/gpu-applications.html?All`.
- Only the applications that are enhanced or certified for the GRID vGPU technologies can take the full benefit of the vGPU processing.

- There are a lot of vGPU monitoring and troubleshooting tools that are available. The very good tools among them include the Microsoft's Process Explorer that helps you in determining the GPU usage and CPU-Z, GPU-Z, and Geeks 3D GPU Caps Viewer which helps you in determining your vGPU capabilities and in testing them.

- You may use software, such as Redway 3D TurbineDemo, for benchmarking and fine-tuning your GPU capabilities and performance.

- The GPU monitoring, testing, and benchmarking tools are not supported in RDP session.

- In case of the Google Chrome browser based GPU solutions, you may find the Chrome browser GPU options by using `chrome://gpu` page.

- In case of the Microsoft Internet Explorer browser based GPU solution, ensure that you use the latest version of the browser. Internet Explorer auto fails over to software rendering on systems whose video card does not support the GPU hardware acceleration, and therefore, the performance will be slower.

- While testing the application performance with GPU, pay attention to the evaluation of the application at each of the Citrix Console session (through XenCenter), at the RDP sessions, and then at the ICA sessions.

Unified Communications Solutions (UCS) - audio and video conferencing applications

The conferencing applications are critical for the online and remote user collaboration, which involves live streaming of the audio and video media content. These applications can directly impact the business productivity. It is a critical challenge for the businesses to support all of the conferencing applications and their availability for a successful collaboration among the internal and the external users. Quite a lot of conferencing applications have been made available in the market, and these majorly include Microsoft Lync, GoToMeeting, WebEx, Softphones, Skype, and so on, and these are generically referred to as **Unified Communications Solutions (UCS)**. The users expect the virtual UCS apps to have the same high definition user experience and responsiveness as that of a locally installed instance.

Challenges with UCS - audio and video conferencing applications

Migrating the UC applications from the physical endpoint to the virtual datacenter desktop environment possess various challenges. A unique challenge with the UC applications is that they closely integrate with the various peripheral devices, such as built-in cameras and webcam for video, and speakers and mic for audio. Furthermore, the user experience depends on the network bandwidth for the live streaming of the audio and the video content. Thus, migration of the UC applications from the physical desktop to the datacenter results in the following major challenges:

- The final destination for the UCS traffic isn't the virtual UCS application, but the end user device. This change results in the additional/duplicate decompression and recompression activities. From the user's device, the audio and video content is compressed and sent to the server. The server decompresses this incoming audio and video content before transmitting it to the user's device by recompressing it. This results in some loss of accuracy while reproducing the audio and video content on the user's device.

- The audio and video data streams compression and decompression activities are CPU intensive, and thus, these increase the load on the physical hypervisors, which impacts the VMs density per hypervisor hosts. This results in a datacenter server scalability issue.

- Furthermore, the UCS audio and video traffic is routed through the datacenter route causing an indirect traffic pattern. This, inevitably, increases the network bandwidth consumption and the server load which results in the audio and video quality degradation due to the transcoding and the incremental latency. This makes the UC applications in the virtual desktops across the WAN connections impractical.

- The virtual desktop connections between the user's device and the datacenter servers typically employ the TCP protocol. However, delivering real-time audio and video usually involves packet loss. Thus, the use of the TCP protocol for the UCS datastreams retransmissions, audio and visual lag, or any sync issues, may even fail or result in an application crash.

- The virtualized UCS application access to the user device peripherals is separated by the virtual layer. The virtual desktop requires including the appropriate compatible drivers for supporting the varying peripherals across the user devices.

XenDesktop® support for UCS (audio and video conferencing) applications

The Citrix XenDesktop has adopted two approaches for accommodating the UC applications in XenDesktop. These approaches are the *Generic* HDX RealTime technologies and the *Optimized* HDX RealTime architectures. We'll discuss both of these options and their high level technical differences.

Generic HDX RealTime technologies

By default, the XenDesktop generic HDX RealTime technologies are available for all the UC applications that are hosted on XenDesktop. These don't involve any modification of the UC applications, rather these use the built-in HDX capabilities for delivering the UC applications with the general possible optimizations. These employ the HDX Optimized-for-Speech codec and the Adaptive Display technologies for audio and video optimizations respectively. As a result, the media processing workload is placed on the XenDesktop hypervisor hosts. Use of Jitter buffering smooth's out the audio's ability of withstanding the variations in the network latencies. Furthermore, the audio latency is addressed by employing the UDP/RTP transport in the ICA protocol. The ICA protocol multi-stream options can be used for assigning the highest/appropriate priority for the audio traffic that enables the QoS routing on the network and reduces the latency in the audio path. HDX RealTime is also enabled with the Echo cancellation capabilities that are required while using the speakers and mics.

Optimized HDX RealTime technologies

Citrix optimized the XenDesktop, as well as partnered with the various UCS application vendors, to address the preceding challenges by enhancing the virtual UCS application performance for delivering the same local-like experience to all the users with the UCS solution of their choice. Citrix came up with improved designs which independently optimize XenDesktop for each UCS solution; thereby delivering the key improvements. They also address the preceding challenges.

- Network optimizations: The UC applications optimized for the XenDesktop transmits the compressed video directly between the user endpoints, avoiding indirect traffic patterns. These applications employ peer-to-peer line of communication that streamlines the traffic patterns and avoids sending any uncompressed video streams over the network. This makes the UC applications robust even across the WAN connections, and it also addresses the server scalability issues.

- Protocol optimizations: The XenDesktop connections are based on the ICA protocol that intelligently separates the audio and video traffic from the virtual desktop traffic. It enables the direct routing of audio and video datastreams between the endpoints over UDP/RTP.

- Server scalability: The peer-to-peer line of communication relocates the compression and decompression activities that are being processed, to the client devices, thereby significantly increasing the hypervisor host scalability in the data center.

The optimized architectures are designed to offload the resource demanding processing activities to the client devices, analogues to the multimedia redirection to the client side processing. In the optimized architectures the media processing engine component is moved to the client devices thus, relieving the processing load from the server side. With the use of the peer-to-peer protocol, the audio and video streams traffic flows directly between the two parties. This minimizes the network bandwidth consumption, avoids latency additions, and provides almost zero degradation of the audio and video quality.

Microsoft Lync is one of the most widely used UCS applications in the XenDesktop environments. The Citrix HDX optimized delivery of Microsoft Lync offers the best performance, scalability, and it also supports cross platforms. Following is a pictorial representation indicating the data flow of Microsoft Lync in the XenDesktop virtual infrastructure by using the optimized architectures with the peer-to-peer protocol, as well as the generic HDX path by using ICA.

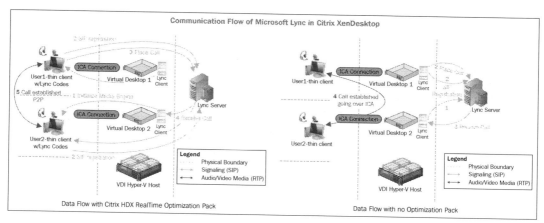

Diagram depicting the data flow of Microsoft Lync in XenDesktop

Local App Access (Reverse Seamless) for the UCS applications

The XenDesktop Local App Access features makes the locally installed desktop applications available to the virtual desktop. This can be another option for making certain UC applications viable on the XenDesktop environments. However, it results in certain limitations, such as the inability of application sharing since, the UC application runs, on the user device and the other user applications run in the XenDesktop virtual desktop.

XenDesktop® and UCS (audio and video conferencing) applications

We'll discuss the XenDesktop optimized applications, as well as the other major UCS applications, which can be implemented in the XenDesktop environment.

XenDesktop® optimized UCS applications

XenDesktop partnered with the major UCS application vendors, including Microsoft, Cisco, Avaya, and Vidyo, and it had their applications optimized for the XenDesktop environments, as follows:

- Microsoft Lync is fully optimized and supported by two methods — the first is Citrix Receiver for Windows Integration with the Lync VDI plug-in, and the other is HDX RealTime Optimization Pack for Microsoft Lync

- Cisco Jabber

- Avaya one-X Agent and Communicator

- VidyoDesktop

Other UCS applications and XenDesktop®

The other majorly used UCS applications have been listed here. These applications haven't yet been optimized exclusively for XenDesktop.

- Citrix GoToMeeting with HDFaces

- AdobeConnect

- Skype

- Cisco WebEx

Configuring the UCS applications in XenDesktop®

We'll discuss how to configure both the generic and the optimized UCS applications for the XenDesktop environment. If the speakers and the microphones are too close to each other, then they will result in echoes and cause disturbances. Headsets are recommended for audio and video conferences.

Optimized for XenDesktop® – Microsoft Lync

Citrix supports two alternate methods for an optimized delivery of Microsoft Lync from XenDesktop.

- Microsoft's Lync VDI Plug-in (media engine) has been designed as a plug-in for Citrix Receiver for Windows. It's the recommended option for the users of the Windows devices. In this scenario, Citrix Receiver for Windows version 4.03, and above, and the Lync VDI plugin need to be installed on the end users Windows devices. The actual Lync client software will be installed on the virtual desktop. The Lync VDI plug-in that is installed on the user's device will efficiently interact with the Lync client software on the virtual desktop.

- Citrix HDX RealTime Optimization Pack for Microsoft Lync is a highly scalable solution, and it is recommended for customers to support the users on Linux, Mac, and Windows devices. It is comprised of two key components.

    - The server side component - Citrix HDX RealTime Connector for Lync, runs in the virtual server environment alongside Microsoft Lync, and it communicates by signaling information over a Citrix ICA virtual channel to the RealTime Media Engine running on the user's device.

    - The client side component - Citrix HDX RealTime Media Engine, is a plug-in for Citrix Receiver, which is available for Windows, Linux, and Mac. It performs all the signaling and media processing directly on the user's device itself.

Both of these components seamlessly integrate with an existing Microsoft Lync environment on the client-side and the server-side.

These are the steps for configuring the Microsoft's Lync VDI Plug-in environment:

1. On the Lync server in the CsClientPolicy policy, configure the EnableMediaRedirection setting to True for all users. Use the following PowerShell command-let to update the status:

   ```
   Set-CsClientPolicy -Identity site:Central -EnableMediaRedirection
   $True (Site level policy)
   ```

2. Install Citrix Receiver for Windows 4.03 or later on the user's device.

3. Install Lync VDI Plug-in on the user's Windows device:

   ○ For a proper pairing of the Lync VDI plugin, the Lync client software must *not* be running on the end user's device

   ○ Ensure that the Lync VDI Plug-in, Office, Citrix Receiver for Windows, and the Windows system are of the same bit, that is, all of them are of either 32-bit or 64-bit

4. Install the Lync Server certificate on the end user's device, as well as on the server hosting the desktops.

5. Install the Lync 2013 full client on all the virtual machines (by installing it on the Master image).

Users can connect to the XenDesktop session and log into the Lync client on the virtual desktop, which will pair with the Lync VDI Plug-in, that is running on the end user's device. Upon successful pairing, the user can see his or her presence on the Lync compatible devices that are connected to the local computer. The user can now place and answer calls as usual.

The following procedure explains how to configure Citrix HDX RealTime Optimization Pack for Microsoft Lync:

1. Install the server side component Citrix HDX RealTime Connector for Lync, as follows:

   ○ Install HDX RealTime Connector on the virtual desktops that are running VDA

   ○ Restart the virtual desktops

2. Install the client side component HDX RealTime Media Engine on the clients' devices, as shown here:

   ○ Install HDX RealTime Media Engine on the user's device, such as Windows, Linux, or Mac

   ○ Install the camera/webcam device and the respective drivers for proper integration and stability

Generic UCS application – Citrix® GoToMeeting

Citrix GoToMeeting is one of the most widely used UCS application. It uses the generic HDX technologies and capabilities for delivering audio and video streams. Citrix currently only supports the audio and recording features of GoToMeeting when it is installed in the XenDesktop environments. A diligent assessment is required for implementing the UCS application by using the generic HDX capabilities in XenDesktop.

The steps shown here will help you in configuring Citrix GoToMeeting in the XenDesktop environment:

1. Download the Citrix GoToMeeting MSI installer from `http://support.Citrixonline.com/meeting/all_files/G2M010013`.

2. Pay attention to the latest note messages, which will tell you what features are supported in the XenDesktop virtual environment.

3. Install the Citrix GoToMeeting software on the virtual desktops that run VDAs or the master image.

4. Install the appropriate audio and video devices, along with their vendor drivers on the user devices.

5. By default, in HDX, echo cancellation is enabled. Its effectiveness is sensitive to the distance between the speakers and the microphone. The devices should neither be too close nor be too far from each other. This setting can be controlled by using the following registry key: `HKLM\SOFTWARE\Citrix\ICA Client\Engine\Configuration\Advanced\Modules\ClientAudio\EchoCancellation`

6. The recommended Citrix Policies for achieving a good performance are as follows:

   ◦ Set **Audio Quality** to **Medium – optimized for speech**
   ◦ Enable **Audio over UDP real-time transport**
   ◦ Ensure **Client audio redirection** is **Allowed** (it is allowed by default)
   ◦ Ensure **Client microphone redirection** is **Allowed** (it is allowed by default)

Important points about Citrix GoToMeeting in the XenDesktop environment are given here:

- Citrix GoToMeeting is not fully optimized for the XenDesktop environment. However, with generic HDX capabilities, the application launches without any glitches in the virtual desktops.

- The Citrix GoToMeeting performance starts degrading when there is an increase in both the number of participants and the number of features in-use (screen sharing, recording, chatting, and so on).

- The CPU load on the hypervisors increases in proportion to the increase in the number of participants and their activities. Even the addition of GPU capabilities doesn't produce any noticeable change.

- GoToMeeting automatically detects if it's running in the XenApp virtual environments and it disables the audio options in the application since GoToMeeting is not supported in the XenApp environments. Following is a registry tweak for experimenting with audio GoToMeeting in the XenApp environments:

```
C:\>reg add "HKCU\Software\Citrix\GoToMeeting" /v XenAppVoIP /T
REG_SZ /F /D true
The operation completed successfully.


C:\>
```

Streaming media applications through HDX technology

It is a common use of a desktop environment to be able to stream media content, which is usually of high quality (HD), at higher speeds or even instantly. It is also of business importance, where the users would need the ability of viewing rich streaming media content of a live or recorded meetings, seminars, online tutorial videos, and entertainment. It is also used as a vehicle for marketing products and services. Providing a rich streaming media experience is critical for the service providers of DaaS. We'll see how the desktop virtualization helps streaming media users in general, and we will discuss the XenDesktop capabilities which provide rich streaming media experiences in particular.

Components of streaming media and its setup in the traditional desktop environment

Streaming media essentially consists of a remote server, which streams the media to the client systems running on their respective Media player applications. As the communication between the remote server and the client system occurs over a network, the network bandwidth plays a key role in the overall end user streaming media experience. The higher the bandwidth, the faster the streaming would be, and this lets the user get uninterrupted streams, and it also enables viewing content in high resolution and high definition. The most common streaming media applications include Flash Player, Windows Media Player, QuickTime, RealPlayer, and so on. These players would run as standalone or as browser add-on applications. As streaming media refers to the incoming data from an external network, they are often subjected to go through the Proxy server for security scanning purposes.

In traditional desktop environments, each desktop user will make a connection to the remote streaming server and the overall network bandwidth will be shared across all the users in the office. In the advanced environments, bandwidth restrictions may be either set per connection or set for the overall network. It is expected that the streaming server and the media player application can optimize the overall performance in case of low bandwidth or overloaded usage scenarios, which usually result in degraded or interrupted streaming media experience.

XenDesktop streaming media capabilities

XenDesktop supports the Citrix HDX MediaStream technology, which provides the streaming media capabilities for the virtual desktops. The HDX MediaStream technologies are to deliver any media format from any media player over any network connection to any device. It includes technologies for streaming the media files to the client's device for playing media through the local codecs with seamless embedding in the remote session. The HDX MediaStream Windows Media Redirection technology improves the performance of the Windows Media player and compatible players, which run on the virtual desktops. The HDX MediaStream Flash Redirection capability provides the IT admins control over the widely used Adobe Flash Player for streaming media. In addition, the other HDX capabilities, such as intelligent network detection and redirection, multicast support, audio delivery over UDP/RTP, and the de-duplication of network traffic at the ICA network protocol level, greatly improves the streaming media user experience in the XenDesktop environment. We'll discuss the Flash redirection for streaming media in detail, as it's the most widely used application for animations, videos, and other applications.

The HDX MediaStream Flash Redirection

The HDX MediaStream Flash Redirection offloads the fetching and processing of Adobe Flash content to the user (Windows or Linux) devices whenever possible. When the Adobe Flash content cannot be redirected to the user device, the technology attempts to gracefully fall back to the server-side rendering. Thus, it reduces the streaming media load at the datacenter server and network levels. This results in a greater scalability of the datacenter resources without impacting the user experience. Furthermore, Flash Redirection is designed to be seamless, which makes it unnoticeable by the users. Configuring Flash Redirection requires both the server-side and the client-side settings. The intelligent network detection and the client side user settings and responses enable the Flash content to be played from the server itself, which is called the server-side rendering/fetching. This behavior is configurable through the client and the service side policy settings.

Following is a pictorial representation of the intelligent network detection of Flash Redirection. It covers the various possible cases and shows the rendering mode used (either on the client-side or on the server-side).

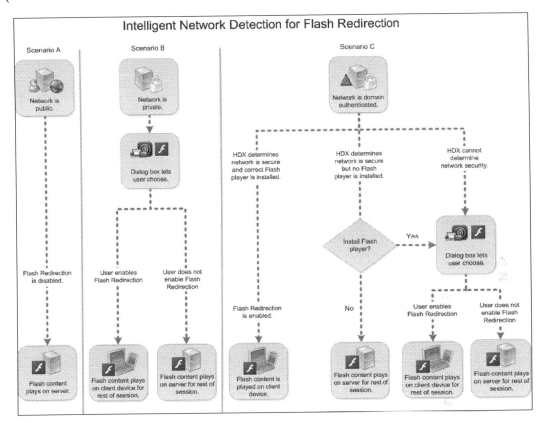

The client-side Flash rendering is most suitable for the business cases where the endpoints have access to reliable and decent speed Internet (say, a minimum of 1Mbps and above). For the scenarios where the endpoints don't have internet access, or have low/unreliable internet access, the server-side Flash rendering works well.

Configuring XenDesktop® for streaming media

Configuring XenDesktop for streaming media essentially involves installing the supported media player software and then configuring the respective policy settings on both the server-side (VDAs) and the client-side. We'll learn how to configure Flash Redirection on both the server-side and the client-side to achieve the Flash acceleration.

Configuring HDX MediaStream Flash Redirection

Configuring Flash Redirection requires both the server-side and client-side settings. The version of Adobe Flash, the XenDesktop VDA, as well as the Receiver used for accessing the desktops can affect the Flash Redirection. The browser's version (and its integration with the Flash Player plugin) will have the largest impact on the specific Flash Redirection behavior that could be experienced in your environment.

- You need to do the following to configure Flash Redirection on the server: by default, the Flash Redirection is enabled on the server side with the optimal default settings. One needs to ensure that the settings shown here are in-place in the XenDesktop policies:

    1. Install Adobe Flash Player on VDA (that is, the master image)

    2. Configure the Citrix XenDesktop **Adobe Flash Redirection** Policies, as follows:

        ○ Ensure, Flash Acceleration (setting name **Flash Redirection**), is **Enabled** (it is enabled by default)

        ○ Set **Flash default behavior** to **Enable Flash acceleration**

        ○ Ensure that **Flash intelligent fallback** is **Enabled** (it is enabled by default)

        ○ Ensure that **Flash event logging** is **Enabled** (it is enabled by default)

        ○ Use the remaining Flash settings for further customizations

- The following steps will show you how to configure Flash Redirection on the user's device:

    1. Install Citrix Receiver.

    2. Install Adobe Flash Player.

    3. While accessing Flash Content, the users will automatically be prompted to allow the Flash content redirection. This setting can be centrally configured by the domain administrator by using the AD Group policies, as explained later.

    4. Upon successful Flash Redirection, the redirected content will be played under a separate sub-process called **HDX MediaStream For Flash Client (v2) EXE** (that is, **PseudoContainer2.exe**).

    5. When you switch to full screen mode, the Flash Player pops out of your virtual desktop and appear same as the local instance.

- Configure the HDX MediaStream Flash Redirection settings on the users' devices with Active Directory Group Policy Objects, as follows:

1. Import the HDX MediaStream for Flash – Client administrative template file `HdxFlash-Client.adm` (which ships along with Receiver installation).

2. Select the **Enable HDX MediaStream Flash Redirection on the user device** setting under the **HDX MediaStream Flash Redirection – Client** section, as shown here:

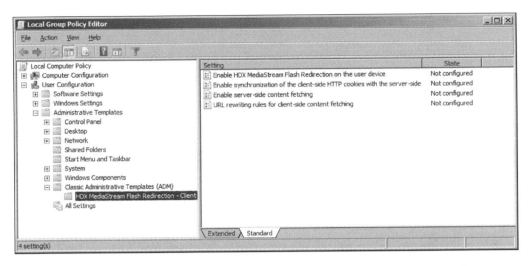

- The following lists the best practices for configuring the HDX MediaStream Flash Redirection:

  1. Ensure that the same Adobe Flash version is used on VDA as well as on the user's device for better optimization. On the user's device, it can be of a higher version than on VDA. If the version mismatches, then the user will be notified that **A different version of Flash Player is required**, as shown in the following screenshot:

2. Adobe ships Flash Player for Internet Explorer as an ActiveX plugin and as a general plugin for all the other browsers. Pay attention to the Flash Player that you are configuring on VDA and the users' devices.

3. Security requirements should be considered while implementing the Flash Content redirection, as the Flash content runs under the Flash player on the user's device.

4. Adobe Flash Player on the 64-bit Internet Explorer is currently not supported. Use the 32-bit Internet Explorer even on the 64-bit operating systems.

5. Use Internet Explorer Compatibility View for the websites that have trouble playing the Flash content. Some of the website specific issues can be resolved by enabling the Emulation mode in Internet Explorer.

Secured Internet access through web filtering

Filtering the user's Internet access is required in highly secured environments for protecting the systems and sensitive information from security risks. For certain businesses, such as financial investments, insurance, government agencies, a compliance policy may make it mandatory to secure the user's Internet access through web filtering. It is also usually requested in case of third party DaaS service provider, to filter the user's web access. Quite a lot of web filtering technologies exist as the physical/virtual network appliance and as a software product. We'll learn how to choose a best match for this and then we will learn how to integrate it with your overall XenDesktop virtual desktop infrastructure.

Web filtering technologies and their options

Web filters have been designed in various forms, which are in accordance with the changing IT security requirements. They are available as a standalone product as well as a featured component of other security software suites. They are available as a physical appliance, virtual appliance, application, and cloud solution. To handle the security of the ever-changing scenarios, most web filters have come up with the categorized lists of websites that are very frequently updated. Any website that user's attempt to visit would usually fall under its respective category. Administrators can define both the allowed websites and the blocked websites rules for the website categories as suitable for their environment. The overhead for identifying and configuring every malicious website is simplified by doing this. It covers the up-to-date statuses of websites. Most of the web filter vendors rely on an open source antivirus engine called ClamAV for detecting trojans, viruses, malwares, and other malicious threats. It's used by Barracuda, Untangle, and so on.

There are also other website categories database providers, such as WebGrade, BrightCloud Web Classification Service, McAfee TrustedSource Web Database, and so on. As a security best practice, almost all of the web filters do not provide any APIs for automation.

 Please refer to http://en.wikipedia.org/wiki/Content-control_software for additional details on the web filtering technologies.

There are plenty of security products and vendors that provide the web filtering applications. There are also Citrix certified web filter products, which are tested for the virtual environments, such as XenDesktop and XenApp. However, web filters mostly fall under the broader scope of the network and security of your overall environment. It requires diligent assessment of both the Citrix certified and the other web filters against your requirements. Following are a couple of the most widely used web filter solution vendors:

- WebSense
- iPrism Web Security (Citrix certified)
- Barracuda
- UnTangle
- WatchGuard
- Linux SQUID proxy

Web filters, along the lines of networking devices, can be majorly configured in the modes shown here:

- The in-line mode: The web filter will be directly connected to a server, as follows:

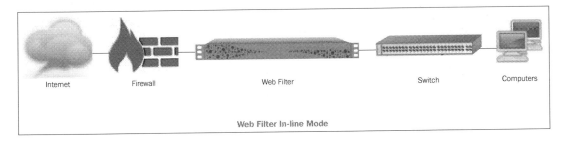

Web Filter In-line Mode

- The forward proxy mode: The web filter will be connected between your LAN switch and your firewall, and it will scan all the LAN traffic, as shown in this diagram:

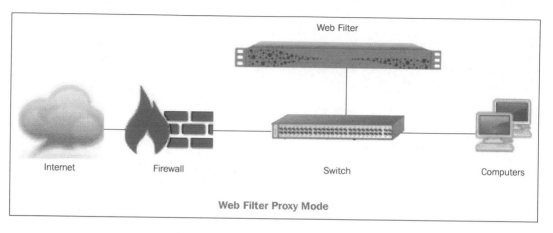

Web Filter Proxy Mode

Integrating web filtering technologies with XenDesktop®

Web filters can be configured in the various modes depending on the kind of web filter solution. In most enterprise environments, the web filter (either in the appliance or the software mode) is installed and configured by either the network or the security teams. The web filters can be integrated into the XenDesktop environments by using the following methods:

- In cases where the web filters are implemented on the network layer as a gateway, all the traffic will be automatically routed through the web filter.

- Usually, the XenDesktop administrators are given the web filter IP and the Port details for configuring them as a proxy server on the virtual desktops. The XenDesktop administrators can configure the web filter proxy details in the Internet Explorer, by using the **Proxy server** option. The IE proxy server settings can be configured in various modes, such as:

    ○ By specifying them in the Master Image IE options
    ○ Updating them through Registry by using the user logon script
    ○ Deploying them by using the Active Directory group policy setting, which is given here:

    ```
    User Configuration\Windows Settings\Internet Explorer
    Maintenance\Connection\Proxy Settings
    ```

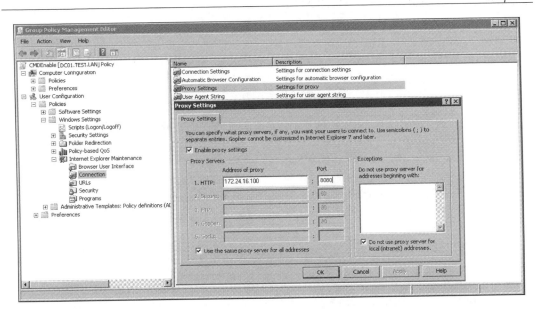

- In cases where web filters are configured on the network as the **WPAD (Web Proxy Autodiscovery Protocol)** servers at DHCP and DNS, all the traffic will automatically be routed through the web filter by enabling the **Automatically detect configuration settings** setting in the Internet Explorer options.

The other major challenge with integrating web filters into the Windows domain and the XenDesktop environment is with user authentication. Most web filters support the user authentication capability, which is usually required by the software itself for the user based licensing model. In order to support the Windows domain authentication, the device is required to integrate with Windows Active Directory or at least support the LDAP to communicate with the Active Directory. If the web filter supports integrated authentication, then no further action needs to be taken by the XenDesktop administrators. In cases similar to these, the software based web filters, such as GFI WebMonitor, suit well.

Further consideration for DaaS service providers

The DaaS service providers have advanced web filtering requirements that are to be met in accordance with several of their customer needs. An ideal solution for this is to consider web filters per customer and maintain its configuration separately. However, it makes the services costlier for the smaller customers. Most of the times, the DaaS service providers require sharing the web filter across customers. This needs more consideration for maintaining the isolation of the user accounts, authentications, network ranges, and so on, for the same web filter.

For easier understanding, let's say that you are a DaaS service provider with two customers each having 10 desktop users. You need to implement a web filtering solution for both the customers. Considering this as a business model, you want to implement a single web filter for both the customers and expand it as the load increases. In this scenario, consider the following:

- Implementing the user authentication will become a major challenge. As an alternate, you can install the web filter in a workgroup (non-domain based) and let both customers' users connect to it as unauthenticated users by using an IP-address.

- Choosing the web filter mode is another challenge. This will have to be setup in in-line, forward proxy, or gateway mode. The in-line mode makes the application to be available to the VMs of system to which Web Filter appliance is connected. Thus, choosing either the forward proxy or the gateway mode will serve the desktop VMs of both the customers well.

- The network configuration of web filter should be done in such a way that it's accessible to the VMs of both the customers. Usually, it should be configured in a separate network, which will be accessible to both the customer networks. Furthermore, installing multiple NICs on web filters and configuring them for each customer will help in separating the customer's traffic.

- Usually the customers, in accordance with their corporate policies, compliance policies, or for any other reasons, need the custom notification message to be displayed when any activity is blocked. Achieving this needs digging into the customization options that are available with the chosen web filter.

Secured virtual desktops through policy restrictions

Restricting the users' access to the virtual desktops by using the administrative policy restrictions is a general practice. By default, the normal Windows domain users have restricted access to the system and they will be prompted for elevated credentials for any administrative activities. However, for certain user groups (such as interns, contractors, or temporary workers) disabling specific features (such as accessing their local/external drives, launching the command shell programs, launching the control panel wizards, downloading executables, and so on) is required. These stringent restrictions can be implemented by using the various built-in Windows Group Policy settings and other firewall applications.

Windows group policies and registry restrictions

Most of the Windows desktop and user policies would be in-place in the Windows enterprise environments. Importantly, these policies can be applied to the Windows desktops and its users in the XenDesktop environment without making any changes. We'll discuss certain settings, which are considered as restrictions, and are most commonly needed and expected to be applied by the service provider under highly secured environments.

The consolidated policy settings listed here are only for reference purposes and they need to be evaluated properly for implementation purposes.

General restrictions

Following are the various general restrictions employed in highly secured environments:

- Hide or remove the clock from the system tray: The Windows system and its communication over a network uses time value for all the communication establishments.

- Remove lock computer: This is required in the scenarios where you are configuring the users so that they are auto logged-in to the desktop VMs and your users don't know their passwords. This is often the case for contractor/ temporary employees or service providers.

- Disable the client drive mapping/access within the session: By default, the user local system drives will be mapped and made available for access in the XenDesktop desktop session. This will let users read and write data from and to the virtual desktop and their local system. Considering data theft and security risk incidents, it's recommended to disable the mapping of the user drives in the virtual desktop. Either use `HKCU\Software\Microsoft\Windows\CurrentVersion\Policies\Explorer` registry setting –or- the Citrix policy **ICA\File Redirection\Client drive redirection** setting for doing this.

- Set **User Access Control (UAC)** to be in the most restricted mode so that any administrative activities by the users will result in administrative credentials prompt.

- Disable all the service control accesses, including start, stop, disable, and so on.

- The software restriction policies are as follows:
  - ° Restrict the execution of all the shell (command shell and PowerShell, and so on) and administrative programs by specifying the file type extensions for the designated file types, such as BAT, CHM, CMD, COM, EXE, HTA, INF, LNK, MDB, MSC, MSI, MST, MSP, OCX, PIF, REG, SCR, VB, WSC, and so on.
  - ° Enable all the system software by allowing unrestricted access to the `.exe` files from the system path, as shown here:
    - ° `%HKLM\SOFTWARE\Microsoft\Windows NT\CurrentVersion\SystemRoot%`
    - ° `%HKLM\SOFTWARE\Microsoft\Windows NT\CurrentVersion\SystemRoot%*.exe`
    - ° `%HKLM\SOFTWARE\Microsoft\Windows NT\CurrentVersion\SystemRoot%System32\*.exe`
    - ° `%HKLM\SOFTWARE\Microsoft\Windows\CurrentVersion\ProgramFilesDir%`

- Start menu and taskbar\turn off user tracking: By default, the Windows system tracks the programs that the user runs. The system uses this information to customize the Windows features, such as showing the frequently used programs in the Start menu. It's not required in the restricted environments.

- Restrict My Computer and its properties: Set the **Remove Computer icon on the desktop** and **Remove Properties from the Computer icon context menu** policies. In a restricted environment, disabling access to My Computer and its properties is often required.

Completely locked down or restricted service provider environments

Following are the general restrictions that are imposed in the service provider environments:

- The system level restrictions are as follows:
  - ° Disable the Windows Automatic Updates
  - ° Prevent access to the command prompt, but do not disable the command prompt script processing

- Restrict Windows Explorer Shell and its components, as shown here:
  - ° Do not list Computers Near Me and Entire Network in Network Locations

- Remove the File menu, Search button, default context menu, **Map Network Drive**, and **Disconnect Network Drive**
- Remove the Folder Options item from the **Tools** menu

- Disable accessing Printer Configurations: Set the options given here under **User Configuration/Administrative Templates/Control Panel/Printers**:
  - Prevent addition and deletion of printers
  - Disable browse the network and browse a common website for finding printers
  - Disable default Active Directory path when searching for printers

- Hide all the system and special folder icons from Desktop and Explorer, as follows:
  - Hide/Remove the desktop icons, such as Computer, My Documents, Recycle Bin, Desktop Cleanup, Internet Explorer, Network Locations, and so on
  - Remove Properties from the context menu of Computer, Documents, and the Recycle Bin icons
  - Prohibit the user from manually redirecting the Profile Folders
  - Do not add shares of the recently opened documents to Network Locations
  - Don't save settings upon exit

- Restrict the user from accessing the Start menu and Taskbar actions by enabling the following settings:
  - Prevent adding, dragging, dropping and closing the Taskbar's toolbars. Do not display any custom toolbars in the taskbar
  - Prohibit adjusting the desktop toolbars
  - Do not keep the history and clear the history of the recently opened documents upon exit
  - Gray the unavailable Windows Installer programs from the Start menu shortcuts
  - Hide the notification area and turn off the notification area cleanup and personalized menus
  - Lock the Taskbar and prevent the grouping of the taskbar items. Prevent the user from being able to make any changes to the Taskbar and the Start menu settings
  - Remove access to the context menus of the taskbar

- ○ Remove and prevent access to the Shut Down, Restart, Sleep, and Hibernate commands. Remove the following from the Start menu:
  - ○ The All Programs list and the Pinned programs list
  - ○ The Common program groups
  - ○ Balloon Tips, as well as the Drag-and-drop and context menus
  - ○ Logoff, Network Connections, User name, User's folders
  - ○ Icon items: Documents, Music, Network, Pictures
  - ○ Menu items: Favorites, Help, Recent Items, Run
  - ○ Link items: Default Programs, Search, User folder, Windows Update

Further resources

Microsoft provides a complete list of the Group Policy Settings Reference for Windows and Windows Server. You can download it from `http://www.microsoft.com/en-us/download/details.aspx?id=25250`.

Citrix® policy restrictions

Some of the Citrix policies that can be configured so as to restrict certain types of accesses to the system, and the devices in session for the users, are as follows:

- Disable the client clipboard mapping: Prevent the clipboard on the client device from being mapped to the clipboard on the server. This will prevent the cut-and-paste data transfer between a session and the local clipboard. Users can still cut and paste data between applications that are running in the sessions.

- Disable all the file redirection options: The file redirection settings allow us to configure the client floppy, optical, fixed, network, and removable drives redirection to the session. Don't allow any of these until they are required. Furthermore, consider disabling the auto connection of the client drives.

- Disable the client USB plug and play device redirection: In view of the security risks caused by the USB devices, it's recommended that we disable the support for the client USB plug and play device redirection to the XenDesktop session.

- Disable the auto creation and redirection of the clients' printers in session: It's not always important to auto create the clients' printers as it delays the session launch time.

- Disable the wait for printers to be created setting: Disable the wait setting as it introduces a delay in connecting to a session till the desktop printers are auto-created.

- Enable Flash Acceleration: It's recommended to enable the Flash redirection for improving the user experience and saving data center resources. However, from a security perspective, the Flash content and player constantly communicate with the desktop, and thus, they will have access to the desktop resources. Always ensure that all the security updates for Flash on the client and the server have been applied.

- Enable the setting ICA keep alive: The ICA sessions are considered as idle and they get disconnected if no user action is detected. In case of broken sessions, this becomes an undesirable behavior. The ICA keep alive setting addresses this issue by automatically sending keep-alive messages to the server, and thus, avoids the session from being disconnected.

- Disable the client COM and LPT port redirections: The LPT port is used by the legacy application that explicitly prints to the LPT port instead of printing objects. The LPT port is not generally needed by the latest applications. Similarly, the COM port is used by specific applications and it is not generally needed. One needs to assess both the COM and LPT port access required applications for the virtual desktops well before making them available to the end users.

Further resources

Either refer to the complete Citrix Policy Reference that is provided and updated by Citrix at `http://support.Citrix.com/article/CTX135039` or you can refer to the Citrix live eDocs at `http://support.citrix.com/proddocs/topic/xenapp-xendesktop-76/xad-policies-settings-wrapper.html`.

Virtual desktops through low bandwidth remote and mobile user connections

Users connecting from their home network or their remote office WAN connections usually experience low bandwidth connections. Also, on-the-go mobile device users may connect from low or inconsistent network connections. The Citrix HDX technologies and the ICA protocol have built-in intelligence of dynamically optimizing to the changing network statuses and speeds. However, in scenarios where the users are constantly connecting from low bandwidth networks, such as WAN, broadband and Wi-Fi, need specific configuration for optimized performance. Considering the remote access from home and mobile networks, a secured external access will fit well with the users who can connect from any device anywhere at any time. This involves creating an externally accessible StoreFront store URL with NetScaler for the HTML5 browser support, which the users can access easily.

Remote access from home PC broadband networks

During off-hours, remote access from the home PC is critical for business users. When the desktops are virtualized, the users still expect to be able to remotely access their virtual desktops from their remote/home PC environments, which are generally connected over a broadband connection. Today's broadband connections provide reasonable speeds and reliability. Thus, the home PC environments provide LAN like capabilities that include a desktop/computer hardware system, a desktop operating system, which supports the Receiver, a consistent Internet connectivity, a secure access to the corporate network through VPN, special firewall rules, and scanning. You can configure the same policy settings as that of local desktops for the home PC access. It includes redirecting Media (all Windows, Flash, UCS applications) and the graphics processing to leverage the user device capabilities, supporting the add-on devices, and so on. Its important to configure the virtual desktops to always be powered-up so that users can connect to it from their home PCs. To achieve this, disable the power management settings at the delivery group that contains the virtual desktops, which are accessible from home PC networks. In case of virtual desktops that are not powered on, XenDesktop will start them when the user connects. However, the virtual desktop startup during the user connection delays the overall connectivity to the desktop. Furthermore, it results in productivity loss in the event that any issues come up while bringing up the desktop. Thus, it's recommended that you ensure a readily accessible desktop, which can be made available for use from the home PC.

Remote office WAN connections

The remote office WAN connections greatly suffer from network latency due to geographical distance between the client and the server systems. Furthermore, the bandwidth availability affects all of the users' experiences as the number of user connections increases. Employing traditional solutions reduces network congestion, and any associated performance issues, to some extent, but it doesn't solve the actual WAN latency issue, as you can see here:

- You can increase the WAN bandwidth
- You can de-centralize the virtual desktops by setting up any one of the following options:
  - The XenDesktop servers in the branch offices
  - A complete virtual desktop delivery infrastructure in the branch offices
- Employing the network router QoS optimization for prioritizing the network traffic and improving the overall quality of service

To overcome the remote office WAN scenario limitations, the Citrix CloudBridge technology accelerates the ICA traffic across the slow WAN links and enables local datacenter experiences to users who are connected through WAN. In August 2006, Citrix acquired the WAN optimization solutions from Orbital Data Systems and enhanced them to form the CloudBridge solution. CloudBridge is a comprehensive set of optimization technologies, which includes the HDX technologies. This combination of the HDX technology and the WAN optimization designed for the HDX technology is one reason for the success of the XenDesktop virtual desktop deployments in the WAN scenarios. In CloudBridge implemented environments, fine-tuning XenDesktop is much simpler. XenDesktop ships a pre-defined set of policies as a template which can be used out of the box. The CloudBridge capabilities include the following:

- Adaptive TCP flow control
- Adaptive compression
- Adaptive protocol acceleration
- Per-application performance monitoring
- Fine-grained QoS
- Video optimization

Furthermore, configure the following settings for reducing the traffic over the WAN connections:

- Configure the audio quality level to low for all the non-optimized UCS applications
- Disable the virtual display settings including wallpaper, menu animation, window contents while dragging, and also reduce frame rate to 10-15
- Reduce the ICA traffic by enabling extra color compression and Twain compression level settings
- Increase the write speeds by enabling the use of the asynchronous writes
- Optimize printing quality limits as feasible

Implement the bandwidth limits either for selective or for the overall ICA traffic so as to balance the session experience of the users.

Mobile users Wi-Fi and telecom network connections

Use of the mobile telecom 3G/4G and Wi-Fi networks is a general practice for mobile computing users. All of these user connections experience a frequent network disconnect, changing security parameters, and are beyond the control of an organization. The BYOD strategy further complicates the management of the end user device environment and configurations. The security management of these mobile devices remains a major concern for IT, which can be addressed by using the **Mobile Device Management (MDM)** solutions.

Delivering the XenDesktop sessions to these mobile devices imposes limitations, such as the following:

- Lack of support for the client side media process for the Windows and Flash based content

- Most of the mobile devices navigation is touch based, which is not currently supported by all the applications

- They come with varying display resolutions and technologies

To configure XenDesktop to best adjust and overcome the preceding limitations and challenges, it's recommended to perform the following steps:

- Enable session reliability for all of mobile users connections so that the users' workspace sessions are auto reconnected, even if they encounter any network glitches or dropouts

- Enable media redirection along with the server side processing for seamless auto fallback in case the device fails to support the client side redirection

- Enable all the other optimization settings (detailed in the preceding section) used for the WAN connection optimizations

- Evaluate each business application for touch based mobile access before making them available to the user community

- Implement the MDM solution that can assess the end device authenticity, security, and capabilities, which may be used for deciding the desktop solution for the respective mobile connections

Citrix is driving the support for slow network connections to new heights by integrating more technologies in HDX. Citrix recently acquired the FrameHawk technology and integrated it with HDX to deliver an unparalleled user experience under adverse network conditions.

High Performance Computing applications

For high workload processing scenarios, including research, scientific computing, and Big Data analytics, a **High Performance Computing (HPC)** is required. In general, such applications are configured on the high performance server systems, which are located in the data center, and then a client side application connects to the server system and presents the UI to the users to operate. These server platforms include co-processors for added computing power, while maintaining the same datacenter space and power requirements. For development teams, working on the HPC capable desktop environment provides a flexible development environment. There are emerging technologies that are under research to achieve the HPC capabilities in the virtual desktops. We'll discuss the currently available option from NVidia and Intel.

High-performance computing and Citrix XenDesktop

Various businesses are looking for HPC capabilities to provide support to their virtual desktop environments and to take the advantage of the consolidated HPC desktop computing from the data center. The Citrix products, and therefore, the XenDesktop, rely on the vendor driver's capabilities to support the HPC computing capabilities to virtual desktops. This avoids the use of the synthetic drivers that are on top, and thus, it avoids serious problems that it would have otherwise encountered. There is no explicit XenDesktop requirement for supporting HPC capabilities. It requires the selected OS, which runs with the supported vendor drivers.

NVidia GRID vGPUs and CUDA

The NVidia GRID GPUs are based on the fastest and the most efficient high performance computing (HPC) architecture called NVidia Kepler. The **Compute Unified Device Architecture (CUDA)** is an NVidia's technology, and it provides a parallel computing platform and programming model, which enables a dramatic increase in the computing performance by harnessing the power of GPU. The NVidia GRID GPUs includes the CUDA cores and the NVidia Quadro drivers that support the CUDA compatible applications. This mix of features makes the NVidia GRID vGPUs a good fit for the HPC requirements. Depending on the use case, you can configure the virtual desktops either with vGPUs or with the pass-through GPU for gaining more computing capabilities with your virtual desktops. NVidia claims that GPU is significantly faster than Intel's Xeon Phi Co-Processor HPC applications.

An important note is that officially the NVidia GRID vGPU technology hasn't yet launched support for CUDA. However, it's experimentally found to be supported running the CUDA applications. The future versions of the vGPU drivers may include the CUDA capabilities support for XenServer.

You will be ready to run the HPC applications after you successfully setup the NVidia GRID vGPU in your XenDesktop deployment, as discussed in the *High-End 3D Business Applications using GPU technology* use case.

Advanced fine-tuning of XenDesktop®

XenDesktop with the FlexCast architecture brings most of the required methods for delivering the desktops to the various user groups across a business organization. Making the XenDesktop experience a complete fit for your user environments requires fine-tuning the XenDesktop capabilities according to your environment's requirements. Here, we'll learn how to fine-tune the various aspects, such as virtual display, seamless mode, local app integration, and so on, which can take your user experience to new heights.

Virtual display

The user experience greatly depends on the quality and the speed of the display on the users' devices. Citrix has always considered the end user experience as the highest priority for the success of the XenDesktop solution.

Citrix® display delivery technologies

Citrix's continued efforts resulted in an evolution of the **Virtual display** delivery technologies. Following are the currently available display delivery technologies that are supported by the latest XenDesktop version 7.x:

- The progressive display
- Legacy Graphics Mode - adaptive display
- The H.264-enhanced SuperCodec
- **Desktop Composition Redirection** (DCR)

XenDesktop supports enabling more than one display technology at the same time, and the HDX encoding intelligently chooses the appropriate technology. Following is a flow chart depicting the HDX encoding selection:

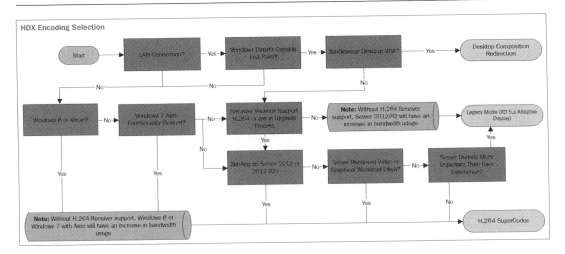

Progressive display

Progressive display was the initial display delivery technology, and it has existed since the launch of the Presentation Server 4.5 version. It employs a lossy compression algorithm, which reduces the fidelity of the rapidly changing images/graphics and the traffic itself. Though not to a great extent, the progressive display also works for server-side video rendering. This results in huge bandwidth savings, which overcomes the client side CPU/media redirection constraints and it makes the application display more responsive to the users. However, it may cause image quality degradation in slow network scenarios. It has been enhanced further and it has been included in all the versions of XenDesktop starting with the 5.x. It is disabled by default and one needs to diligently evaluate and then enable it through the Citrix policies. When the progressive display is enabled, it automatically disables the adaptive display.

The Citrix progressive display policy settings include the following:

- The ICA\Visual Display\Moving Images\Progressive compression level
- The ICA\Visual Display\Moving Images\Progressive compression threshold value

Legacy graphics mode - adaptive display

The adaptive display (legacy graphics mode) is the successor of the progressive display, and it is enabled by default for all the XenDesktop versions 5.5 and above. Progressive display, when enabled, takes precedence if the adaptive display has not specifically been enabled in the Citrix policies. It's recommended to specifically enable both of the policies. The adaptive display policies tune the various graphics settings as per the available bandwidth, thereby providing the most optimal end-user experience. When the legacy mode is enabled, VDA reverts to the XenDesktop 5.x settings, allowing the adaptive display technology to take effect. It's a long proven technology, which can deliver a rich user experience by using a balance of CPU and bandwidth.

The adaptive display is recommended where the end points cannot be updated to support the H.264 codec and delivering Windows 7 or Server 2008 R2. With limited capabilities, it's available for Windows Server 2012 and above, but it can't deliver the aero desktops, and it is not supported on Windows 8 and above because of changes introduced in the OS.

- The Citrix adaptive display policy settings include the following:
    - The ICA\Graphics\Legacy Graphics Mode
    - The ICA\Graphics\Display memory limit
    - The ICA\Graphics\Display mode degrade preference
    - The ICA\Graphics\Dynamic Windows Preview
    - The ICA\Graphics\Image caching
    - The ICA\Graphics\Maximum allowed color depth
    - The ICA\Graphics\Notify user when display mode is degraded
    - The ICA\Graphics\Queuing and tossing
    - The ICA\Graphics\Caching\Persistent Cache Threshold
    - The ICA\Visual Display\Max frames per second
    - The ICA\Visual Display\Still Images\Extra Color Compression
    - The ICA\Visual Display\Still Images\Extra Color Compression Threshold
    - The ICA\Visual Display\Still Images\Heavyweight compression
    - The ICA\Visual Display\Still Images\Lossy compression level
    - The ICA\Visual Display\Still Images\Lossy compression threshold value

- ◦ The ICA\Visual Display\Moving Images\Minimum Image Quality
- ◦ The ICA\Visual Display\Moving Images\Moving Image Compression
- ◦ The ICA\Visual Display\Moving Images\Progressive compression level
- ◦ The ICA\Visual Display\Moving Images\Progressive compression threshold value
- ◦ ICA\Visual Display\Moving Images\Target Minimum Frame Rate

H.264-enhanced SuperCodec

The H.264 SuperCodec was initially a part of HDX 3D Pro. The H.264 SuperCodec uses deep compression allowing for the delivery of the server rendered video in the low bandwidth connections. The H.264 SuperCodec is enhanced to include the H.264 encoder, which supports the new display architectures of Windows 8. The codec runs completely on the server CPU, provides a great user experience, provides a fully Aero enabled desktop on any device, low bandwidth consumption, and a greatly improved delivery of the server rendered video. It's the default technology that is used for Server OS VDAs and devices that do not support the latest DCR technology. This feature will be disabled if the visual quality policy with a lossless setting is enabled. In which case, the H.264 compatibility mode will be employed. All the supported end points can be forced to use the H.264 codec by disabling the DCR. This is recommended, especially when accessing the server rendered video or graphical content.

However, as the SuperCodec is optimized for Receiver clients that support H.264, the clients without this support may see an increased bandwidth usage. It's always recommended to use the latest and a complete installation of Receiver to ensure that all the features are supported by the client devices. Further, due to the H.264 processing, it needs increased CPU requirements on VDA.

The Citrix H.264 display policy settings are as follows:

- The ICA\Visual Display\Visual quality
- The ICA\Graphics\Display memory limit
- The ICA\Graphics\Display mode degrade preference
- The ICA\Graphics\Dynamic Windows Preview
- The ICA\Visual Display\Moving Images\Target Minimum Frame Rate
- The ICA\Desktop UI\Desktop Composition Redirection

Desktop Composition Redirection

DCR is the latest display technology from Citrix, and it supports the latest Windows display features. It's based on the aero redirection feature, which was introduced in XenDesktop 5.x.

It allows the offloading of the DirectX commands used by the Desktop Windows Manager to the user's Windows device, thereby reducing the CPU load on the server. Since the Desktop Windows Manager is always on in Windows 8 and above, DCR is the default setting for the capable end points. It provides a great user experience, full Aero enabled desktop, and low server CPU consumption (higher server scalability).

However, it's available only on DirectX that is capable of the Windows end points and it requires a high bandwidth. It is neither supported by the Server operating systems nor by HDX 3D Pro VDAs. Due to its high bandwidth requirements, it's recommended only in LAN or for the remote home user that is on broadband environments. Unlike Windows 7, the aero feature is always on (can't be disabled) in Windows 8, and by using DCR, you can offload it's processing to the client resources.

The Citrix Desktop Composition Redirection display policy settings include the following:

- The ICA\Desktop UI\Desktop Composition Redirection
- The ICA\Desktop UI\Desktop Composition graphic quality

The HDX display delivery technologies comparison

Following is a pictorial representation of the major and latest display technologies, and their key strengths:

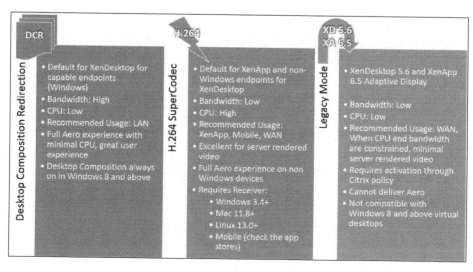

Integrating local applications

The Local App Access, which is also called Reverse Seamless, is a much awaited feature that it lets the user's desktop local applications be visible during the virtual desktop session without needing to switch away from the virtual desktop session window. The Reverse Seamless technology was first introduced and patented by RES as a product called **RES Virtual Desktop Extender (RES VDX)**. Citrix got this technology's patents licensed from RES and developed it further for its products.

Business use cases for Local App Access

This feature is required for the various business use cases, such as:

- To support a local application that cannot be hosted in XenDesktop. It is recommended for applications such as a DVD copying software, watching TV by using a tuner card, connecting to a FireWire device, and so on.
- Application that requires a hardware utility, which can't be attached to the virtual desktop hosts at the datacenter.
- Supports **Bring-Your-Own-Apps (BYOA)**, which lets the users access their favorite applications during the desktop session.
- Support the UCS apps that haven't yet been adapted to use the HDX optimized architecture for the client-side media processing.
- Eliminates the double-hop latency when the applications are hosted separately from the virtual desktop by putting the shortcut to the published application on the user's Windows device.

Configuring Local App Access

At a high-level, configuring Local App Access involves major steps, which cover both the client side as well as the server side configurations. Once this configuration is all set, all the client application shortcuts will appear in the user desktop on the VDA. Apart from letting the users use all the local applications that are available in the XenDesktop session, there is also a provision for IT to control only the published local applications, which are to be mapped to the user's session.

Enabling Local App Access

Following are the steps for enabling the Local App Access. Enabling Local App Access on the client's device that is running the Receiver can be done during the Receiver installation or by using the group policy settings, as follows:

- During the Receiver installation, use /ALLOW_CLIENTHOSTEDAPPSURL=1, while installing the Receiver software. For example, CitrixReceiver.exe / ALLOW_CLIENTHOSTEDAPPSURL=1.

- The Group Policy setting: Enable **Computer Configuration** > **Administrative Templates** > **Classic Administrative Templates (ADM)** > **Citrix Components** > **Citrix Receiver** > **User experience** > **Local App Access settings,** as shown here:

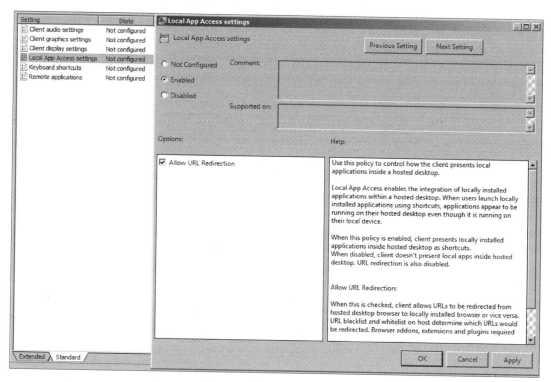

- Enable the Local App Access on the XenDesktop server side by using Studio, as follows:

```
ICA\Local App Access\Allow Local App Access
```

After enabling this feature, all the client application shortcuts will appear in the desktop on the VDA.

Enabling only local applications access that is published in Studio

In very restrictive and high security environments, you don't want to make all of the users' local applications accessible during the XenDesktop session. Instead, you want to allow only certain applications, which have been either centrally defined or centrally allowed through Studio. XenDesktop supports this capability for only allowing the published local applications to be accessible during the sessions. This involves the following server-side configuration changes to be made on the delivery controller:

- Enable the extra option **Create Client-hosted application** under the Delivery group for the Applications in Studio through a registry key, as shown here:
  - Set the registry key `HKLM\SOFTWARE\Wow6432Node\Citrix\ DesktopStudio\ClientHostedAppsEnabled` to 1 for enabling the Local App Access (using 0 will disable the Local App Access), and then, restart the controller server.

- Publish the Local app through the **Delivery group\Applications** tab**Create Client-hosted application** in Studio, as follows:
  - In the **Location** section, enter the full executable path of the application as it is present on the user's local machine. Specify any arguments as appropriate.
  - In the **Shortcut** section, select whether the shortcut to the local application on the virtual desktop is visible on the Start menu, the desktop, or on both of them.
  - Specify the other values in the rest of the **Create Client-hosted application** wizard sections.

Current limitations of Local App Access

As this technology is evolving, it is currently limited to the following capabilities:

- The Local App Access has been designed only for full-screen, so it causes confusion for multi-monitor users, who have virtual desktops spanning across all the monitors.
- Some applications have unexpected behavior, such as:
  - The applications that require elevated permissions cannot be launched as the client-hosted applications
  - It can't launch the local applications that support only single-instances

○ The full-screen applications are not supported

○ The Shortcut functionality is not supported. Including the system level shortcuts like My Computer, Recycle Bin, Control Panel, Network Drive, as well as folder shortcuts, are not supported.

○ Applications cannot be launched using COM

- The local desktop folder that is in a VDA session does not allow users to create new files.

Controlling seamless and in-browser access

In certain scenarios, you would like to ensure that the XenDesktop ICA session desktop viewer is launched either within the browser window or in the seamless (out of the browser) mode. The seamless Window mode launches the desktop viewer and it is visible on the user taskbar just as any other local application. The desktop viewer toolbar has by default been configured to launch in the seamless mode. Its behavior is controlled by the `ConnectionBar` configuration entry in the `.ICA` file. This setting is defined in `\inetpub\wwwroot\Citrix\Store\App_Data\default.ica`. In the restricted environments, it's expected to disable the desktop viewer, and thus, change its options by disabling the seamless mode.

The `ConnectionBar` when set to `1`, enables the desktop viewer seamless mode. It disables the desktop viewer, and thus, results in the in-browser session when it is set to `0`. This setting can be configured for all the ICA sessions either by adding this entry to `\inetpub\wwwroot\Citrix\Store\App_Data\default.ica` or by programmatically appending this entry during the `.ICA` file generation from the StoreFront or the Web Interface. In addition to this, use `DesktopViewer-ForceFullScreenStartup=true` to force the desktop viewer to always start in the Full Screen mode in spite of the users receiver settings on the device. Following is a screenshot of the `.ICA` file containing the `ConnectionBar` value set to `1`, which lets the XenDesktop session be seamless or out of the browser.

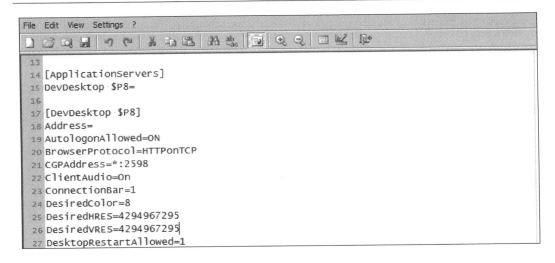

Provisioning instant virtual desktop sessions

Connecting to a virtual desktop usually causes a delay, when compared to having instant access in case of physical desktops environments. The time it takes for users to get a successful virtual desktop session running is one of the key factors that affect the physical to the virtual desktop migration projects. Citrix has addressed this issue for the application session by introducing it as a session prelaunch feature. It's now also integrated with XenDesktop 7.6, however it is still limited to the application delivery groups. Hopefully, Citrix may support the session pre-launch for the desktop sessions.

In the interim, one can apply the same application session prelaunch concept to the desktop sessions for speeding up the user connectivity to the virtual desktops. The solution can be based on using the XenDesktop SDK for programmatically launching the virtual desktop session whenever the users login to Receiver. Keep them parked in a disconnected state until the user requests the desktop. Upon the user desktop launch attempt, the disconnected session will immediately connect and it will become active. This is only an informational and a high level technical architecture idea for the advanced customization of the XenDesktop environment for meeting the respective business use case requirement.

Summary

In this chapter, we learned how XenDesktop can be configured for meeting the various advanced business use cases, and we also learned the fine-tuning of the XenDesktop policies for specific use cases. This deep understanding will help you in designing XenDesktop for any specific business requirement. It will also give you a focused understanding of specific capabilities of XenDesktop when it comes to achieving required performances and results.

In the next chapter, we'll develop a deep understanding of the networking concepts for XenDesktop.

Networking for XenDesktop®

In this chapter, we'll discover various network layers, and their roles and configuration for building optimized XenDesktop environments. As networking is responsible for connecting various distributed components required for successful connectivity to the virtual desktop, there exists a great scope to further enhance XenDesktop reliability, security, and performance at this layer. XenDesktop networking also includes both network virtualization concepts as well as Windows networking. Getting the networking configured correctly can be a key factor for the success of your overall XenDesktop deployment.

We'll start with understanding networking concepts in general as well as virtualized environments. Then, we'll dive deeper into the layers of networking involved in the XenDesktop environment. Here is a quick outline of topics we'll discuss in this chapter:

- The role of networking in XenDesktop
- XenDesktop and layers of networking
- Network layer components and configuration
- Virtualization layer network components
- Windows networking
- Citrix-recommended network performance tuning

We will not cover networking on Cloud service platforms such as AWS and Windows Azure. It's assumed that you have a basic understanding of layered TCP/IP communication flow, general network, and Citrix terminology, including firewalls, gateways, proxy servers, load balancers, web servers, NAT, DMZ, SSL certificates, DHCP, DNS, PXE, TFTP, ICA, and so on.

The role of networking in XenDesktop®

Networking itself is a broad domain that includes various technologies covering physical/virtual appliances, specialized devices, and components, along with their management software solutions. Networking is needed and implemented in every system for communication. Networking components, protocols, and technologies are built on industry standards and operate mostly independent of the networked devices platform. XenDesktop, being Windows-based technology requires certain network configuration for its successful operation. Before we get on to networking, we'll take a high-level overview of users connecting and using virtual desktops over the network. This will give you an understanding of various networking used during various stages of successfully connecting and using virtual desktops.

In *Chapter 2, Understanding the XenDesktop® Architecture in Detail*, the *Working of FMA components to deliver virtual desktops* section details intranet access via StoreFront. We'll be extending this and looking at the overview of this access from public/external access via NetScaler. For completeness, I am including the steps that are common to both modes of access. We'll be covering the network components that are used in this overall process.

Overview - extranet access via NetScaler connecting to virtual desktops

Providing users access to XenDesktop resources from external network involves implementing Citrix NetScaler (or others supported by Citrix) in a DMZ. NetScaler communications are secured using SSL/HTTPS. By using NetScaler external access, users can connect to their virtual desktops from anywhere, without needing VPN for connecting to their corporate network. With the use of NetScaler appearance on the frontend, there will be additional operations that take place in the overall virtual desktop delivery process workflow.

At a high-level, major differences between extranet access and intranet access are:

- Users access the desktop over secured SSL port
- Authentication takes place at NetScaler, if authentication is not configured at NetScaler, then it will be handled at StoreFront
- Controller issues and verifies STA tokens
- Desktop's private IP address is represented by VIP on NetScaler and is shown encrypted in the `launch.ica` file

The following is the workflow of users accessing XenDesktop resources externally. For ease of reading, I am including all the steps that are common and discussed in the intranet access case. *Italicized* are the common steps for both internal and external access.

Phase 1 - User authentication and resources enumeration

The following sequence of steps takes place during user authentication and resources enumeration:

1. The user logs on to the NetScaler Gateway secure SSL URL that is publically accessible.

2. NetScaler authenticates the user's credentials against the configured Active Directory domain controller server.

3. NetScaler forwards the validated user credentials to the StoreFront store website, which can be over a virtual address hosted by a load balancer.

4. Upon receiving the request from NetScaler, StoreFront retrieves the user's credentials from the authentication service of the NetScaler.

5. *StoreFront authenticates the user against the Active Directory domain that it is a member of.*

6. *Upon successful authentication, StoreFront checks the application subscription data store for existing user subscriptions and stores them in memory.*

7. *StoreFront forwards the user credentials, as part of XML query, to the controller,* which can be a virtual address hosted by a load balancer.

8. *The controller queries Microsoft Active Directory with the end user's credentials to verify user authorization, that is, the controller fetches the user security group memberships to find resources that the user's had access to.*

9. *The controller then queries the site database and determines which applications and desktops the user is allowed to access.*

10. *The controller sends an XML response to the StoreFront site, which contains the enumerated list of all resources (desktops or apps) available for the user within that XenDesktop site.*

11. *StoreFront web store pages display the desktops and applications that users can access* after passing through the NetScaler.

Phase 2 - Virtual desktop allocation and connection establishment

The following sequence of steps take place during virtual desktop allocation and establishing a connection:

1. The user selects an application or desktop from the list.

2. *The request is sent to StoreFront through NetScaler.*

3. *StoreFront passes the user resource selection to the controller.*

4. *The controller queries the status of desktops within that group. The controller then determines the proper VDA to host the specific application or desktop. It communicates the user's credentials and all the data about the user and the connection to the VDA.*

5. *The VDA on the selected desktop accepts the connection and sends all the information needed to establish the session back to the controller.*

6. *The controller forwards this connection information to the StoreFront site (in an XML format).*

7. StoreFront also requests the **Secure Ticket Authority (STA)** that runs on the controller.

8. STA generates a unique ticket (it is valid only for 100 seconds by default). This ticket contains the details required to identify the requested resource, including resource name, user, domain, server address, and port number, and thus avoids appearance of this sensitive information in the .ICA **(Independent Computing Architecture)** file over external networks.

9. *StoreFront combines all the connection information,* including the STA ticket, *generates an* .ICA *file (by default named as* launch.ica) *and delivers this information to the Receiver.*

10. The receiver saves the .ICA file on the user's device. Using the saved connection settings of the .ICA file, the receiver connects to NetScaler.

11. NetScaler contacts the STA running on the controller for validating the STA ticket found in the .ICA file.

12. The STA on the controller validates the ticket and responds to NetScaler.

13. NetScaler then makes a connection to the VDA on the user's behalf, and the *VDA notifies the controller that the user has connected successfully.*

14. *The controller queries the Citrix license server to verify that the end user has a valid ticket.*

15. *The controller passes all the session policies to the VDA, which then applies those policies to the virtual desktop while the user logs on with his active directory profile.*

16. *Citrix Receiver displays the virtual desktop to the end user* via NetScaler. NetScaler acts as proxy between the user and the XenDesktop resource in the data centre and secures all communication.

17. *The controller writes this connection information to the site database and starts logging data to the monitoring database.*

The STA service was introduced as a separate component with an initial version of Secure Gateway 1.0 and later integrated into the XML service in Presentation Server Version 4.0. This complete XML service has been rewritten in .Net as part of FMA and has been made part of Broker Service on the Controller server.

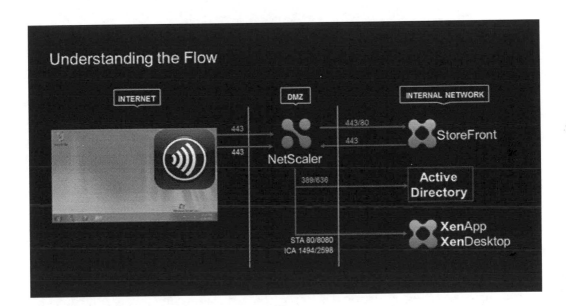

Communication ports used across XenDesktop®

The following are the various network ports used for communication across all of the XenDesktop components. It's critical that access to these ports is allowed between the components for a successful connection at that level. If any of this access fails, it impacts communication throughout that path and can even result in failure in connecting to the virtual desktops.

The following diagram will help XenDesktop administrators and engineers to easily trace communication issues and work with networking teams.

Ports

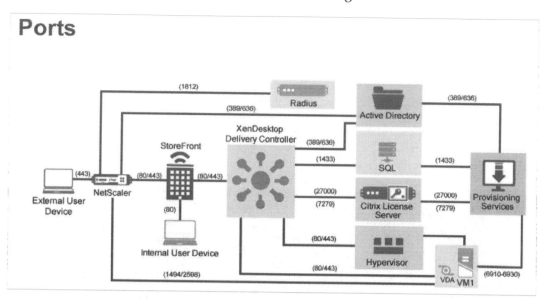

For an exhaustive list of current service, protocol, and port usage, you may refer to the list of Service Name and Transport Protocol Port Number Registry (http://www. iana.org/assignments/service-names-port-numbers/service-names-port-numbers.xhtml) maintained by **Internet Assigned Numbers Authority (IANA)**.

XenDesktop® and layers of networking

In the preceding section, we took a more detailed look at processes involved in successfully connecting to virtual desktops. You can classify the levels and layers of networking involved in various modes. Based on specialization and administration scopes, we can classify them as layers of network, virtualization, and Windows networking. We will discuss the high-level overview of networking concepts and you'll need to refer to the respective component/technology vendor document for a more detailed understanding.

Networking in a traditional desktop environment

In a traditional physical desktop environment, each desktop is connected to a network through the physical NIC. Similarly, desk IP-phones are also connected using physical cables. There isn't any virtualized layer of networking while the Windows and network layers exist. The desktops are connected to ports on switches via physical cables. These physical switches are configured with DHCP server details that allocate IP addresses to the desktops. The desktops then register with the configured DNS server and obtain a DNS host record entry. With DHCP and DNS entries, one can access the desktop over the network using either the IP address or DNS host name. Usually, desktops and servers are segregated by allocating separate switches and dedicated IP address subnet ranges for easier management.

The DNS and DHCP infrastructures play a key role in making desktops and servers accessible to each other over the network. Most Microsoft technologies specifically rely on a proper DNS resolution for network access and certain automated jobs. To accommodate various security and access requirements of teams, desktops are primarily classified into user workstations (production), test lab workstations (QA), and remote workstations (home PC systems). Typically, user and test lab workstations are located within the office premises and are connected in LAN. Remote workstations, either company-provided or user-owned, connect to the corporate office network via secured VPN access. In corporate enterprise environments, all of the network's incoming and outgoing traffic is sent through Firewall at the network layer. Firewalls will scan and allow only network traffic that adheres to corporate secure access policies.

Networking in virtual environments

The purpose of XenDesktop is to consolidate and virtualize physical desktops that are usually located within the corporate office LAN. As part of desktop virtualization, the desktop's networking components also become consolidated and virtualized. The virtual desktops hosted on any of the virtualization technology (such as XenServer, ESXi, and Hyper-V) will be assigned with virtual NIC (vNIC). The vNIC is connected to the virtual switch (vSwitch), which in turn is connected to the high-speed physical NIC of the host server.

The following diagram shows networking components and flow in virtual environments, indicating the vNIC, vSwitch, and physical network adapter. Virtual network components and their management solutions are named and designed differently across virtualization technologies.

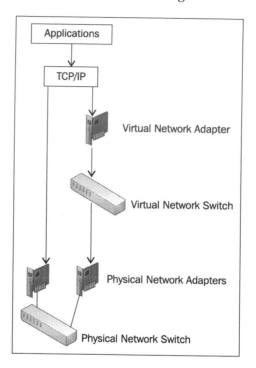

In general, virtualization technologies offer the following logical network classes that give all the basic networking needs required for VMs and their management at a host level. These are formed by grouping of ports on vSwitch for network traffic segregation.

- VM networks: These are the networks that are isolated or have direct access to logical network or direct dedicated access to physical NICs

- Management networks: These are networks dedicated to virtual host management traffic

- Custom networks: Custom logical networks can be created based on vLAN/ Subnet scopes; for example, it's general practice to create separate logical network for storage devices to isolate their traffic

For desktops running mission-critical business applications and server-hosted desktops, virtualization technologies offer great features, such as storage or live migration of VMs (virtual desktops or servers), high availability clustering, and resource pools for efficient utilization of resources. Implementing these features imposes various network requirements, such as having same or equal-capacity and features-enabled NIC cards in the hosts, NIC teaming or binding for high availability of network access, and so on.

Windows networking

Apart from configuring IP addresses and DNS entries, XenDesktop requires Windows-level networking for all of its components, including virtual desktops. Windows networking has a broader scope that includes various network specifications for the different technologies that it supports. Windows networking primarily includes the following technologies that fall in need as your XenDesktop deployment becomes more advanced. All of these are Windows server-side technologies involved with respective client-side components or configurations. Not all of them are core networking concepts, but configuring these technologies involves an advanced networking setup to function properly.

- Active Directory Domain Level:
    - Domains for Windows network management and Trusts
    - Sites and Subnets
    - AD integrated DNS, global catalog, and AD replication
    - Time Sync, domain user profiles, and roaming profiles
    - AD Group Policy management
    - AD Federation Services for user single-user sign-on
    - AD Certification Services for internal certificates management

- Windows Server Level:
    - The DHCP server
    - Windows Firewall
    - Windows services with network system access
    - Windows updates
    - DFS, iSCSI services, and network shares for remote file access
    - Windows KMS and license activation services
    - Windows Failover Clustering

- ○ SQL Server Instances, remote database access, replication and clustering
- ○ IIS web services
- ○ Windows Remote Desktop Services (RDS)
- ○ WinRM for PowerShell remoting
- ○ Network print and document services
- ○ Windows Deployment Services for PXE network boot

- Windows Desktop Level:

  - ○ Windows Firewall
  - ○ Windows services with network system access
  - ○ Windows updates
  - ○ Windows remote desktop and remote assistance
  - ○ User Access Control (UAC)
  - ○ Windows Defender or Endpoint Protection Solutions
  - ○ Internet Explorer options such as trusted sites and proxy settings
  - ○ WinRM for PowerShell remoting

Configuring these server-side and desktop technologies needs a diligent setup that enables communication in the Windows domain.

Challenges in configuring networking for XenDesktop®

In the previous sections, we looked at the various layers of networking with a wide range of technologies involved for successful enterprise deployment of XenDesktop. In large enterprises, it's general practice to build teams specialized on specific key technologies. These key technologies include XenDesktop, Windows server-side technologies, storage, network, security, and so on. Considering the scope of your XenDesktop deployment, you need to coordinate with various other specialized teams. This becomes a challenge where XenDesktop administrators need to make other teams understand the network requirements needed at various levels. It takes time to build the right configurations needed for successful operations of your XenDesktop deployment. On the other hand, most XenDesktop administrators don't have a deep understanding of the wide ranges of networking technologies involved. XenDesktop deployment becomes more efficient as the XenDesktop team build deep understanding on the backend network technologies.

Network layer components and configuration

The network layer is the first layer involved in the process of the user connecting to virtual desktops from the external network. We'll start with the URL that is used to launch the XenDesktop StoreFront store URL and cover till the user access reaches the virtual desktop located on a corporate internal network.

In most large enterprises, all of these networking activities are handled by a specialized network team and these fall out of the XenDesktop administrator's scope. Having the functional knowledge of these components enhances your understanding and eases isolating any network-related operational issues.

External networking

Unlike intranet access, external access requires a URL formed with a proper domain name followed by a URL path that will resolve to the NetScaler Gateway. This external access requires the following components to be properly set up and verified:

For example, let's assume your external XenDesktop URL is `https://nsacg.mycorp.com/` in which:

- `mycorp.com` is your corporate domain name
- `nsacg.mycorp.com` is your NetScaler Gateway external DNS record, assigned with an external/public IP address
- `https` indicates that it's a secure site, so either a wildcard (`*.mycorp.com`) or an explicit host certificate (`nsacg.mycorp.com`) can be used
- The URL `https://nsacg.mycorp.com/`, after passing through your firewall, will reach your NetScaler Gateway, which intelligently retrieves the complete gateway URL configured on the serving StoreFront servers
- The gateway auto redirects the main URL to the complete NetScaler Gateway URL

We'll cover all of the components that are involved in the preceding process covering the network layer.

The domain name provider

The root and top domain on the Internet are managed by the **Internet Assigned Numbers Authority (IANA)**, a department of **Internet Corporation for Assigned Names and Numbers (ICANN)**. It is responsible for global coordination of the DNS root, IP addressing, and other Internet protocol resources. The generic top-level domain names are available from ICANN accredited registrars, usually referred as **Internet service provider (ISP)**. There are several hundred accredited registrars located across the world, such as GoDaddy, Network Solutions, DreamHost, BigRock, and so on; the complete latest list of registrars is available at `http://www.internic.net/alpha.html`.

You need to buy your website a top-level domain name; in our preceding example, it's `mycorp.com`. If the exact name you want is not available, then you need to choose an alternate domain name that is available for you to buy. After getting your domain name registered with the registrar, you need to specify at least two external **Name Servers (NS)** that contain the DNS entries for your domain and its hosts/resources. For all attempts to access your website, `mycorp.com`, on the Internet, your registrar will redirect them to your external name servers to provide further responses. The registrar will ensure that all queries for your domain are redirected to reach your NS servers from anywhere in the world.

A typical domain name registration (in our `mycorp.com`) may look like the following:

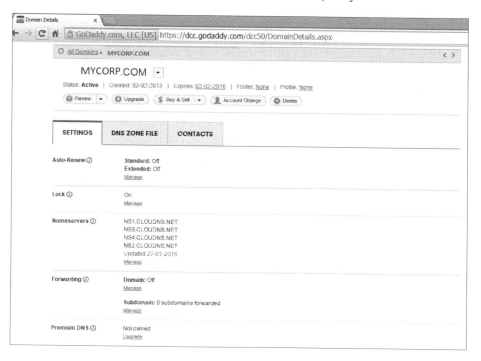

External DNS

External DNS servers are generally referred as NS. With the advancement of cloud solutions, there are now various options to host your NS servers/services. These days, most popular registrars are providing external DNS services, and there are also free cloud-based external DNS service providers such as `cloudDNS.net`. However, most enterprises maintain their own external NS servers that respond to all of their domain queries on the Internet. These servers are typically placed in DMZ behind the corporate firewall. Most enterprises prefer these NS servers to be based on security-hardened Linux (non-Windows) servers running with DNS services only. These servers are generally configured on physical hardware with high throughput to handle the huge volume of external queries. In the case of large, reputed, and geographically distributed enterprises, it's usual practice to place dedicated NS servers in each high-traffic location. This also provides failover and load-balancing capabilities for your NS services.

The DNS service on NS servers needs to be configured to service all host and resource name resolution under your domain name. This involves the following usual DNS activities:

- The root DNS zone named as `mycorp.com`

- The zone will have regular DNS SOA and its zone-level settings

- The list of all its subdomains and their NS servers' details:

    - Include NS records of other subdomains for cross-domain resolution

    - Set the NS record to the root domain NS servers to redirect any subdomains to the main domain

- Resource records for NS, www, mail, ftp, and other remaining server host entries

- It's general practice to enable replication of zone files across all the NS servers in the enterprise

- If you need to maintain differing values for the same DNS name records, you may not enable zone file replication and manually create and update the respective entries on each of the NS servers

A typical NS server root DNS zone file may look like this:

```
1 @          IN       SOA ns.mycorp.com.   operations.mycorp.com.   (
2                          2010071003  ; serial
3                          10800    ; refresh 3 houstonrs
4                          1800     ; retry 30 minutes
5                          86400    ; expire
6                          86400 ) ; minimum ttl 1 day
7
8          IN   NS   ns.mycorp.com.
9          IN   NS   ns1.houston.mycorp.com.
10         IN   MX 20    mail.mycorp.com
11         IN   TXT "v=spf1 mx a:us.mycorp.com -all"
12         IN   TXT "v=spf1 mx include:aspmx.pardot.com ~all"
13
14         IN   A    74.125.227.10
15
16 ; Sub domains:
17
18 london  IN   NS   ns.london.mycorp.com.
19         IN   NS   ns1.houston.mycorp.com.
20
21 houston IN   NS   ns1.houston.mycorp.com.
22         IN   NS   ns.london.mycorp.com.
23
24 ; Resource records:
25
26 ns       IN   A    74.125.227.8
27 ns1      IN   A    74.125.227.8
28
29 www      IN   A    74.125.227.10
30 nsacg    IN   A    74.125.227.11
31
32 ftp      IN   A    74.125.227.20
33
34 mail     IN   A    74.125.227.201
35 mail     IN   MX 0     mail.mycorp.com.
```

The root DNS zone file of mycorp.com

Secure Socket Layer (SSL) certificates

By default, all communication between web servers and client systems occurs over a clear text connection. This causes data in the communication to be exposed and an attacker will be able to see the communication taking place. This results in unintended disclosure of information, which is a serious security threat. To prevent this, SSL or the newer **Transport Layer Security** (TLS) protocols are used to secure communication between the client and the server.

SSL Certificates have a key pair consisting of a public and a private key. These keys work together to establish an encrypted connection. The other attributes/properties (such as subject, common name, and so on) of a certificate are used for the identity of the certificate/website owner. The SSL certificate encrypts web communications between client and server systems. SSL communication is also referred to as secured web access that uses the https protocol over 443 port. In addition to securing the communication between the client and the web server, SSL also confirms the identity of the web server to the client systems. This process is widely used on the Internet today to ensure that the client is dealing with the entity that the website claims to represent.

How Secure Socket Layer (SSL) certificates secure communication

When you access a website secured with the SSL certificate, it performs the following sequence of steps to establish the secure/encrypted communication between the client and the server:

- The web browser on the client system connects to the web server secured with SSL and requests the server to identify itself.
- The server sends a copy of its SSL certificate with the server's public key to the client browser.
- The browser verifies the SSL certificate root against a list of trusted CAs it knows. If the browser trusts the SSL certificate, then it creates a symmetric session key using the server's public key. This key is then encrypted and sent back to the web server.
    - As part of the SSL certificate validation, it verifies the provided certificate common name matches/valid for the website that is being accessed.
    - This also validates that the certificate is not expired or revoked.

- The web server decrypts the symmetric session key using its private key. This provides an acknowledgement that is encrypted with the session key to start the encrypted session.
- Using the session key, the server and browser now encrypts all transmitted data.

Third-party Secure Socket Layer (SSL) certificates

During the process of establishing SSL secured connection, we learned that the browser on the client system verifies the SSL certificate presented by the web server, against a list of trusted **Certificate Authorities (CAs)**. A certificate authority is the server that issues the SSL certificates. In order for your SSL certificate to be valid for client systems, the certificate root CA must be in the list of trusted CAs on the client system. In the case of websites accessed over the Internet, you can't configure all the client systems with your root CA. Thus, to address this, there are publicly available CA services known as third-party. These third-party root CAs are preconfigured to ship with the web browsers that are widely used on the client systems. Thus, almost all of the client systems can access the third-party root CAs and validate the certificates issued by them.

Popular third-party SSL certificate service providers include Verisign, DigiCert, Entrust, and Thawte, and so on. You can purchase the SSL certificates for your public websites from these vendors and have them deployed for your websites. You don't have to make any configuration changes to the client systems. In our example, the SSL certificate for `https://nsacg.mycorp.com/` should have the common name matching `nsacg.mycorp.com`.

Installing and binding an SSL certificate for your website

Upon purchasing an SSL certificate from a third-party CA vendor, you'll receive your certificate (`.cer` file) along with its private key (`.pfx` file). Upon downloading these files to your web servers, launch IIS Manager, navigate to **Server Certificates**, right-click and select **Import the Certificate**, and point it to the downloaded `.pfx` file. Upon successful import, you'll find the new entry for your certificate in the list of **Server Certificates**.

Launch the IIS manager and follow these steps:

1. Select your website, right-click, and select **Edit Bindings**.
2. Click **Add** to create a new binding for your website.
3. In the **Add Site Binding** wizard, choose:

    ° **Type** to be **https**
    ° **Port** as **443**
    ° Select respective SSL certificate from the dropdown list of SSL certificates provided in the wizard

The following is a screenshot of where you bind the SSL certificate to your website hosted on IIS:

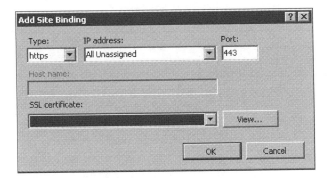

Planning IP addresses and VLANs

The IP address is the key identification for locating systems or devices on the network. As each system requires a unique IP address, these IP addresses will quickly become exhausted as the number of systems and devices on the network increases. A well-planned IP addressing model should be used to avoid the IP address crisis being a bottleneck for overall network scalability. We'll see types of IP addresses, required considerations, and recommendations for proper IP address planning to support scalability.

Types of IP addresses

Depending on Internet access requirement, IP addresses are classified into public and private IP addresses. Direct Internet access is provided by a public IP address and indirect internet access is gained for private IP address systems.

Public addresses

Public addresses are assigned by **InterNIC** (operated by ICANN, also known as **Network Information Center (NIC)**). Public addresses consist of class-based network IDs or blocks of CIDR-based addresses (called CIDR blocks) that are guaranteed to be globally unique to the Internet. Routers of the Internet are programmed or updated with the routes of assigned public addresses that enable traffic to the assigned public addresses to reach their locations. Traffic to destination public addresses is reachable on the Internet.

Private addresses

Each system on a network connected to the Internet, requires an IP address that is globally unique to the Internet. However, as the Internet grew, organizations connecting to the Internet, required a public address for each node on their intranets. This resulted in a huge demand on the pool of available public addresses.

The Internet designers found that not all nodes of organizations needed direct access to the Internet but that they still needed IP addresses that did not duplicate with already-assigned public addresses. To solve this addressing problem, they reserved a portion of the IP address space and named this space the private address space. An IP address in the private address space is never assigned as a public address. Because the public and private address spaces do not overlap, private addresses never duplicate public addresses. This solved the IP addressing problems and these private address spaces are reused across organizations. The use of NAT/PAT-supported gateway/router or proxy systems enables private IP nodes to access the Internet.

The following are three private IPv4 address blocks specified in RFC 1918 by:

1. 10.0.0.0/8: This is a single block of the class A network and is referred to as 24-bit block. The allowed range of IP addresses is 10.0.0.0 to 10.255.255.255 (totaling to 16,777,216 IP-addresses). This comprises of 24 host bits and 8 network bits. Its subnet mask is 10.0.0.0/8 and in decimal is 255.0.0.0.

2. 172.16.0.0/12: This is a block of 16 contiguous class B networks. The allowed range of IP addresses is 172.16.0.0 to 172.31.255.255 (totaling to 1,048,576 IP-addresses). This comprises of 20 host bits and 12 network bits. Its subnet mask is 172.16.0.0/12 and in decimal is 255.240.0.0.

3. 192.168.0.0/16: This is a block of 256 contiguous class C networks. The allowed range of IP addresses is 192.168.0.0 to 192.168.255.255 (totaling to 65,536 IP-addresses). This comprises of 16 host bits and 16 network bits. Its subnet mask is 192.168.0.0/16 and in decimal is 255.255.0.0.

Choosing public and private IP addresses

Depending on externally facing services, you need to buy a set of public/external IP addresses that are resoluble globally on the Internet. Similar to domain names, public IP addresses are provided by ISPs. In the case of enterprise data centers, the data center facility provider allocates requested public IPs to customers. Usually, public IP addresses are used for external facing services hosted in DMZ and incoming requests are sent to appropriate intranet systems using NAT/PAT technologies.

Usually, the external IP addresses to be administrated are few in any organization compared to their private IP addresses. Choosing or designing a private IP addressing scheme for your internal network plays a key role and is mostly defined by the number of hosts to be accommodated in a given network. For example, you require to set up separate networks for the POC test lab, training room, QA lab, and so on. Each of these scenarios will have varying number of systems and durations to be supported. Depending on the number of hosts, you need to choose the closest private IP address space. You should also consider the estimated growth of the systems in the requirement so that the chosen address space can easily scale.

Virtual LAN (VLAN)

A VLAN is a concept of logically grouping devices/systems with a common set of requirements, independent of physical location. VLANs have the same attributes as a physical LAN but allow you to group and manage endpoints even if they are not located physically on the same LAN segment. VLAN traffic is mutually isolated on the network and is set up at switch or router devices. VLAN greatly simplifies your network design and VLAN membership can be configured through software without physically relocating devices or connections. Today's most enterprise-level networks use the concept of virtual LANs for efficiently managing advanced networking requirements for various services and technologies. VLANs are fully controlled by networking teams.

Firewall

Firewall is a core component of the networking layer and plays a key role in enforcing corporate security policies at the perimeter level. It's usually configured as the first system (by an internal IP address such as 172.22.1.1) in your network. It's the frontend server that is configured to intercept both incoming and outgoing communication traffic, and this server enforces the security access policy configured with allow and block settings. Firewall is a broad technology to configure and administer. It's available from many vendors among which Cisco, Juniper, Barracuda, and so on are the widely known. There are various advanced features offered by these vendors and we'll cover the core features that are required for understanding the network flow in XenDesktop connections.

Network Address Translation (NAT)

As the name implies, NAT is a capability of firewall where it maps an external IP address to an abstracted and secured corporate internal IP address. The simplest form of NAT is one-to-one IP-address translation. However, due to the limited external IPv4 addresses, most enterprises implement one-to-many NAT at routers, where a single external address corresponds to all internal IP addresses.

In our example, we have `nsacg.mycorp.com` pointing to 74.125.227.11 (as shown in the screenshot of *Root DNS zone file of mycorp.com*). When `nsacg.mycorp.com` is accessed externally, it will resolve to the 74.125.227.11 external IP address. On the firewall, you can configure the NAT rule that translates all traffic of 74.125.227.11 to an internal IP address of your Access Gateway server. NAT is not required if your access gateway server is configured in the **DMZ (demilitarized zone)** zone with an external IP address. In our example, `nsacg.mycorp.com` is a NetScaler Gateway configured on the NetScaler that is in DMZ. However, NATing becomes a key player in securing environments that do not run NetScaler and would like to have external access to corporate services such as StoreFront, mail server for OWA, and so on.

Port forwarding/redirection

Port forwarding is an application of NAT to redirect requests from one IP address and one port combination to another. Port forwarding plays a key role in masquerading the ports used by services that are accessed from external networks. For example, to allow secure shell access from the Internet to your server running on the corporate secure network. The secure shell uses standard TCP port 22. In highly customized and secured environments, you can configure the secure shell service to use a custom port that will be redirected to the server running the secure shell on port 22. This way, you can avoid secure shell access attempts from unknown sources to your secure shell server.

In our example, port forwarding is required to redirect the http (port 80) access attempts to secure http (port 443) port to the NetScaler Gateway. With this, you don't have to take care of autoredirecting user requests from `http://nsacg.mycorp.com/` to `https://nsacg.mycorp.com/`. This is required in case of DaaS service providers, where their customers allow only http requests to your service.

Port overloading

Port overloading is also referred to as NAT overloading or **Port Address Translation (PAT)**. Port overloading maps a single public IP address with different ports to different multiple internal IP addresses. This particularly comes in handy when you have a single external DNS name/external IP address that needs to connect to different servers inside the corporate network. In this case, you can map different ports of an external IP address to each of your servers on the internal network.

In the case of virtual desktop environments, this comes in handy when you are configuring a web service for external access that is pooled on a virtual desktop or server VDAs. You can configure single external IP address to connect to different server VDAs by using different ports.

Real-time monitoring

It is often the case that firewall and its features are configured and updated as the organization grows. The troubleshooting and testing/verification of the firewall rules becomes more difficult as the firewall configuration advances and becomes more complex. To help network administrators, almost all firewalls feature real-time traffic monitoring capability. Real-time monitoring provides an instantaneous log of all active traffic crossing on the firewall. As the volume of traffic is huge, you can apply filters to monitor the status of the selective traffic. This will help you determine whether there is any blocking or request denial taking place at the firewall.

Real-time monitoring is useful when your online users complain that their external access is not working or working partially from certain networks. You can apply various filters, such as incoming or outgoing traffic, source or destination network, access protocol, port, access times, and so on, to find the intended traffic status. Based on the statuses found in real-time monitoring, you can update or set up firewall rules to allow/block the required access from an external world.

Audit logging

To trace complex firewall-level access issues reported at random times or during off hours, you need to audit all the network logs periodically and analyze them for reported behaviors. To facilitate this, firewalls support auditing the logs by collecting them into a file on the network share. This facility of archiving the logs to a network location is referred to as syslog. It is by default disabled and needs to be manually configured. It is important to note that enabling syslog will result in an added load on your firewall devices. Enable syslog only for the required duration and ensure that the configured network location has enough disk space, as these files fill up rapidly.

Configuration replication

Enterprises spanning multiple locations globally will have firewalls placed at each of their data centers. It becomes a difficult task to manually keep track of changes to firewall and apply them across all firewalls globally. To ease management and administration, most of the firewalls support replication of their configuration to other firewalls on the network. However, setting up firewall configuration replication requires firewalls to be of the same model/level. Further replication is intended only for global configuration and one needs to diligently choose the policies and exclusions that are being replicated globally.

Citrix® NetScaler

NetScaler is a sophisticated networking solution acquired and further developed by Citrix. NetScaler is designed with cloud features such as multitenancy, load balancers, SSL, and so on. The NetScaler product is an application switch that performs application-specific traffic to intelligently distribute, optimize, and secure Layer 4-Layer 7 (L4–L7) network traffic for web applications.

Components and architecture

The NetScaler core components include:

- Virtual servers: The NetScaler Gateway virtual server is an internal entity that is representative of all the configured services available to users. The virtual server is also the access point through which users access these services. You can configure multiple virtual servers on a single appliance, allowing one NetScaler Gateway appliance to serve multiple user communities with differing authentication and resource access requirements.

- Authentication, authorization, and accounting: You can configure authentication, authorization, and accounting to allow users to log on to the NetScaler Gateway with credentials that either the NetScaler Gateway or authentication servers located in the secure network, such as LDAP or RADIUS, recognize. Authorization policies define user permissions, determining which resources a given user is authorized to access. Accounting servers maintain data about NetScaler Gateway activity, including user login events, resource access instances, and operational errors. This information is stored on the NetScaler Gateway or on an external server.

- Network resources: These include all network services that users access through the NetScaler Gateway, such as file servers, applications, and websites.

- The virtual adapter: The NetScaler Gateway virtual adapter provides support for applications that require IP spoofing. The virtual adapter is installed on the user device when the NetScaler Gateway plug-in is installed. When users connect to the internal network, the outbound connection between NetScaler Gateway and internal servers uses the intranet IP address as the source IP address. The NetScaler Gateway plug-in receives this IP address from the server as part of the configuration.

- User connections: Users can log on to the NetScaler Gateway by using the NetScaler Gateway plug-in, Receiver, and the NetScaler Gateway web address.

The following is an architectural diagram of the NetScaler traffic flow:

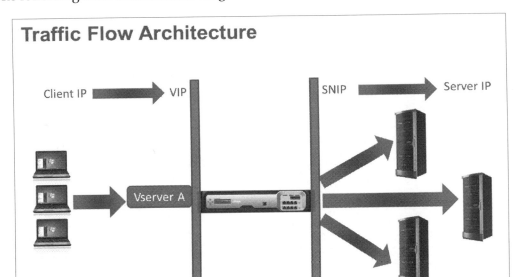

The underlying core functionality of NetScaler is called Request Switching technology. The NetScaler appliance separates the application layer HTTP request from the TCP connection on which the request is delivered. Request switching enables NetScaler to multiplex and offload TCP connections while maintaining persistence of connections and thus manages the traffic at the application layer requests.

NetScaler deployment and its working

In a typical deployment, NetScaler is configured with an access gateway, load balancer for StoreFront and DDC XML services. NetScaler is usually equipped with two NIC cards and is physically connected to a switch in the data center. NetScaler is networked to be accessible from both internal and external networks by configuring the available two NIC cards accordingly. Most commonly, NetScaler is deployed in the inline (two-arm) mode between clients and servers. A virtual server configured for gateway handles the client requests. In this mode, client systems reside on the public/external network and the XenDesktop component servers exist in the corporate private network. NetScaler securely manages the communication between them.

A virtual server on NetScaler is an entity that acts as a point for delivering NetScaler features. External clients use virtual servers to access applications services hosted on the servers. The virtual servers abstract the internal servers by using a single IP address to which the clients connect. User connections are terminated at the virtual server and NetScaler initiates its own connection with the internal servers on behalf of the client. All the external access requests reach the access gateway service running on the NetScaler. The gateway passes the requests to the load-balanced virtual server for StoreFront web services. StoreFront services, upon successful validation of user credentials, forwards the user request to a load-balanced virtual server for XML services that runs on the controller servers. A controller server controls all further communication that takes place across the internal XenDesktop component servers.

For easier understanding, the following is a diagram of a logical view of the NetScaler deployment in the inline mode:

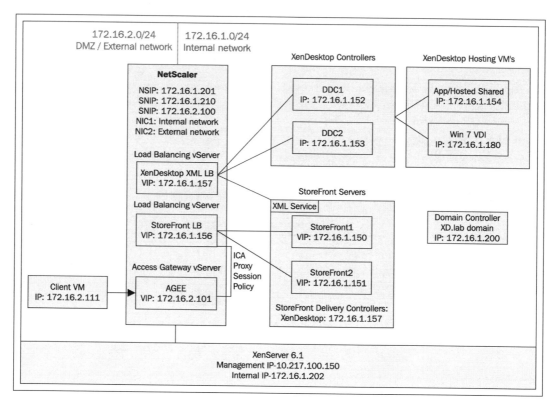

NetScaler features

NetScaler is a highly sophisticated and feature-rich network solution for XenDesktop. There are many great features and capabilities that can be implemented with NetScaler in the broader scope. For the scope of this section, we'll cover the high-level overview of features that are recommended and often employed in XenDesktop deployment.

Global server load balancing (GSLB)

The global server load-balancing feature lets you load-balance flow of the traffic to the website hosted on geographically separated web servers supporting disaster recovery, load balancing based on load or proximity of servers, or persistence. It's very common practice for enterprises to hold more than one data center hosting the service to make services highly available and recoverable. In our example, `nsacg.mycorp.com` is the web URL, which will be load-balanced across the web servers in multiple data centers running the website. By configuring GSLB for `nsacg.mycorp.com`, you can implement effective load-balancing at data center level, provide disaster recovery, and ensure continuous availability of applications by directing client requests to the closest or best-performing data center, or to surviving data centers in case of an outage.

To configure GSLB, both data centers should be using NetScaler appliances preferably of the same model, deployed in the same mode (inline/two-arm mode). NetScaler appliances need to be configured as authoritative DNS servers for the `nsacg.mycorp.com` domain.

Load balancing

The load balancing feature distributes the client's requests/traffic across multiple servers and improves the efficiency of resource utilization and avoids single-server overloading. Traffic management using the load-balancing feature is possible from layer 4 (TCP and UDP) through layer 7 (FTP, HTTP, and HTTPS). NetScaler features various algorithms, referred to as load-balancing methods, to intelligently determine how to distribute the load across the servers configured for the load-balanced service. The default method is the least-connections method which is widely used.

Load balancing is recommended and widely used for the StoreFront store web URL and XML service running on controller servers. The load balancing feature can be enabled via **NetScaler console** | **Configuration section** | **System** | **Settings** | **Configure Basic Features** and then by selecting the **Load Balancing** checkbox.

The following is the pictorial representation of load-balancing architecture:

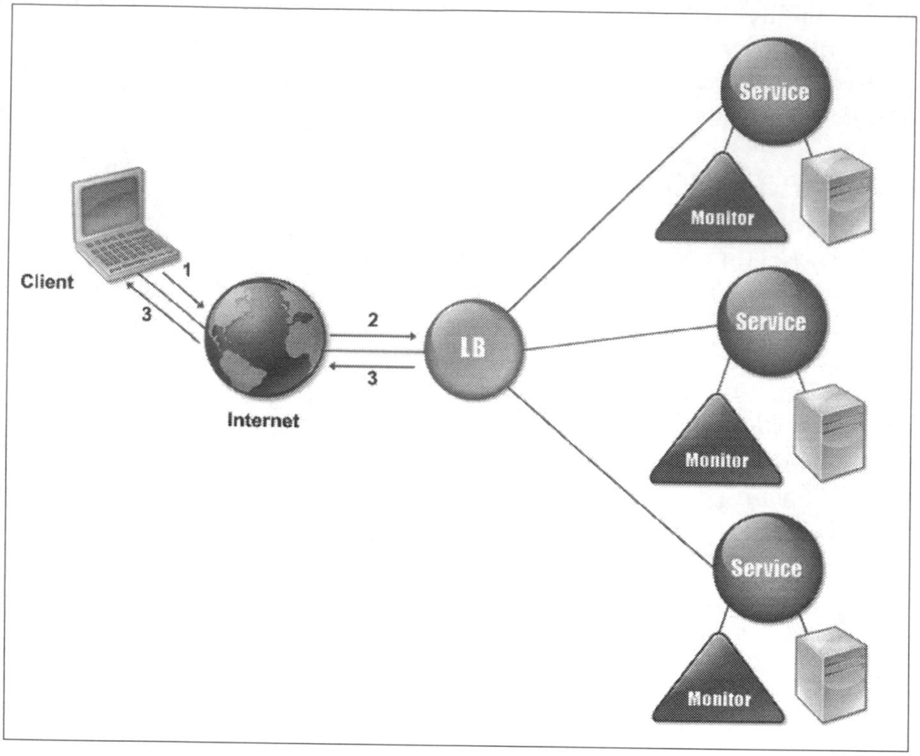

NetScaler Gateway

NetScaler Gateway is a secure remote access solution and provides user authentication while allowing users to work from anywhere. NetScaler Gateway provides users with an externally accessible URL configured with an external DNS and external IP address; in our example, it's `https://nsacg.mycorp.com/`. NetScaler Gateway is configured as a virtual server, when deployed in DMZ, it intercepts traffic from the Internet; NetScaler Gateway decrypts SSL connections from the user device and authenticates a user before network traffic reaches the secure network.

Configuring NetScaler Gateway requires an external IP address and SSL certificate matching the external DNS name, authentication protocol, and StoreFront or Web Interface URL. In our example:

- The external IP address used is 74.125.227.11 (defined in the *External DNS* section of this chapter); it's configured as vIP for NetScaler Gateway virtual server on the NetScaler appliance

- The external DNS name used is nsacg.mycorp.com
- The SSL Certificate that should be used is: nsacg.mycorp.com (or wildcard cert: *.mycorp.com)
- The authentication protocol: LDAP to authenticate with Active Directory
- The StoreFront URL: StoreFront FQDN, relative path to store URL, STA URL

The role of NetScaler

We have seen the key features and functioning of NetScaler configured for the XenDesktop environment. Behind the firewall, the NetScaler plays a key role in global website load-balancing for gateway URLs, load-balancing for StoreFront service and XML Controller services. These features provide enterprises with disaster recovery, high availability, scalability, load-balancing, and other benefits. Furthermore, NetScaler is designed for XenDesktop by Citrix and has various monitoring and logging integration.

Citrix® CloudBridge

Citrix CloudBridge provides a unified platform that connects and accelerates applications and optimizes bandwidth utilization between branch offices and enterprise data centers and public clouds. CloudBridge delivers superior application performance and user experience for branch and mobile workers through a broad base of features that include the following:

- Unique enhancements for the Citrix XenDesktop user experience
- Secure, optimized networking between clouds
- Acceleration of traditional enterprise applications
- Unparalleled visibility into per-application performance
- Sophisticated traffic management controls and reporting
- Faster storage replication times and reduced bandwidth demands
- Integrated video delivery optimization for branch offices
- The adaptive TCP flow control
- Compression, de-duplication, and protocol acceleration
- Cloud connectivity and optimization

The CloudBridge architecture

A typical architecture of CloudBridge installation between data centers usually includes installation of CloudBridge devices at each of the data centres, as shown here:

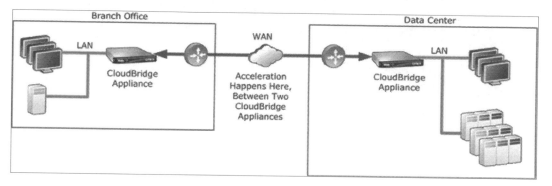

Web proxy / filter servers

Web filtering is an advance requirement in highly secured environments. We've covered this in detail under the *Web filtering technologies and their options* section of *Chapter 6, Configuring XenDesktop® for Advanced Use Cases*. I am including this reference here since web filtering technologies fall under the scope of networking, and you may need to work with your networking team for getting it set up.

Virtualization layer network components

The network components of the virtualization layer for the most part fall under the scope of infrastructure virtualization and are mostly pre-existing in an established environment. Furthermore, depending on the virtualization platform chosen, terminology and specific concepts will differ. We'll cover general virtualization networking, since XenDesktop component servers and virtual desktops are based on a virtualized infrastructure.

The host/management network

It is general and recommended best practice to separate virtualization host management traffic from typical virtual machines traffic by using dedicated NIC. The management network is designated for the exclusive use of virtualization software communication with virtual machines. This is required to ensure that virtualization software doesn't suffer communication issues due to virtual machines overloading the network bandwidth. Generally, all virtualization host servers are grouped into a separate subnet for easier management.

Another important consideration for host server networking is choosing the right hardware and software for connecting to a high-speed storage area network. The advancements in network device hardware, drivers, and virtualization technology support have uncovered various possibilities in configuring access to storage. The early advancement was the host bus adapter which offloads the iSCSI packets processing from the CPU to the HBA, whereas NICs don't do TCP/IP offloading. Now, there exists Ethernet HBAs, iSCSI HBAs, software iSCSI over standard NICs, and **Converged Network Adapters (CNAs)** that support both Ethernet and fiber channel.

There are further considerations for choosing host NICs if you are planning to implement storage or VM Live migration (VMotion, XenMotion, and so on) capability in your deployment. You can define custom logical networks that correspond to individual or teamed physical NICs. For each logical network, you can assign separate network configurations (such as a different range of IP addresses, subnet mask, and gateway).

NIC teaming/bonding

NIC teaming is also called as NIC bonding. NIC teaming configures two NICs together and so they logically function as one network card. Both NICs have the same MAC and IP addresses. This enables sharing network traffic load, bandwidth aggregation, increased network throughput, and passive failover in case of NIC hardware failure or network outage. NIC teaming is supported by all the major virtualization technologies vendors. For high-availability requirements, NIC teaming is recommended.

Commonly, NIC teaming is employed for connectivity to storage devices to overcome unplanned physical damages and network outages. Host servers will be equipped with recommended **HBA (Host Bus Adapter)** or capable NICs to connect with the **SAN (Storage Area Network)**. As part of high-availability for storage, HBAs or NICs are teamed. The NIC in a team is usually connected to different physical switches to avoid single-network path failures due to physical damages and network outages.

The virtual machine network

Virtual machines on a host can be running either XenDesktop component servers or desktop systems. For all server VMs, you may allocate a dedicated NIC configured with your server subnet network. Similarly, you can allocate the logical network that is configured with your desktop subnet network. Based on the logical network assignment, virtual machines obtain their network configuration. In general, the desktop subnets are configured with DHCP for automatic IP address assignment, whereas servers are manually configured with a static IP address.

The key parameters when specifying the IP address details include use of the DHCP server, or IP address with subnet/vLAN, gateway, and DNS server details. As the master image is used for provisioning VMs in XenDesktop MCS, the networking configuration of the master image VM needs to be configured with proper settings and its ideal to set the desktop master image to use DHCP.

Full Internet access

Enterprise networks are usually locked down with network access restrictions. In case of DaaS service provider scenarios, there will be more added restrictions to Internet access. However, in setting up new applications or troubleshooting certain issues, it is desired to verify behavior by allowing full Internet access to the virtual machine. This requirement can be addressed either by implementing a proxy server or using a separate network with full Internet access on the host server. For troubleshooting purposes, set the virtual machine to use the full Internet network. Once the required access is found, you can have that access allowed in a proxy server so that access will be available to all VMs that use the proxy server.

Windows networking

In the Windows layer, networking at operating system and application level involves configuring Windows server-side technologies and client-side configurations. These server-side networking technologies includes DHCP, DNS, Active Directory, IIS web sites and servers, file shares, remote desktop services (RDS), and so on. The core networking services such as DNS, DHCP, and Subnets can be hosted on non-windows platforms as well as in an advanced hybrid enterprise scenarios. For the scope of this section, we'll cover all network services hosted in Windows platforms alone.

Windows server technologies have a broader scope and can directly affect users; these are maintained and administered by dedicated skilled professionals on those technologies. XenDesktop administrators should be closely working with them and should also have a fair understanding of almost all of the Windows server technologies.

Dynamic Host Configuration Protocol (DHCP)

DHCP is the primary networking component in any network as it assigns the IP address, which is required for any device to come onto the network. **Dynamic Host Configuration Protocol (DHCP)** is a standardized network protocol used by computers to dynamically attain an IP address and required network configuration, and then maintain them automatically. The client and DHCP server follows the **DORA (Discover, Offer, Request, and Acknowledgement)** process for this communication. By default, the DHCP allocates IP addresses with eight days of lease period. Clients must renew their IP addresses before the lapse of the lease period.

The following is the flow chart of the DHCP renewal process that explains the detailed steps involved:

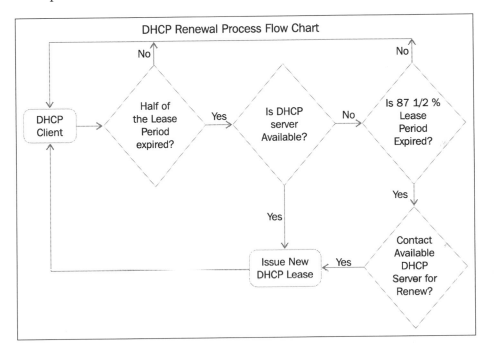

DHCP for multiple networks and subnets

DHCP communication uses packet broadcasting on the network. However, router devices don't support these broadcast communication across the networks, thus DHCP servers are restricted only to the network that they are in. To make DHCP server serve the requests from clients across various network segments/subnets, you may configure any of the following:

- Use RFC 1542 compliant routers that support broadcasting communication across segments

- Set up the DHCP server in each of the network segment/subnet

- Use DHCP relay agents

Configuring DHCP

The DHCP server is a server role in the Windows server, which can be added/ removed using the server manager. The installation involves specifying the following:

- Network connection binding, choosing which NICs to be used for serving the DHCP requests, and so on

- DNS server settings, including the DNS domain name suffix, primary and secondary DNS servers

- WINS server details

- Creating a scope

- IPv6 setting if you are planning to use it

- Authorizing the DHCP server using enterprise administrator credentials

DHCP comprises of scopes that represents a range of IP addresses which can be assigned to computers requesting the IP addresses. A scope is typically defined with a start IP address, end IP address, subnet length, and subnet mask. The scope also supports exclusion of IP address ranges to address any custom setup or advanced configurations. Scopes upon creation also needs to be activated to take effect.

Linking DHCP and DNS

By default, the DHCP server integrates with DNS servers that are specified during the installation of the DHCP server role. This simplifies deploying DNS settings to computers on the network. Upon successful DHCP IP address allocation to the client, the DHCP server automatically updates the DNS servers with a respective host (A) and pointer (PTR) records. You can configure this setting in the **DHCP Console | IPv4 Properties | DNS** tab, as shown here:

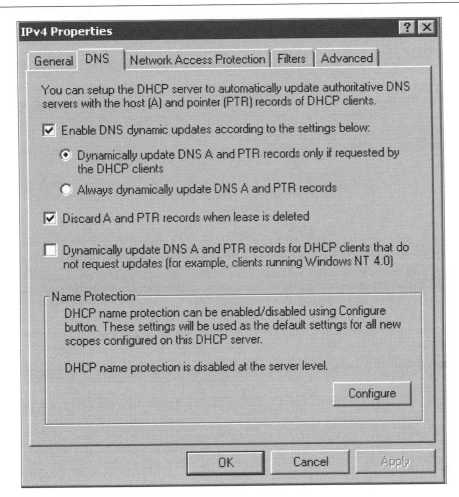

DHCP for XenDesktop®

We would need IP addressing to be configured for both XenDesktop component servers as well as for virtual desktops. As standard practice for any other server systems, it's recommended not to use DHCP for server systems and manually configure them with static IP addresses. For virtual desktops, it's recommended that you use DHCP so that it will auto configure IP addresses for the growing number of virtual desktops. The master desktop needs to be set to use the DHCP so that all the provisioned desktops will be set to use DHCP. For use cases to retain the IP address, you may want to use DHCP reservation for respective virtual desktops.

DHCP for XenDesktop® using provisioning services

Provisioning services use DHCP to allow PXE boot to streamed virtual desktops. During PVS installation, you can specify the DHCP server to be used for the IP address assignment. DHCP also plays key roles in letting the provisioning services locate the TFTP server and Bootstrap file details. Configure the following shown DHCP server options:

- **066 Boot Server Host Name**
- **067 Bootfile Name**

The following is a screenshot of DHCP server option 66 and 67:

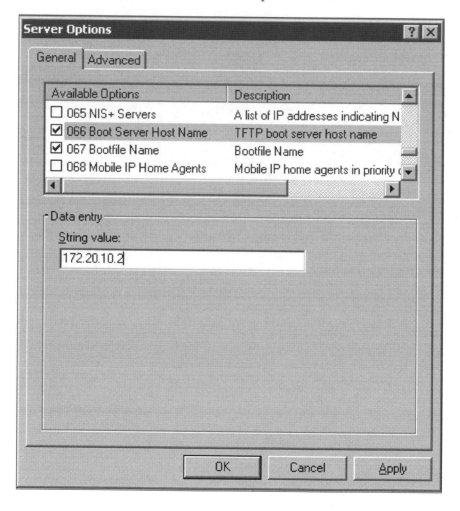

Active Directory (AD) and domain membership

AD is the directory service for Windows domain networks that are designed to manage the Windows infrastructure. AD authenticates and authorizes all users and computers in a Windows domain. An AD structure is an arrangement of information, about all network objects. The AD instance consists of a database and respective services. AD is included as a role of Windows server operating systems and Windows servers running the AD role are called as **Domain Controllers (DCs)**. AD at the top level consists of forests, domain, sub-domain, site, and trusts. A geographical deployment of AD is defined as a site that consists of subnets/networks. You'll define all the private networks that you are using for Windows systems in your AD site. If your deployment spans across the geographical locations, you'll configure AD sites for each of them with all the used subnet entries. These details will be replicated across the sites as part of the AD replication. AD uses and integrates with LDAP, Kerberos, and DNS services and provides network time for a complete domain.

Virtual desktops and AD membership

All virtual desktops of XenDesktop run Windows operating systems and require an end user to authenticate with the AD to log in to the virtual desktop session. In order for user login to be successful, the virtual desktop should be a member of the AD domain and should have valid domain trust to allow the user access to networked resources. With domain membership, virtual desktops must have a proper time value set, which is critical for a successful user login using Kerberos that uses time value.

Domain Name System (DNS)

DNS plays a key role in Windows networking. The active directory domains tightly integrate with DNS to an extent that an AD is worthless without a DNS in its domain. DNS is a hierarchically distributed naming system for devices, services, or any resource connected to the Internet or a private network. In simple terms, DNS is a kind of phonebook/database that maintains the list of mappings between computer names and IP addresses. Once an IP address is assigned by the DHCP server, a computer automatically gets registered in DNS which is configured on the DHCP server or in its TCP-IP preferred primary/secondary DNS servers.

Configuring DNS

DNS is installed during AD installation and can also be installed as a server role from the server manager. During AD installation, a DNS primary zone with a name matching your Windows domain name is created as the AD integrated zone and server is set as the primary DNS server for the AD domain.

Post-installation, you can manually create a corresponding reverse lookup zone for your networks and subnets to support reverse name lookup. The reverse zone provides you the reverse lookup wherein you can resolve an IP-address to its DNS record. You can choose the NIC interfaces of the DNS server to serve DNS requests. You can add or remove the list of other DNS servers and manually specify servers to receive zone file transfers.

DNS zones

A DNS namespace consists of zones that define scope, that is, the machines that fall under that zone. The DNS zone is a text/database file (NTDS.Dit) that defines which machines it knows about in the namespace. When integrated with AD, DNS zone files are automatically replicated as part of AD replication across the sites.

Types of DNS zones

The following are the four basic types of zones supported by Windows DNS:

- Active Directory integrated zones: DNS DB is stored as an AD object. This supports DNS zone transfers via AD replication. If all DNS servers are DCs, you don't require secondary zones.

- Primary zone: This is a master zone in a non-AD integrated DNS network. All DNS updates run through this server and this server communicates to secondary zone server for pushing updates.

- Secondary zone: Is a read-only copy of primary zone. An explicit zone transfer is required for pulling up updates from the primary zone.

- Stub zone: This is a special zone where you only have a list of DNS servers for DNS servers and other domains. Usually, preferred while you set up communication between two domains in separate forests. Stub zone auto-populates a list of all active NS servers for the configured domain.

Classification of DNS zones

Depending on the type of data stored, DNS zones are classified as follows:

- Forward lookup zone: This looks up a host IP address by host name, that is, it maps a host name to host the IP address.

- Reverse lookup zone: This looks up a host name by host IP address, that is, it maps a host IP address to a host name.

- Stub zones: This contains a list of all available NS servers to be contacted for external domain name resolutions.

- Conditional forwarders: This contains a list of NS servers to which a DNS request has to be redirected based on the domain name for external domains.

- Root (dot) "." zone: The existence of root "." zone designates a DNS server to be root hint server and is usually deleted. If you do not delete this setting, you may not be able to perform external name resolution to the root hint servers on the Internet.

Types of DNS entries

DNS zones contain records for each resource and services on the network. DNS supports various entries to indicate differing types of resources and records. The most commonly used DNS records are:

- Host/A record for the host address
- The PTR record for a domain name pointer
- SRV for server selection
- NS for an authoritative name server
- MX for a mail exchange server
- CNAME for a canonical name for an alias
- SOA record marks the start of a zone of authority

The DNS resource record types are specified in RFC1035 by IETF and are maintained by IANA. The complete list can be found on the DNS parameters page (`http://www.iana.org/assignments/dns-parameters/dns-parameters.xhtml`).

Features of Windows DNS

Windows DNS service lets you configure the following features that extend DNS resolution for other known domains and for all public domain requests:

- Conditional forwarders is a feature that lets you redirect all DNS requests to other internal/external domain DNS servers by domain names. You need to manually maintain the list of servers added for DNS redirection in conditional forwarders.

- Root hints is a feature that lets the DNS server direct requests to external Internet world NS servers, for all DNS queries that can't be resolved internally.

- Forwarders is a list of internal DNS servers to be used in case a query is not resolved in the current DNS zone.

- In the case of AD-integrated zones:

    ○ DNS updates are secured

    ○ DNS zone transfers are taken care of by AD replication

    ○ Backward compatibility to support existing secondary zones

    ○ This supports multi-master replication, that is, DNS updates can be done on any of the AD-integrated DNS server and they get autoreplicated to other servers

Virtual desktops and DNS

Virtual desktops communicate with controllers and other Windows network resources via their DNS names. It's critical that your virtual desktops are able to communicate with your DNS server to resolve the names of network resources. If there exist multiple, conflicting, and invalid DNS entries for any resource, it's possible that access to the resource fails. In case of name resolution failures, you can access network resources explicitly via the IP address.

You may use a DNS CNAME for deploying configuration of critical services to Windows desktops so that client-side configuration remains the same across the data centers. You can specify a list of actual servers, DNS or IP address entries that are used when CNAME resolution is attempted on the network.

Internal SSL certificates

In case of scenarios to secure web connections within your private network, you can deploy an enterprise CA within your domain using AD certificate services. Using the internal CA, you can issue and renew SSL certificates that can be used for securing your internal web sites. In this case, systems on your private network verify certificate root CAs with your internal CA.

IIS hosting StoreFront sites

Internet Information Services (IIS) is a flexible, secure, and manageable web server designed by Microsoft for Windows platforms. All web-based applications or technologies developed for native Windows use IIS as their default web server technology. Similarly, the XenDesktop web access solution StoreFront server is based on the IIS web server. In our example, external user requests for `https://nsacg.mycorp.com/` after passing through firewall, NetScaler, will be routed to the StoreFront Store website running on internally hosted StoreFront servers IIS web service. Upon receiving the user request, the IIS website will attempt to load the respective site pages and render the pages back to the NetScaler, firewall, and the user browser.

IIS is an advanced technology with broad options to define for customizing, securing, and fine-tuning overall website performance. Specifically, IIS uses application pools to run linked websites. The application pools run the actual web server processes that are isolated from other application pool processes. This is a major architectural change and great improvement in IIS that lets you restart your website without affecting other web services running on the same server.

IIS is included in all Windows servers as a server role. The IIS server runs IIS admin service on the server, and you can manage websites hosted in IIS using the IIS manager console application. By default, IIS website files and contents are saved under `C:\inetpub\wwwroot` path on the server. The IIS logs all of its activities to the log file located in path `C:\Windows\System32\LogFiles\W3SVC1\exyymmdd.log`.

Windows Firewall

Windows Firewall is a built-in component that provides firewall software functionality at Windows networking layer. It is part of both Windows desktop and server operating systems and runs as a service named Windows Firewall. However, as most enterprises implement firewall at network layer, Windows Firewall at Windows layer is never used in real time and thus set as disabled in most environments.

In the case of environments using Windows Firewall, one needs to diligently configure the firewall rules. Windows Firewall ships with most of the widely used access rules that can be used to quickly allow or disable access to and from the system. It also works as an application blocking/control suite. Windows Firewall uses network profiles domain, private (home and work), and public to selectively apply the rules for these network types. Firewall can be disabled or enabled for each of these network profiles.

Windows Firewall and XenDesktop®

In the case of using Windows Firewall on either XenDesktop component servers or on virtual desktops, diligent attention has to be made to configuring firewall rules and ensuring all required system, protocol, and port access is allowed between XenDesktop servers and virtual desktop systems. The overall network port defined in the *Communication ports used across XenDesktop* section earlier should be implemented across systems using Windows Firewall.

In most desktop environments, it's general practice to implement endpoint solutions such as Symantec endpoint protection or McAfee antivirus and have Windows Firewall disabled. These endpoint solutions provide easier and more centralized management of security policies across the endpoints. Both Windows Firewall as well endpoint protection solutions will incur an additional load on the desktop. If misconfigured, these will drastically degrade virtual desktop performance or may even render the desktop unresponsive or unusable. It's highly recommended to work with your network and security teams in choosing and configuring firewall components for your Windows desktop environment.

Citrix® recommended network performance tuning

Citrix recommends the following configuration to improve the network performance of XenDesktop:

- Consider enabling the following features on network adapters. Most network adapters will have these features enabled by default.
    - Large send offload
    - TCP checksum offload
    - Receive side scaling
    - Dynamic virtual machine queue to reduce CPU usage of network I/Os from virtual machines

- Use a dedicated private network for live migration traffic. This will minimize the time required to complete live migrations and ensures consistent migration times. Enable **Single Root I/O Virtualization (SR-IOV)** on this dedicated network only, if the network adapter supports it. SR-IOV reduces network latency, CPU utilization, and increases the network throughput. In addition, it increases the number of *receive* and *send* buffers on each network adapter involved in the migration, which can improve migration performance.

- Virtualization technologies support creating multiple virtual network switches. Each virtual switch is associated with a physical network adapter. If the host system has multiple network adapters, virtual machines with network-intensive loads can benefit by having their workloads divided between the virtual switches for better use of the physical network adapters.

Summary

In this chapter, we gained a deeper understanding of networking for XenDesktop, including the networking involved at various layers in overall XenDesktop deployment. We took a deep dive into each layer of networking and discovered the relevant components, concepts, and technologies used in XenDesktop. This high-level understanding on the broad scope of networking helps you design networking components and architecture to improve the performance of your XenDesktop deployment. In larger enterprises, where you don't have scope to administer these networking components, you will be able to easily coordinate and verify these configurations.

In the next chapter, we'll dive deeper into the monitoring and troubleshooting of XenDesktop where your network understanding and skills learned in this chapter will be applied.

8
Monitoring and Troubleshooting XenDesktop®

In the earlier chapters, you learned about deploying and configuring XenDesktop environments. In this chapter, you'll learn about monitoring and troubleshooting XenDesktop, which form the ongoing XenDesktop operations that become part of the help desk or support team workflows. Although monitoring and troubleshooting have their specific scope of handling and tools, they still go hand in hand towards the common goal of resolving XenDesktop issues and stabilizing the deployment. Diligently handling the operational issues gives us an opportunity to identify the deployment loopholes, fine-tune the deployment for the real-time use cases and load, and increase the efficiency of overall end user experience.

We'll start by going through an overview of monitoring and troubleshooting XenDesktop. We'll then deep dive into each monitoring and troubleshooting procedure, detailed with suitable examples of use cases. The following is a brief list of tools and applications that you'll be learning:

- Citrix Director and EdgeSight
- Citrix Studio
- **Citrix Insight Services** (**CIS**) and Citrix Scout
- Citrix HDX monitor
- Citrix Diagnostic Toolkit
- XDDBDiag, XDPing, and CDF Control
- Citrix Print Detective

Overview of monitoring and troubleshooting XenDesktop®

Monitoring and troubleshooting are general, ongoing operations after the deployment of any major technology. In large enterprises, these operations are handled by dedicated resources or teams. All major technology vendors provide specialized tools for both monitoring and troubleshooting purposes. The support teams use vendor-recommended tools and their documentation to troubleshoot issues effectively. Effective monitoring requires learning and configuring technology-specific tools to track performance and other metrics. Troubleshooting requires an understanding of how the chosen technology works, as the deeper you understand a technology, the more complex issues you can solve. For a quicker response in addressing the issues, you need to have monitoring configured for every component and a configuration that is involved in successfully delivering the XenDesktop sessions to users. We'll see what solutions Citrix provides to monitor and troubleshoot XenDesktop environments. As virtual desktop infrastructures involve a broad scope of technologies, such as Windows desktop and server OSes, virtualization, storage and networking, and so on, having hands-on experience and an understanding of these areas helps you to identify and resolve issues specific to your environment, and beyond the usual scope of troubleshooting tools.

We have seen that XenDesktop has evolved over the years with lots of improvements and features. Citrix has greatly simplified monitoring and troubleshooting XenDesktop through a dedicated and remotely accessible web-based solution called Citrix Director. Citrix also enhanced and merged the early monitoring technology designed for legacy IMA architecture, called EdgeSight. The merger of these two fine technologies provides XenDesktop administrators with a single pane of window to monitor and troubleshoot large XenDesktop environments.

Apart from Director and EdgeSight, Citrix also provides a number of tools for specific troubleshooting purposes. We'll cover all the Citrix-provided tools, along with the general troubleshooting steps involved in the case of external user access.

A deep dive into monitoring and troubleshooting XenDesktop®

Citrix is largely committed to simplifying and supporting complete automation to monitor a XenDesktop environment. The release of integrated Director and EdgeSight indicates that, Citrix is going to bring all monitoring and troubleshooting under this single solution going forward. We'll dive deep into the Director and EdgeSight architectures, deployment options, and configurations. Then, we'll cover the specialized XenDesktop troubleshooting tools provided by Citrix. You will also learn about troubleshooting of external access by users.

Citrix® Director and EdgeSight®

Director is a web-based administration solution designed for support / the help desk to access both up-to-date real-time data from the VDAs, as well as historical data from a site's database. Citrix acquired EdgeSight, the monitoring software, from Reflectant software. Director now includes EdgeSight as its integral component and includes most of its features. EdgeSight's features include performance management for both health and capacity assurance, and historical trending and network analysis. This network analysis is powered by NetScaler HDX Insight, which identifies bottlenecks due to the network, in a XenDesktop environment. These new built-in end user experience analytics features help define long-term capacity management, resource planning, and assurance of service-level agreements. This integrates complete monitoring and managing tools into a single, unified solution. Director and EdgeSight help XenDesktop IT support increase operational productivity and efficiency through a more holistic view of the Citrix environment. From resolving user issues more quickly to planning more accurately for future needs, IT support and management team gains the insight and actionable data it needs to deliver the best support to users and businesses.

Director supports shadowing using Microsoft Remote Assistance (not ICA shadowing), which can be enabled during the installation of Director on the server side. This lets you view and interact with user sessions to provide remote support. On the virtual desktop, VDA software installation turns on Remote Assistance by default, and it can also be enabled via Group Policy. However, client-side Flash rendering cannot be shadowed.

Architecture

Director is one of the core components of XenDesktop that was introduced in XenDesktop 5, which was a major version featuring XenDesktop's adoption of the FMA architecture. It's a web-based solution developed in .NET, and supports the integration of monitoring modules for Citrix technologies, such as HDX insight from the NetScaler, which provides detailed network-level debug information. These advanced capabilities are enabled with the Platinum license of XenDesktop. Currently, the Platinum license extends Director to include EdgeSight performance management and Network Analysis provided by HDX Insight. The Director framework also integrates with the Active Directory environment, which facilitates configuring delegated administration to define role-specific access to XenDesktop administrators in large enterprise environments.

Director provides a dashboard that summarizes real-time machine issues, usage metrics, HDX information, and host and controller health information. Information is displayed according to aggregation from multiple sources, including XenDesktop controllers, Citrix profile management, **Windows Management Information (WMI)**, and Active Directory. It allows administrators to manage the environment from a centralized tool. Director can connect and monitor multiple sites, but does not load-balance between controllers. Although a single Desktop Director server can manage the environment, it is recommended that redundant Director servers be configured and load-balanced to ensure that the management console is always available. It is also recommended to install Director on a separate **IIS (Internet Information Services)** web server in large-scale environments. In a multisite XenDesktop deployment, ensure that the system clocks are synchronized on all the servers where controllers, Director, and other core components are installed. The sites might not display correctly in Director if the clocks are not in sync.

The following is an architecture diagram of Desktop Director communicating with controller services as well as the NetScaler HDX Insight service:

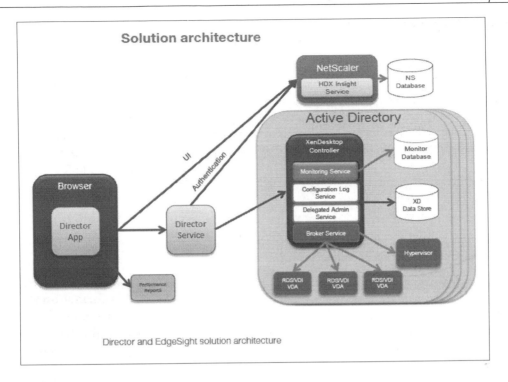

Director and EdgeSight solution architecture

The Citrix® monitoring service

Citrix introduced a new service called monitoring service in XenDesktop 7. It is built on the FMA service SDK and adheres to the stateless service model of the XenDesktop controller services. The Citrix monitoring service on the collector server collects instrumentation in the VDAs and the Broker service as events. The events are pieced together into a data model. The data is stored in a logical monitor database, which can either be in the XenDesktop site database for small deployments, or in a separate database for larger enterprise deployments. Customers can pull data from the ODATA API to convert into CSV format. From the virtual desktop, Director provides rich WMI data from VDA, such as perfmon, event logs, hardware data, and policy reports. The Director user should have local administrator access on VDA. It uses WinRM, which is enabled by default on Windows 7. WinRM uses port 5985 and it's a SOAP service. Director's event-based monitoring provides key data for troubleshooting, including session usage, logon performance, connection, and machine failures. EdgeSight integration provides the capability to build historical data that enables historical trends, experiences comparison, and provides access to details and exporting data.

Here is a pictorial representation of the communication flow from VDA and the Broker service on the controller to the monitoring service. The monitoring service saves event-based information in the monitoring database in a defined structure, which is used by Director to retrieve the information.

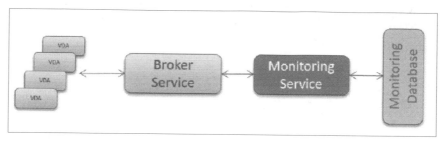

Installation

We have covered the installation of Director in the *Installing Citrix Director* section of *Chapter 4, Implementing a XenDesktop® Environment*. The installation tasks involve specifying the controller and its database, choosing Windows Remote Assistance, and allowing the HTTP and HTTPS ports in Windows Firewall. In the master image (VDA), installation of the VDA software, by default, enables Remote Assistance, which is required for successfully connecting to the user session via the Windows Remote Assistance feature in Director. Director communicates with the specified controller by default. It automatically discovers all other controllers in the same site and fallbacks to them if the controller you specified fails. You should specify only one controller address for each site that you will monitor.

When installed with a non-Platinum license, Director will notify you about the upgrades to Platinum edition features, which include **EdgeSight performance management** and **Network Analysis**, as shown here:

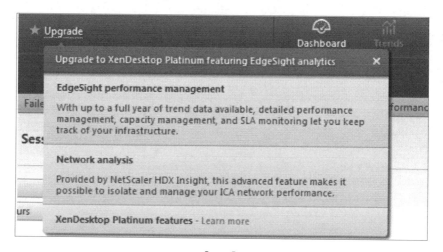

It is recommended to implement SSL on the IIS website hosting Director to secure the communication between the browser and the web server running Director. This can be implemented independently of the Director configuration, using either internal or third-party SSL certificates. Configuring Director for advanced scenarios, such as supporting multiple sites or multiple AD forests, can be done through the IIS manager. The Director service automatically logs off all users of Director and restarts when you change a setting in IIS.

EdgeSight® performance management

EdgeSight performance management doesn't involve the setup of additional components, and is available for XenDesktop Platinum license environments. Performance management builds and retains historical data, which is shown under the trends view of the Director. In non-Platinum environments, Director retains historical data only for the past 7 days, and cleans up the rest. In a Platinum license environment, it retains all of the historical data that needs to be groomed for database performance in large environments and long runs. For Desktop as a Service (DaaS) providers, this historical trend data helps build efficient long-term capacity and resource planning, and the assurance of service-level agreements.

EdgeSight® network analysis

EdgeSight provides network analysis by leveraging NetScaler HDX Insight, which provides Citrix desktop administrators with the ability to troubleshoot and correlate issues related to poor network performance. It's one of the XenDesktop Platinum license's features and requires NetScaler Insight Center to be installed and configured to enable EdgeSight network analysis. NetScaler Insight Center doesn't need any license, and interacts with the HDX Insight, which is an Enterprise or Platinum feature of NetScaler. In short, to enable EdgeSight Network Analysis, you need:

- XenDesktop 7 and above with the Platinum license
- NetScaler 10.1 and above with the Enterprise or Platinum license

Configuring EdgeSight® network analysis in Director

The Insight Center communicates and gathers information related to XenDesktop deployment from HDX Insight. It provides a robust analysis of the Citrix ICA protocol between the client and the backend Citrix infrastructure. NetScaler Insight Center is a virtual appliance provided by Citrix. It can be set up on any of the popular hypervisors, such as Citrix XenServer, VMware ESX, or Microsoft Hyper-V.

Linking the Insight Center virtual appliance with NetScaler

Once you bring up the Insight Center virtual appliance on a hypervisor, follow these steps to complete its configuration:

1. Navigate to the IP address of the Insight Center virtual appliance in a browser and click on the **Get Started** button.

2. In the **Configuration** section, key in the NetScaler IP (not the VIP) and credentials to authenticate Insight Centre access to the NetScaler.

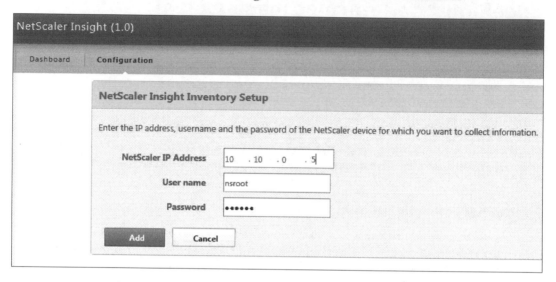

3. Click on **Add**. Then, your NetScaler should appear in **Inventory of Devices**.

Linking Director Server with Insight Center

Linking Director Server with the Insight Center virtual appliance is currently supported through a command-line utility called DirectorConfig.exe. This tool ships along with Director installation, and can be located at C:\inetpub\wwwroot\ Director\tools\DirectorConfig.exe. Follow these steps to complete the setup:

1. Run C:\inetpub\wwwroot\Director\tools\DirectorConfig.exe with the /confignetscaler parameter in Command Prompt.

2. In the **Enter Machine name** prompt, specify the NetScaler Insight Center machine name, in either FQDN or IP address format.

3. Then, provide the NetScaler root username and password to authenticate.

4. Choose the connection type, either HTTP or HTTPS, using the options provided.

5. Following is a screenshot showing all the above steps:

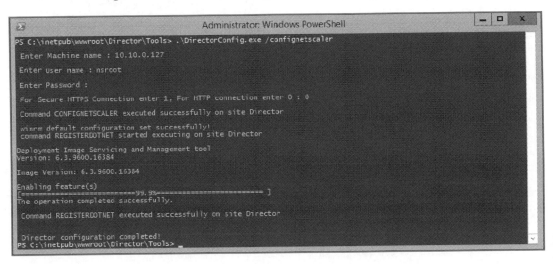

Configuring Delegated Administration

Delegated Administration is one of XenDesktop's features that apply to the Director Console as well. The Delegated Administration model offers the flexibility to match organization-specific needs to delegate administration activities using role-based and object-based control. Delegated administration employs three concepts: administrators, roles, and scopes. Using these, granular permissions can be set. These permissions are based on the administrator's role and the scope of the role. They determine what is presented in the Director interface to administrators and the tasks they can perform. Delegated administration can be configured in Citrix Studio under the **Administrators** sub-section of **Configuration** section. Studio ships a set of built-in roles defined with widely used permissions for those roles.

For example, users in the built-in **Help Desk Administrator** role will see an interface tailored to help desk tasks. This role allows helpdesk administrators to search for the user and display their activity, such as the status of the user's applications and processes. The permissions to view and kill user applications and processes enable helpdesk to quickly resolve issues by performing any of these: ending an unresponsive application or process, shadowing operations on the user's machine, restarting the virtual machine, or resetting the user profile. The following is a screenshot of Citrix Studio as it shows up the built-in **Help Desk Administrator** role definition, which details the permissions this role is allowed to perform in Director:

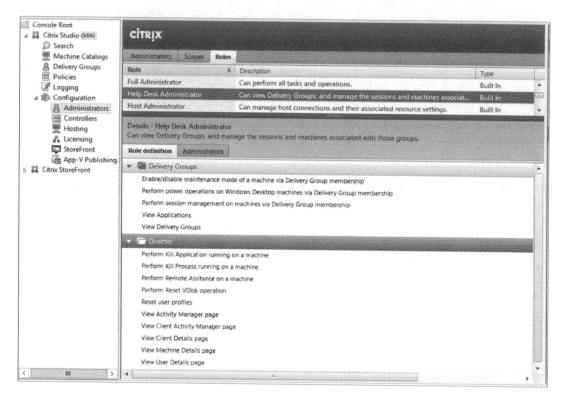

XenDesktop®'s built-in administrator roles for Director

Here is a brief table of built-in roles and their permissions, which determine how these XenDesktop administrators use Director:

Administrator role	Permissions in Director
Full Administrator	Has full access to all views and can perform all commands, including shadowing a user's session, enabling maintenance mode, and exporting trends data. Can perform all tasks and operations.
Delivery Group Administrator	Can deliver applications, desktops, and machines. Can also manage the associated sessions.
Read-only Administrator	Can see all objects in specified scopes, as well as global information, but cannot change anything.
Help Desk Administrator	Can view Delivery Groups and manage the sessions and machines associated with those groups. Cannot access the Dashboard, trends, or filters views. Cannot use the power control options for server OS machines.
Machine Catalog Administrator	No access. This administrator is not supported for Director and cannot view data. Can create and manage Machine Catalogs and provision machines.
Host Administrator	No access. This administrator is not supported for Director and cannot view data. Can manage host connections and their associated resource settings.

These roles are located in Citrix Studio under the **Configuration** section, in the **Administrators** subsection, and then the **Roles** tab.

Using Director and EdgeSight®

Upon successful installation, Director is automatically configured with localhost as the server address, and communicates with the local controller by default. Director can be accessed remotely via a website using URL: `https` or `http://<Server_FQDN>/Director`. Only configured administrator users can log on to Director, and they must be Active Directory domain users. Based on the role and permissions assigned, Director provides different views of the interface tailored to particular administrators.

The dashboard view

Director uses views that are used to fetch specific information from the monitoring database and present to users in an intuitive, graphic web page. By default, Director launches with the dashboard view, which gives an overview of the current status of virtual desktop sessions. Here is a screenshot of the default dashboard view of the Director Console:

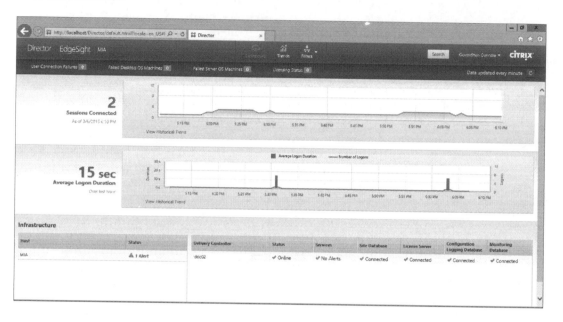

The trends view

Director also ships a trends view, which provides critical metrics from configuration logging, as well as the EdgeSight performance and HDX Insight capabilities. The trends view aggregates the events that took place in the past 2 hours. These metrics provide an overview about **Sessions, Connection Failures, Failed Desktop OS Machines, Failed Server OS Machines, Logon Performance, Load Evaluator Index, Hosted Applications Usage,** and **Network** statistics, as shown in the following screenshot. These results from the trends view can be exported to either PDF or CSV format.

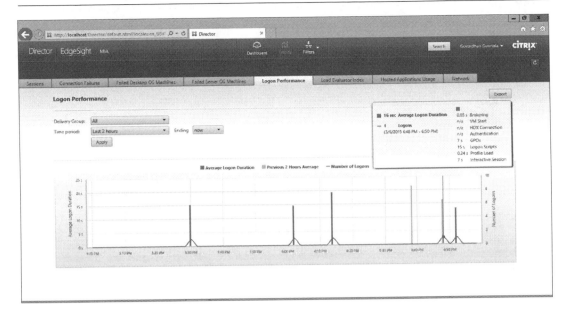

The filters view

The filters view can be used to build a custom search for some specific information needed. Filters can be applied to the **Machines**, **Sessions**, and **Connections** information. The filters view helps us to drill down to specific details and presents a table of results. In it, it is easy to see exactly who has been affected by the failures, which machines are affected, the reason for failure, the time of failure, and many more details. Global actions can be performed from this page, enabling a quick remediation of issues.

Predefined filter views

The filters view includes a set of predefined subviews under three major sections to quickly find the failures in the environment. The following is the list of them:

The first section is **Machines**, which includes these subviews:

- **All Machines**
- **Failed Machines**

  ○ **All**

  ○ **Failed to Start**

  ○ **Stuck on Boot**

  ○ **Unregistered**

  ○ **Maximum Load**

The next section is **Sessions**:

- **All Sessions**

The third section is **Connections**:

- **All Connections**
- **Failed Connections**
  - ○ **All**
  - ○ **Client Connection Failures**
  - ○ **Configuration Errors**
  - ○ **Machine Failures**
  - ○ **Unavailable Capacity**
  - ○ **Unavailable Licenses**

Custom filter views

Apart from predefined filter views, Director also provides an exhaustive list of parameters that you can use to build your custom filter. Say that you want to find all the connection attempts that failed due to the virtual desktop being in maintenance mode. You can quickly build your filter views, as shown in the following screenshot. You can have your custom created filter view saved for later reference:

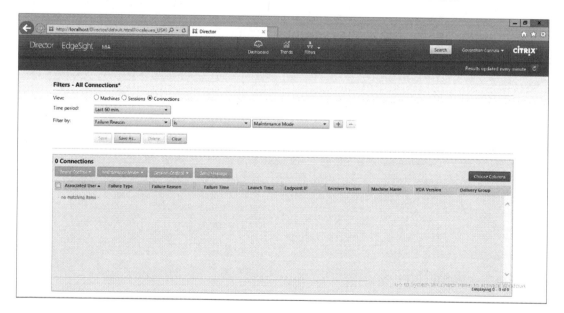

Shadowing user sessions

Shadowing is a very handy and effective troubleshooting tool for helpdesk teams to address end user issues. It allows administrators to remotely connect to an active user session, view all of the user's activity, and take control of the session. This unique capability helps coordinate with users in handling runtime issues that a user may experience within the session.

The **Shadow** feature is available under **Activity Manager**, which can be launched from various filter view results against session records. To launch **Activity Manager**, navigate to **Filters | Sessions** and click on **All Sessions**. In the resulting session list, click on the hyperlink value for either **Associated User** or **Endpoint Name**, which will launch **Activity Manager**. Here is a screenshot of **Activity Manager**, showing the **Shadow** button to start shadowing that particular user session:

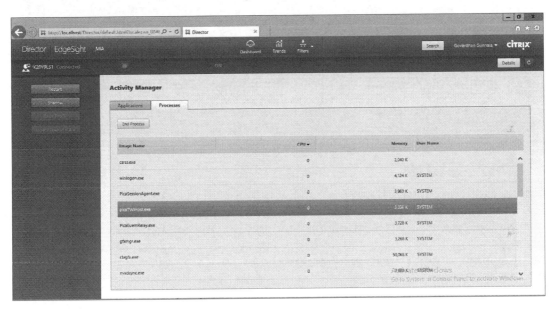

Monitoring licenses

Director includes the monitoring of Citrix XenDesktop licenses as well. You can view the License server and **Licenses Status** under the **Dashboard** view. The **License Server** section under **Licenses Status** lists all the licensing alerts and **Recommended Actions**. The **Delivery Controllers** section lists the actual license servers, their overview, and detailed status information, as shown in the next screenshot. The **Details** tab should show **The License server is operating normally and not in the grace period.** as long as your license server is working and there exists the required licenses on the server to serve the user sessions.

Citrix® Studio

Citrix Studio provides the interface for XenDesktop administrators to view and update the XenDesktop site configuration. Although Studio is not a monitoring or troubleshooting tool, any XenDesktop configuration issues can be effectively fixed through it. We'll cover the configuration **Logging** in detail and an overview of the other troubleshooting capabilities of Studio.

Common tasks for testing the XenDesktop® environment

Upon the first-time launch, Studio starts in the **Common Tasks** pane, which lets you build the XenDesktop site in a guided procedure. The **Common Tasks** pane features the test option at each level of **Site configuration**, **Machine catalogs**, and **Delivery groups**. These tests are used to verify the XenDesktop site during its initial configuration, but are mostly forgotten or overlooked in later stages. To run these tests, perform the following steps:

1. Log on to your controller server and launch Studio.

2. Click on **Citrix Studio (<sitename>)**. In the right-hand-side pane, you'll see these tabs:

    ○ **Common Tasks**

    ○ **Actions**

    ○ **PowerShell**

3. The **Common Tasks** page will have the following subsections populated, with respective entries related to your environment:

    ○ **Site Configuration**

    ○ **Machine Catalogs**

    ○ **Delivery groups**

4. Each of the subsections will have a button used to test its configuration:

    ○ **Test Site…**

    ○ **Test Catalog…**

    ○ **Test delivery group…**

5. When you click on any of these Test option buttons, they will perform a series of predefined tests and provide the results showing the count of **successful tests**, **warnings**, and **failed tests**.

6. It also provides an option called **Show report** for viewing the detailed results of the tests. The following is a screenshot of a successfully completed **Test site** option:

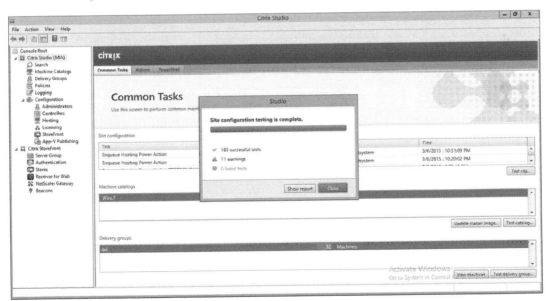

7. Here is the screenshot of the results page from **Show report**:

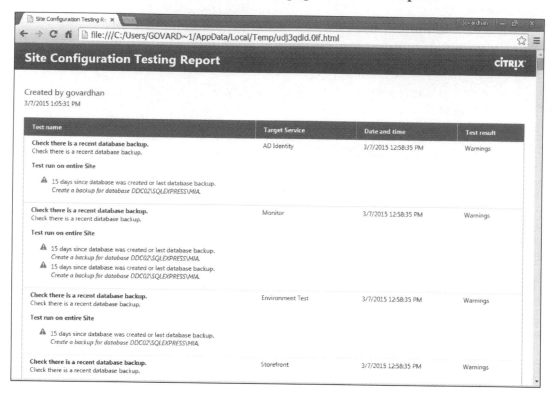

Search

The **Search** option in Citrix Studio lets you search and view the instantaneous status of the overall sessions in the XenDesktop site. The results of the search are classified into **Desktop OS Machines**, **Server OS Machines**, and **Sessions**. Similar to the custom **Filters** view in Director, the **Search** option provides various parameters to filter the results, and you can save your custom search for later usage. Say that you want to find all virtual machines that are unregistered and not under maintenance mode. The following is a screenshot of the search query in Studio that finds all virtual machines that are unregistered and not under maintenance mode:

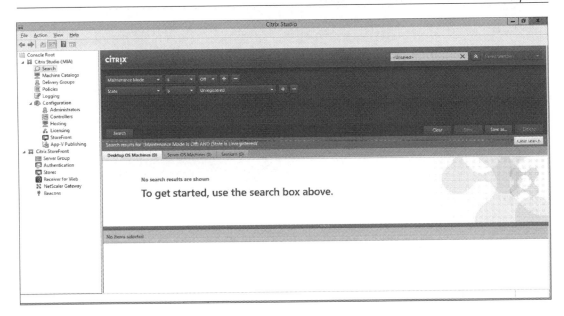

Configuration Logging

Configuration Logging is a long existing feature of XenApp that was introduced in the legacy Presentation Server 4.5 version. Citrix introduced it to XenDesktop as an integral feature since its early versions. Configuration Logging is enabled by default. As the name says, Configuration Logging captures the XenDesktop site configuration's changes and administrative activities in the database. By default, Configuration Logging uses the XenDesktop Site Configuration Database. It's recommended to use a separate database for Configuration Logging, particularly in large deployments.

With Configuration Logging, you can view or store information for administrator activities and desktop configuration changes, including image updates, Machine catalog creation, and Delivery group changes. This information plays a helpful role in scenarios such as these:

- Diagnosing and troubleshooting problems that surface after a configuration change. You can review the recent configuration changes and work on reverting to verify that your environment returns to its previous state.

- Streamlining the XenDesktop change management workflows and building a track of changes over time.

- Reporting and reviewing the administration activities for audit purposes.

Enabling and disabling Configuration Logging

The Configuration Logging feature can be administered from Citrix Studio. It can be enabled or disabled through the logging preferences set for your site. To enable or disable it, launch Citrix Studio, navigate to **Logging**, and right-click on **Preferences**. In the **Logging Preferences** window, you can set it to either **Disable** or **Enable**. You can also change its database location, as shown here:

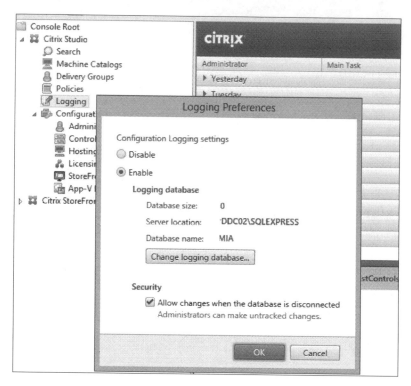

Accessing Configuration Logging data from Director

Configuration Logging information can also be viewed in Director, with the **Trends** view interface, which provides notifications of configuration changes to administrators who do not have access to XenDesktop Citrix Studio. The trends view provides the historical data of configuration changes over a period of time. This helps administrators assess what changes occurred, when they occurred, and who made them, while finding the cause of an issue.

The trends view represents the configuration information in three categories, listed here:

- **Connection Failures**
- **Failed Desktop OS Machines**
- **Failed Server OS Machines**

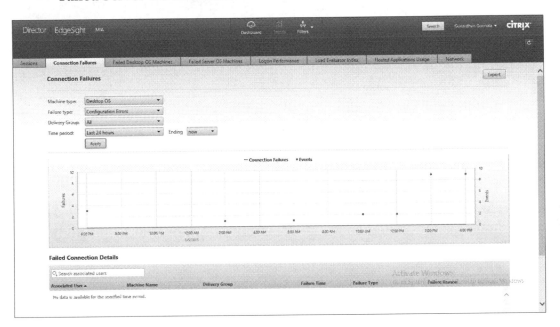

Creating reports from Configuration Logging

The nice thing about Configuration Logging is that it supports exporting Configuration Logging information into either CSV or HTML for quick report generation. Reports can be generated from Studio by right clicking on **Logging** section and selecting **Create Custom Report** option. Report creation provides date filters with defined values of **All**, **Last 24 hours**, **Last 7 days**, and **Last 4 weeks**, and also supports a custom date range.

In the next screen, you can select the format of the report as CSV, HTML, or both. **Create Custom Report**, with the format and location options, is shown in this screenshot:

Citrix® Insight Services (CIS)

Citrix Insight Services (CIS, formerly known as **Tools as a Service (TaaS)**) is an initiative from Citrix focused on, making the support of the Citrix environment as easy as possible. It is a free online tool that analyzes log files, profiles the virtualization environment, and scans for hundreds of known issues. Yet, it takes only minutes to deliver a clear, actionable advice customized to the customer environment. It includes tools that are focused on data collection and are designed to lower the impact on the environment in terms of disk space, prerequisites, and performance during the data collection process. It analyzes your configuration and gives you best-practice advice, with links to relevant articles or white papers. CIS also suggests hot fixes, patches, and updates with red/yellow/green colorized indication for easy prioritization. Furthermore, CIS isn't only for troubleshooting. It's also a great way to perform a quick health check of your environment, so you can spot any issues before they become real problems. A frequent analysis of your environment logs using CIS is recommended. However, you need to ensure that your data privacy policy allows you to upload your environment details for analysis.

Citrix® Collection Tools for Citrix® Insight Services

Citrix has made available separate tools for each of its key technologies' diagnostic log data collection. Citrix collectively refers them as Collection Tools. The following is the current list of Citrix Collection Tools for its various products:

Product	Log collection tool	Citrix knowledge base article explaining the tool
XenDesktop/ XenApp	Citrix Scout	http://support.Citrix.com/article/ CTX130147
XenServer	Server Status Report / xen-bugtool / fdisk –l	http://support.Citrix.com/article/ CTX125372
NetScaler	Collector Script	http://support.Citrix.com/article/ CTX127900
Provisioning services	PVSDataTools	http://support.Citrix.com/article/ CTX136079
CloudBridge	Show Techsupport tool	http://support.Citrix.com/article/ CTX135546
CloudPortal Business Manager	The CloudPortal Business Manager (CPBM) admin utility	http://support.Citrix.com/article/ CTX200176
Citrix Insight Services	All products tools	http://support.Citrix.com/article/ CTX135408

Using Citrix® Insight Services

Citrix Insight Services currently provides analysis for both 5.x and 7.x versions of XenDesktop, NetScaler, and XenServer. It is available for all customers who have signed up for the MyCitrix account. Using CIS mainly involves these steps:

1. Log on to the CIS website (TaaS.Citrix.com) with your MyCitrix account.

2. Run Citrix Scout on the controller server, which generates the log files.

3. Upload the files to the CIS website, either manually, or with the upload option provided by the Citrix Scout tool.

4. Upon successful file upload, the uploaded data will be auto-analyzed by the CIS analysis engine against a list of known issues and best practices.

5. You'll receive an e-mail once the analysis is completed. You can check the personalized report, including next-step resolution recommendations.

Given next is a screenshot of the results of a XenDesktop log analysis by CIS. The **XenDesktop Overview** section shows **Health Check Summary**, **Environment**, **Collection Overview**, and **Controller Overview**. **Diagnostic Report** of **Health Check Summary** showing **0 Issues** indicates that your environment is doing all good.

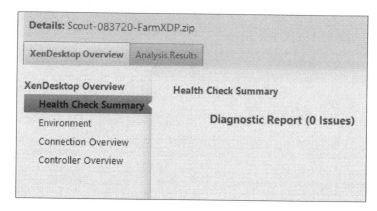

Citrix® Scout for XenDesktop® diagnostics

Citrix has bundled various XenDesktop and XenApp diagnostic and debugging tools under the roof of a single tool called Citrix Scout. Citrix Scout is supported on XenDesktop 5.x and above. Starting from XenDesktop 7.1, Scout is preinstalled on all controller servers, and can be found in the `Citrix` folder on the Start menu app.

Included Citrix® tools

Scout includes the other standalone and earlier tools such as **Citrix Diagnostic Facility (CDF)** Control, XDPing, and XDDBDiag. The following is the complete list of other Citrix tools that are included in Scout. All of these tools can be located within the `Scout` folder, as shown here:

```
C:\>dir "C:\Program Files (x86)\Citrix\Scout\Current\Utilities\*.exe" /d
/b

CDFControl.exe

LicInventoryCheck.exe

paexec.exe

XADSInfo.exe

XDDBDiag.exe

XdPing.exe


C:\>
```

Key data points collected

The information collected by the Scout tool includes the following key data points:

- Hardware details, such as information on BIOS, the computer, and its peripheral devices

- Software details, such as the OS, service packs, hot fixes, drivers, group policies, and so on

- Windows application and system event logs

- The Windows system registry

- XenDesktop site-specific data includes Broker details, Hypervisor details, License server information, XDDBDiag output, and so on

- Controller system details, such as CDF Traces, Citrix binaries and services information, controller and VDA configuration and log files, XDPing output, and so on

Running Citrix® Scout

Citrix Scout can be run on the controller server. The user running Scout on the controller must be a local administrator, as well as a domain user for each controller being queried. Scout can also be run from the command-line interface, and is located at `C:\Program Files (x86)\Citrix\Scout\Run.exe`. A successful run of Citrix Scout involves the following steps:

1. Launch Citrix Scout from the Start Menu Apps list, which will run `C:\Program Files (x86)\Citrix\Scout\Run.exe`. The Scout application shows the XenDesktop Site and DDC server in the left pane with a sub list of the data points that will be gathered.

2. Define the Collection settings for Scout using the Scout configuration settings wizard. It lets you define settings such as **Report folder**, **Event Log** selection, **CDF trace file settings**, **Machine Settings**, and an option for specifying **Proxy server** if it's in use in your environment, as shown here:

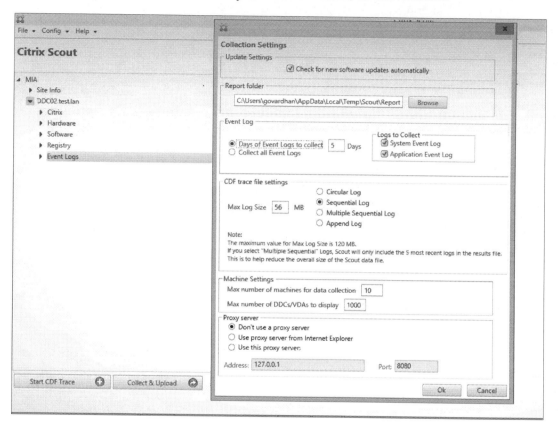

3. Click on **Start CDF Trace** to capture and include the CDF traces in the collection:

   1. A new window with option the **Select machines to gather CDF traces from** will be presented, listing all of your virtual desktops and controllers.

   2. Select the controllers and VDAs to be queried from the listed machines, and click on **Continue**.

   Upon completion, the CDF trace files are written to `tmp\<site-farmname>\<hostname>\Citrix\CDFControl Traces` in the folder. All the CDF Trace files created will be included in the final ZIP file.

4. Click on **Collect & Upload**:

   1. Select the controllers and VDAs to be queried from the listed machines, and click on **Continue**.

   2. During machine selection, you can define the settings to be used for querying that machine. These settings include enabling the **WinRM Configuration** for VDAs to be queried remotely and also enabling verbose logging for XenDesktop services, as shown here:

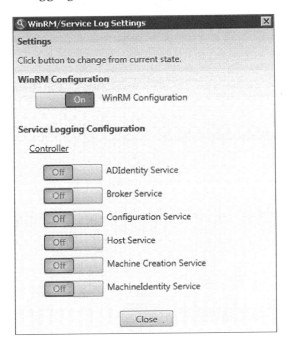

   3. Upon successful data collection, you'll be presented with the **Save** option to provide an alternate filename and location of the zipped file.

   4. Once the file is successfully saved, you'll be presented with the dialogue box to upload the files to the CIS web site.

   5. Click on **Continue** to proceed. Provide your MyCitrix account to get authenticated into the CIS website, and click on **Upload**.

6. Then, exit the Scout application, during which you can choose **Delete all temporary file on exit**, and also **Delete saved collection results on exit**, as shown in the following screenshot:

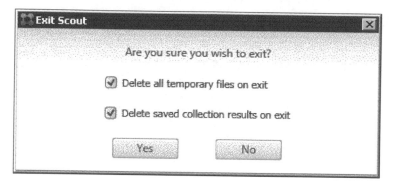

PowerShell command-lets

Citrix has made an automated interface to manage XenDesktop configurations, as well as logs gathered by its monitoring services. You can use the XenDesktop PowerShell SDK to monitor or retrieve the instantaneous status of a XenDesktop environment. We'll cover all the XenDesktop PowerShell-based command-lets and options in the next chapter, which is focused on the XenDesktop PowerShell SDK. I am making this reference here so that you'll be aware of command line interface support which can be used in troubleshooting and automation requirements.

Citrix® troubleshooting tools for XenDesktop®

So far, you have learned about the comprehensive set of enterprise-level XenDesktop monitoring and troubleshooting tools from Citrix. You'll now learn the individual tools available for troubleshooting XenDesktop's operational issues.

How to troubleshoot XenDesktop® issues

In most cases, effective troubleshooting usually requires following the correct procedure and tools. Before we get into the technicality of the tools available for XenDesktop troubleshooting, here is a quick review of how to troubleshoot XenDesktop issues.

Refer to the right documentation

All major technology vendors provide decent documentation on enterprise-level applications, and I should say that Citrix really does a great job on maintaining the documentation of its technologies. In most enterprises, the helpdesk or support team is provided with the required documentation about the product and its setup in the environment. Help desk support team builds a list of known issues and fixes documentation, which serves as an internal knowledge base for operational issues. Always follow the internal documentation first and refer to the vendor documentation for reference or advanced troubleshooting.

It's also recommended to have documentation written to educate end users on how to use your XenDesktop environment and its features from both within the LAN and VPN over the public Internet.

Understand the XenDesktop® architecture and its setup in your environment

Apart from general support / helpdesk knowledge base articles, understanding how XenDesktop works strengthens your XenDesktop troubleshooting skills. Knowing how it is setup in your environment further simplifies the troubleshooting of issues and limits turnaround times to meet the SLA defined. Keeping a track of the latest changes in your environment helps you to quickly correlate the issues resulting as a side effect. Build a deep understanding of the XenDesktop FMA architecture and always have — and refer to — an updated XenDesktop architecture implemented in your environment handy.

XenDesktop troubleshooting can be made effective by the following:

- Understanding your organization's desktop environment and use cases by different groups of users
- Both a high-level overview and a deep component-level understanding of the XenDesktop FMA architecture
- As XenDesktop is a Windows based technology, the more your knowledge on Windows technologies, the better you can resolve Windows-related issues

Understanding the nature of issues

A support professional's first task involves understanding and correctly classifying the issues reported. In general, most issues that arise while using any technology are majorly related to:

- Lack of knowledge of usage by end users
- Product misconfiguration and malfunctioning
- Operating environment failures, such as in the hardware, network, and so on

When handling XenDesktop issues, you should be able to classify/isolate them according to their root cause. Most of the common XenDesktop issues can be specific or related to the following:

- User-level- or user-profile-related
- User-sessions- related, such as runtime issues
- Application level
- Machine level—includes both Windows and VDAs related
- Citrix- or Windows Group policy level
- Delivery group or Machine catalog level
- XenDesktop Site level:
  - Windows or Citrix Licenses-related
  - Virtualization-hosts-related
  - Storage-related
  - Database-related
  - XenDesktop component server level, such as Storefront, controller and other servers
  - Related to XenDesktop server-side services
- Data center level:
  - Servers hardware and physical networking level
  - Network-related, such as Firewall, NetScaler, external DNS and others
  - Related to NetScaler or other load balancing services, if used
  - Active Directory level, including sites, trusts. and replication
- Related to any other third-party technology (if used), for example, AppSense for managing application and user settings

Citrix® HDX monitor

HDX monitor validates the functionality and configuration of the HDX stack, which is one of the core strengths of XenDesktop. All of the HDX stack that can be validated includes latest HDX virtualization technologies, such as MediaStream for Flash and HDX RealTime features. For example, suppose you have deployed a new policy setting to enable Session Reliability for your virtual desktop connections. You can verify the effect of your policy change by running HDX monitor against your virtual desktop machine or sessions, which shows whether the policy setting got applied to the virtual machine or session.

HDX monitor plays a key role in validating and ensuring that your HDX configurations are successfully deployed. Its built-in analyzing capabilities capture data and identify potential problems in the state, configuration, and/or performance of HDX technologies in your environment. It also suggests corrective action that can help resolve the problem or improve performance. For example, it detects when multimedia redirection is in use and whether your endpoint device supports it or not. It also can tell you what audio codec you are using and its bit rate.

Plus, HDX monitor has the ability to diagnose XenDesktop sessions via the WMI diagnostics interface, both locally and remotely from any machine in the domain. The latest HDX monitor 3.x provides better configurability, validation of expanded components, and many more alerts. HDX monitor is designed for ICA HDX diagnostics and doesn't yield any results if run under Console or Remote Desktop sessions.

Features of HDX monitor

HDX monitor ships with very handy and self-explanatory features that include the following:

- **Generate report**
- **Export**
- **Support forum**
- **Change target**
- **Settings**
- **About**

HDX technologies supported

The following are the current HDX technologies covered by this tool:

- **Thinwire (Graphics)**
- **Direct 3D (Graphics)**
- **Media Stream (also known as RAVE)**
- **Flash**
- **Audio**
- **USB devices**
- **Mapped Client Drives (CDM)**
- **Branch repeater**
- **Printer**
- **Client**
- **Smart card**
- **Scanner**
- **System**

Using HDX monitor

Using HDX monitor is exceptionally simple, and it intuitively displays the results. You'll start loving it more as you keep using it. HDX monitor is supported by XenDesktop 5.5 and above. An important point to note is that it doesn't make any changes to the HDX. The following are a few brief notes and screenshots to help you get started with using this tool, and the look and feel:

1. HDX monitor can be currently downloaded from the CIS page at `https://taas.Citrix.com/hdx/download/`.

2. It does not require administrative rights to install or run. Some HDX features data can be accessible and shown only when run with elevated access. Install HDX monitor on virtual desktops or any machine in the domain that has access to virtual desktops.

3. Upon launching, HDX monitor presents **HDX Settings and Performance**, which lists all the HDX features and their runtime performance rating index. Also, at the bottom of the screen, you can see the overall **HDX Index Score** value, the maximum value being 10, as shown in this screenshot:

4. Upon clicking any of the components listed, you'll be taken to the detailed view of that feature, as shown here:

5. Using its **Settings** page, you can further define various parameters under **Performance Counter**, **HDX Components**, **Monitor**, **Logging**, and **Alerts**. The following is a screenshot of the **Settings** page, displaying the HDX Component's section options:

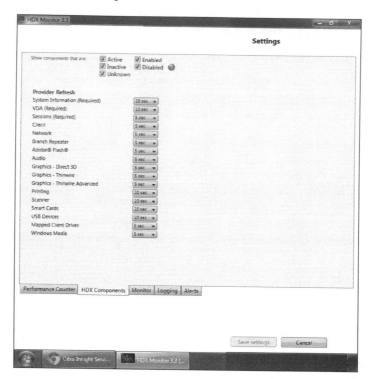

6. The remote virtual desktops should have WinRM enabled for this tool to run remotely. To remotely run HDX monitor using WinRM, choose **WinRM** by going to **Settings | Monitor | Access Type**. On the virtual desktop, you can enable WinRM by running the `winrm quickconfig` command as an administrator.

Citrix® Diagnostics Toolkit

The **Citrix Diagnostics Toolkit (CDT)** is a suite of tools and automation options designed with easy-to-use, built-in menus and shortcuts to quickly and effectively configure data collection and integrate third-party tools for more robust and comprehensive debugging sessions, though each of the tools included is available as an independent standalone application. It's available in both 32-bit and 64-bit editions for the respective platforms. It's enhanced to support XenDesktop 7.x. It serves as the comprehensive set of Citrix tools, and you are advised to use this toolkit with guidance or assistance from Citrix support teams.

Suite of tools included

During the installation, the tools most commonly used for that product will be deployed, based on the options that you select during the CDT installation wizard:

- Citrix Scout: http://support.Citrix.com/article/CTX130147
- IMA Helper: http://support.Citrix.com/article/CTX133983
- CDFMonitor: http://support.Citrix.com/article/CTX129537
- XDPing Tool: http://support.Citrix.com/article/CTX123278
- Citrix Quick launch: http://support.Citrix.com/article/CTX122536
- Citrix Print Detective: http://support.Citrix.com/article/CTX116474
- PortICA Log Enabler V3: http://support.Citrix.com/article/ctx118837
- The Receiver Clean-Up utility: http://support.Citrix.com/article/CTX137494
- The XenDesktop site checker: http://support.Citrix.com/article/CTX133767
- Citrix Policy Reporter Tool: http://support.Citrix.com/articlc/CTX138533
- XDDBDiag for XenDesktop: http://support.Citrix.com/article/CTX128075
- Citrix Web Interface Tracing: http://support.Citrix.com/article/CTX136629
- DSCheck Maintenance Assistant: http://support.Citrix.com/article/CTX137608
- Seamless Configuration Helper Tool: http://support.Citrix.com/article/CTX115146
- DSCheck Maintenance Assistant v1.2: http://support.Citrix.com/article/CTX137608
- XenApp Load Balancing Diagnostic Tool: http://support.Citrix.com/article/CTX124446
- Citrix Receiver Diagnostics Tool for Windows: http://support.Citrix.com/article/CTX141751
- SystemDump 3.1 for 32-bit and 64-bit platforms: http://support.Citrix.com/static/oldkc/CTX111072.html
- XenDesktop Controller Service Log Enabler V3: http://support.Citrix.com/article/CTX127492

- StressPrinters 1.3.2 for 32-bit and 64-bit platforms: `http://support.Citrix.com/article/CTX109374`
- Citrix DumpCheck utility (command-line) version 1.4: `http://support.Citrix.com/static/oldkc/CTX108890.html`

The **XenDesktop Tracing Tools** (CDF Tracing) option is selected by default during the installation. A `.ctl` file with all the trace modules for XenDesktop DDCs is created in the `\CitrixDiagnostics\XenDesktop Tools\` folder.

XDDBDiag

XDDBDiag (short for XenDesktop DataBase Diagnostic) is a command-line tool that is now included in Citrix Scout. XDDBDiag performs a consistency data check on the data as well as a connectivity verification of the XenDesktop database. It outputs the diagnostic data in a compressed comma-separated value (`.csv`) file named `<computername>_XDDBDiag_Output.zip` in the current directory of the tool. It supports various parameters to run against a local or remote SQL server used for the XenDesktop database.

This tool collects the following important details about the XenDesktop environment:

- Site information
- VDA information
- Current connections / connection log
- Hypervisor connections
- Citrix policy information
- Desktop groups
- Controller information
- SQL information

It can be downloaded from Citrix at `http://support.Citrix.com/article/CTX128075`.

XDPing

The XDPing (short for XenDesktop Ping) is a command-line tool that checks for the causes of common configuration issues in a XenDesktop environment. It primarily helps to determine connectivity issues between the controller and the VDAs. This tool can also be used to verify configuration settings on both the XenDesktop Broker and VDA machines, both from the console and remotely. It's also built into the Citrix Scout.

When you run this tool on the VDA, it will run through various connectivity checks and report you the status of the following major data points:

- Local machine
- User
- Local machine time
- Domain controller (or controllers) time
- Network interfaces
- WCF endpoints — BrokerAgent
- Workstation devices
- DNS lookups for local machine
- Client details
- Event log check
- Windows firewall settings
- XenDesktop farm
- Registry based configurations
- Controllers (manually specified)
- Summary

A sample output of a successful XDPing run will look like this:

```
C:\>Users\govardhan\Desktop\XDPing\XdPing.exe


XDPing 2.2.0.0
Created by Citrix Systems Engineering and Escalation teams.
Help us improve this tool by providing feedback through http://twitter.
com/CitrixEscEMEA.


Checking version : You are using the latest version.


------------------------------------------------------------------
Local Machine::

  NetBIOS Name = XDVM01
  OS Version   = Microsoft Windows NT 6.1.7601 Service Pack 1
```

```
   Platform      = X64 Platform


   Computer Domain: Test.lan
     Role        = Member Workstation
     Membership = Verified, SID
  :S-1-5-21-2967284573-3965547089-2029033641-1140 [OK]



-----------------------------------------------------------------
User::


  User Name      = govardhan
  User Domain    = TEST
  Authentication = Kerberos [OK]
  Groups:
     TEST\Domain Users
     Everyone
     BUILTIN\Users
     BUILTIN\Administrators
     NT AUTHORITY\INTERACTIVE
     CONSOLE LOGON
     NT AUTHORITY\Authenticated Users
     NT AUTHORITY\This Organization
     LOCAL
     TEST\Domain Admins
Unable to translate group name from SPID  S-1-18-1
[WARNING]
     TEST\Denied RODC Password Replication Group


-----------------------------------------------------------------
..
...
...
-----------------------------------------------------------------
```

Registry Based Configurations::

Registry based Controller list (ListOfDDCs) : [Not Conigured]

[Configured]

   Controller : DDC01.Test.lan

- -

Controllers (manually specified)::

  Controller: DDC01.Test.lan:0

    DNS Lookup(DDC01.Test.lan):

      Host Name = DDC01.Test.lan

      Address #0 = 172.20.16.29 (rDNS: DDC01.Test.lan) [OK]

    Ping Service: /Citrix/CdsController/IRegistrar

      Connect = Unable to open connection to DDC01.Test.lan:0

[ERROR]

  ListOfDDC is set in the c:\personality.ini file to enumerate DDC list
[OK]

- -

Summary::

    Checking version : You are using the latest version. [OK]

    Unable to translate group name from SPID S-1-18-1 [WARNING]

    NetRemoteTOD from Test.lan failed! - Error: The service has not been
started [ERROR]

    Unable to obtain time from domain controller. [ERROR]

    Connect = Unable to open connection to DDC01.Test.lan:0 [ERROR]

Number of messages reported = 5

C:\>

CDF Control

The **CDF (Citrix Diagnostic Facility)** control is an event tracing tool for the controller/consumer that captures CDF trace messages resulting from the various Citrix tracing providers. CDF Control is now included in Citrix Scout and is available on the controller servers. It can also be installed on any Windows server system. It should be run with local administrator access for all of its features to be functional. This tool provides options to choose the **Trace Categories** modules, and then buttons called **Start Tracing** and **Stop Tracing**. As the tool runs, it instantly updates **Controller Stats** and **Consumer Stats** with the appropriate counters, as shown here:

It also supports features such as remote tracing and a broad set of filters to refine the results. The options page of this tool lets you customize the tool behavior, as shown in the following screenshot:

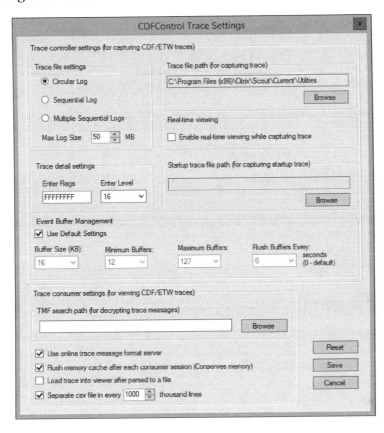

Citrix® Print Detective

The Citrix Print Detective is a specialized tool for troubleshooting printing issues in a XenDesktop environment. It enumerates all the printer drivers from the specified Windows machine, including driver-specific information. Helpdesk and support teams can use this tool to detect how printers and their drivers are deployed on virtual machines. It also supports an option to delete the specified print drivers. Furthermore, it gives log file capabilities and provides a command-line interface. Here is a screenshot of **Print Detective**, showing the available printers and drivers:

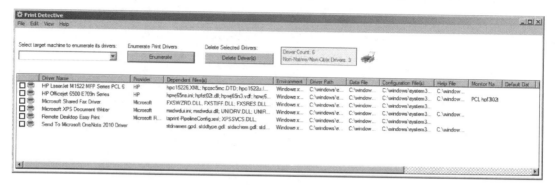

XenDesktop® Site Checker

XenDesktop Site Checker is a XenDesktop PowerShell-SDK-based tool that enumerates XenDesktop 5 site brokers, services, hosts, assignments, catalogs, and provisioning tasks and schemes. It performs extensive service running statuses and checks whether the service instances are registered or not. It provides the ability to enable logging for each service. It also provides some advanced management tasks that aren't available in Desktop Studio. Furthermore, it provides detailed information about each component that it checks, and logs any script that is executed by the tool. However, this tool is currently supported only on 5.x.

Troubleshooting knowledge for issues out of the scope of XenDesktop

Apart from what can be handled by the aforementioned Citrix-provided XenDesktop troubleshooting tools, certain issues are beyond the scope of these tools and need other domain-specific knowledge and debugging skills. Most of such issues generally fall under the Network, Virtualization, and Windows domains. In most enterprises, these domains and their technologies will have their specific monitoring setup, as well as troubleshooting procedures to be followed.

Network tracing for external access issues

If you suspect that the issues reported could be related to the network layer, you'll be able to trace the entry points where the access is failing. This is mostly the case if your deployment has external access set up. In this case, you'll have to work with your network team to enable verbose logs and analyze them to correlate to the issue at the hand. The most helpful logs will be the following:

- Firewall logs
- NetScaler logs
- StoreFront web server logs

Troubleshooting at the virtualization layer

Virtualization has become a key infrastructure platform in most enterprises, and it ships with advanced monitoring and troubleshooting procedures. In most enterprises, independent of the virtualization platform used, there will be dedicated monitoring set up, as well as a team to handle the virtualization infrastructure. You should be able to at least verify the following activities with respect to the virtualization platform:

- Access and connectivity to the virtualization hosts
- Storage connectivity status to the virtualization hosts
- Virtual machine management tasks, such as restarting during hung or crash states
- Viewing the virtual machines and virtual host logs
- Verifying the network configuration of the hosts and VMs

Troubleshooting at the Windows layer

What a user needs out of the virtual desktop is access to the functional Windows applications, data, settings and preferences, security, and privacy of their access. With respect to XenDesktop, troubleshooting Windows layer issues requires minimum knowledge of the following concepts:

- Users profiles
- Users sessions
- Application issues
- The Windows operating system
- Runtime session issues
- Filesystems and the registry
- Server-side technologies

Summary

In this chapter, we started off by defining monitoring and troubleshooting in general, and then you learned the broad range of XenDesktop's troubleshooting tools available from Citrix. The "deep-dive" knowledge of these tools helps you to keep your XenDesktop environment operating at a higher efficiency and performance. We also covered the minimum of other domain knowledge required for handling the issues that fall out of the scope of XenDesktop tools.

In the next chapter, you'll learn how to automate XenDesktop tasks using the PowerShell SDK, and also the command-lets that help troubleshoot XenDesktop issues.

XenDesktop® PowerShell SDK for Automation

In the earlier chapters, we learned about implementing XenDesktop and its administration through manual GUI procedures. In this chapter, we'll discover the command-line mode for automating procedures involved in managing the XenDesktop environments. Similar to any other Windows-based technologies, Citrix provides a PowerShell-based SDK as well that lets XenDesktop administrators implement the automation.

We'll start off with understanding the terminology, including SDK, PowerShell, and automation in the context of XenDesktop. We'll dive deep into implementing new automations and also learn how to use SDK command-lets for troubleshooting purposes. The following is a list of topics we'll learn in this chapter:

- PowerShell SDK for automation:
  - The purpose of SDK
  - PowerShell and its capabilities
  - PowerShell for XenDesktop
  - The role of automation for IT
  - Tools for developing automation using PowerShell SDK

- Using the XenDesktop PowerShell SDK:
  - Installation and configuration
  - Running SDK command-lets
  - Creating PowerShell scripts
  - Automation using PowerShell scripts

- Dive deep into the XenDesktop PowerShell SDK:
  - Key notes about using PowerShell
  - The structure of the latest PowerShell SDK
  - A complete reference of PowerShell SDK
  - Troubleshooting and commonly used SDK command-lets

It is assumed that you will have an intermediate and higher level of PowerShell's usage and its knowledge.

PowerShell SDK for automation

Citrix SDK for XenDesktop is based on the Microsoft Windows PowerShell language, which lets you perform all of the administrative tasks that you can do in Citrix Studio, and even more tasks that can't be performed with Studio alone. This PowerShell-based SDK lets you automate XenDesktop administrative tasks, operations, and also integrate with other Windows technologies or programming platforms.

The purpose of SDK

As widely known, SDK stands for Software Development Kit and is also termed as DevKit. SDK generally consists of one or more **Application Programming Interfaces** (**API**) that are shipped in the form of libraries (.dll files) with an interface to a particular programming language. SDKs are provided by the software product vendors to their developer communities. SDKs include detailed documentation, debugging, and respective development tools. It's primarily aimed at software developers to build software that reuses, extends, or customizes functionalities to their business requirements. APIs are also referred to or used from the supported scripting languages by IT administrators and system engineers, to automate the daily or recurring operational tasks.

PowerShell and its capabilities

PowerShell is a Microsoft Windows task-based command-line shell and scripting environment, especially designed for system administration. It's built on the .NET Framework, enabling IT professionals and power users to control and automate the administration of the Windows operating system and applications that run on Windows. For a long time, Windows IT professionals suffered the difficulties of manually running ever-increasing system administration activities through GUI or semi-automated modes. Microsoft has come up with PowerShell as the new Shell interface with a highly readable syntactic language. PowerShell was developed considering the features and capabilities of Shell and Shell scripting languages that are already existing in non-Windows (*nix) operating systems. PowerShell has now emerged as the new de facto standard for both command-line and scripted modes access to Windows operating systems and Windows-based applications/technologies.

PowerShell is continuously evolving and its latest version in use is PowerShell 4.0. PowerShell 4.0 ships as a Windows Management Framework by default with Windows 8.1 and Windows Server 2012 R2. All major releases of PowerShell are supported, and each major release has backward compatibility with the preceding versions. The following are some of the key technologies that PowerShell integrates and interacts with.

PowerShell and .NET framework

As PowerShell is built on .NET framework, and it inherently features most of the .NET capabilities. The primary attribute is everything in PowerShell that is an object. PowerShell supports both procedural as well as object-oriented programming syntax. PowerShell features intrinsic support for .NET objects to leverage the vast set of .NET objects and information available in them.

PowerShell and WMI

The **Windows Management Instrumentation (WMI)** has been the long existing feature of Windows operating systems for management. PowerShell supports and integrates with WMI that lets you access the broad information within WMI and its remote access capabilities.

PowerShell and COM

The **Common Object Model (COM)** is Microsoft's early technology for supporting interoperation between software, regardless of the original language. The .NET Framework and its developments are slowly replacing the use of COM. PowerShell supports the COM objects as well and lets you automate the application level tasks execution.

PowerShell Remoting and WinRM

For an efficient enterprise level system administration, it's a highly required capability to manage the systems remotely. PowerShell ships with a capability called PowerShell Remoting that lets PowerShell users execute the commands remotely. PowerShell Remoting is supported via the **Windows Remote Management (WinRM)** feature.

The Windows Remote Management (WinRM) feature is a Microsoft implementation of WS-Management Protocol, a standard **Simple Object Access Protocol (SOAP)**-based, firewall-friendly protocol that allows hardware and operating systems from different vendors to interoperate. The Windows Remote Management (WinRM) runs as a service on Windows systems, which supports the execution of remote commands. WinRM is supported on Windows 7 and above.

Target audience for PowerShell scripting

As explained in the previous section, PowerShell is designed for system administration and its automation is primarily done by Windows IT professionals. Being a scripting language, it interfaces with the Windows on top of .NET Framework and WMI, which simplifies programming for IT professionals. However, the Windows software developers find it more efficient to directly interact with an SDK based on native .NET APIs instead of PowerShell that runs on top of .NET. Depending on the scope of requirement, either IT professionals or software developers can work on implementing the PowerShell-based solutions.

PowerShell for XenDesktop®

Microsoft has integrated PowerShell in all of its core technologies, such as Active Directory, MS Exchange, SQL Database, SharePoint, Azure, IIS, and so on, and made some of the operations available only via PowerShell. Microsoft's Common Engineering Criteria prescribes that new server and product management tools must be based on Windows PowerShell. This resulted in the wide adoption of PowerShell across the industry, and in-line with this shift, all the major Windows based technology vendors, such as VMware, Citrix, Symantec, CA technologies, and even cloud service providers, such as Amazon Web Services, have started supporting PowerShell-based access to their technologies.

Citrix also provides PowerShell SDKs for all of its technologies, including XenDesktop. The common platform of PowerShell helps to develop automation that can interact not only with XenDesktop, but also with other Citrix and Microsoft technologies. Using PowerShell SDK for XenDesktop, you can perform all the administrative actions that can be performed using Studio, along with tasks that can't be performed using Studio. XenDesktop includes several options and features that can only be configured via PowerShell. Citrix Studio features the built-in PowerShell prompt to quick launch the PowerShell from Studio.

Role of automation for IT

One of the top priorities for IT professionals today is to reduce the operational costs and improve the efficiency of managing the ever-growing scale of enterprises. Enterprises while implementing and integrating multiple technologies in their environment find various gaps to be filled in to bridge the gap and adhere to the existing operational and compliance terms. For example, as you know we use Active Directory user groups for assigning desktops to users in XenDesktop. In an environment, it may be dictated that no individual user should be assigned the desktops, and only user groups need to be used. This requires XenDesktop administrators to periodically monitor XenDesktop assignments. To address this, you can set up a scheduled task that runs a PowerShell script daily, which queries all the desktop assignments and e-mails them to the support team list. There exist plenty of such requirements, which can be automated for efficient handling.

Automation primarily consists of a tool (.exe) or a script that runs a sequence of commands or code block, either locally or remotely, on a predefined schedule. In this chapter, you'll learn how to author PowerShell scripts for automating XenDesktop operational activities.

Tools for developing automation using PowerShell SDK

PowerShell ships with a built-in editor for authoring PowerShell scripts and modules. There also exists good third-party tools and editors with additional features to help the PowerShell developers. The following is a quick list of tools for the PowerShell developers.

Microsoft PowerShell ISE

Windows PowerShell **Integrated Scripting Environment** (**ISE**) is a free and default PowerShell script editor that ships along with PowerShell and is part of Windows Management Framework. It enables you to write, run, and test the scripts and modules in a graphical and intuitive environment. The key features include syntax coloring, tab completion, IntelliSense, visual debugging, Unicode compliance, context-sensitive Help, Script browser, and Script analyzer.

PowerGUI

PowerGUI is a Dell software product available in both Free and Pro editions. The free edition provides all of the basic features and capabilities similar to PowerShell ISE. It's one of the most widely used editors by the PowerShell developer community.

Visual Studio extensions

Most of the Windows core developer professionals use the Visual Studio software for their Windows software development. It's a comprehensive development platform that supports all of the .NET programming and its languages.

PowerShell tools

Microsoft PowerShell tools is an extension that integrates PowerShell with Visual Studio. Using Visual Studio, users can develop PowerShell scripts and automation within it.

Citrix® Developer

Citrix Developer is a Visual Studio Extension pack provided by Citrix. It provides several Citrix Solution Kits for developers to get started quickly with building on top of the Citrix APIs. This extension also includes a menu to the Citrix Developer online communities with easy access from within the IDE.

The PowerShell community – CodePlex and PowerGUI

The key benefit with PowerShell is that its wide usage has generated a great community across the world that helps you achieve your requirements. You can find vendor or product-based communities that focus on specific technologies. Here, we discuss the most active and commonly contributed communities.

CodePlex (https://www.codeplex.com/) is Microsoft's free open source project hosting site. You can find various PowerShell modules and extensions shared by the PowerShell community. You can also share your own PowerShell modules and scripts for the community.

The PowerGUI (http://en.community.dell.com/techcenter/powergui/m/ powerpacks) community shares their scripts and modules as PowerPacks, which can be auto-detected and loaded by the PowerGUI editor. It contains the modules developed for Dell technologies, and also includes modules for common Microsoft technologies.

Using the XenDesktop® PowerShell SDK

In the previous section, we learned the terminology and quick foundational introduction to the concepts of PowerShell SDK for XenDesktop automation. We'll now see how to get the environment set up and will start authoring PowerShell scripts using XenDesktop PowerShell SDK command-lets.

Installation and configuration

We'll see the quick installation and configuration steps required to install and configure both PowerShell and XenDesktop PowerShell SDK.

Installing and configuring PowerShell

PowerShell ships by default with the latest Windows Server and desktop operating systems. With each recent release of Windows operating systems, Microsoft has released a newer version of PowerShell. In fact, the upcoming Windows 10 release is supposed to ship the latest PowerShell Version v5. Starting with the PowerShell 2.0 release with Windows 7 and Windows Server 2008, Microsoft has integrated and made PowerShell available by default on the systems. For the earlier versions of Windows, PowerShell needs to be installed manually. Also, on Windows 7 and above, you can manually update PowerShell to the latest version by installing the Windows Management Framework. You can perform the following steps to install and make PowerShell available for the script execution:

1. Download the required version of Windows Management Framework from Microsoft Download Center (`http://www.microsoft.com/en-us/download/`).

2. Ensure that the recommended version of the Microsoft .NET Framework is installed on the system.

3. Run the PowerShell installer as a local administrator and restart the computer.

4. Verify the version of PowerShell on the system using the following command:

   `$PSVersionTable`

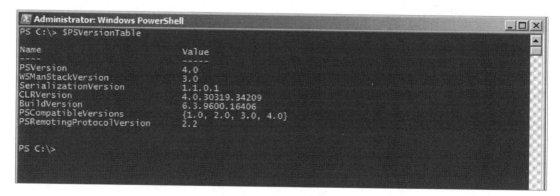

5. By default, PowerShell allows the execution of command-lets but not scripts, as a security measure. You need to enable script execution via PowerShell ExecutionPolicy. You can set the ExecutionPolicy to one of the supported value as appropriate to your requirement. The supported values include AllSigned, RemoteSigned, or Unrestricted. The ExecutionPolicy can be set using following command which can only be set by the members of the administrators group:

   `Set-ExecutionPolicy -ExecutionPolicy <DesiredPolicySetting>`

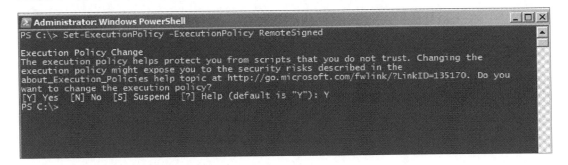

6. Enable PowerShell Remoting: By default, PowerShell configures Windows
   systems to initiate remote commands on other computers. The latest
   Windows Server 2012 and above are also configured to receive the remote
   commands and no further configuration is needed. However, on the earlier
   Windows operating systems, PowerShell Remoting can be enabled by
   administrators using the following commands:

   ```
   winrm quickconfig (this command can be run from command shell as
   well) (OR)
   ```

   ```
   Enable-PSRemoting -force
   ```

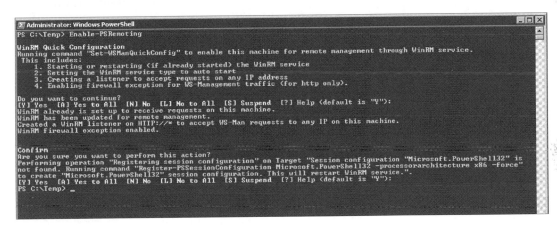

Installing and configuring XenDesktop® PowerShell SDK

The PowerShell SDK for XenDesktop has been in existence, since XenDesktop 4. The latest XenDesktop PowerShell SDK consists of various PowerShell Version 3.0 snap-ins that are installed automatically along with either the Controller or Studio components installation. The latest SDK in XenDesktop 7 is backward compatible only with XenDesktop 5, but not with XenDesktop 4 since it is based on IMA. For easier differentiation, the XenDesktop 5 snap-ins are named with V1 at the end, while the XenDesktop 7 snap-ins are named with V2 at the end. Both .V1 and .V2 snap-ins work with the current latest version of XenDesktop 7.x.

The PowerShell SDK snap-ins can be located under separate subfolders of the `C:\Program Files\Citrix` path. XenDesktop PowerShell SDK currently ships the following snap-ins:

- Citrix.AdIdentity.Admin.V2
- Citrix.AppV.Admin.V1
- Citrix.Broker.Admin.V2
- Citrix.Configuration.Admin.V2
- Citrix.ConfigurationLogging.Admin.V1
- Citrix.DelegatedAdmin.Admin.V1
- Citrix.EnvTest.Admin.V1
- Citrix.Host.Admin.V2
- Citrix.MachineCreation.Admin.V2
- Citrix.Monitor.Admin.V1
- Citrix.Storefront.Admin.V1

Running SDK command-lets

Once you have PowerShell successfully installed with XenDesktop snap-ins, you can load and run any of the SDK snap-ins and command-lets. The following sequence of steps is used to load XenDesktop snap-ins in the PowerShell environment and then, execute the XenDesktop command-lets:

1. **Manually load and use XenDesktop snap-ins**. Launch PowerShell and load the XenDesktop snap-ins that you require in the PowerShell environment using the `Add-PSSnapin` command-let, as shown in the example that follows:

   `Add-PSSnapin Citrix.Broker.Admin.V2 (OR)`

   `Add-PSSnapin Citrix.* (to load all of the Citrix snap-ins)`

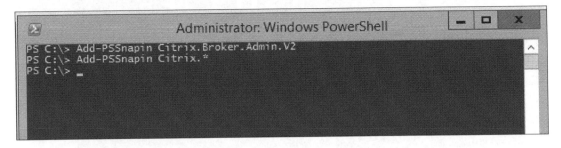

2. **Use Launch PowerShell from Studio, which automatically loads the XenDesktop snap-ins**. For easier invocation, Citrix provides a quick button named **Launch PowerShell** from the Studio itself, which launches the PowerShell Window with XenDesktop snap-ins preloaded. The following screenshot shows you where you can locate the **Launch PowerShell** from Studio:

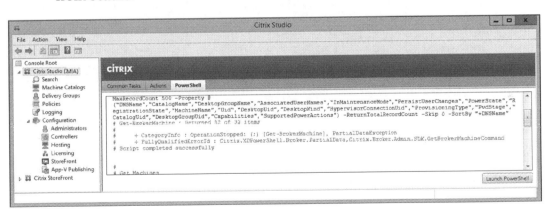

3. Verify that the XenDesktop snap-ins are successfully loaded by running the following command-let:

```
Get-PSSnapin Citrix.* | ft -Auto
```

4. On the successful loading/importing of XenDesktop snap-ins, you can access the XenDesktop command-lets and their associated help.

5. You can further get a list of command-lets that are available with each, or all, of the XenDesktop snap-ins using the following command:

```
get-command -module <XenDesktop snap-in name>
```

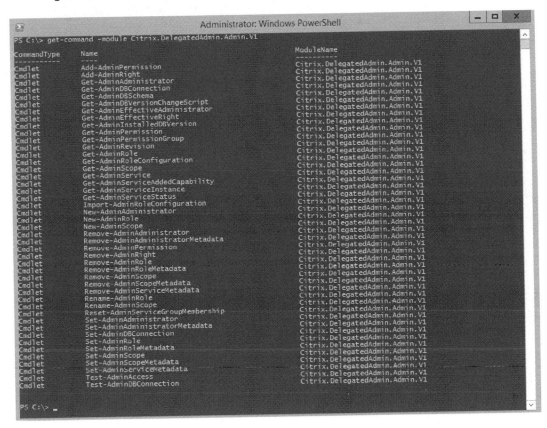

6. You need to follow a proper syntax while framing the command-let for the execution with values from your environment. If you are running the command-let for the first time, pay attention to its help documentation, frame a proper command line, and then execute it. The following command is a quick PowerShell SDK command execution, along with its help documentation:

```
get-help <XenDesktop command-let name>
```

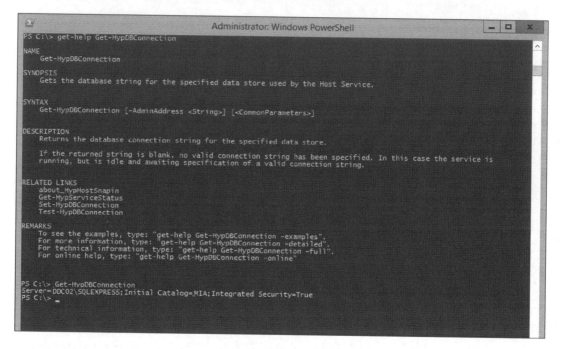

7. That's all! You have now learnt how to load the XenDesktop snap-ins, explore the command-lets, get the command-let help documentation, and execute your first PowerShell SDK command-let.

Creating PowerShell scripts

Now that you have learnt how to execute the SDK command-lets, we'll see how to author PowerShell scripts based on SDK command-lets. We'll learn how to quickly get on to authoring your own PowerShell scripts that can be used for automation. The following recommended procedure is used to develop PowerShell scripts for the XenDesktop automation:

1. Understand and analyze the task's requirement that you want to automate.

2. Locate the required command-lets and refer to its help documentation. A complete reference of XenDesktop version-specific command-lets can be found at the Citrix website. You can refer to the XenDesktop 7.6 command-lets documentation at `http://support.Citrix.com/proddocs/topic/XenApp-XenDesktop-76/xad-commands.html`.

3. Learn the invocation syntax used by Citrix Studio to perform the respective XenDesktop operations. Studio, in fact, runs respective command-lets for every action you perform, and it maintains a clean log of the PowerShell SDK commands that it has run.

4. You can locate the Studio log under the **PowerShell** tab of the Studio top-level node. The following screenshot of the Studio log shows the execution of the **Get-BrokerMachine** command-let, when you click on the **Search** section of Studio:

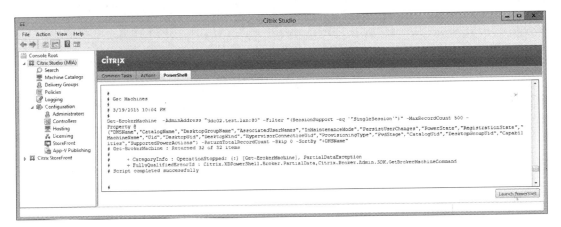

5. It is recommended that you collect the Studio PowerShell log for the operations that you want to automate, and then reuse the same code with your customizations.

6. To create your own script:

   1. Create a new file and save it with the `.ps1` extension.

   2. In the first lines of the file, import the XenDesktop snap-ins using the Add-PSSnapin command-let.

3. Add your XenDesktop command-lets along with tested arguments and clean comments, as follows:

```
Get-Machines - Notepad
File  Edit  Format  View  Help
#
# Get Machines  - Following is commandlet syntax from Studio log to list the machines.
# I've updated the command to run against my Collector server (ddc03.qalab.lan) in my test lab
#
#
Get-BrokerMachine  -AdminAddress "ddc03.qalab.lan:80" -Filter "((Uid -eq 2) -and (SessionSupport -eq
`"SingleSession`"))" -MaxRecordCount 2147483647 -ReturnTotalRecordCount -Skip 0
#
#
```

4. Test run any of your scripts in a test environment to validate that it's working as expected.

Automation using PowerShell scripts

Once you have authored your PowerShell scripts with the SDK commands, you can set them up to run automatically on a defined schedule, which becomes an automation task. You can set up the automation job execution using various tools, such as the Windows default **Scheduled Tasks** feature that is often used for setting up the automation. While setting up a script for automation, pay attention to the following factors:

- Ensure that your PowerShell location is defined in the system path variable. Use the absolute path to refer to PowerShell.exe.

- Provide the proper command-line parameters and their values.

- Specify a suitable schedule for the script execution. It's recommended that you schedule the automation tasks to run during off hours of your desktop usage.

- Ensure that you use an appropriate user account with the required access to run the script on the server.

- Ensure that you implement the logging into a file with proper error handling, so that a single command failure may not stop or affect the execution of the remaining commands in the script.

- Ensure that you capture the command's success and failures output to avoid runtime issues.

- It is recommended that you implement e-mailing the output of failures to the support team list, to address any runtime issues.

- If you are using commands to run against remote servers/systems, ensure that PowerShell Remoting is enabled and configured on the target system.

- Avoid writing/setting values via the automation unless they are rigorously tested and verified.

- Implement clean up of temporary files and stuck up process to avoid overloading the system.

A deep dive into the XenDesktop® PowerShell SDK

PowerShell SDK can be best utilized by users having both PowerShell scripting skills and the XenDesktop architecture understanding. We'll cover some of the advanced details about XenDesktop SDK, and will also learn the most widely used commands of PowerShell SDK.

Key notes about using PowerShell

It is implicit that XenDesktop administrators should learn/know the usage of PowerShell command-lets to make use of XenDesktop SDK. This makes XenDesktop, but not scripting aware, professionals to lag in using the SDK efficiently. The following quick PowerShell usage tips let you easily get started with PowerShell:

- Ensure that you are running the recommended version of PowerShell. If you are running an older version, but your script is using the latest PowerShell capabilities, the script execution may fail with errors.

- PowerShell is case insensitive. Command-lets are capitalized for readability purpose only.

- Command-lets use the notation of Verb-Item syntax, for example, **Get-BrokerMachine**.

- PowerShell also supports the execution of system commands and other tools that you run in Command Prompt cmd.exe.

- PowerShell (as well as its built-in editor ISE) is available in both x86 (32-bit) and x64 (64-bit) versions. By default, x64 Version of PowerShell is used on x64bit systems.

- Most of the command-lets will have a shortened form of a syntax called as alias:

    ○ By default, PowerShell ships with useful aliases for commonly used command-lets, and these aliases are called system level aliases. For example, the shortened alias for the **Add-PSSnapin** command-let is **asnp**.

    ○ PowerShell also supports the creation of a user's own aliases using the **New-Alias** command-let, as shown in the following command. These aliases are user-specific and are called user aliases:

    ```
    New-Alias  <aliasename>  <Command-let full name>
    ```

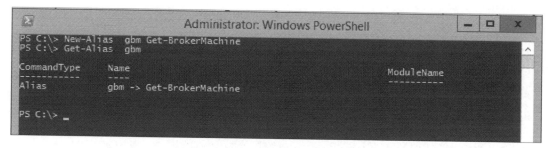

    ○ You can find a list of aliases available in the PowerShell environment using the **Ge-Alias** command-let, as shown in the following command:

    ```
    Get-Alias  <aliasename>
    ```

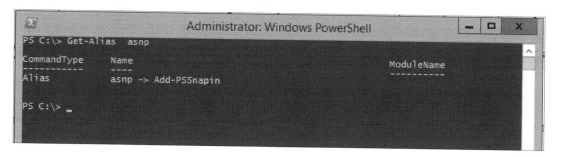

- PowerShell snap-ins are now legacy and are replaced with modules. Citrix is now adopting modules for the XenDesktop SDK, as discussed in the next section.

- The following command-lets can be very helpful for you to navigate through the new modules and command-lets:

    ○ Get-PSSnapin or Get-Module

    ○ Get-Command

    ○ Get-Help

    ○ Get-Member

- In cases where you need to set up your PowerShell script as .exe for automation, you can use the **PS2EXE** tool to convert your PowerShell script to an .exe file.

Structure of the latest PowerShell SDK

Citrix is constantly enhancing the PowerShell SDK with new capabilities. XenDesktop SDK snap-ins and modules are now very well-organized.

Folder structure

At a high level, all of the XenDesktop SDK files are located under the C:\Program Files\Citrix path. The SDK is split into separate snap-ins for each service on a controller. The individual snap-ins are segregated within the folder and follow a structure, as follows:

- The folder level corresponding to a component or feature is named with the notation of C:\Program Files\Citrix\<componentname or featurename>\.

- The component or feature-specific Snapin is located in a subfolder as C:\Program Files\Citrix\<componentname or featurename>\snapin.

- The `Snapin` folder consists of all the SDK code library files related to that component. Suppose that you are working on MCS, you can locate all the library files of MCS-specific PowerShell module `Citrix.MachineCreation.Admin.V2` in the `Snapin` folder, as shown in the following screenshot:

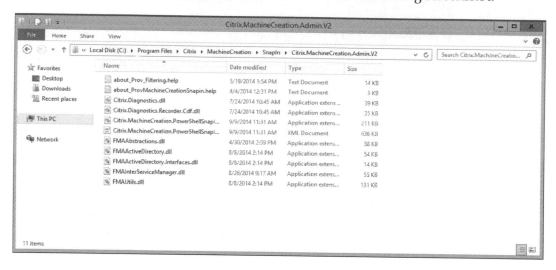

PowerShell Module adoption

The use of snap-ins for PowerShell has become legacy and Microsoft recommends that you use modules instead. While most of the XenDesktop PowerShell SDK is still based on snap-ins, Citrix has introduced a new module for XenDesktop administration named `Citrix.XenDesktop.Admin` in XenDesktop 7. This module is installed and can be located under the following path:

```
C:\Program Files\Citrix\XenDesktopPoshSdk\Module\Citrix.XenDesktop.
Admin.V1\Citrix.XenDesktop.Admin
```

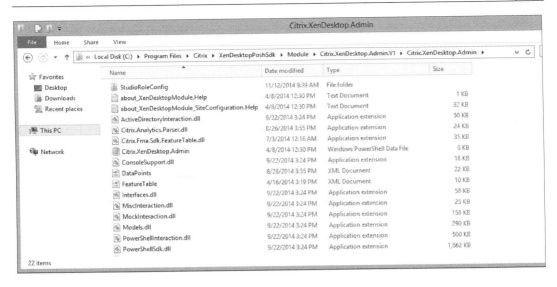

You can load and verify this module in your PowerShell environment using the following command-lets. Also, note that you can't manage PowerShell modules using the PSSnapin command-lets. To help you understand, the following screenshot explicitly shows the use of the Get-PSSnapin command-let that fails to locate the `Citrix.XenDesktop.Admin` module:

- To load the PowerShell modules, use the `Import-Module` command-let:

  `Import-Module -Name <module name>`

- To find the successfully loaded PowerShell modules, use the `Get-Module` command-let:

  `Get-Module -ListAvailable -Name <module name>`

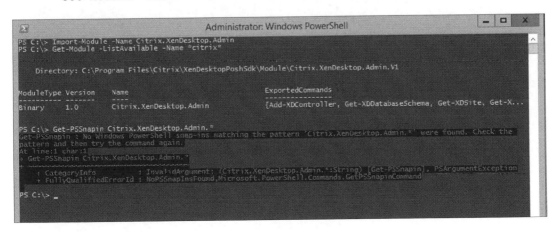

A complete reference of the PowerShell SDK

As mentioned before in this chapter, a complete reference of XenDesktop version-specific command-lets can be found at the Citrix website. You can refer to the latest XenDesktop 7.6 command-lets documentation at http://support.Citrix.com/proddocs/topic/XenApp-XenDesktop-76/xad-commands.html. Always refer to the Citrix documentation for XenDesktop version-specific SDK details. To quickly find and learn about the new command-lets or modules, ensure that you search in the Citrix website.

Troubleshooting and commonly used SDK command-lets

While the XenDesktop PowerShell SDK brings you a broad set of command-lets to achieve various specific tasks, the most commonly used are retrieving the configuration values and status checking. The following is a list of common requirements along with an example of command-let to use.

Get the license details

Use the following command-lets to get the license details, including server name, edition, model, port, and license usage by active sessions:

```
Get-BrokerSite | Select-Object license*
```

```
PS C:\> Get-BrokerSite | Select-Object license*

LicenseEdition                   : PLT
LicenseGraceSessionsRemaining    :
LicenseModel                     : Concurrent
LicenseServerName                : 172.2.16.72
LicenseServerPort                : 27000
LicensedSessionsActive           : 0


PS C:\> _
```

Use the following command-lets to get the current status of your XenDesktop licenses:

```
Get-BrokerController | Select-Object licens* | fl
```

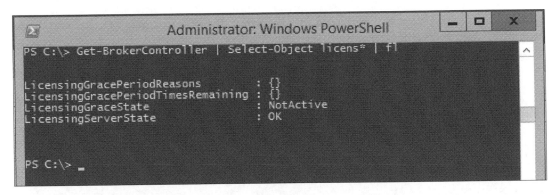

Get XenDesktop® Site details

Use the following command-lets to get XenDesktop Site details, including controller servers, controller version, OS version, and active roles hosted by the controllers:

```
Get-BrokerController | Select-Object * -exclude Licen*,Last*,*ID,*Map
```

Get XenDesktop® Site Services details

XenDesktop runs individual services for each of the FMA core components and features. Thus, there exists separate command-lets to check the status of each of these individual services. All the service status checking command-lets end with `ServiceStatus` at the end. You can list all of the service status checking command-lets using the following command-let:

```
Get-Command *servicestatus
```

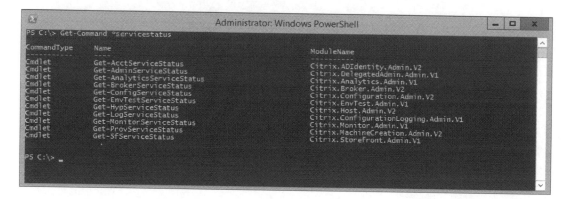

The following is an explicit list of service status command-lets along with a quick description:

- **Get-AcctServiceStatus**: This returns the current status of the **ADIdentity Service** on the controller

- **Get-AdminServiceStatus**: This returns the current status of the **DelegatedAdmin Service** on the controller

- **Get-AnalyticsServiceStatus**: This returns the current status of the **Analytics Service** on the controller

- **Get-BrokerServiceStatus**: This determines the current state of the **Broker Service** on the controller

- **Get-ConfigServiceStatus**: This returns the current status of the **Configuration Service** on the controller

- **Get-EnvTestServiceStatus**: returns the current status of the **EnvTest Service** on the controller

- **Get-HypServiceStatus**: This returns the current status of the **Host Service** on the controller

- **Get-LogServiceStatus**: This returns the current status of the **Configuration Logging Service** on the controller

- **Get-MonitorServiceStatus**: This returns the current status of the **Monitor Service** on the controller
- **Get-ProvServiceStatus**: This returns the current status of the **Machine Creation Service** on the controller
- **Get-SfServiceStatus**: This returns the current status of the **Storefront Service** on the controller

Use the following command-lets (a bit long, but is a single liner):

```
Get-Command *servicestatus | Select-Object -Property Name | ForEach-
Object { $_.Name; invoke-expression $_.Name | Select-Object -Property
ServiceStatus } | fl
```

These command-lets will be used to automatically:

- Get the list of service status checking command-lets
- Execute the retrieved command-lets
- Return each service name and its current status

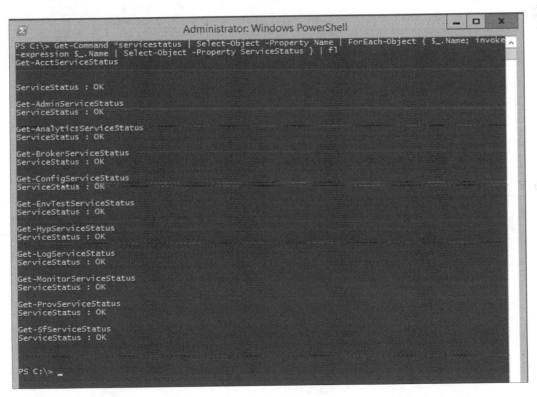

Test XenDesktop® Site services

XenDesktop SDK features an explicit environment test module that ships a great bunch of very useful command-lets to troubleshoot site-wide issues, and also to verify the health status of the site services. The following command-lets fetches all of the services and performs the availability test, and provides you with great status details:

```
Get-Command *servicestatus | Select-Object -Property Name | ForEach-
Object { $_.Name; invoke-expression $_.Name | Select-Object -Property
ServiceStatus } | fl
```

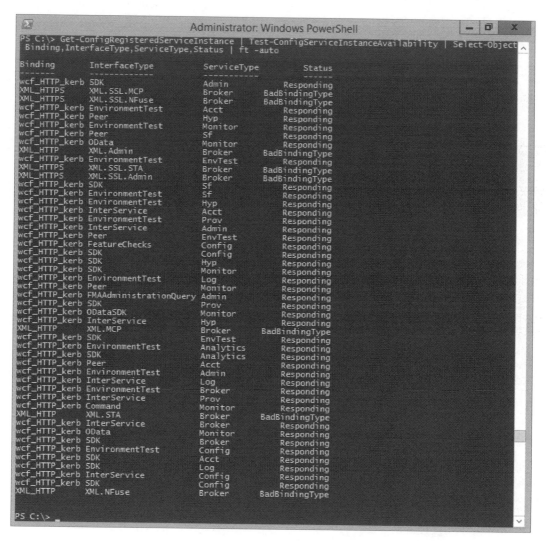

Get the XenDesktop® database details

XenDesktop uses the database to store and access all of its services configurations and data in their own database space. Use the following command-let to list the database being used by all of the XenDesktop services:

```
Get-Command Get-*DBConnection | Select-Object -Property Name | ForEach-
Object { $_.Name; invoke-expression $_.Name } | fl
```

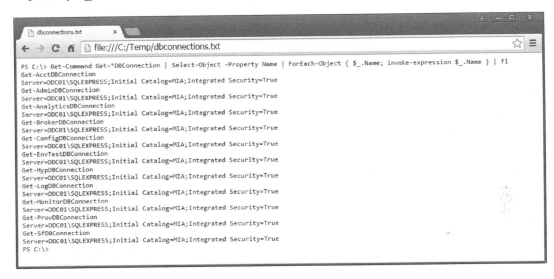

Get virtual desktop details and status

For all queries related to virtual desktops, the Get-BrokerDesktop command-let would be your way to go. It retrieves a great amount of information related to virtual desktops, user sessions, and end user details. You can get virtual desktop details, including machines names, IP addresses, VDA versions, client host names from where the users are connecting from, and many more.

Consider the following command-let:

```
Get-BrokerDesktop | Select-Object MachineName,IPAddress,OSType,AgentVersi
on,RegistrationState,PowerState,SessionState,SessionUserName,ClientName,C
lientAddress,ClientVersion | ft
```

This is a quick command-let that provides you with:

- Virtual machine details, including machine name, IP address, OS, and power state
- VDA details, agent version, registration state

- Session details, session state, session user name
- End user system details, client name, client address, client version

Use the following command-lets to find all users who have been using the desktop sessions for more than a day with the machine name, session start time, and overall duration of the session:

```
$d = (Get-Date).AddDays(-1); Get-BrokerDesktop -Filter { StartTime -le
$d } | ft MachineName,SessionUserName,StartTime,@{Label='Duration';
Expression={(Get-Date) - $_.StartTime}}
```

Get the XenDesktop® admin and user details

Use the following command-lets to get the XenDesktop admin users details:

```
Get-AdminAdministrator
```

Use the following command-let to list all of the XenDesktop users:

```
Get-BrokerUser | select FullName
```

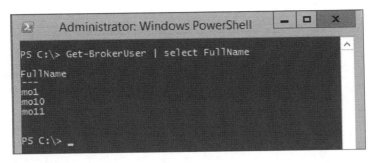

There exist many command-lets that enable command-line access to the complete XenDesktop environment. You can further build custom and advanced queries using these broad set of the built-in command-lets. Essentially, while using command-lets that update your environment (usually, starts with Set-*, New-*, Add-*, Remove-*, and so on), they should be performed with due diligence in the production environments.

Summary

This chapter equips you with the today's most sought out skill of mastering XenDesktop, that is, using PowerShell to automate your XenDesktop setup and operations. You will now be able to access the vast XenDesktop information through the PowerShell command-lets, understand the existing PowerShell automation scripts, and also set up new automations in your environment as required.
This ability to automate enables you to easily manage the growing XenDesktop deployment(s) in large enterprises.

In the next chapter, you'll discover yet another important feature, the App-V integration and how to deliver App-V-based applications through XenDesktop.

10
XenDesktop® and App-V Integration

In the last chapter, we discovered how to install a XenDesktop deployment, and we also learned some of the basic tips about its sizing and configuration.

In this chapter, we will introduce the Microsoft App-V technology and we will learn how to integrate it in a XenDesktop environment.

In this chapter, we will cover the following topics:

- Understanding the Microsoft App-V infrastructure
- Creating virtual application by using App-V
- Delivering applications based on App-V with XenDesktop

Understanding the App-V infrastructure

The **Microsoft Application Virtualization (App-V)** technology is used for virtualizing applications.

Originally, this solution was known as Soft-Grid and it was developed by Softricity, which was acquired by Microsoft in 2006 and its name was changed to App-V.

App-V enables applications to be deployed to any supported client from a publishing server. With App-V, it is not necessary to perform a local installation of the applications because the applications are streamed to the end users either on demand or pre-installed in a local cache.

An App-V application is contained in a *bubble*. In this situation, the application does not directly make any changes to the underlying operating system's file system or Windows registry.

Users obtain access to the virtualized application by using the App-V client, which is installed locally on the user's machine. The user experience is similar to the traditional locally installed application, as the extensions for the application are integrated into the user's desktop shell by the App-V client.

Microsoft App-V is an additional component, and its users require a separate license for it. Licensing is user-based and it is either acquired by licensing **Microsoft Desktop Optimization Pack (MDOP)**, and is available as a subscription for the Software Assurance customers, which allows it to be used on the clients' operating systems, or as a part of the **Microsoft Remote Desktop Server Client Access License**, which allows it to be used on the Remote Desktop Servers.

If you are familiar with Citrix products, then you would know that Citrix Streaming is Citrix's version of Microsoft Application Virtualization. Citrix Streaming will not be developed and supported anymore.

The App-V components

A Microsoft Application Virtualization infrastructure is based on the following components:

- App-V Management Server: This server is the central location for managing the App-V environment.

- App-V Database Server: This server is the location of the SQL Server Data Store, which is used by the management server for storing the configuration data.

- App-V Publishing Server: This server is used for authenticating the users and the computers. This is also used for delivering the appropriate virtual applications to the users.

- App-V Desktop Client: This software agent is installed on a Windows desktop operating system and it is used for managing and publishing applications for the user.

- App-V Remote Desktop Services Client: This software agent is installed on a Remote Desktop Services server, and it is used for managing and publishing the application on a hosted shared desktop environment.

- App-V Sequencer: This tool is used for creating a virtual application. It acts like a recorder, which registers the installation and the configuration phases of a traditional local application, thereby providing you with the virtual package called the *bubble*: it will be available to you at the end of the creation process.

The following image shows you a schema of the App-V infrastructure:

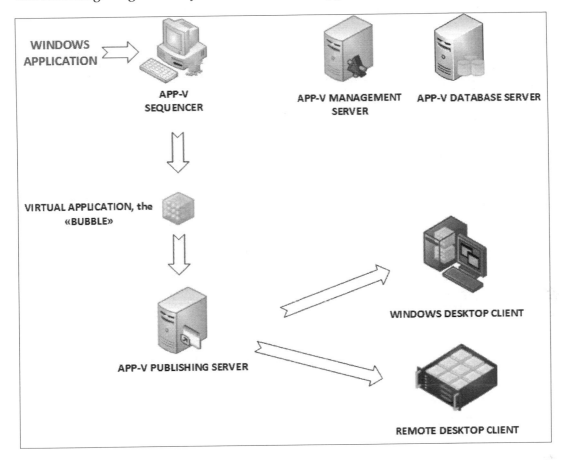

You do not have to satisfy any particular additional requirements for installing Microsoft App-V. The following operating systems are supported by Microsoft App-V:

- Windows Server 2008 R2 Service Pack 1
- Windows Server 2012
- Windows Server 2012 R2

The SQL Server versions shown here are supported by Microsoft App-V:

- SQL Server 2008 R2 Service Pack 3
- SQL Server 2012 Service Pack 2
- SQL Server 2014

You can install and configure the App-V client on the following desktop operating systems:

- Windows 8.1
- Windows 8
- Windows 7 Service Pack 1

The App-V client for Remote Desktop Services can only be installed on the Remote Desktop Services enabled servers.

> You can find out more about the system requirements from
> `https://technet.microsoft.com/en-us/library/`
> `dn858695.aspx` and `https://technet.microsoft.com/en-`
> `us/library/jj713458.aspx`.

Management Server requires IIS. So, install the IIS role by using the Server Manager that has the features given here:

- The common HTTP features, such as static content and default document
- The application development features, such as ASP.NET, .NET extensibility, ISAPI extensions and ISAPI filters
- The security features, such as Windows authentication and request filtering
- The management tools, such as IIS management console

All the infrastructure servers have to be joined to an Active Directory Domain.

The next topic, which will be discussed in this chapter, is creating a virtual application by using App-V and distributing it by using the Citrix XenDesktop.

> The installation of the App-V infrastructure is beyond the scope of this book. If you need more information about the installation process, then visit `http://social.technet.microsoft.com/`
> `wiki/contents/articles/16754.how-to-install-and-`
> `configure-the-app-v-5-0-management-server.aspx`.

Creating virtual applications using App-V

Previously in this chapter, we learned that the App-V Sequencer tool is used for creating virtual applications in App-V.

The creation process is called sequencing. Properly sequencing applications is critical for a successful App-V implementation.

You have to create the sequencer machine before beginning to create the App-V packages. Usually, the sequencer machine is created by using a virtual machine, and this is the best approach as you can use snapshots for this purpose.

When you work with App-V, you will discover that the applications will be sequenced multiple times, by mistake, or by configuration changes. In these situations, using a virtual machine and snapshots is very useful, because you will be able to reduce the development time and you can even get back to a clean situation.

[Create a base snapshot before you start sequencing the applications.]

When you create the sequencer machine, configure it in order to match the operating system configuration of the App-V client.

In this section, we will sequence the 7-Zip application by using a Windows 8.1 machine, in order to discover how the sequencing process works.

To start the sequencing process, follow this procedure:

1. Launch Microsoft Application Virtualization Sequencer, and then click on **Create a New Application Package**.

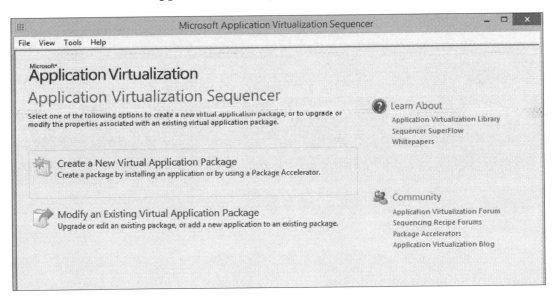

2. Select **Create Package (default)** as the creation method, and then click on **Next**.

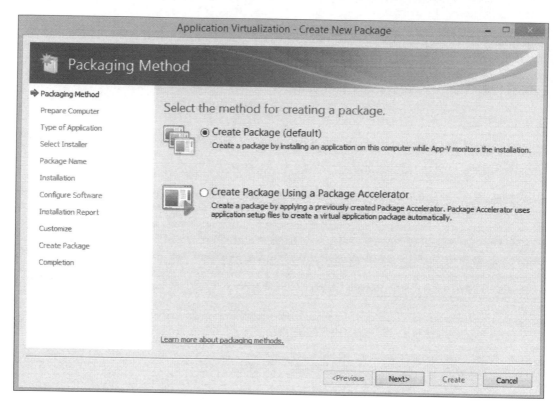

3. The sequencer examines the machine in order to identify the potential conditions that might prevent successful sequencing. In our example, Windows Defender is running, and it should be stopped before continuing with the process. Click on the **Refresh** button to confirm that no other issues were detected.

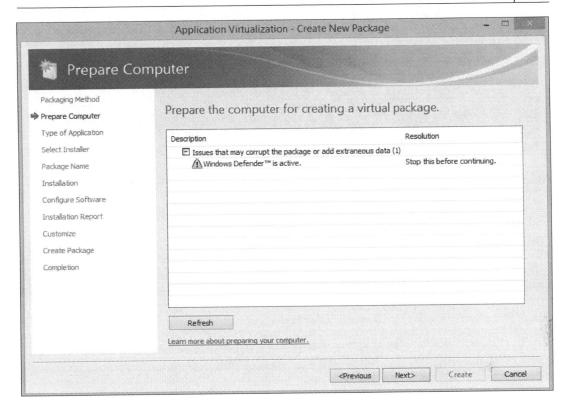

4. Now, click on the **Next** button to continue.

5. On the **Type of Application** page, the standard application type is the default selection. You use this selection when you want to sequence standard applications, such as Microsoft Office.

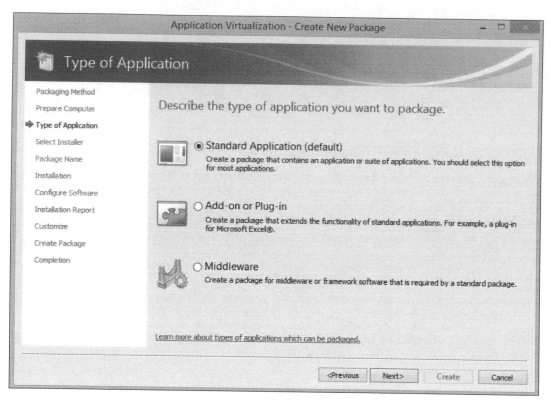

6. The wizard will now prompt you to select the installer for the application. In this example, we have selected the 7-Zip installer.

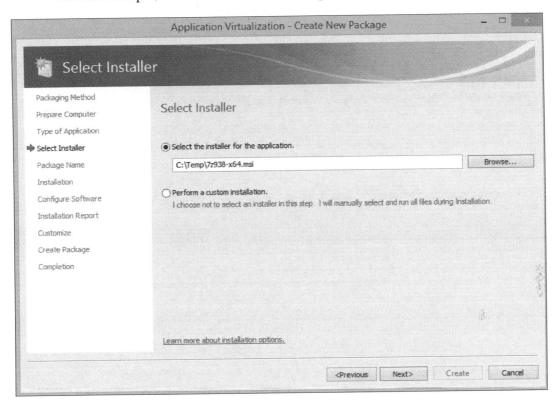

7. Click on the **Next** button to continue.

8. Now, the wizard will prompt you to type a name for the sequenced application. This name will be used for identifying the application in the management console. In our example, we have typed 7-Zip.

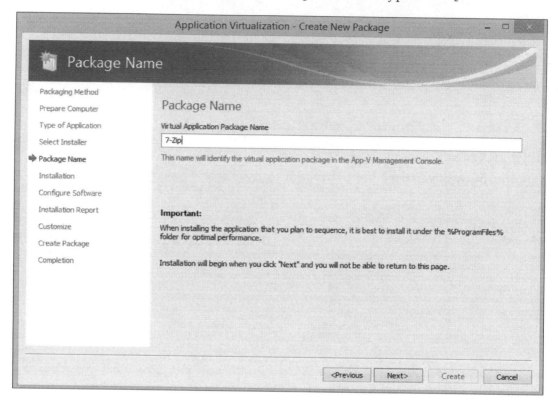

9. Click on the **Next** button to start the sequencing process. Then, the wizard will launch the installer. In this example, the 7-Zip installer will be launched.

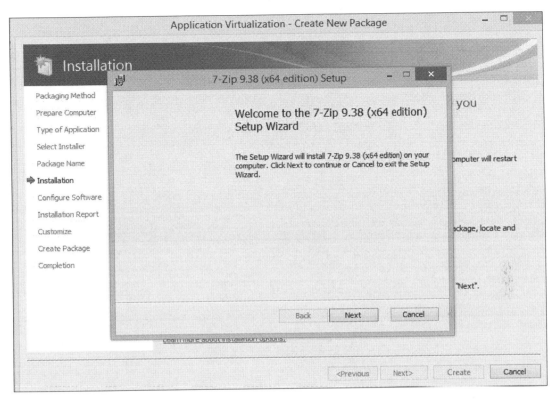

10. Complete the installation of your application.

 Some applications, such as Adobe Acrobat Reader, will require you to select an option for choosing how you would like to manage the application updates. It is the best practice to disable the automatic updates in a sequenced application.

11. When you have finished installing the applications, select the check box **I am finished installing.**, and then click on the **Next** button.

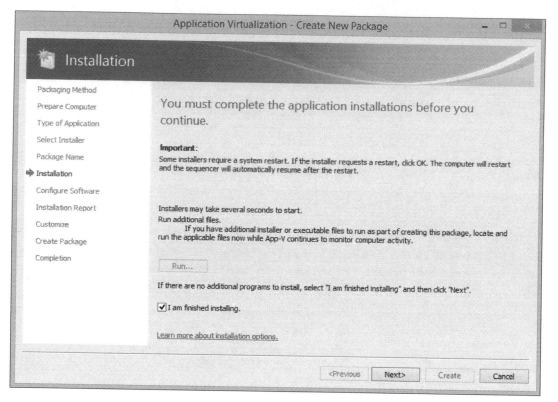

12. The wizard will collect the system changes applied by the installer, and then it will require you to configure the software. This phase is very important as you have to often do the post-installation configurations, such as crating the ODBC connections, accepting the license agreement, and so on.

13. Select the application that you want to run, and then click on the **Run Selected** button.

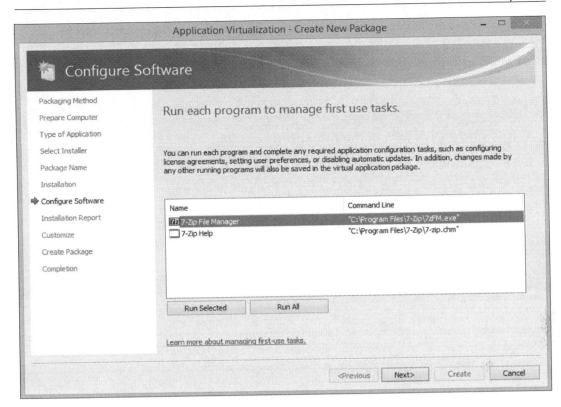

 It is the best practice to launch each application multiple times in order to be sure that all of the post-installation tasks have been completed.

14. When you have run all the applications and made the required configurations, click on the **Next** button to continue.

15. The wizard will now display a report about the issues detected during the sequencing, and they will be categorized by their severity.

   If issues are detected, then you can double-click on them to see the details. In our example, no issues were detected.

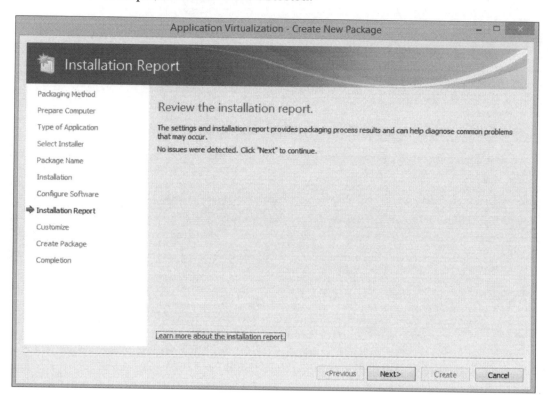

16. Click on the **Next** button to continue.

17. Now, you are ready to create the virtual package. By default, the wizard will select the **Stop Now. Create a basic virtual application package (default)** option for you. If you want to customize the package, then select **Customize. Further configure the virtual application package.**.

In this example, we have used the default selection.

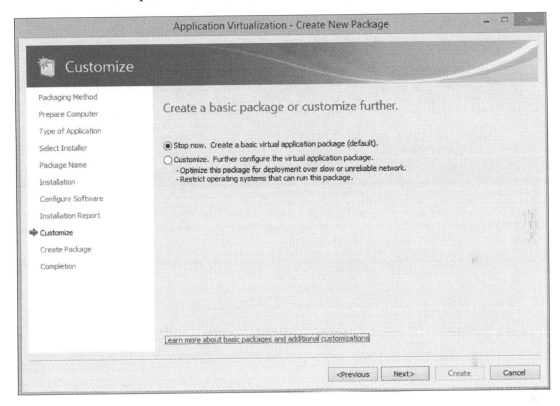

18. Click on the **Next** button to continue.

19. Now, you can save the virtual package. On the file system, set a location for the wizard for creating the package. You can also type a description for the package. This is useful for remembering the history of the sequencing process.

   In our example, we have saved the package in the `C:\App-V Packages` directory by using the `7-Zip.appv` package name.

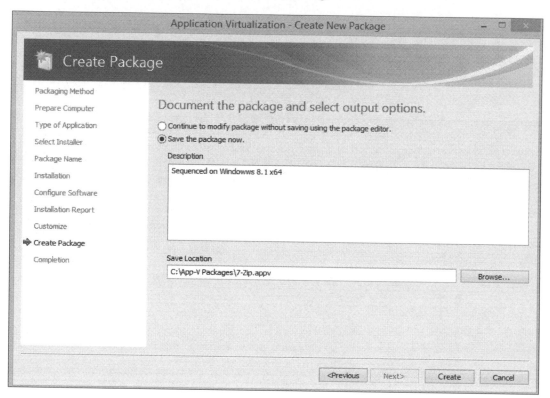

20. Click on the **Create** button to save the package.

21. Next, the wizard will display the **Completion** page. Here, you can find messages and information about the package creation report, categorized by their severity.

   In our example, a warning will inform us that some files were excluded by the package.

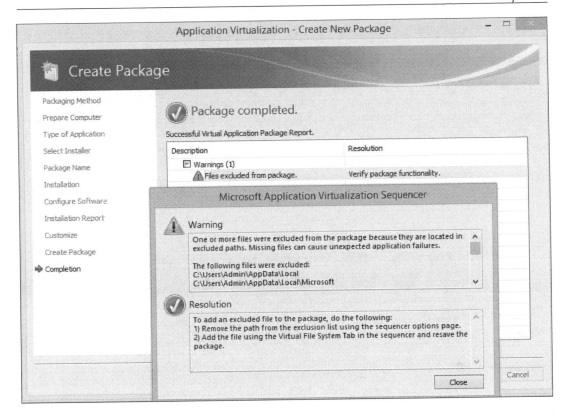

22. Click on the **Close** button to finish the sequencing process.

You can get more information regarding the sequencing process and the best practices for the App-V 5.0 from a Sequencing Guide, which is available on the Microsoft web site. You download the guide from http://download.microsoft.com/download/F/7/8/ F784A197-73BE-48FF-83DA-4102C05A6D44/App-V%205.0%20 Sequencing%20Guide.docx.

You can also find out more about this by visiting https://technet.microsoft.com/en-us/library/jj713468.aspx.

Delivering App-V applications using XenDesktop®

In the previous section, we discovered how to create a basic App-V application.

Now, we will learn how to configure XenDesktop for delivering these types of applications.

To deliver the App-V applications, you have to configure the App-V publishing by using Citrix Studio.

To do so, follow the procedure shown here:

1. Open Citrix Studio, and then click on **Configuration – App-V Publishing**.

2. On the **Action** panel, click on the **Add App-V Publishing** link.

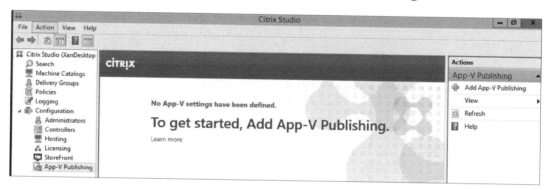

3. Now, the App-V publishing server settings dialog box will be displayed. Here, you have to insert the URL for the App-V management server and the App-V publishing server according to the following syntax: `http://fqdn_server:tcp_port`, where `fqdn_server` is the fully qualified domain name of the App-V management, or publishing server, and `tcp_port` is the port that is used for connecting to the server.

   After you type the server's name, click on the **Test connection...** button to make sure that you can access the servers.

 The TCP port is set during the installation of the App-V server components.

In this example, we have used the `appv-mgmsrv.contoso.local` server, which acts as the management and the publishing server.

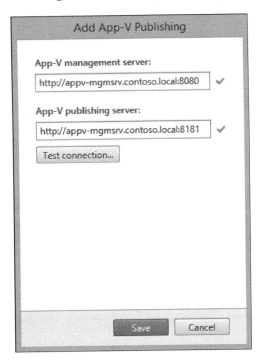

4. Click on the **Save** button to confirm your settings.

Now, if you want to deliver the App-V applications, then you will have to create a delivery group by using Citrix Studio. Note that for doing this, you will have to either create or configure an Applications or a Desktops and Applications delivery group type.

We learned how to create a delivery group in *Chapter 5, Delivering Virtual Desktops and Optimizing XenDesktop®*.

In this example, we have used a delivery group named Windows Apps, which is used for delivering the App-V applications.

To publish the applications, follow these steps:

1. In Citrix Studio, click on the delivery group that you want to use.

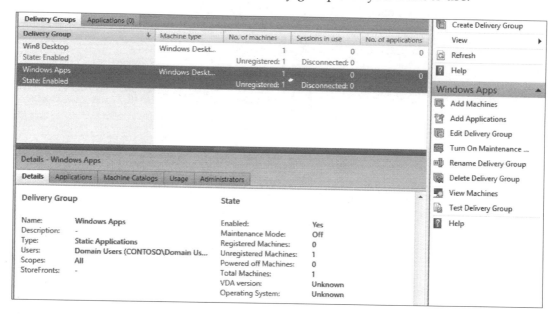

2. Click on the **Add Application** link, which will be available on the **Action** panel.

3. The Create Application wizard will be launched, and then, the Introduction page will be displayed. Click on the **Next** button to continue.

4. The wizard will display all the discovered App-V applications. Select the applications that you want to publish. In this example, we have delivered **7-Zip File Manager** and **7-Zip Help**. We have already sequenced these applications at the beginning of this chapter.

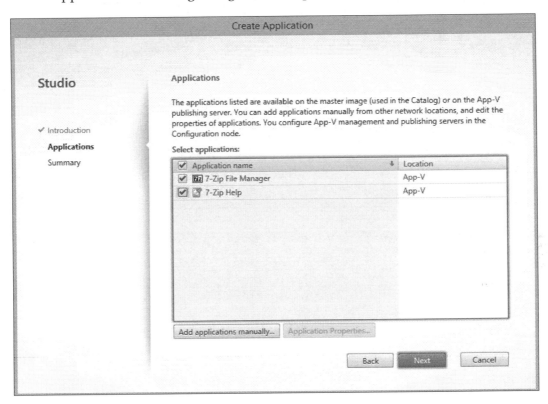

5. Click on the **Next** button to continue.

6. Click on the **Finish** button to complete the publishing process. Now, the App-V applications will be available for delivery through the Windows Apps delivery group.

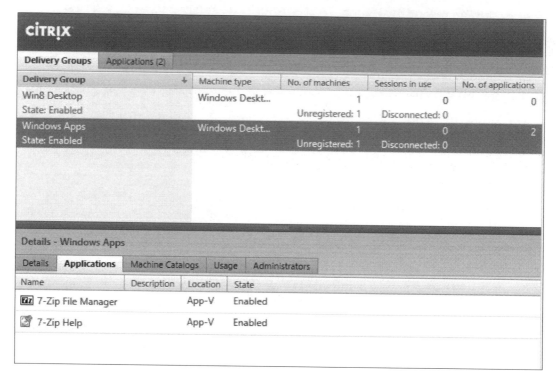

Installing the App-V client

In the previous section, we learned how to configure XenDesktop for publishing the App-V applications. Now, we will discover how to install the App-V client on a Windows machine. The App-V Client is required for starting the virtual applications.

In this section, we will focus on the installation of the App-V client when it is used with the standard images.

When working with standard images, you should install the App-V client as follows:

- Enable the Shared Content Cache: The shared content cache allows you to directly stream from a content shared source without having to stream the App-V package to every user's machine, thereby saving your storage resources.
- Enable Package Scripts by using PowerShell.
- Set the PowerShell ExecutionPolicy to RemoteSigned: The AppV client module provided by Microsoft is not signed and this allows PowerShell to run the unsigned local scripts and command-lets.

For installing the App-V client with an enabled shared content cache, follow this procedure:

1. Open Command Prompt with administrative privileges on the Windows machine.
2. For installing the client, execute the following command:

   ```
   appv_client_setup.exe /SHAREDCONTENTSTOREMODE=1 /q
   ```

   - The `/SHAREDCONTENTSTOREMODE=1` parameter will enable the Shared Content Cache
   - The `/q` parameter will install the client in the silent mode

 If you install the client on a Windows 7 machine, then you should also install Windows PowerShell 3.0 and Microsoft .NET Framework 4.5 before starting the App-V client setup.

For enabling the Package script and setting the PowerShell ExecutionPolicy to RemoteSigned, follow this procedure:

1. Open Windows PowerShell on the Windows machine.
2. Import the App-V client module by executing the command, as shown here:

   ```
   Import-Module AppVClient
   ```
3. Enable Package Scripts by executing the command as follows:

   ```
   Set-AppvClientConfiguration -EnablePackageScripts 1
   ```
4. Set ExecutionPolicy to RemoteSigned by executing the following command:

   ```
   Set-ExecutionPolicy RemoteSigned
   ```

For more details regarding the App-V and Citrix integration, visit `http://www.microsoft.com/en-us/download/confirmation.aspx?id=40885`.

Summary

In this chapter, we learned some concepts about the App-V infrastructure. We also discussed how to integrate App-V with XenDesktop. We discovered how to install the App-V client into a standard image and how to use the App-V sequencer for creating the virtual applications package.

App-V is a very powerful solution for delivering applications but it requires time and patience, especially when working with the sequenced packages.

Sequencing is an art, and if you want to test it, then take your time and enjoy it!

In the next chapter, we will cover the XenDesktop licensing. We will also learn how to allocate the Citrix licenses.

11

XenDesktop® Licensing

In the previous chapter, we discovered how to integrate Microsoft Application Virtualization in a XenDesktop environment.

In this chapter, we will cover the following topics on Citrix Licensing for XenDesktop:

- Understanding Citrix licensing
- Discovering XenDesktop editions
- Allocating Citrix licenses

Understanding Citrix® licensing

Citrix products, such as XenDesktop, require you to buy some licenses according to your needs, and Citrix offers licensing programs designed to meet these needs.

For commercial, public, and private organizations, you can buy licenses according to the following programs:

- An EASY License
- The Enterprise License Agreement

Citrix also provides programs for the education and government sectors.

You can acquire licenses for your Citrix environment by participating in the Citrix Volume Licensing. Using Citrix Volume Licensing, Citrix provides software licenses and Citrix products such as downloads, and permits you to save money rather than acquiring retailed boxed licenses.

The EASY License Program is ideal when you have to license Citrix products for very few users. It does not require a minimum amount or quantity, so you can buy Citrix licenses on an as-needed basis.

The Enterprise Agreement, on the other hand, is appropriate for organizations with more than 250 users, and requires a minimum investment that can also vary by the geographic area.

The Enterprise Agreement offers you different levels according to your needs and initial investment. When you place your first Citrix order, you receive a discount, starting from 25 percent of the suggested retail price and according to the assigned level.

This discount is also applied to the additional orders. You can acquire licenses for all the Citrix products and the agreement is valid for three years; but, it is flexible, because you can increase the discounts if you buy new qualified licenses.

When you participate in a Citrix license program, you need to perform a registration using the Licensing Program Registration available on the MyCitrix.com portal.

You can do this registration yourself or ask your Citrix partner to do this for you. You will need to create a MyCitrix account if you do not have one.

When you have to buy a Citrix license for XenDesktop, you can acquire the following two types of license:

- A user\device license
- A concurrent license

A user license gives your users access to virtual desktops from an unlimited number of devices, while a device license gives access to a virtual desktop that is granted to an unlimited number of users from a single device.

Each user license has to be associated with a specific user ID. When a user ID is shared between multiple users, you need to have a license for each user.

In the same way, a device license has to be assigned to a specific device.

Usually, you should select this license model when your users have to connect from multiple devices; for example, a computer located in the main office and a smartphone.

On the other hand, you should select the device license model when you have users that connect from a single machine, such as a thin client.

User and device licenses remain assigned to a user or device until 90 days of inactivity have passed.

If you need to release a user or device license, you can use the udadmin utility. You can find more details at http://support.citrix.com/proddocs/topic/licensing-1110/lic-admin-cmds-list-deletes-user-device-r.html.

The concurrent license is usually used when you have concurrent user or device connections. In this case, a single license is assigned when a connection is established to the Citrix XenDesktop environment.

When the connection ends, the license is returned, and can be immediately assigned to another different user if needed.

You can acquire a concurrent license when you have to license Citrix products for occasional use.

You can find more details on Citrix licensing at http://www.citrix.it/buy/licensing.html.
You can also read the XenDesktop FAQ licensing guide available at http://support.citrix.com/article/CTX128013.

Microsoft licensing for virtual desktops

When you implement a virtual desktop infrastructure, you have to also consider Microsoft licensing.

When you have devices or users accessing a virtual desktop environment based on Windows operating system, you have to license those devices or users, using Microsoft VDA or Windows Software Assurance.

Indeed, Windows client Software Assurance gives you the right to access a virtual desktop environment at no additional charge. Software Assurance is either included with some Microsoft Volume Licensing programs, such as Enterprise Agreement, or it is an option you can acquire when you are buying Microsoft licenses.

You can find out more information on Windows Assurance at http://www.microsoft.com/licensing/software-assurance/faq.aspx.

The Windows VDA subscription license provides the right to access virtual Windows desktop environments from devices that are not covered by Software Assurance for Windows, such as thin clients.

Each user or device must be licensed separately. When you license a device, multiple users can access a virtual desktop environment from that device.

When you license on a per user basis, a single user can access a virtual desktop environment from any device.

> You can find more details on Microsoft licensing for virtual desktop environments on the following white papers:
>
> You can refer to Licensing Windows desktop operating system with virtual machines at `http://download.microsoft.com/download/9/8/D/98D6A56C-4D79-40F4-8462-DA3ECBA2DC2C/Licensing_Windows_Desktop_OS_for_Virtual_Machines.pdf` and Windows 8.1 and Windows RT 8 at `http://download.microsoft.com/download/9/4/3/9439A928-A0D1-44C2-A099-26A59AE0543B/Windows_8-1_Licensing_Guide.pdf`.

Discovering Citrix® XenDesktop® editions

Citrix XenDesktop is offered in three different editions:

- VDI
- Enterprise
- Platinum

The VDI edition is ideal for organizations that want to approach virtual desktop infrastructure, without the need to deliver published applications or shared hosted desktops.

In the VDI edition, the Citrix standard HDX optimization feature is included.

The Enterprise and Platinum editions provide you with an enterprise-class virtual desktop solution, and enable you to deliver virtual desktops, published applications, hosted shared desktops, Cloud integration, provisioning services, and so on.

Furthermore, with the Enterprise and Platinum editions, you can deploy your XenDesktop environment on popular Cloud management platforms, including AWS or Citrix CloudPlatform-based public or private cloud services.

On the Citrix website, you can find an exhaustive matrix listing all the features available in each edition. You can refer to it at

`https://www.citrix.com/go/products/xendesktop/feature-matrix.html.`

Allocating Citrix® licenses

Citrix licenses are managed through MyCitrix.com website.

When you buy licenses, you receive a confirmation e-mail containing instructions on how to activate them.

Licenses have to be activated and allocated to a license server, using the License Server Management Console.

In this section, we will discover how to allocate Citrix licenses.

To allocate licenses, we need to complete the following tasks:

1. Log on to MyCitrix.com website using your MyCitrix account. In the following screenshot, you can see an extract of the home page of MyCitrix.com:

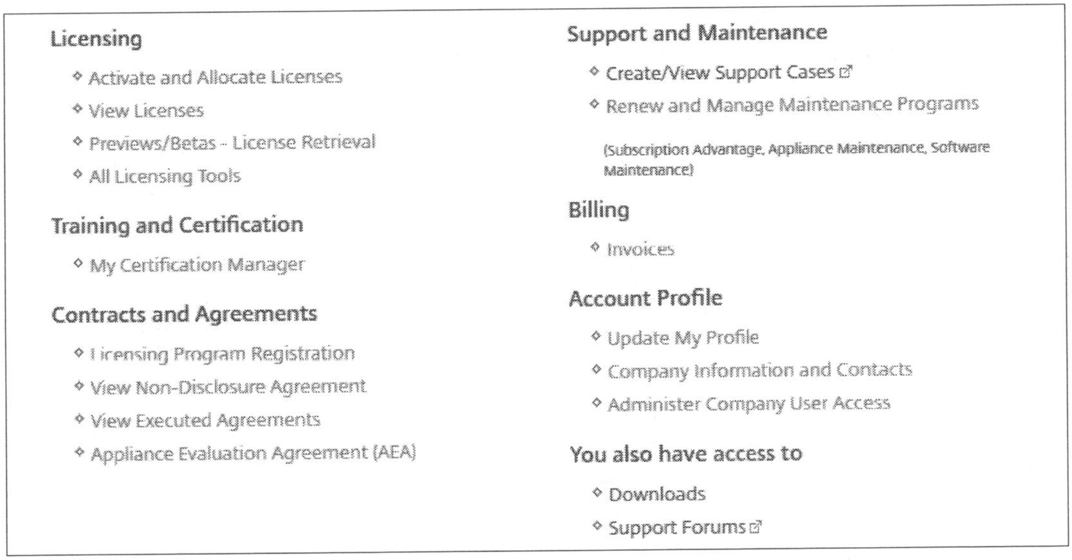

Licensing

- ◇ Activate and Allocate Licenses
- ◇ View Licenses
- ◇ Previews/Betas – License Retrieval
- ◇ All Licensing Tools

Training and Certification

- ◇ My Certification Manager

Contracts and Agreements

- ◇ Licensing Program Registration
- ◇ View Non-Disclosure Agreement
- ◇ View Executed Agreements
- ◇ Appliance Evaluation Agreement (AEA)

Support and Maintenance

- ◇ Create/View Support Cases ☑
- ◇ Renew and Manage Maintenance Programs

    (Subscription Advantage, Appliance Maintenance, Software Maintenance)

Billing

- ◇ Invoices

Account Profile

- ◇ Update My Profile
- ◇ Company Information and Contacts
- ◇ Administer Company User Access

You also have access to

- ◇ Downloads
- ◇ Support Forums ☑

2. Click on the **Activate and Allocate Licenses** link. Here, you will find all the licenses you have bought. If you do not see the licenses, you will have to allocate them. To do this, click on the **Single Allocation** tab. In the following screenshot, you will see that no licenses are available:

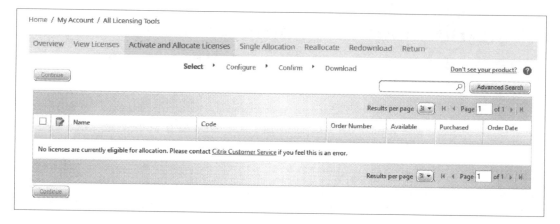

3. On the **Single Allocation** page, insert your license code; you can find this on the order mail that you receive from Citrix:

4. Click on the **Continue** button to proceed.

5. Now, the wizard will ask you to insert the name of the server, which is acting as the Citrix license server:

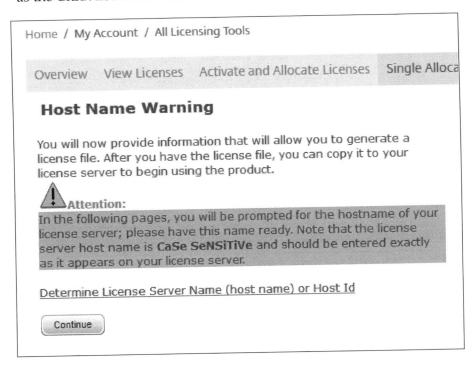

6. Click on the **Continue** button to proceed.

7. Type the hostname of the license server on the **Host ID** field. Note that the name is case sensitive, so pay attention when you type the name.

Do not use the Fully-Qualified-Domain-Name here!

In this example, we typed XD-CtxDC. You can also change the number of licenses to be allocated. When using a trial license, you will receive **99** licenses from Citrix. By default, the licensing system selects all the available licenses for you; you can change this value according to your needs.

8. Click on the **Continue** button to proceed.

9. The following wizard shows you a confirmation page:

10. Click on the **Confirm** button. The system prompts you to download the license file that you have to upload on the license server:

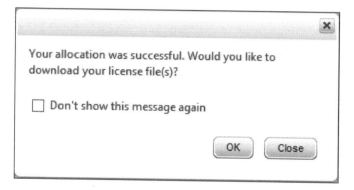

11. Click on the **OK** button to download the file. This file has to be uploaded on the Citrix License Server.

The file that you download looks similar to the following:

> If you want to find out more information on license management, you can visit `http://support.citrix.com/proddocs/topic/licensing-11121/lic-license-files.html` and `https://www.citrix.com/buy/licensing/management.html`.

After the allocation, you have to connect to the Citrix license server and upload the license file.

To complete this task, you need to follow this procedure:

1. Copy the license file to the server hosting the Citrix Licensing services.

2. Open the Citrix **License Administrator Console**, and click on the **Administration** tab.

3. Log on to the Administration page using an account with administrative privileges. Typically, the user used for performing the Citrix Licensing installation:

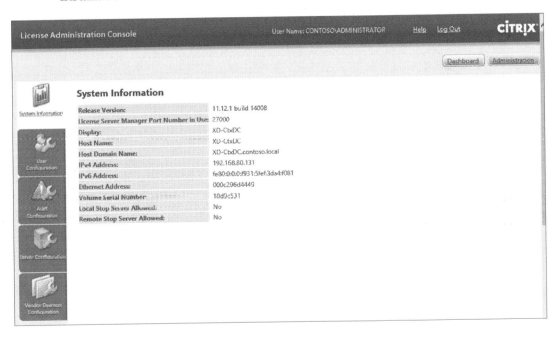

4. Click on the **Vendor Daemon Configuration** button.

5. Click on the **Import License** button.

6. Click on the **Browse...** button to select the license file you want to import, which you copied in step 1. You can also click on the **Overwrite License File on License Server** checkbox, if you want to overwrite the same file that you could have uploaded previously:

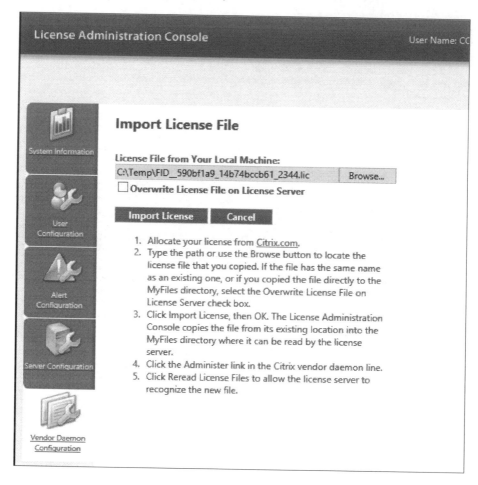

Click on the **Import License** button to continue. You will receive a confirmation, informing you that the import process has been completed successfully:

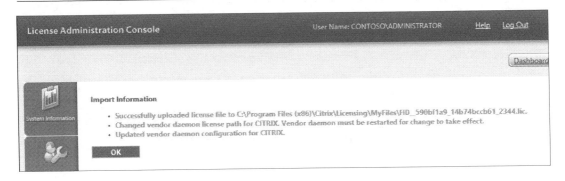

7. Click on the **OK** button. The **Vendor Daemon Configuration** page will be displayed.

8. Now you have to instruct the Vendor Daemon to reread the license files. To do this, click on the **Administer** link:

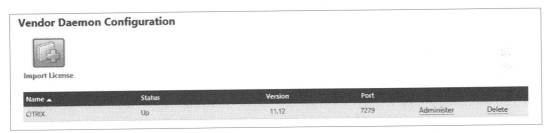

9. Click on the **Reread License Files** button:

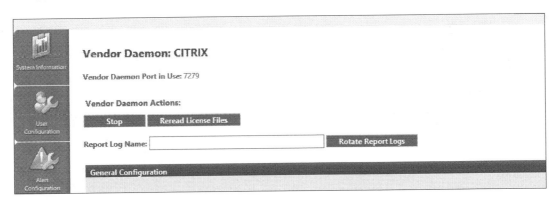

10. The Vendor Daemon informs you that the reread process completed successfully:

11. On the Dashboard page of the Citrix License Administrator console, you can now see the new licenses. In the following screenshot, you can see the **99** Evaluation licenses that we allocated previously in this section:

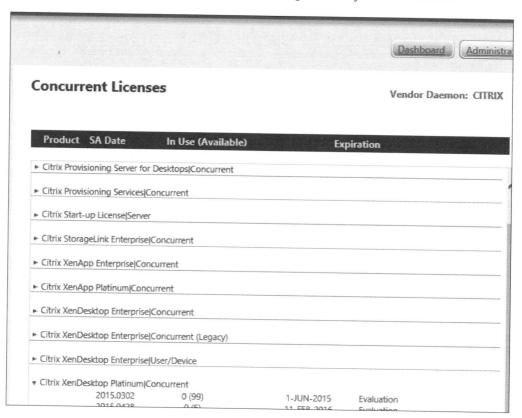

Summary

In this chapter, we learnt some concepts about Citrix licensing and discussed how the Licensing program works.

We also discovered how to allocate Citrix licenses using MyCitrix.com website.

This is the last chapter of the book. We learnt how a XenDesktop infrastructure is composed, and how to design and install a high-available and scalable virtual desktop environment.

We also introduced some concepts about Citrix networking, and how to monitor and maintain your XenDesktop environment.

Index

C

M

N

Thank you for buying
Mastering Citrix® XenDesktop®

About Packt Publishing

Packt, pronounced 'packed', published its first book, *Mastering phpMyAdmin for Effective MySQL Management*, in April 2004, and subsequently continued to specialize in publishing highly focused books on specific technologies and solutions.

Our books and publications share the experiences of your fellow IT professionals in adapting and customizing today's systems, applications, and frameworks. Our solution-based books give you the knowledge and power to customize the software and technologies you're using to get the job done. Packt books are more specific and less general than the IT books you have seen in the past. Our unique business model allows us to bring you more focused information, giving you more of what you need to know, and less of what you don't.

Packt is a modern yet unique publishing company that focuses on producing quality, cutting-edge books for communities of developers, administrators, and newbies alike. For more information, please visit our website at www.packtpub.com.

About Packt Enterprise

In 2010, Packt launched two new brands, Packt Enterprise and Packt Open Source, in order to continue its focus on specialization. This book is part of the Packt Enterprise brand, home to books published on enterprise software – software created by major vendors, including (but not limited to) IBM, Microsoft, and Oracle, often for use in other corporations. Its titles will offer information relevant to a range of users of this software, including administrators, developers, architects, and end users.

Writing for Packt

We welcome all inquiries from people who are interested in authoring. Book proposals should be sent to author@packtpub.com. If your book idea is still at an early stage and you would like to discuss it first before writing a formal book proposal, then please contact us; one of our commissioning editors will get in touch with you.

We're not just looking for published authors; if you have strong technical skills but no writing experience, our experienced editors can help you develop a writing career, or simply get some additional reward for your expertise.

Citrix® XenApp® 7.x Performance Essentials

ISBN: 978-1-78217-611-4   Paperback: 120 pages

Tune and optimize the performance of your farms with the new improved XenApp® architecture

1. Monitor your infrastructure using the new tools, and learn how to optimize the end-user experience.

2. Discover the new FlexCast Management Architecture of XenApp® 7.5 and its components.

3. Explore the new features designed for mobile and remote users.

Getting Started with XenDesktop® 7.x

ISBN: 978-1-84968-976-2   Paperback: 422 pages

Deliver desktops and applications to your end users, anywhere, anytime, with XenDesktop® 7.X

1. Build a complete and secure XenDesktop® 7 site from the ground up.

2. Discover how to virtualize and deliver accessible desktops and applications to your end users.

3. Full of clear, step-by-step instructions with screenshots, which will walk you through the entire process of XenDesktop® site creation.

Please check **www.PacktPub.com** for information on our titles

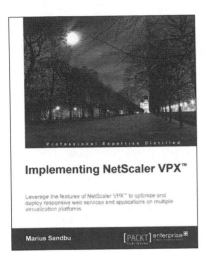

Made in the USA
Middletown, DE
11 May 2016